BEHOLD!
THE LAMB OF
GOD

Who Takes Away
The Sin Of The World.

---

365 Daily Devotional

CINDY JOANNE BALCH

Copyright © 2015 by Cindy Joanne Balch

BEHOLD! THE LAMB OF GOD
WHO TAKES AWAY THE SIN OF THE WORLD.
by Cindy Joanne Balch

Printed in the United States of America.

ISBN 9781498435369

All rights reserved solely by the author. The author guarantees all contents are original and do not infringe upon the legal rights of any other person or work. No part of this book may be reproduced in any form without the permission of the author. The views expressed in this book are not necessarily those of the publisher.

Unless otherwise indicated, Scripture quotations are taken from the New International Version (NIV). Copyright © 1973, 1978, 1984, 2011 by Biblica, Inc.™. Used by permission. All rights reserved.

Scripture quotations are taken from the New American Standard Bible (NASB). Copyright © 1960, 1962, 1963, 1968, 1971, 1972, 1973, 1975, 1977, 1995 by The Lockman Foundation. Used by permission. All rights reserved.

Scripture quotations are taken from The Message (MSG). Copyright © 1993, 1994, 1995, 1996, 2000, 2001, 2002. Used by permission of NavPress Publishing Group. Used by permission. All rights reserved.

Scripture quotations are taken from the King James Version (KJV) – public domain

Scripture quotations are taken from the New King James Version (NKJV). Copyright © 1979, 1980, 1982 by Thomas Nelson, Inc. Used by permission. All rights reserved.

Scripture quotations are taken from the Good News Translation (GNT). Copyright © 1992 American Bible Society. Used by permission. All rights reserved.

Scripture quotations taken from the Amplified Bible (AMP) (E-version). Copyright © 1965 by Zondervan Publishing House. Used by permission. All rights reserved.

www.xulonpress.com

*This book is written
to help you survive life's 'heart breaking moments'
in a dangerously changing world.
We were never intended to make this journey
through life alone. God will walk right beside you all the way
if you will just ask Him. He longs for you to get to know Him.*

"Children are an anchor that holds a mother to life."
-Sophocles-

This book is dedicated to my children. To my son Dr. Rocky Balch, a Surgeon and West Point grad. Proud mama doesn't begin to express all of your accomplishments in life. I would let you take out my gallbladder anytime. To my beautiful daughter Jennifer Balch, single mom extraordinaire to twins. You are beautiful both inside and out. I know it hasn't been easy for you and I am so proud of you. To you both, I am so blessed God chose me to be the one you call 'Mom.' Many years ago I took you on a journey you never asked to go on. It was a painful time for all of us. With the Lord's help we survived. Once again I ask your forgiveness. A very special thank-you to my daughter-in-law Susan Balch, a wonderful wife and mom. Thank-you for helping me pick out the book cover.

This book is also dedicated to my three grandsons, twins Cody & Austin and my third little guy Hunter. My three little 'peanuts.' Of all the things I have done over the years, being grandma to the three of you has been the absolute biggest blessing of my entire life. I love this grandma stuff! Just thinking of you brings a smile to my face. I love you to the moon and back!

To my mom, every day I wish Heaven had a telephone. I know you would knock over St. Peter, if necessary, to answer my call. You were my anchor to life and my prayer warrior. You spent an eternity on your knees on my behalf and shed more than a few tears at the throne of God. My heart hurts every day I spend without you.

To my sisters Kathy and Georgia, your absence in my life has been one of life's most painful experiences. My heart hurts for all of the moments in life we could have shared and didn't or weren't able .

To my nieces Jan Hernandez & Lynda Stoodley. You are always on my heart and in my prayers. You both have always been there when I needed you. I hope you feel the same.

To my dear friends Linda and Lee McCown. We have been through the good, the bad and the ugly over the years and have survived it all. My heart still hurts at the loss of your son Danny. I loved him as if he were my own. I am so proud of your daughter Erin. She has become a beautiful young woman and mother.

A very special thank-you to Craig Jorgensen and Taina Allen. Craig, who I have known since kindergarten and Taina is a beautiful Critical Care nurse I have worked with over the last 10 years. Their encouragement to keep on writing proves that you never know how important a simple word of encouragement to someone at just the right time can be. It can mean the world to them. It may be so important it can mean the difference between them giving up or pressing on. I pressed on because of your encouragement.

And finally, to those precious few I trusted with my heart, who stood by me when times got tough, and to those who didn't, it's okay, because Jesus never left my side.

From my heart to yours...
Cindy

INTRODUCTION
LIFE 101

How do you survive life's most painful moments when life hurts, love hurts, truth hurts, everything hurts? People hurt. I hurt. You hurt. Life hurts people. Hurting people hurt people. The pain goes on and on and on…Yet, through all of the pain God still has a good plan for each one of our lives. Every day, His plan is slowly unfolding. Notice the 'slowly' part. There are no instant fixes. Your life if surrendered to Him will unfold according to His plan. In fact, He won't even consider my plan or yours. He will not leave loose ends in our life. If His love doesn't get our attention than "ouch moments" will, at least temporarily. Oh, some days we get this temporary insanity and think we know better how to run things. We interfere with what God is trying to do, but He will succeed. God is kind and loving but He also knows how to elbow His way into our life when necessary, especially those places we have put up "No trespassing" signs. "Ouch, Lord, stop." Some days we doubt. We question God, sometimes when we should and sometimes when we shouldn't. Like Noah, "Build an ark."…a what Lord?" If I could see His plan for me through His eyes, I might still hurt, I might be scorned or laughed at but I would never lose hope. Never. How many watched the ark float away in the rain, those who had laughed and mocked Noah? Not so funny after all.

The greatest measure of a man's faith is to be able to trust God when the feelings aren't there. When it *seems* that He is not there. You are all alone. At least you think you are. Friends have deserted you. Moments or seasons in life when you find yourself in the midst of something that appears hopeless. Something I can't reason my way through, bluff my way through or manipulate my way through. Moments when emotions let you down, when sense and reason seem to fly right out the window. At times like these is when I say some of the stupidest things. You question your own sanity. When you make a decision in life that looks good to everyone, everyone that is except God. Have you run from God? Silly notion, but we all try it. We also find ourselves as Jonah did. Swallowed up by trouble and spit out and right back where we started from. Or you find yourself in the Lion's den and it doesn't take you long to figure out those lions are very, very hungry. Or you find yourself standing in the midst of a storm and you don't know how to swim and it's much too late to learn. Think of Joshua. He was instructed to march around Jericho 7 times then blow trumpets. I am certainly not a military strategist, but that has to be the worst war strategy in the world…unless of course you are God. When the circumstances get so overwhelming we may find ourselves close to despair. We think we have great faith until God sends us a reality check. There is no limit to the damage the enemy would do to us if given the chance. If God let down His hedge of protection for just a moment and the devil thought God wasn't looking he would destroy you. Jesus will gently remind you that He has your back.

We turn to God for help when the foundations of our life are shaking only to realize that it is God who is doing the shaking.

There are times when our world is suddenly upside down and inside out. At times like these it is difficult to believe that after the hurt my heart will ever sing again, "It is well with my soul." Maybe not without tears and maybe not without an ache deep in my heart, but I will sing again. He promises I will. He says, I shall not be moved. It does not say I shall not hurt, but I shall not be moved. After it's over that part of me that will sing to Him through the sorrow and the tears is that part of me He has changed. All along He has been at work. He may have seemed silent, but He was not. God does not always work in the "spectacular" but often behind the scenes. The moment the child of God gets down on their knees and asks for God to intervene in their life as only He can, then all of heaven shouts Hallelujah! Suddenly, you find yourself in a place of stillness and peace. The war between you and God is over. Instead of being His adversary you are now His soldier. You can have a peace that sadly most will never know because they do not know Him. They never even give Him a chance. It's a peace God gives in return for my growing weary of trying to tell Him how to run things and simply choose instead to rest in His arms. Safe. Secure. Accepted. Loved. Okay, that in this life there will be questions I may never get answered. Contentment doesn't mean I don't want to see things change, it simply means I am okay until God does move to change things. Sometimes, ignorance is bliss, sometimes it is deadly.

Life hurts. Truth hurts, but then it begins to heal. Aren't you glad God doesn't give up on us as easily as we give up on Him or give up on ourselves?

Ask...He longs to give.
Give...He longs to multiply.
Believe...He longs to bless.
Surrender...He longs to take His rightful place in your life and mine.

Remember...your life...your eternity... depends on what path you choose. You can't blame your decisions on anyone but yourself. You are all alone on judgment day standing before your Creator. The party is over. The balloons have wilted, the music has died, and the people are gone. It is a day of accountability, not a day of excuses. You can follow the crowd where wide is the road that leads to destruction or choose to follow JESUS down that narrow path that He says leads to life. How do you find that narrow path? Good question. "I AM the way, I Am the truth, and I AM life." How simple is that? Follow Him.

You don't need to pack much for the journey because He has promised to provide you with whatever you need along the way, when you need it. So, buckle your seat belt, sit back, hold on and try to relax and for goodness sake try not to scream! Warning! It will get very scary some days. One day He will be let you sit in His lap all comfy, cozy, secure, not a care in the world. Next day you might find He has pushed you out of your comfy little nest and suddenly you wish you had paid close attention when He was trying to teach you to fly. You find yourself falling, desperate you start flapping away, just when you know this is the end of the road you feel His everlasting arms underneath. He scoops you up. Places you back in your comfy little nest just long enough to take a deep breath and calm down and then... He pushes you out again.

This time is different, however, because this time you know He will catch you. It doesn't usually happen as soon as you would like, but He will catch you. The more He pushes the greater our faith becomes. He proves His faithfulness over and over again.

A life that was once in free fall....becomes flying
lessons for the Christian.

As we journey through this book day by day we will learn to fly a little higher until we are soaring through the Heavens with unshakeable faith. But first...first He must break us. Brokenness is God's plan for all of us. He must get rid of the junk in our life. He changes our attitude. We stop saying, "For me to live is stuff," and we begin to say "For me to live is Christ." We think there is someone we can't forgive. He will show us that with His help we can. The Corrie Ten Boom kind of forgiveness. She was an amazing woman, a survivor of the Holocaust. She was able by God's grace to reach out a hand of forgiveness to the German soldiers, who murdered her sister and parents. We may have given up on a dream...He will help make it come true no matter how many years have gone by.

Why does God break us? That is another very good question. Let me tell you a little story about "Jesus had a little lamb"...

Years ago on a Sunday school wall, I saw it for the very first time. I have never forgotten it. Its image is burned into my heart forever. Its memory will never fade. It is a picture of Jesus with a little lamb wrapped around his neck and shoulders. Actually, it's not the picture so much as the explanation of the picture I heard one day that had its greatest impact on me. I stared at the picture and wondered why that particular lamb was lucky enough to be carried by the Lord until I found out luck had nothing to do with it.

As the story was told, in ancient times the shepherds would care for their sheep in the fields. They would make sure they were well fed, well watered and above all protected from harm. Sheep have many predators and adversaries. Occasionally, there was one lamb that refused to stay by the Shepherd's side. He would begin to wander. Maybe the grass looked greener on the other side. "Just this one time won't hurt..." I fell for those lies too. The Shepherd sensed the lamb's danger and would bring him back time and time again. Gentle discipline was not working and neither was love. The Shepherd in these cases would break the little lamb's legs and carry the lamb around his neck and shoulders until the legs healed. This lasted a considerable amount of time. Some of us heal quicker than others. Some of us 'get it' sooner than others. By the time the lamb's legs had healed he was completely dependent on the Shepherd for *everything*.

This little lamb was broken in love and so was I. God will pursue you and do whatever it takes, even break your heart and life into little pieces as He did mine.

Pieces only He can put back together. When all the king's horses and all the king's men couldn't put Humpty together again...The KING of kings can...and He will.

This story is a sobering illustration of brokenness. Brokenness is all about OBEDIENCE. You can't separate the two. Sin causes pain. Obedience brings life and peace.

Everyone has problems. Everyone, but our God specializes in people with insurmountable problems.

This book has been on my 'bucket list' for a number of years because God has placed in my heart a desire to help people not make the same mistakes I have. If someone learns from my mistakes it will turn something bad into a blessing. Our God specializes in doing just that.

This devotional is not for the faint hearted, but it is for the weary, the broken, the hopeless, and most important for the "whosoever will." Our world is getting more frightening with each passing day. God is the only safe harbor we have from the storms of life. No matter what happens in your life or mine, He is in control! Keep your eyes on Him. Wise men still seek Him.

In His love,
Cindy Joanne Balch
Author of, The Journey Is Too Great For Thee.

I can walk with God this New Year or go it alone.

"Choose this day, Whom you will serve... but as for me
and my family, we will serve the LORD."
Joshua 24:15

JANUARY 1

❄

How is your vision? When giants come into your life this New Year, and they will,
who will you see clearer...God or the giants?

"...holding on to faith and a good conscience. Some have
rejected these and so have ***shipwrecked their faith***."
I Timothy 1:19

The events of the world are shouting you will need great faith this New Year. You will face many giants. Some old, some you have been struggling with for years and just can't seem to overcome. You can be sure some new giants will rear their ugly heads this year too. When you see the giants, is your first instinct to run, or to reach for your slingshot? Faith reaches for the slingshot, fear runs away. The very first thing a soldier must know, "Who is my enemy?" Why is it so important for us to identify our enemy and what difference does it make? It's important because these enemies of our soul, steal our peace, disrupt our lives, and they can destroy us. We find ourselves living in constant turmoil. If you can't identify the enemy you will never win the battle. You are defeated before you begin. Satan is the number one enemy of mankind. He is dangerous because the Bible says he comes to us clothed as an angel of light. He is masqueraded as something good, not like at Halloween where he is depicted in a red suit with a pitchfork. Many don't like the teachings of a devil who wants to kill, steal and destroy us, but to be a victorious Christian you must face the truth that he exists and he is out to harm you and your loved ones. This will change your life and your battle strategies. Never put your focus on Satan, always keep it on the LORD this coming year. It is so easy to get caught up trying to slay giants on your own and placing your focus on your circumstances, instead of on the God of your circumstances. Some of life's battles we are called to fight and some we are not. Some battles are God's alone to fight. Wisdom is knowing when to stand your ground and when to stand back and 'let God.' How many of us consider **ourselves** to be our own worst enemy? I came across this poem years ago and wrote it in my Bible so I would never forget it:

I walked along an alien path with eyes that would not see.
I raged and cursed and fought against an unknown enemy.
Anger, sorrow, pain and fear, all paved my tortured road.
Until, at last I prayed to God to ease my weary load.
A light came shining from His heart, a light to help me see.
My enemy came into view, the one I fought was me.

This New Year, do everything you can to keep your focus on God. Satan's job is to distract you, don't let him. One of his greatest deceits is getting us to focus on ourselves, me, me, me. Begin to see everything in life as coming from God. He always places Himself between you and the enemy. Thought for the day: Who are you boxing with? If it's with yourself, stop! It will be a lose, lose situation. God loves you. He died for you to have a victorious life! He has provided everything you will need to face the giants in your life this year. Everything. You will never have to fight alone. Show the world exactly who you are... a child of the Living God, a soldier in the army of Jesus Christ. Start this year by throwing your boxing gloves away and picking up God's armor instead, you'll be glad you did.

"When Christians feel safe and comfortable, the church is in its greatest danger."-unknown-

January 2

There is a rebel in the heart of all of us...

"Do not rebel against the Lord, and don't be afraid of the people of the land."
Numbers 14:9

Imagine yourself standing in front of a mirror with a pair of boxing gloves on, boxing with your own reflection. Now, isn't that just dumb! But that is exactly what we do. It's sad to think how much heartache we can bring upon ourselves; heartache and trouble that God never intended for us to experience. He tries over and over to warn us of trouble up ahead if we continue down the road we insist on taking. Many of us insist. He makes attempt after attempt to show us the right road to take, but we choose to turn a deaf ear to Him. Maybe, we can't hear Him because we have gone so far in the opposite direction from Him, that His voice can no longer be heard. Many of us don't want to hear what He has to say because it will require a change in our life. A change we don't want to make. So, we choose to ignore His still small voice. It can be too painful to take an honest inventory of our lives because we know we won't like what we see. God knows, unless we are willing to face the truth about ourselves we will never be set free. We can look in the mirror, see the enemy, and walk away and go about our business as if nothing has happened. Satan wants to keep us in the darkness, but God wants to shed His light on the sin so we will clearly see the dangerous path we are on. Most of us prefer the darkness. We reach for another drink or pill to ease the pain, but the monsters inside scream louder. We tell ourselves, "I could quit if I wanted to." We have fooled ourselves for so long, and who in their right mind wants to go through the pain involved in seeing yourself as you really are? We quickly put our "religious mask," or our "nothing is wrong with me, everything is ok, mask," back on so no one will see the real us. We can pretend just a little longer.

Why on earth would we be our own enemy? Isn't that just a double kind of stupid? Yes! **The real question is who or what is behind all of this deceit?** Most of us want to live good lives. Lives of peace and contentment, but somehow we find ourselves doing things and saying things we never thought we would say or do. How do we find ourselves going from having one little 'social' drink to being unable to get through the day without one? How can we wake up in the morning promising ourselves today we are going to keep our anger under control, only to find ourselves five minutes later yelling at the kids and kicking the dog? Only God can change our hearts. When we accept Him as Lord and Savior, we become new creatures, all things have passed away and all things become new. He gives us a new perspective in life. He gives us a new 'want to.' Don't live life by looking in the rear view mirror.

"It takes more courage to repent than to keep on sinning." –unknown-

JANUARY 3

"Sometimes the worst of times are designed by the enemy of
God to get you to give up on God's clear direction because he
knows of the powerful and wondrous blessings that are ahead."
-Chip Ingram-

"You prepare a *feast* for me in the presence of my enemies."
Ps.23:5

As the story goes a family had gathered at the dinner table and the little girl was told by her father it was her turn to say grace. Her rebellious little heart got the better of her and she turned to her father and said, "No, I don't want to." She was then instructed to go stand in the corner until she was ready to obey and say grace just as she was asked to. Finally, the little girl shuffles back to the dinner table, with her head hanging down, mumbling to herself. She gets up in her chair, bows her head and she prays, "Dear Lord, thank you for preparing this food in the presence of my enemies."

Who is the enemy? Don't you sometimes feel like this little girl? Confused, bewildered. What in the world is happening? Why is your life suddenly falling apart at the seams? The best known Psalm in the Bible is the 23rd Psalm. "The Lord is my Shepherd....He prepares a table before me in the presence of my enemies." Obviously the little girl was familiar with this scripture, but did she understand it? Do we understand it? Why do we have to go through life with enemies, for crying out loud, isn't life hard enough anyway? Have you found yourself fighting battles and you don't know why? Nothing seems to go smoothly anymore. Are you finding yourself being deceived, more and more, by others? Have you ever thought someone was your friend only to find out they aren't and even worse, they never were. You ask yourself, "Is everyone pretending?" You don't know who the enemy is anymore. So you find yourself distrusting everyone. Have you ever asked someone, "How could you do that to me? I thought you were my friend." Have you ever felt that bitter sting of a 'Judas' kiss on your cheek? Pause and think about the ONE who promises to NEVER leave you. NEVER forsake you.

"A child of God should never let adversity get him
down, except on his knees."
-Mae Nicholson-

JANUARY 4

❋

Who really is my enemy?

"O Lord, I have so many enemies; so many are against me."
Psalm. 3:1

It is very important to our own daily survival that we answer this question and answer it correctly. Our life may depend on it. Our eternity depends on it. We look around us and the enemy seems to be everywhere. The enemy can be found right in our homes, they might even be lying next to us in bed. The enemy is next door, in the work place, at church, in the grocery store, or in the worst place of all... in the mirror.

What can we do to protect ourselves? Remember this: **God always warns. Always.** If we are heading in a wrong direction in life, He will warn us or send someone to try and stop us. One way His warnings come to us are by, what I call the **"Road signs" of life**. They are our map through the dark, scary places in life for those times we can't seem to find our way. Just like regular road signs on the highways, these are used for the same purpose; "Caution," "Yield," "Bump up ahead." "Dip," "Slow down," "Road block ahead," "No trespassing," or "Do not Enter." All of them are given for our protection and to ensure we have a safe journey. Simple statements, sent to warn us, usually just a few short lines, but with years of wisdom woven into them. In my first book, "The Journey Is Too Great For Thee," I filled the book with these "Road signs." I believe they give wisdom and direction to weary travelers on the road of life. They strengthen you for the journey. They keep you from giving up or quitting. Some of these "Road signs" came right from the Bible, and some were quotes I have gathered over the years, from other weary travelers. Those who started on a journey alone and found life to be too tough, too scary and too hard to make alone. If we can learn from their experiences, we will be prepared for the battle, when we meet the giants along the road of life. I hope these Road signs, over the following days and weeks, will help make your journey a little easier and much safer.

God never intended for us to journey through this life without His help. But, many of us try, only to get bitterly disappointed in the end. Life's journey is too long, too hard and too scary to make alone, so God offers to go with us. Unfortunately, too many people turn down His offer, turn down His protection and turn down His love. They go it alone. They choose to take on the giants of this world on their own and lose.

Life is filled with enemies we **will** meet along the pathway of life. Not may meet, but will meet. They usually come at the worst possible time. David had his Goliath, Jonah his whale, Elijah had his Jezebel. Giants are inevitable. All of us will experience a "Judas" in our life at one time or another. We may get kissed more than once. Are you going to kiss back or wisely surrender them to God? Determine today to live a life of faith, of trust in a God who can never fail you. A God who loves you more than you could ever imagine.

January 5

*Life's battles are inevitable, how prepared
we are to fight them, is optional.*

"Do not be afraid! Don't be discouraged by this mighty army
for the battle is not yours, but God's."
2 Chronicles 20:15

God's plan is to prepare us for battle ahead of time. He doesn't want us to wait until we see the vicious right hook the enemy is throwing at us. What is the best way to prepare? Simply put;

KNOW YOUR ENEMY !

Webster's dictionary defines "enemy" as: hostile person, opponent, armed foe or hostile force; attacker, adversary, foe, competitor or rebel. (Ooh, this is not a nice person.) Does it sound like anyone you know? If you have read your Bible, it should. Remember the comedian Flip Wilson, and his famous line, "The devil made me do it," and he would laugh and so would the audience. In light of the tragic scene played out in the Garden of Eden, maybe it's not so funny after all. Sound familiar? Have a bite...yum! "You'll be like God." "God didn't really mean that, did He?" "It's just an apple." "Come on, just one little bite." And the whole world was turned upside down and our lives were turned inside out. It wasn't the fruit that caused the problem, it was disobedience to God. God said, "Don't do it." Satan said to Eve, "Oh, phooey, God didn't really mean it." And Eve believed the enemy. She chose to listen to the enemy instead of to her Creator. What a dummy, we think to ourselves, and we go out and do exactly the same thing. We fall just as hard for his lies. We reach for the apple and take a big juicy bite. Then the bottom drops out of our life and we wonder why. Duh! Disobedience! We tend to convince ourselves that occasional disobedience is no big deal. Maybe God won't notice. He does and it is a very big deal to Him. Obedience is a command, not a suggestion. When we really, really want something we think God does not want us to have, that is when we disobey the most. Sad thing about us is that sometimes we are willing to suffer the consequences to get what we want, when we want it. We don't want to wait for God's timing or His wisdom. Blinded by our own desires, we reach for the forbidden fruit. What have you reached for recently you know you shouldn't have?

JANUARY 6

If heaven had a post office with wanted posters on its walls, Satan's face and his demon followers would be plastered all over it.

"For the thief comes only to steal, kill and destroy. I came so that they may have and enjoy life, and have it in abundance (to the full, till it overflows)."
John 10:10

The thief, Satan, is mankind's Public Enemy Number One. He is not just the Christian's enemy, but he is also the enemy of the unbeliever. The main theme of this devotional is to help you recognize and know the enemy and then take him very seriously. To live triumphant, despite the enemy's repeated attacks and to be obedient to God's Word. This will prepare you for the daily battles of life. He is so devious and cunning; it may be very difficult at times to recognize him and the evil he brings into our lives. Sadly, there are even some Christians who laugh at the thought of a devil. They laugh their way to defeated lives. They may be saved, but they are defeated and powerless.

Every enemy that we will come across in the pages of life, Satan is behind them in some way or another.

Remember that, please. Satan is a very powerful foe. He goes to church more often than most of us do. He knows God's word better than we do. He has one goal for you and me, "to replace God in our life." He doesn't care how or with what, but he wants to get our focus on anything, but God. It could be bad things, or good things; drugs or he will attempt to get us to work too much. Work isn't in and of itself bad, unless it causes you to be out of balance in your life. Satan will do his best to get us discouraged and to doubt God. He offers "very attractive" alternatives to God's plan for our life. He wraps sin up in some very pretty packages. It's like finding a beautifully wrapped package. You can't wait to tear it open and see what's inside – only to discover inside is dog poo. Now I know what you're thinking. That's just disgusting. You're so right, but it was all I could think of. Unfortunately, sin is like that. It comes irresistibly wrapped. We think we are getting one thing only to discover we are getting something we never bargained for. We end up with something worthless and stinky. You'll find lots of it in the pigpen of life.

Satan will try to wear us down, to tire us out. He will send blow after blow to take us down. He will do whatever it takes to keep us off our knees. What is the good news? Jesus came to give us an 'abundant life!" You must choose whom you will follow. Thought for the day: "What has been keeping you off your knees lately?

January 7

Satan will never give up. He will be back...

"All men need a faith that will not shrink when washed
in the waters of affliction and adversity."
–unknown–

Satan has been at this game of deceit for thousands of years. He knows what works and what doesn't. He will never retire. He will distract us. He will try to take our eyes off Jesus and onto ourselves. He will get us into rebellion......remember? "Have a bite....yum!" He will try to get us into self-sufficiency. "I don't need God." He will attempt to keep us from forgiving others because he knows that will imprison us, in a prison without walls. He will make addictions **look attractive and harmless**, like pornography, until he gets you hooked. He will get us into worrying, fretting, and doubting, and then he will go in for the kill. He will get our minds on wrong thoughts, negative thoughts. Who do you think it is that makes us think, "I don't need God, I can do it alone?" He will bombard your life and mine with "enemies." Who tells us to "get even" instead of forgive? Who whispers to us, "Don't let them get away with that, you better get them before they get you." Who knows that the more pain he can bring into my life will cause me to doubt God more and more? Lies, lies and more lies, because Satan is a LIAR. Sad part is we think these thoughts are our own. They are not. Even sadder is we believe them. Think about the guy who really believes he's Julius Caesar and then goes on a killing spree. That man is no different from the man Jesus casts the demons out of 2000 years ago. They both are Satan's prey. They both allowed Satan access to their minds and they both fell for the enemy's lies and paid a very heavy price. Thought for the day: Do you have stinking thinking? What have you been thinking about lately? How to bless someone or how to get even?

January 8

Satan goes to church more than most of us;
and he knows the Bible better than most of us do.

"If you would not have affliction visit you twice,
then listen at once to what it teaches."
-James Burgh-

Satan will do everything he can to get you off balance. He is fighting a deadly battle. He wants your soul, but he will settle for your peace and joy. He'll knock you down, and then he'll knock you down again. If he can't get you with the first punch, he'll send another and another. He'll get you so caught up in the fight that you will lose sight of everything else. He will play mind games with you. "Did God really say?... Satan will do everything he can to try to pull you right out of the arms of Jesus. He will try to make you think it's possible, but it isn't. There isn't a demon in hell that can separate us from God's love. Not for even one minute. The forces of hell can never cause God to lose His eternal grip on His child. The enemy knows his time is short and he knows his fate. He knows hell is real, he knows Jesus wants to save you from its fires, but he will try to take as many lost souls with him, as many as he can successfully deceive.

Satan doesn't hang out in bars, he hangs out in churches.
Does he attend your church? Does he follow you to work?....Think about it. I know he's followed me a few times more than I would like.
"The church is the only institution supernaturally endowed by God. It is the one institution of which Jesus promised that the gates of hell will NOT prevail against it."
-Chuck Colson-

That is a bold prophetic statement, "The gates of hell will not prevail against the church of Jesus Christ. In the true church, TRUTH prevails. Truth isn't always popular, but it is the very foundations a believer stands on. The moment the body of Christ begins to compromise in the doctrines of Christianity, we no longer have the true church, but a charlatan, a deceiver, a harlot of what once was. It is imperative to protect the doctrines of the church with your very life. The Apostles died for this very reason. They boldly proclaimed that Jesus Christ was and is the Son of God, and their message never changed, regardless of what came against them. They chose to suffer rather than to deny their Lord. Is there any area of your life you are compromising God's Word? Who do you say Jesus is? It is the most important question you will ever be asked.

January 9

*When Satan speaks to us about God, he lies; when Satan speaks to
God about us he tells the truth.*
– unknown-

"Truth often hurts, but it is the lie that leaves the scar."
-unknown-

Satan's already got the drunk and the drug addict fooled, so he goes off to church every Sunday to find the "religious hypocrite." He's looking for the one who says one thing and lives another. Then he goes in for the kill. They never saw him coming. They never knew what hit them. Truth comes to them and they bat it away like it's an unwanted pest.

Sin did not start in the Garden of Eden, it started in Heaven. Now, that may shock you. I know it shocked me, but it is true. I always thought it was "all about that darn apple." However, Lucifer, Angel of God, Son of the Morning as he was once called, got the bright idea that he should be exalted above God. He figured he should be the one worshipped, not God, and the battle began. Lucifer said, "I will exalt myself above the throne of God." "I will...I will...I will...," he said, and God threw him out of heaven.

Sad thing is, one-third of all the angels in heaven agreed with him, and they all were cast out of heaven to the earth. Lucifer became Satan, and the angels became demons of darkness. This began the war between good and evil, light and darkness. It is a war that will continue to rage until Jesus returns. What is the war about? It's all about you and it's all about me. This deadly war is over our souls, yours and mine. The most precious thing we possess, our will and our very lives, and Satan is out to destroy them.

The choices we make on this earth, and the one we choose to follow, the one we believe, will determine who wins the battle for our soul, God or Satan. It is an act of the will to choose or reject the gospel message – but make no mistake, everyone will make a choice. Have you made your choice yet? Tomorrow may not come for you. Our times are in His Hands.

"If anyone would tell you the shortest, surest way to
happiness and all perfection, he must tell you to make
it a rule to yourself to thank and praise God for everything that
happens to you. For it is certain that whatever seeming
calamity happens to you, if you thank and praise God for it, you
turn it into a blessing." –William Law-

The thankful heart begins by accepting that Jesus has paid your sin debt in full and then thanking Him for saving you. He stands ready to save anyone who will bow their head and ask for forgiveness for the way they have lived their life apart from Him.

JANUARY 10

*God has a good plan for our lives. Trouble is
most of us want Him to bless 'our' plan.*

"Paul had been shipwrecked, whipped, beaten, stoned and imprisoned.
Through everything, his faith enabled him to maintain perspective. He
realized that as long as he was doing what he was supposed to do, his
being labeled a success or failure by others didn't really matter."
-John Maxwell

God's plan is a good plan, to give us hope and a future. (Jer. 29:11) Most of us in our arrogance think our plan is better. God has a plan, we have a plan and Satan has a plan. Satan's plan is to kill, steal and destroy us and he doesn't care how he does it or how long it takes. He isn't in any kind of hurry. He knows that one drink today will lead to two tomorrow and more the next day until he finally has you hooked. We have become our own worst enemy and it has been with the devil's help. We aren't innocent in all this. **We have the power to choose.** God never takes that away from us. It grieves Him when we choose the enemies lies over God's truth, but He will always let the choice be ours, even when it's wrong. This is why men end up spending eternity in hell...they made a choice and it was the wrong one. They did not take God's warnings seriously.

God does not play games. He takes our lives very serious and He wants us to take Him very seriously. Why? Because He knows that without Him we are no match for the enemy. Through the centuries, Satan has brought down the best starting with Adam and Eve. There are some pretty famous people on his hit list. Adam and Eve, Abraham, Noah, Peter, Judas...you, me. Whether you know it or not, your name is also on his list.

"Everyone who breathes, high and low, educated and ignorant, young and old, man and woman, has
a mission, has a work. We are not sent into this world for nothing; we are not born at random; we
are not here, that we may go to bed at night, and get up the next morning, toil for our bread, eat
and drink, laugh and joke, sin when we have a mind, and reform when we are tired of sinning, rear
a family and die. God sees every one of us; He creates every soul...for a purpose."
-John Henry Newman-

Find your purpose in life, God's purpose for you in life. The sooner the better, and hold fast to it.
Satan threw everything he possible could at the Apostle Paul but nothing destroyed his faith. There are some things in life we cannot compromise, our faith being one of them. We must settle in our hearts before the persecution comes how we will respond. If we wait to decide as adversity hits, it is too late. Adversity has a way of showing us just how much we really believe or disbelieve something. As the song says, "I have decided to follow Jesus, no turning back, no turning back." You're either all in or you're not in at all.

January 11

Satan is behind all of the evil in this world...all of it.

"Against the dark background of man's failure and sin, the CROSS shows
us the measure of God's passion against evil and the measure of God's
passion to redeem His sinful children."
-W.H.T. Gairdner-

Never forget who the author of evil is. Who do you think whispers in your ear? "It's just a little lie, no one will know." Who do you think gets your focus off your wife and kids at home, and on the cute little thing at the office? "Have a bite......yum!"... Temptation comes in many different forms. There is a good reason Satan is called the "deceiver....liar...father of lies...destroyer," just to name a few. He wants to get your focus off of God and on "self." The moment he succeeds, we are in rebellion towards God and headed down a path that will lead to our destruction. Walking away from God is never a good idea. Never.

It's so easy to view someone who disagrees with us as hostile or our adversary. How hard is it to view ourselves as hostile or as a rebel? It's difficult to view ourselves as competitors with God or even rebellious towards Him. "Me in competition with God?" you may be saying? "That's ridiculous!" Yet, we spend so much of our life trying to help Him run His universe, don't miss that, 'His' universe, while at the same time trying to get God to keep His hands off of our lives.
"The God of the universe has need of nothing."
-Clement of Rome.-

If you still have any doubt, after looking at Jesus hanging there on the cross for our sins, then you do not understand the price God paid to free you. His Son was hung there naked, spit on, laughed at, cursed, even His clothes were gambled for, and some dare to use His name as a swear word. Maybe, thinking about it this way might help, what if you were asked to give up your own child to pay for the sins of the world the way Jesus did, you would say no, I would say no, God said, "Yes," they are worth it.

January 12

Know thy enemy...

"From God we receive both our freedom and morality.
A godless society will have neither."
-Drake Raft-

There are those who foolishly make God their enemy because they are unwilling to take Him seriously. They make that foolish choice to live their whole life "indifferent" to Him, "doing their own thing," leaving God out of every major decision in life, doing what "feels good" and then wondering why their life turned out the way it did. It started empty and it will end empty. That big hole in the heart of man remains vacant until the day we let Him into our heart to fill it. That's what salvation is all about, God filling up that big empty hole in our life, taking away our sin and replacing it with Himself. When we end up with an empty life, who is our enemy under these circumstances? We again, are our own worst enemy. We have believed the lies of our number one enemy. He has defeated us once again... because we have allowed him to. It's all about choice. Who are you listening to?

God is our true friend, who always gives us the counsel and comfort we
need. Our danger lies in resisting Him; so it is essential that we acquire the
habit of hearkening to His voice, or keeping silence within, and listening
so as to lose nothing of what He says to us. We know well enough how to
keep outward silence, and to hush our spoken words, but we know little of
interior silence. It consists in hushing our idle, restless, wandering imagination,
in quieting the promptings of our worldly minds, and in suppressing the crowd
of unprofitable thoughts which excite and disturb the soul."
-Francois Fenelon-

Thought for the day. "God has never lost a battle and He has never tied one." -Bill Krishner-

Christians can already proclaim victory because of whom we serve. Jesus meant it when He said, the gates of hell would never prevail against His church. Period.

January 13

"We are too Christian to enjoy sinning and too fond of sinning to enjoy Christianity. Most of us know perfectly well what we ought to do; our trouble is that we do not want to do it."
-Peter Marshall-

""Do little things as if they were great, because of the majesty of the Lord Jesus Christ, who dwells in thee; and do great things as if they were little and easy, because of His Omnipotence."
-Blaise Pascal-

We know the right thing to do, but we don't always want to do it. What a sad statement that is, but how true, "we don't want to do it." We especially rebel when it comes to things like forgiving someone who's wronged us, or putting others above ourselves. Ouch ! This is why life hurts.

For the next few days, we will take a journey through the corridors of time. We are going to take a long, penetrating look at the enemy of us all. We are going to see Satan as God sees him and his fallen angels. We are going to study his tactics of warfare. We are going to learn to take him very seriously.

"For we are not wrestling with flesh and blood (contending only with physical opponents), but against the despotisms (oppressive, tyrannical), against the powers, against (the master spirits who are) the world rulers of this present darkness, against the spirit forces of wickedness in the heavenly (supernatural) sphere." (Eph. 6: 12 Amplified Bible)

Who is our fight against? This verse makes it real clear. We are fighting against "spiritual beings," that do most of their work through humans. Humans who allow them access to their lives. We aren't supposed to be fighting one another, but because of selfishness, pride and the unwillingness to forgive, those things we allow in our lives, we end up in a battle against one another. We get defeated again. All of hell breaks out in laughter.

Thought for the day: You have a very real enemy. He wants to destroy your life and your family. Don't let him. Learn to fight back!

January 14

"You will know the truth, and the truth will set you free."
John 8:32

"If I profess with the loudest voice and clearest exposition every portion
of the truth of God except precisely that little point which the world and
the devil are at that moment attacking, I am not confessing Christ, however
boldly I may be professing Christ. Where the battle rages, there the loyalty of
the soldier is proved; and to be steady on all the battlefield besides, is mere
flight and disgrace if he flinches at that point."
-Martin Luther-

Our enemies don't scare God, but they can scare the living daylights out of you and me...**but only until we learn the truth about them.** The truth is what Satan wants to keep you from knowing. His power is in the lie. It is in the lie that is believed. Remember the pretty package filled with you know what?...the stinky stuff of sin. Truth is what sets us free from its grasp. The more truth we know the freer we become. God says it and Satan knows it is true. Once we know the truth about our enemy, victory is just around the corner.

Buckle your seatbelt...God is about to turn 'all us cowards' into some 'mighty, giant slayers.' Long ago, God took the young shepherd boy, David, and made him into a King, **but first** God had to teach him how to slay a few giants. He needs to do the same for us. Look out Goliath! When the world saw David they saw a shepherd boy but when God looked at David He saw a Giant killer. What does God see when he looks at you?

Oops! Don't forget your slingshot...

"We're in spiritual combat – cosmic combat
for the heart and soul of humankind."
-Chuck Colson-

JANUARY 15

When the pain no longer serves a purpose; the healing begins.

"God whispers to us in our pleasure, speaks to us
in our conscience, but shouts in our pain. It is His
megaphone to rouse a deaf world."
C.S. Lewis-

God sends the good times and He allows the bad times to come our way. Now, we may not like that statement, but it is true, nevertheless. All are from His loving Hand; the good, the bad and the ugly. Some of life can get pretty ugly. It has been said that, "Trials don't make a man, they reveal a man." The real us doesn't come forth until the bottom literally drops out of our life. We believe ourselves to have great faith, until a sorrow or trial hits our life that knocks the wind right out of our sails. We have fooled ourselves into thinking we are these great spiritual giants, until God shows us the truth about our faith, or rather lack of it. Here's a little story I read a while back that speaks volumes about where our hearts are:

"During my hardest trial, I kept asking the Lord, "Why me, Lord... why, me?"

Then a friend gently put his arm around my shoulder and asked me, "Do you ask God, "Why, me?" during the good times? "Why, me?" during those times of health, great prosperity and blessing? I bowed my head and wept. I humbly asked for His forgiveness."
-Unknown-

I think this little story reveals a lot about us. We think we deserve the good things in life, not the heartaches or losses that at some point in time, come to us all. We have to remember, we live in a world of sin and sinners.

"Let me not beg for the stilling of my pain,
but for the heart to conquer it."
-Rabindranath Tagore-

January 16

*Humpty Dumpty had a great fall...so did Adam & Eve.
So did you and I.*

"God originally created man in His own image, and free from sin; but, through the temptation of Satan, he transgressed the command of God, and fell from his original holiness and righteousness; whereby his posterity inherit a nature corrupt and wholly opposed to God and His law, are under condemnation, and as soon as they are capable of moral action, become actual transgressors."
-James Boyce, 1858-

"Humpty Dumpty sat on a wall, Humpty Dumpty had a great fall"...familiar, silly childhood lyrics but do you ever feel like him? Have you found yourself feeling lost and broken by the world and the people in it. Have you been sitting on a wall of 'indifference' or 'indecision'? Maybe, on a wall of rebellion? If the answer is yes to any of these questions then you are headed for a big tumble. Somewhere down the road you fell for the lie that you don't need God in your life? You decided that you're going to run things yourself? It's no wonder your life is so out of balance. You are teetering on the wall, swaying back and forth between faith and unbelief, between obedience and disobedience. You have one foot in heaven and one foot in the world, and unhappy in both. Something has got to give. The enemy has you right where he wants you. The saddest part is, the enemy has wreaked havoc in your life and you are unaware of his presence. You are out of balance with yourself, the world around you and especially with God. There is good news though, when you start to feel like Humpty Dumpty and all of the Kings horses and all of the King's men, can't put Humpty together again.... Please remember that, "the KING of kings still can." God is still in the fixing business. He is still in the miracle business, too. He can heal broken hearts and broken lives that no one else can. He is the only One I know, who can put Humpty Dumpty back together again. He is the only One I know who can put you and me back together again.

JANUARY 17

❈

Wars and rumors of war...

"The wars that rage within the world are a reflection
of the wars that rage inside people."
-Leighton Ford-

"There will come wars and rumors of wars," says Jesus, in Matthew 24. Keep in mind that on this earth there are more wars raging than you know. Not only are there wars in Afghanistan and Iraq, but there is also a war of much greater magnitude raging in the spiritual realm. The fact it is unseen makes it no less deadly. In fact, it makes it more frightening because you can't see the enemy. You are not sure who the enemy is. Think back to the film clips of the Vietnam war when little children holding grenades approached our soldiers. The soldiers let down their guard and were killed. If we let our guard down because someone looks safe, we too will be destroyed. God's word is very clear that the enemy disguises himself, but he is a wolf in sheep's clothing. The war in Iraq is no different. Men disguising themselves as pregnant women, with bombs strapped around their waists, blowing up market places and killing hundreds. Deception is an especially deadly tool in Satan's war chest.

Who can you trust? Who is the enemy? Sometimes it is almost impossible to be sure. The stakes in this spiritual battle are high, also. The battle I am referring to is between God and Satan. It is a battle between the forces of good and evil, right and wrong, light and darkness. God has an enemy and any enemy of God is also our enemy. Satan's mission is to kill, steal and destroy. His goal is to steal you and me away from our Creator. When Adam and Eve were placed in the Garden of Eden by God Himself, there was never any question who they belonged to or to whom they were accountable. The questions started after the serpent, Satan, entered into the picture. Satan doesn't care how he takes us down, or how long it takes. What does steal mean? It means to take something that does not belong to you. Satan's plan is to steal us away from God and His plan for our life. You must not let him. God will protect you if you will just ask Him.

January 18

"Why, why, why God?..."

"God will often use the desert of quiet faithful service, or the prison of injustice, to permanently transform our self-confidence into Christ-confidence. It is only when control is out of our own hands and we are thrust blindly into God's arms that He is free to teach us that He can be completely relied upon."
-Tim Burns-

We all have questions about life. Tough questions. Unanswered questions. Baffling questions. Why does it have to hurt so much? Why does life have to be so hard most of the time? Why are there only few moments of ecstasy compared to days, months and even years in the pits? Why? Why? Why, God? Why do I seem to have so many enemies? Why do some people with cancer recover and other's die? Why is it that my neighbor's child gets a scholarship, and my child ran away from home? Why did my son die in the war for the right of another to burn the flag and shake his fist at all that America stands for? Painful questions followed by even more painful "whys?" "If you loved me Lord, why would You let this happen?" We painfully conclude, "God must not love me," and we start down the path that leads away from God, looking for some answers. Time to take an inventory. Where is the path you are on leading you to? The bible talks about two paths, two roads we can all take, in fact, we must choose one or the other. The wide road, leads to destruction. Many are found traveling this road, it is where the popular crowd is found, the compromisers, the 'do your own thing' crowd gather. One person you will never find on this road is Jesus. The 'narrow' road is where you will find Him. Very few choose to travel this road. It is the harder of the two. It requires obedience to God, it requires patience, waiting on God to reveal His plan, it involves above all, trust in a God you cannot see, to direct you to a place you do not know. That is faith! It is the way of truth, and often times the way of suffering. On this road, God will require you to give up your life and surrender it to Him. It is not always and easy thing to do but it is always the wisest choice. He leads, we follow. It is as simple as that.

"It must be remembered that there is spiritual wickedness at the back of all confusion and discord in the work of God. The servant of Christ must, therefore, practically recognize that his warfare is with these satanic beings and must be waged on his knees."
-D.E. Hoste-

JANUARY 19

Every one of us is on a journey...not all of us are traveling with God.

"I believe Jesus Christ to be the Son of God. The miracles which He wrought establish in my mind, His personal authority, and render it proper for me to believe whatever He asserts. I believe, therefore, all His declarations, as well when He declares Himself to be the Son of God, as when He declares any other proposition. And I believe there is no other way of salvation than through the merits of His atonement."
-Daniel Webster-

With life comes many battles. I hope these daily reminders will help to give you a better understanding of some of those difficult questions we all have. Life isn't fair and it never will be, at least not until God makes things right again, and He will. Now, that may discourage you, because we want things done now. We are a microwave society. We want out of our pain and we want out of it now. God will act, but He usually doesn't do it in our timing, but He will do it. You can count on it. Why? because our enemies are His enemies and because He said so.

Keep in mind that there will always be some questions we will <u>never</u> have answered to our satisfaction, this side of heaven.

Why did Adam and Eve do what they did? Why couldn't they have just left that darn apple alone? Why the Hitler's and the Saddam Hussein's of the world? Why are there terrorists who are allowed to kill the innocent? If that weren't bad enough, they claim to do it in the name of God. How on earth do you fight against an enemy like that? It has to start in the hearts of men. We must continue to get the good news of the gospel of Jesus Christ out to a lost world. It is what will change the world. It will first change the heart of each man that hears it, and eventually change the heart of a city, a state, a nation. The gospel is unpopular with the world. Many over the centuries have been put to death proclaiming it. They gladly went to their deaths rather than to deny the Lord who bought them with His precious blood.

"I believe there are many accommodating preachers....Jesus Christ did not say, "Go into the world and tell the world that it is quite right." The gospel is something completely different. In fact, it is directly opposed to the world."
-C.S. Lewis-

Many unanswered questions... Accept it and go on with life. Who have you told about Jesus, lately? What is it you want out of life? What do you seek most in life? "But seek first His kingdom and His righteousness, and all these things will be given to you as well."
-Matthew 6:33-

What have you been struggling with that you need to finally accept that it will never change or you will never get it back, and you need to release it to God and move on?

January 20

*Some things in life just can't be humanly reasoned out
no matter how hard we try or how smart you think you are.*

"Pride made the soul desert God, to whom
it should cling as the source of life, and to
imagine itself instead as the source of its own life."
-Augustine of Hippo-

Not only some of the bad times in life can't be explained, but also some of the good things have no explanation, either. For instance, travel back with me 2000 years ago to the day the ten lepers came to Jesus to be healed. Jesus' heart broke to see these broken lives and He knew that even though they would not return to thank Him (except one), He still chose to heal all ten of them. That's God love. That's His grace in action. We think we deserve the 'good stuff' life has to offer but none of the bad.

Someone once said, **"When you don't understand, and you can't trace His hand, trust His heart."** When there are things we can't seem to figure out using our own earthly wisdom and we don't see any trace of God's hand in our circumstances, then we are to fall back on who He is. He isn't just a God of love, He is love. He cannot make a mistake.

God in His infinite wisdom does not reveal all, but He will always reveal enough of Himself, so that we may be assured that He is still on His throne and no one is going to push Him off of it. He will speak to your heart that He is in control and always will be, and He will reveal whatever is necessary for your survival.

Have you lost the joy and peace in your heart? Have you forgotten how to laugh and enjoy life because you're too busy fighting giants? I hope to put courage back into your life, put a smile back on your lips and the peace back into your heart, once again, or maybe for some of you, for the very first time. Today, make a choice to walk away from trying to figure it all out. That is God's job and He is very good at it. He doesn't need our help, so be wise and throw yourself a retirement party.

January 21

*Courage: When only you and God
are aware of how really scared you are.*

"Let the fact of what our Lord suffered for you grip you,
and you will never again be the same."
-Oliver B. Greene-

Life may start as a fairy tale starts, "Once upon a time..." but it sure doesn't always end with... "And they lived happily ever after." Some won't. In fact, many of us won't because of the choices we've made or didn't make.

Somewhere along the way your castle comes crumbling down. You try to rebuild and it's not easy. This time you are forced to build moats and big walls around your castle in order to keep the giants out. Reality begins to set in, and you find that not everyone has your best interests at heart. Not everyone is your friend. Not everyone lives happily ever after. Cinderella loses her shoe and no one cares, much less bothers to return it. There is no Prince Charming, no Easter Bunny, no Santa Claus and no Tooth Fairy. More lies from the enemy. Our romances fall apart, even after you've had to kiss a bunch of ugly, smelly frogs. Our loved ones die, or they choose to leave us. Some kids don't have enough food, much less get presents at Christmas time, and we are no richer for having lost our teeth. Santa Claus and the Tooth Fairy must have gotten our address mixed up with someone else's. Disappointment after disappointment causes us to begin to question life. We quickly figure out this growing up stuff is for the birds and besides that, it hurts. We begin to ask the big "WHY & WHAT?" Why am I here? And what am I supposed to be doing now that I'm here? The mundaneness of life or its chaotic pace, takes its toll on us day after day. We shake our fist at a silent heaven or turn away from God, in despair. We develop an attitude of indifference. We give up. Maybe there is a God, maybe there's not. If there is I'll leave Him alone if He'll leave me alone. Not really understanding the impact of those words or the consequences of a life lived without God. God knows each and every fear we face, and why we face them. He never once has asked us to face them alone.

"Jesus does not give recipes that show the way to God as
other teachers of religion do. He is **Himself** the way."
-Karl Barth-

Learn to practice His presence. Get up each morning, and say "Good morning Lord, it's a beautiful day you have made, help me to bring glory and honor to Your name today."

January 22

Surrounded by the enemy...

"Faith takes God without any ifs. If God says
anything, faith says, "I believe it;" faith says, "Amen" to it."
-D.L. Moody-

Enemies everywhere! Most of the time, you don't even know who you're fighting anymore or what you're trying to protect yourself from. Have you found that trying to make it through life on your own can be too hard and very, very scary at times? Have you found yourself traveling down that "road of selfishness," pleasing "self," and all along feeling a gentle tug at your heartstrings, knowing that it's God doing the pulling? He gently whispers to you "Don't go that way, follow Me." "I am the Way."

Please don't miss that. It's not just me saying, Jesus is the way. It's Jesus Himself saying it. You either believe Him or you don't. Please take note what He is not saying. He isn't saying He is one of many ways, He is saying, "I am **THE WAY**," the **only** way. You may be thinking how narrow minded that is. Yes, it is, but truth by its very nature can be very limiting. Who does He invite? ***Whosoever*** will call upon the name of the LORD will be saved. Last time I looked I was a '***whosoever***' will and so are you. That is all inclusive. It includes you, me, your neighbor, a prisoner in jail, a housewife, farm worker, doctor, janitor, it includes everyone...

"Either sin is with you, lying on your shoulders, or it is
lying on Christ, the Lamb of God. Now if is lying on your
back, you are lost; but if it is resting on Christ, you are free,
and you will be saved. Now choose what you want."
-Martin Luther-

So, the next time someone tells you how narrow minded you Christians are, ask them if they are a 'whosoever will' or a 'whosoever won't.'

"The Son (Jesus Christ) is the radiance of God's glory and the exact representation
of His being, sustaining all things by His powerful word. After He
had provided purification for sins, He sat down at the right hand of
the Majesty in heaven."
Hebrews 1:3

JANUARY 23

*Trouble with most of us is we are much too busy trying to find
an answer other than God and there isn't one.*

"No founder of any religion has dared to claim for himself
one fraction of the assertions made by the Lord Jesus Christ about Himself."
-Henry J. Heydt-

The sooner you can get a revelation, "There isn't any answer to life apart from God," you will have saved yourself a truckload of grief and sorrow not to mention wasted years.

How many of us view God as our enemy? Well, maybe you wouldn't put it quite that harshly, but really, isn't anyone who interferes with our plans, our hope our dreams, or stands in the way of us getting what we want, our enemy? Oh, we may attempt to give God our "to do list" or "our just can't do without list," but when He doesn't come through like we think He should, we turn our backs on Him and try to fix it ourselves. Most of life's battles are our attempts to get what we want, when we want and how we want. We don't like it when God says, "No," to some request of ours, especially when it's something we really, really want. Has He said "No," even after you have begged and pleaded with Him, thinking you know better what you need than He does. You are just sure its something you've got to have. How many times have you looked elsewhere for the answer, when God has given you a resounding, "No," to some request of yours. Did you then tell yourself, "I don't need God?" Well, God has ways of "**touching your circumstances**" to make you realize He is the One person you can't live without. We were never meant to travel through this life on our own. We were never meant to travel even one moment without Him at our side. He is always there, whether we acknowledge the fact is another matter. He leads, we follow. Trouble with that is, we know He's going to take us to places we don't want to go and ask of us things we don't want to do. Ouch! It's going to hurt and we know it. Our attitude quickly changes. "Ok, God, I'll go there with you but I won't to that place," as if we have a choice. Well, guess where God is going to take us? Yep, right to the place we didn't want to go. Is it because He's a mean God that just loves to see His children miserable? No, it's because the 'place' should **never** be our focus. He wants us to learn that as long as He is with us, that is all that really matters. Our focus should be on God and nothing else. He doesn't ask for our partial obedience either, He requires **total surrender.** As God touches more and more of our circumstances as only He can do, surrender starts to look better and better. Jesus claimed to be the Son of God who takes away the sin of the world, coming again one day, not as a babe in a manger, but as judge of all mankind.

"He said that He was Lord of the Sabbath; He claimed to forgive sins; He continually identified
Himself, in His work, His person and His glory, with the One He termed His Heavenly Father;
He accepted men's worship; and He said He was to be the judge of all men at the last day, and that
their eternal destiny would depend on their attitude to Him."
-J.N.D. Anderson-

January 24

Following in His footsteps...

"If I could hear Christ praying for me in the next room, I would not fear a million enemies. Yet distance makes no difference. He is praying for me."
-Robert Murray M'Cheyne-

Where will Jesus lead us to if we choose to follow Him? To answer that question let's see some of the places He has been. His footsteps can lead to the lion's den. Who in their right mind wants to tag along for fear that we might be their next meal? Never mind that He has the ability to shut the lion's mouths if He wants to. Either way it's going be a very scary trip and we know it, so we don't want to go. So, we try to figure a way to get out of it. We begin to rationalize or reason our way out of obedience. Big mistake!

"Follow Me," Jesus says, again. Sounds like a piece of cake, until you find out where He's going next. His footsteps take us to the sick and wounded. People we would rather forget than help. "Let someone else take care of them," we mutter to ourselves. We refuse to let their desperate need, invade our safe, comfortable little world of denial. How many times have you seen those poor starving children on TV and immediately changed the channel. Then you feel guilty because you did, but your guilt was short lived. Just because you changed the channel does not mean the children are no longer hungry. That's the first sign of a heart beginning to grow cold towards the things of God, a heart that is becoming cold and indifferent. Instead of choosing compassion, we choose self. You don't want to know there are people out there without enough food, especially children, because you might have to make a choice to help them or turn your back on them. Many choose to turn their backs. We may not be able to do something spectacular, but we can make a difference by changing one life at a time.

"To the hurting, He is the great Physician.
To the confused, He is the Light.
To the lost, He is the Way.
To the hungry, He is the Bread of Life.
To the thirsty, He is the Water of Life.
To the broken, He is the Balm in Gilead."
-Calvin Miller-

Who is He to you? What is it that you need most today? He will meet that need and more.

January 25

Help...fire! Oops! No, it's a storm...no, it's an earthquake...

"Jesus came treading the waves; and so He puts all the swelling tumults of life under His feet. Christians – why afraid?" -Augustine of Hippo-

Today, we will learn more about following Jesus. How about following Him through a fiery furnace? Want to go there? Yikes! Me neither. But sometimes that is exactly where God leads. Not only is it hot, but He allows the enemy to heat it up seven times hotter. "Lord, what are you doing?" we shout over the crackling flames. But, guess what? He knows exactly what He's doing. He's into miracles, not into turning His children into crispy critters. I believe He **allows** the fire to get heated up, to show us that even though it may look as if things are getting worse, or totally out of control, He can handle them.

"The wise man in a storm prays to God, not for safety from danger, but for deliverance from fear."
-Ralph Waldo Emerson-

What do you pray for when a storm strikes? I pray, "Help! Lord." Ever been in a boat when a storm hit? I have been in some pretty bad weather on the Pacific Ocean, sailing with my dad to Catalina Island, and it scared me half to death. Waves coming up over the edge of the boat, sure you are about to be 'Jaws' next snack or the next episode on Gilligan's Island. A simple life jacket was all that stood between me and Jaws. God offers us a life jacket in this life, Jesus. We need only put Him on, being clothed in His righteousness, not our own.

Remember the night the disciples went through a very bad storm on the Sea of Galilee? The worst part is Jesus is the One who sent them into the storm in the first place. He told them to get in the boat and He would meet them on the other side. He knew they were walking right into a storm of huge magnitude, a storm beyond their control, but not His. When the storm hit, they were sure there would be no "reaching the other side," for them. They were scared to death and they should have been, as far as I'm concerned, but then Jesus comes walking to them on the water. I have to chuckle at this. Were the disciples more afraid of the storm or of Jesus walking on the water? They thought they saw a ghost. The Bible says there is only one thing we have to fear, and that is fear God. Hugh Black has said, "The fear of God kills all other fears."

"The fear of the Lord is the beginning of all wisdom." (Proverbs 1:7).

"Happy the soul that has been awed by a view of God's Majesty, that has had a vision of God's awful greatness, His ineffable holiness, His perfect righteousness, His irresistible power, His sovereign grace." -Unknown-

Jesus did not leave the disciples alone on that angry sea that night. He was watching them the whole time even as the waves threatened to take them out, still he watched. When He said, "I will see you on the other side," He meant every word of it. Only He has the power to calm the sea. He promises to get you to the other side too.

January 26

Getting out of the boat...

"The remarkable thing about fearing God is that
when you fear God, you fear nothing else, whereas
if you do not fear God, you fear everything else."
-Oswald Chambers-

I can't help but think Peter had to have at least one screw loose to ask Jesus, "Let me come to you, Lord." What? Are you crazy Peter? Stay in the boat where at least you're a little safer, (at least until we all sink.) That's kind of like being on an airplane that's crashing and being glad you're sitting in the back of the plane. Duh! The back of the plane is going down too. But no, Peter probably had a deeper, more intimate glimpse of who Jesus really was and because of this was able to get out of the boat and try what no man had ever done before, "walk on water." Remember, however, who Peter was walking to. It makes a big difference how brave you're willing to be when you know that it's Jesus waiting for you. Bad news is, the very moment Peter took his eyes off the Lord he started to sink. Blub! Blub! Blub! was the sound of Peter's lack of faith. "Peter, you shouldn't have looked at your circumstances." God's grace is what carries us through the most bitter of circumstances. His grace is what sustains us. It is nothing found in ourselves, but by His merciful grace He brings us through, especially when we are willing to get out of the boat.

"Grace puts its hand on the boasting
mouth, and shuts it once for all."
-C.H. Spurgeon-

Who in their right mind couldn't have seen those giant waves and not been scared half out of their wits? Answer: Someone with faith. "Peter you should have kept your eyes on the Lord." Advice is cheap...especially when it's not me getting wet. We can criticize Peter all we want but you have to admire him. He had to have real guts to get out of the boat in the first place. How many of us would have gotten out of the boat? Would you? Me neither. Not only does God give us flying lessons at the most inopportune time, but He also gives us boating lessons so we can learn to swim in the storm.

JANUARY 27

When the storms of life are overwhelming...

"Sorrow is one of the things that are lent, not given. A thing that
is lent may be taken away. Joy is given; sorrow is lent;...then it will
be taken away and everlasting joy will be our Father's gift to us, and
the Lord God will wipe away all tears from off our faces."
-Amy Carmichael-

When God sends the storm it is priceless...there is a precious insight in this story of the Apostles getting into the boat as Jesus commanded and Peter getting out of the boat, walking on the water to His Lord, I hope you didn't miss. Not only did Jesus send them into the storm, He knew it would overwhelm them. Has He ever sent you into one of those kinds of storms? Yes, me too. He knew they would be afraid. He knew I was afraid. How do I know? I knew because I must have reminded Him at least a hundred times. "Lord, I'm afraid. I can't do this." "Yes you can," He would whisper back. He also knew that nothing less than His presence would allay their fears and mine. After challenging Peter to do something he thought would be impossible, and Peter took Him up on His offer, then Jesus simply spoke and the seas were calm. Has He ever challenged you to do the impossible while you were in the midst of a trial? Did He come through for you? Of course He did. He promises to. What was the disciple's reaction? "Even the winds obey Him." Think of that. All of nature is subject to Him. No wonder the Bible proclaims that if men refuse to praise Him then the very rocks will cry out. They will be unable to remain silent. Wow...don't you wish you could have been there that night?

I hope you saw this wasn't just a story of Peter walking to Jesus on the water, but there was so much more. If Jesus sends us into a storm, He will meet us in the middle of it. Especially when we are the most scared and then He will calm the storm for us, just like He did for His disciples.

"Now to Him who is able to do immeasurably more than all we
dare to ask or even imagine, according to His power that is at work within us,
to Him be glory in the church and in Christ Jesus throughout all
generations, forever and ever."
-Ephesians 3:20-21-

God knows there will be times our faith may start out strong and then falter because of some unforeseen circumstance. At those times He stands more than ready to reach out His hand and lift us out of the water and encourage us not to give up because He is with us.

January 28

Well, well, well...

"Our attitude towards sin is more self-centered than God-centered.
We are more concerned about our own 'victory' over sin than we
are about the fact that our sin grieves the heart of God."
-Jerry Bridges-

One day Jesus took a trip to a well. There Jesus met up with a woman who had been married a gazillion times and was now living with some man she was not married to. The others had all kicked her out. You see, in those days, if the wife burnt the toast then she was soon toast herself. All the man had to say 3 times was "I divorce you," "I divorce you," "I divorce you." We would have kept ourselves at a safe distance from her, but not Jesus. The other women in the town wouldn't even come to the well when she was there. Maybe, they were afraid their husbands would be 'her gazillionth and one.' We would have passed judgment on her, but not Jesus. He offered her living water instead. We would never have allowed the likes of her into our church, but not Jesus. He offered her something she couldn't find anywhere else, forgiveness and a glimpse into the very heart of God. If you want to change the way you are living, God says you can, with His help.

Concerning Sin...
"Man calls it an accident, God calls it an abomination.
Man calls it a blunder, God calls it blindness.
Man calls it a defect, God calls it a disease.
Man calls it a chance, God calls it a choice."
-Unknown-

We need to start calling sin what God calls it. He paid a very heavy price for us to diminish its effects on our way of living and on our eternal destiny. God gets to define sin, not man. How about following Jesus to '<u>your</u>' church? Yep, I said 'your' church. What would He find? Are you squirming in your chair yet? It makes me very squirmy too. Does your church let 'sinners' in? Mine does, how do I know? because they let me in. Newsflash! We are ALL sinners. In fact, one day Jesus turned to the 'religious' Pharisees of His day and said they were white washed sepulchers, filled with dead men's bones. As you can imagine, Jesus' words didn't go over so well with these guys. In their own eyes, they were the holiest men on the face of the earth yet, they denied Jesus was the Son of the Living God.

"Original sin is the only rational solution of the undeniable fact of the deep, universal and early
manifested sinfulness of men in all ages, of every class, and in every part of the world."
-Charles Hodge-

Who do you say that Jesus is? Settle that question this side of eternity, you won't have a chance once this life is over.

January 29

*If I can sit in a church service and not be moved by God speaking then
either I am not listening or I am in rebellion.*
-unknown-

"The unexamined life is a life not worth living."
-Socrates-

Makes you pretty uncomfortable doesn't it, just the thought of Jesus walking into your church? What do you think the reaction to Him would be? If it's anything other than falling on your face before Him, you are definitely in the wrong church. Would He find you with a Bible in your hand? Or is it sitting at home on your coffee table collecting dust? Just there for show or to impress company how "spiritual" you are? Would the sermon just tickle your flesh and make you "feel good" that you played church today or was it a "life changing sermon?" Did it challenge you to love those who hate you? Ouch! Those who lie about you? Ouch! Those who cheat you? Ouch! And the very worst one of all, did it command you to put other's before yourself. Not just suggest it might be a good idea, but command you to esteem others greater than yourself. Ouch! Ouch! Ouch! Lord, stop. Commanding us to forgive all of our enemies, no matter what they did. Ouch!

"No more soul-destroying doctrine could well be devised
than the doctrine that sinners can regenerate themselves, and
repent and believe just when they please. As it is truth both of
Scripture and of experience that the unrenewed man can do nothing
of himself to secure his salvation, it is essential that he should be
brought to practical conviction of that truth. When, thus convinced,
and not before, he seeks help from the only source whence it can be obtained."
-Charles Hodge-

We love to put manger scenes in our churches at Christmas time to remember His birth. Many churches have crucifixes with Jesus hanging on the cross to help us remember His death, but were He to walk into our sanctuary, just the glory of His presence would be all the light we would need. Not only was He born into a world that didn't want Him, but even the religious people of His day had a part in putting Him to death. But, let us never forget those wondrous words, "On the third day I will rise again," and that's just what He did. That's still not the end of the story because He said, "I will come again and take you unto Myself, that where I am, you may be also." See, why it's so important to choose the right church? When He does return, where will He find you? Will you be somewhere you shouldn't or will you be sitting on ready for His return? He is coming again.

"One of the outstanding glories of the gospel is its promise of eternal security to all who truly
believe it. The gospel presents no third-rate Physician who is competent to treat only the
milder cases, but One who is capable of curing the most desperate cases."
-A.W. Pink-

January 30

What are you doing here?

"In times of trouble, remember that God is:
Too kind to be cruel,
Too wise to make a mistake, and
too deep to explain Himself."
-Unknown-

How about following Jesus to the pigpen? What??? Yes, you heard me right, to the pigpen. It used to be one of my favorite places. I use to hang out there a lot and I was never quite sure how I got there, sometimes. What are we going to find there, you may be asking yourself? You're going to find a dirty, broken, stinky child of God who decided one day that he didn't need God telling him how to run his life anymore. Sound familiar? We all have moments like that. Some of us have months and even years. He wanted to have some fun. He was tired of all those rules of God, "Thou shalt 'not' this..." and "thou shalt 'not' that," "Thou shalt, not, not, not." We don't like to hear that. He was going to try some of the "Thou shalts... But they didn't have anything to do with God. "Thou shalt...do thy own thing...party on...live for self...and the list is endless.

I think the story of the Prodigal son will always be my very favorite story in the whole Bible. It gives hope to us all. It isn't just a story about rebellion and sin, but it is the story of a Father's magnificent, unconditional love for His child who had gotten himself into a pretty big, stinky mess and didn't even know it until it was too late. Even though you or I may wander away from God or choose to deliberately walk away, He will not leave us happy and content in our sin. He will **'touch my circumstances'** so that I will one day long to return home to my Father. Why? Because He loves me and because He doesn't give up on me as easily as I give up on myself or others. He won't leave me in the pigpen unless I insist. Some of us insist. Some of us stay in the pigpen so long, we begin to sound like them, "oink, oink." Unfortunately, we begin to smell like them too. Sin stinks. We don't belong there. We don't know it but God does. He patiently waits for us to come to our senses and head back home. "I will go to my Father." He made a choice. A good choice will always get us out of the mess we have found ourselves in.

"Faith is often found and strengthened right at the point of greatest disappointment."
-Rodney McBride-

January 31

*You can take a thousand steps away from God, but
it only takes one step to return home.*

"The discerning heart seeks knowledge, but
the mouth of a fool feeds on folly."
-Proverbs 15:14-

All it takes to head back home is a decision of the will. "I don't want to live like this anymore, I will return to my Father." "I will..." and you will find your Father waiting for you with open arms. He won't even ask you to clean up before He throws His arms around you. He will love you just as you are. Hopefully, you will have found the experience in the pigpen so awful you will never choose to leave the Father's house again. Some do, however.

Let's follow Jesus to the night Peter denied he ever knew Him. It was the night the world determined to put to death the Son of God. This is another one of those unanswered questions. How can Peter be walking on the water to Jesus one day, telling Him he would follow Jesus to death if necessary and then a few days later tell people he doesn't even know Him? Fear causes us to do some pretty crazy things. I have to hang my own head in shame on this one. There have been times God has provided something for me only He could have done and I was a victorious, unstoppable saint. Then just a little while later, when I found myself in another impossible situation, wondering if God really exists, and if He did, would He help me? I can imagine your head is hanging down a bit right about now, too. Thank God, this is not the end of the story or of Peter. After Jesus was put to death and raised from the dead, and the women saw Him, He told the women, "Go tell the others and Peter," that He had risen and was alive. Now, why would Jesus single out Peter? I think it's because He knew Peter's heart. He knew Peter's heart was broken. The Bible says, "Peter went out and **wept bitterly**." Peter knew he had failed Jesus and he had failed himself, just to save his own hide. Peter had given up on himself, but Jesus didn't. It's the same with you and me. Jesus won't give up on us either. Peter thought his service to the Lord was over, only to find that it was really just beginning. Peter was forgiven. How do we know that? Jesus allowed Peter to be the one to preach the unforgettable sermon on the day of Pentecost. Filled with the power of the Holy Spirit, Peter delivered a message that has touched the hearts and minds of millions, through all these centuries. "Jesus died for you and was raised again on the third day and is alive." He has conquered death for you so that you can conquer life for Him. We are more than conquerors in Jesus who loved us.

"New things will always come along. Some will be good;
some will be better. But according to God, only one
thing will be best. He sent His Son into the world to live
a perfect life and go to the cross to bear His wrath for
sinners like you and me."
-C.J.Mahaney-

February 1

*God plus one (me or you) is **always** a majority.*

"We have lost the sense that we are at war and that is why we are so often defeated. It's not that Christians don't want to win. They don't even know they are at war."
-David Jeremiah-

Are there battles, skirmishes or an outright war in the forecast of your life? This book is about surviving those battles, but you won't survive if you don't know who your enemy is.

Let me say that again just in case you might have missed it. If you don't know who it is you are fighting, you're going to lose. Not just lose, but get creamed. Do you know if you are going to be on the winning side? You can know. You see, there are those of us who have read God's word and already know God wins. Thank the Lord, that is why we don't have to wonder if it's all going to turn out ok. With Jesus, we know it will. With Jesus you can't lose. Without Him, you are already defeated. It's a done deal. Satan is defeated and he knows it. Don't miss that. He knows he is going to lose and he is very angry. His time is short and he is going to take as many lost souls with him, as he can. Are you one of them? Is a loved one on Satan's 'already has' list? Pray for them! Intercede for them! Do not give up. All of heaven will be behind your prayers shouting a hearty AMEN! Let it be so! If you just refuse to give up.

February 2

*Are you on God's side or do you
just think you are?*

" We say- "If I really could believe!" The point is – If I
really will believe. No wonder Jesus Christ lays such emphasis on
the sin of unbelief. "And He did not mighty works there because
of their unbelief." If we really believed that God meant what He said-
what should we be like! Dare I really let God be to me all that He says He will be?
-Oswald Chambers-

Remember, those chilling words of Jesus, "Depart from Me, I never knew you..." Those words will be spoken some day in the future, will they be directed at you or someone you love? As you continue to read you may find out you've been on the wrong side all along. It's better to find out now then to waste your whole life fighting for the wrong cause. You might be very sincere in your efforts, but nevertheless, you are sincerely wrong. The stakes are too high on this one, not to be on God's side and know it. It might surprise you and it might scare the living daylights right out of you when you see the battle from Heaven's perspective. Actually, battle isn't a strong enough word, "war" is more like it, a "raging" (violent) war. Satan is a deadly adversary. Don't ever forget that, please. Anyone who's out to devour you is evil. Pure evil. The good news is Jesus has conquered him. He is a defeated foe and I plan to be in the balconies of Heaven cheering as he is thrown into the lake of fire. I pray you will be right beside me with a front row seat.

"God meets you in your weakness, not in your strength.
He comforts those who mourn, not those who live
above desperation. He reveals Himself more often in
darkness than in the happy moments of life."
-Dan Allender & Tremper Longman III-

Some days we are weak. Some days we are stronger. Every day we need Jesus. Some days we are more aware of that need than other days.

FEBRUARY 3

*Giants don't scare God and He doesn't
Want them to scare you either.*

"The Christian's faith isn't a leap into the dark. It is
a well-placed trust in the Light of the world, JESUS."
-Ravi Zacharias & Kevin Johnson-

What do I mean when I refer to "giants?" Giants are anything in life bigger than us. Anything or anyone out to destroy us; get us off track; turn us away from God; or cause us to doubt God and His love. In a nutshell, it's anything that separates you or me from God, whether intentional or unintentional.

Trials, storms and heartaches come to us all. Not one of us will escape them. We usually look at them as "the enemy." How we respond to them is the key to our survival. Don't miss that. It doesn't matter what enemy you are up against. What does matter is your response. Do you fall to pieces at the first sight of blood on the battlefield of life or do you stand your ground and look up, to the Commander of Heaven's armies for help?

One minute life seems rosy and the next minute it seems to be spinning out of control. Some of life's storms are inevitable, some we bring on ourselves. Those are the hardest. Some of us are so pigheaded we give God no choice but to discipline us, and He will use storms, trials, giants, whatever it takes to get us back on His path. Some storms God never intended for us to have to go through them. Unfortunately, we choose the long hard road through life instead of the straight and narrow path.

**We choose a much harder path through life
than God ever intended for us to take.**

Don't skip over that word, **'choose.'** It's a very important 'life' word. It means "I am responsible for my life." With choice comes accountability. I can choose to go down the road that has lots of giants on it or I can choose to follow Him. Many choose the giants. I've been down that road myself, but there is good news. You don't have to stay on that road. You can get off of it at any time. God will help you. It's all about choice. Choose to go home. Your Father is waiting for you.

February 4

God's way is a straight and narrow path, but we choose to make it crooked by the choices we make or don't make.
-unknown-

"He that won't be counseled, can't be helped."
-Benjamin Franklin-

Most of the "messes" in our lives are self-orchestrated, even though we may be tempted to blame them on others. We are usually the one responsible for the messes we find ourselves in, and it's all because of bad choices. We wanted something so bad we would do anything to get it, regardless of the consequences. We can suddenly or maybe even slowly over a long period of time, find ourselves in a world of hurt. Those are the most painful. We wake up one day and our life has come apart at the seams. We wonder what in the world happened. Simply said, we chose to ignore God and His many warnings and now the consequences have come knocking on our door. Bad choices bring with them a whole lot of pain, not sometimes, but every time.

You will try to get rid of the pain your own way, only to find yourself running out of ways to deaden that pain deep inside you. Will you be able to do it? No. God will not let you. God will never leave you content in your sin. He will never leave you satisfied without Him. Never. That is how He can use the messes we create to draw us to Himself. If I had the ability to fix my own mess, I would have no need of God.

When things are going along just great, how many of us bother to give God a second thought? Not many. It's a different story, however, when the bottom drops out from under us and its, "Lord, help! Where are You?"

Have you realized that there's more to life than what you have been experiencing, but you won't take the time to find out what that something is? Maybe, you're afraid to find out. I was. In my heart I knew God was after me, but I was more concerned with what I would have to give up. Everyone knows Christians don't have any fun, or so we think. Because there are all those stupid rules and stuff, just to spoil our fun. We never see God's Hand of protection in all those "stupid rules and stuff," until it's too late. Then we piously ask a friend as we cry on their shoulder, "Why did God let this happen to me?" Wouldn't it have been easier to just do what He said in the first place? Think about it.

God does not want us to live hurt. He is still in the healing business.

February 5

Success isn't measured by what we achieve. It is better measured by what we had to give up in order to get it.

"My definition of success: choosing to enter into the arena of action, determined to give yourself to that cause which will better mankind and last for eternity. Success is more than just power or not violating the rights of others; it is the privilege of contributing to the betterment of others."
-John Maxwell-

Did the successful business man have to sacrifice his integrity or his family in order to "keep up with the Jones'." Was it worth it? Who are the Jones' anyhow? They are just people trying to keep up with the Smith's and on it goes. Some friend of yours might think it was worth it, but God never would. It's impossible for us to measure the damage done to children who have no father around, but God knows. An empty, empty, child with a life filled with "stuff." "Stuff," instead of hugs. "Stuff," instead of a listening heart of a parent. "Stuff," instead of your precious time that lets a child know just how important he is to you. How many kids could have been saved with a simple hug, a kind word and "I love you?" How many? I think the number would sicken us. The really sad part is that it doesn't matter what the stuff is. It could be a new car, but a genuine hug at the right time is priceless. A car can't wipe away a tear or put a bandaide on a heart that is broken.

It's all up to each of us. It's all about the choices we make or more importantly, the choices we don't make. Ask yourself if you ever had to compromise your integrity or your reputation to succeed. If you did, you just lost. Any kind of compromise and you are a loser.

Have you been doing your own thing? Have you put God on the back burner? Found you have no time for Him? Can you imagine how silly that is? No time for the God of the Universe? "Sorry, God, I have better things to do." What could be so important in someone's life to make them turn their back on God? Nothing! Absolutely nothing! Again, we choose.

So, He leaves us to fight the giants on our own. What you need to realize is that because God loves us so much there will come a time in our life when His patience runs out on our rebellion. He leaves us to find out that we are not very good at fighting giants. He will allow a few giants to overwhelm us to teach us we can't make it through life without Him. My question is, "Why would anyone want to?"

"Success has ruined many a man."
-Benjamin Franklin-

February 6

God does not play games. He is playing for keeps.

"Christians get excited about the return of Jesus. Oh, happy day! Yes,
it is a happy day for the saved, but for the unsaved the return of Jesus
is the worst of all conceivable calamities."
-R.C. Sproul-

How many of us treat life like it is a game. We think we can make those "important" decisions in life, later on. For some, later on never comes. We fool ourselves into thinking we can get serious about God "stuff" after we have had a little fun. We try to stay in contact with Heaven with a quick prayer here and another quick prayer there. We want to know God is there, "just in case." Sadly, most of us treat God as our back-up plan. Many of us treat Him like some personal vending machine in the sky. "God give me this," "God I need that." "Hurry, God." "What's taking you so long, Lord?" We get angry or we get irritated at the slowness of Heaven. So, God decides to give us a little reality check by sending a few giants our way. What we don't realize is that there is a line God draws for each of us and He says "Don't cross over it." How close are you to that line right now? If you can't answer that question you are already in bigger trouble than you can imagine. Just over that line is big, scary giants that will wreck and ruin your life. I can guarantee you that you won't like what's on the other side.

Our own conscience sounds a warning. God has made us like that. Our conscience confirms to us that such a line does exist. If you cross that line you are probably trying to run away from Him, but you will find yourself coming face to face with Him. We think we can run from Him, but we can't. We end up confused and running in circles. We may look over our shoulder only to see we are being pursued by giants, big scary giants. God may use these giants to get you back on track. It will hurt. There is nothing worse than God using our enemies to discipline us. Believe me, He will if we force His Hand. His discipline can hurt a lot. It's designed to deliver a wallop, so we will think twice before walking away from Him again. When He is finished, however, I promise, you won't be afraid of giants. **They will be afraid of you.** If the courage is deep in your heart and not just on your lips, you can slay any giant under any circumstances. God will be there to hand you the slingshot.

February 7

What will God have to do to get us going in His direction?
...whatever it takes.

"We (Christians) have no business letting the world get us down. When I start
feeling down, I turn to the last chapter of the Book of Revelation.
There is no way I can ever, ever stay down when I have read that last chapter."
-Ken Hutcherson-

It is time to get serious with God, now. Not tomorrow, **now.** Has God ever sent one of His attention getters into your life? "Giant," attention getters? You know the kind, where you suddenly find yourself in the belly of a whale or thrown off your donkey, face down in the dirt of life? It worked for the Apostle Paul and for Jonah. As Paul was brushing the dirt off his face, the first words out of his mouth were, "What would you have me to do, Lord?" In our modern day English, Paul said, "Ouch! Well, you've certainly got my undivided attention God, what do you want me to do?" And Jonah, well, he very quickly decided he needed to take a little trip to Nineveh, after all. Can you think of any little heavenly skirmish you've been in lately? Then you find the battle has only just begun. Why? Because you're fighting with God and you may not even realize it. Are you weary from fighting life's battles? Are there too many giants in your life? Then maybe it's time to put down the boxing gloves. Stop fighting with others, yourself and God and take a long, hard, **honest** look at your life and **take responsibility** for how you got to where you are. Taking responsibility for your life and your choices is called "repentance," if you are truly sorry. That is something God will forgive in a heartbeat. Do you know you are forgiven? Consider this, God will send us to 'Giant Slaying' school until we pass with an A+.

February 8

Caution! Detour ahead....

"When we choose to sin, there will be consequences. However, that's where our choice in the matter ends. We choose to sin, but God is the One who chooses our consequences. He decides what happens because of our sin, how many times it will happen, and how long it will last."
-Tony Evans-

I took one of those detour roads God said not to, more than once, it led me right to the pigpen. I can be a very slow learner at times. I found myself foolishly, skipping and singing all the way there. I was completely oblivious to the neon sign God had placed there for anyone who cared to take notice, "Danger ahead." Never once looking for God's warning signs along my path, like "Caution" or "Stop." The pigpen wasn't where I thought I was going. Please don't miss that. I did not think I was headed for the pigpen. I was headed for a good time, but sin is very deceitful. It can look real good. It makes you think you're getting one thing when you are really getting something else. Something you never bargained for, a whole lot of trouble. Unfortunately, my children ended up taking that journey with me, a journey they never asked to take. I too, foolishly believed that I didn't need God. I wanted to do things "my own way" and live life like I pleased. Sad thing is; God let me. Please don't miss that last statement, **God let me.** He doesn't force us to do things His way. He let me choose. I chose, and He reluctantly let go of my hand and said, "Well, ok then, have it your way." He was probably thinking to Himself, with a tear slowly making its way down His cheek, "Well, there she goes again." Maybe you don't think God cries? Think again. The shortest verse in the Bible is, "Jesus wept." Why did He weep? His heart broke because the people walked away from Him to "do their own thing." Has that day come yet where you would rather do His thing than your own thing?

"You can only serve one master...and you need to decide who it's gonna be."
-Steve Campbell-

February 9

Jesus wept...

"He is bread to the hungry, water to the thirsty,
a garment to the naked, healing to the wounded;
and whatever a soul can desire is found in HIM."
-John Flavel-

Jesus wept. What a mind boggling statement. The Creator of the universe wept. Son of the living God, He wept at Lazarus' tomb. Why? Because the people didn't believe He was the Son of God, with power over death, power to raise the dead back to life again. Power to change a life. Power to heal a broken life. Even after Jesus had raised Lazarus from the dead, did the people bow down and worship Him? No, the religious men began even harder to plot His death. It was the religious men plotting this evil, not the scum of the earth, but the pious, hypocritical Pharisees, who proclaimed one thing and lived another. They did it all in the name of God. (Sound familiar? Religious men, persecuting and killing others, all in the name of God.) No wonder Jesus called them whitewashed sepulchers. They looked okay on the outside, fooled everyone, everyone except Jesus that is. You can't fool Him, He knew what was on the inside of them. What's on the inside of us is more important to God than what is on the outside. He is interested in the heart. These guys had some major heart trouble. Can you imagine how wicked their hearts had to be to plan the death of the Son of God, who just showed beyond a shadow of a doubt, not only who He was, but that death isn't the end? People haven't changed; we still would rather do our own thing than follow Him. We pretend to be "religious." We wear crosses around our necks, we help out in some committee at church, but we still don't know Him. We have lots of head knowledge, but no heart knowledge of who He is. We still don't believe Him to be who He claimed to be. What will it take to convince you?

In the beginning (before all time) was the Word (Christ) and the Word was with God, and the Word was God Himself. (John 1:1 Amplified Bible)

We still break God's heart with our rebellion, our disobedience and most of all, our unbelief. I quickly found out too, that I was not very good at slaying giants on my own.

Our lives are a sum total of our responses to God, whether in obedience or rebellion. We do what we know is wrong and still expect something good to come from it. I am a firm believer that God always warns us ahead of time, "Don't do that," (Thou shalt not!) or He will send someone into our life to warn us. Most of us turn a deaf ear to our own peril. Are you listening?

February 10

God always warns. Always...

"No matter what limitation or circumstance you find yourself
up against in life, God who can empower you and gift you to
go past what you thought was possible...when you are at the
end of yourself, that's the time He can do His best work."
-Henry Cloud & John Townsend-

We can listen and obey or we can just listen... then turn away to our own folly...and pay a very big price. Most of us choose folly. I did. God offers us plan A. We choose plan B because it's **easier**. Plan B rarely includes God. Instead of making right choices we usually end up making easy ones. There are too many giants on God's path and who wants to run into giants? So, we turn our back on Him and go our own way. Big mistake! Sin always comes with a price tag. Usually, it's a very costly one. By His grace and love, I found that I didn't have to stay in the pigpen. He had purchased my way out, Himself. He has also purchased yours. I thought I was in the pigpen to stay. How did I get out? Grace. His grace. His amazing grace. His grace found me...even in the pigpen. It will find you too.

God gives each of us life and then our journey begins. Our journey ends with our death and in between our journey's beginning and ending, life's choices are made. Have you found that one 'seemingly insignificant' choice has brought you a lifetime of heartache? Unfortunately, most of us, myself included, spend most of our life convincing ourselves that we don't need God. "I'll try this and if that doesn't work, I'll try that".......all the while trying to drown out the voice of God calling, pleading, "Don't take that road, you won't like where it takes you." We struggle; we fight life's battles one after another until finally one day we realize **"God doesn't play games. He is playing for keeps."** He takes our life very seriously and wants us to also. There is a line God draws and He warns us not to step over that line. Why? Because there are more giants on the other side, then you could ever imagine. He knows that whatever is across that line will hurt us, and because He loves us, He wants us to have a good life. Sadly, God will never force us to choose what's right. He leaves the choice up to us. He lets us cross that line He has drawn for our protection, if we insist. Most of us insist.

"Every choice we make in life has the
possibility of changing our lives forever."
-Jimmy Houston-

Choose wisely the first time.

February 11

"God, stop telling me what to do!..."

*"Every time we say "yes" to God we will get
a little more sensitive to hearing Him the next time."*
-John Ortberg-

We all eventually have to answer the question: **"Does God have a right to tell me how to live my life?"** Be careful how you answer it, the quality of your life depends on your answer and so does your eternity. We try everything we know to deaden that pain deep inside each one of us. We turn to drugs, alcohol, sex, gambling, pornography, work, whatever we can find but the pain only increases. It screams louder and louder. Sin can be fun for a while, but at some point God's patience runs out on our rebellion and the fight is on because God knows how much we have to lose even when we don't. God says "Do it My way," we say, "Nope," and the fight is on. Jonah said "No," to God and found himself in the belly of a whale. God touched Jonah's circumstances and after being swallowed up and spit out, Jonah finally agreed with God. "Think I'll go to Nineveh after all," he said. He ended up obeying God, eventually, but he took the long, very painful route of obedience. He bought himself a lot more trouble than he bargained for, the very moment he told God, "No." Zig Zigler has summed it up like this, "When we disobey God, we always lose." Not sometimes, always. Disobedience immediately takes us out of the will of God for our lives. We have put ourselves in a place God never intended for us to go. Sorrow and regret are found on the pathway of disobeying what you know to be right. There are only two choices for the Christian, obey or don't.

*"No sin, no matter how momentarily pleasurable,
comforting, or habitual, is worth missing what God has for us."*
-Beth Moore-

FEBRUARY 12

Once upon a time there was a Prodigal son and there was a pig...

"As we pass through life, dirt will land on us.
How long we let it stay there is up to us."
-Michelle McKinney Hammond-

My favorite story in the whole Bible is the wayward son who turned his back on his loving father. The Prodigal son said, "Father give me my inheritance, I am done with all of you. It's time for me to go out and see the world and have myself some fun!" "I'm going to do my own thing," "Let's party"...and he did. He woke up one day and found himself in a pigpen. What's the moral of this story? Walk away from God and find yourself with the pigs. Funny thing is you may not even realize you are in the pigpen. It can look real good at first. Sin usually does. It can be fun too. You may be living "high on the hog".....no pun intended. You may have a fancy house and some fancy cars. Your garage may be full, but your heart is empty. Where is the pigpen? Anywhere that God is not.

Never wrestle with a pig. Both of you will get dirty. The pig likes it.

What's the difference between the Prodigal and the pig? The child of God will never feel at home, never be content in the pigpen. He knows he doesn't belong there. He longs to be clean again. There will always be that tugging of the Lord on the believer's heart, a still small voice, speaking deep into the spirit and the very soul, "Please come home."

Visited any pigpens lately? What kind of stinky place are you in right now? You can get out you know, but remember, God does not offer any quick fixes. He doesn't use band aides either. Choice got you into the pigpen and choice will get you out. The moment you are willing to stop trying to run the universe and put Him back on the throne of your life, He will begin to put the pieces of your life back together again. You will have help fighting those giants off, that use to defeat you in the past.

God never intended for any of us to journey through this life on our own, but many of us do. He will leave us alone if we insist, but it will break His heart and eventually our own. Have you answered that all important question yet, "Does God have the right to tell me how to live my life?" Well, does He? Be careful how you answer, your eternal future is at stake. Your answer will come the moment you are willing to put down the boxing gloves, open up your heart and listen for His voice, "Follow Me." If you follow Him He will lead you out of the pigpen to His home someday. Exchange pigs for angels, straw for streets of gold and uncertainty for nail scarred Hands of love that would rather die than to live without you.

FEBRUARY 13

Remember: God will never leave you content without Him. Never.

"The Lord of the universe stands ready to pick up your life and give it significance, a sense of fulfillment beyond anything you have ever experienced. Your heart has got eternity in it...and you will not be fulfilled until you know you are making an eternal difference with the one life you have."
-Ron Hutchcraft-

Only God can give your life real significance. You may search and search but it always comes back to Him. Others let us down, He will not. Others will disappoint us and leave us. He promises NEVER to leave or forsake us. It is by His grace and mercy we take our next breath. Freedom comes in this life when we realize God is in control, not me, He is. Not a sparrow falls from a tree branch that God does not take notice of. He even counts the stars in the heavens and calls them all by name. That is mind boggling when you realize there are billions and billions of stars. How much more important are you than a sparrow? Jesus asked that question, not me. You may experience some occasional "happy moments," but without Him you will never find the kind of peace you have been searching for all of your life, this side of heaven. Why? because peace doesn't exist, without Him. Like it or not life is all about choices. By not choosing, you chose. Choose Him and let Him put the song back in your heart. The next giant you meet will flee before you because he will see God at your side and a big old slingshot in your hand. Now, that's a reason to sing. God takes us to giant slaying school right after our flying and boating lessons...that is if we pass them. If not we get to take them over and over and over again until we do. One thing about God, you never fail His tests. He just repeats them until you get what it is He is trying to teach you. Thank God He doesn't give up on us and he doesn't want us to give up on ourselves or others. None of us is hopeless as long as God is still on His throne. He can change things in a heartbeat. Something we may have spent years praying for can get answered in the next 5 minutes. Expect great things from God. Expect an answer! Why bother to pray if you don't expect God to answer?

"No matter how far along our spiritual pilgrimage we may have come, we need to be shown again and again that humble, ordinary things can be very holy and very full of God."
-Elisabeth Elliot-

February 14

Almost ok...

"God's love, pouring through the lonely life of Jesus, runs
deeper, wider, and farther than any loneliness of the human heart.
Prayers from our lonely, troubled lips mix with the prayers of the
risen Christ on our behalf. He understands our expectations – and our
grief when those expectations fail to materialize."
-Bonnie Keen-

Almost ok....isn't ok. What a sad phrase. 'Almost ok' means life hasn't quite worked out the way I thought it should. It means the losses I experience, far outweigh the gains. 'Almost ok' means that the loss is so great it becomes too hard for the human mind to comprehend a God of love allowing it to happen. It means that I am trying to live with one foot in the world and one foot in heaven, and unhappy in both. I am playing at Christianity and not taking God seriously. It means, somewhere down the pathway of life I have compromised with sin. I have made some wrong choices with some very bitter consequences.

Why is it that the Apostle Paul was 'ok' in a stinky, dirty, cold prison and I can live in a beautiful home and not be ok? Could it be because my happiness is wrapped up in things, in the "stuff" I have. Am I living for the moment with no thought for tomorrow? Am I living only for today? 'Almost ok' means, I am doing my "own thing" and expecting God to bless it. It means I have compromised what I know to be right. Somewhere down the road I decided that I knew better than God how I should live my life. I believed this so much so, that my own life contradicted my own beliefs. Those who don't know God watch our lives very closely. They are very uncomfortable around followers of Jesus because it convicts them of their sinful lifestyle. Danger comes when I begin to rationalize and reason away my behavior. I have an excuse for every bad thing I do now. I have become so comfortable in my sin I no longer can hear the whisper of His still, small voice. My conscience has become hardened and cold to the voice of God. Almost ok, means God will **soon** be shouting in order to get my undivided attention. I have been seeking momentary pleasure that God knows will bring me a lifetime of pain. Don't miss that. The consequences of some sins will linger for a lifetime.

Almost ok means God will soon be forced to **touch my circumstances** in a way that will force me to choose. He will touch us in a way that will leave a lasting impression. Determine not to live life almost ok, but in the power of God who died that you might have life and live it abundantly. The choice is always yours to make.

FEBRUARY 15

*The very moment you choose your way over God's way,
you are headed straight for the pigpen.*

"Don't presume to direct your own life on your own terms.
Discovering the will of your Creator and Savior – and walking in
that will, may not be the most "secure" way to live, according to
the world's standards. But, I assure you of this: It will be the most
fulfilling thing that could ever happen to you."
-Jack Hayford-

Does God give up on us when we end up in the pigpen? No. No. No. A thousand times no! We may give up on ourselves, but He never will. His eyes of love have followed us all the way to the pigpen. We may not be able to hear His voice still calling to us until the pain is so bad, it drowns out everything else. Why so much pain? The pain results as **natural consequences to bad decisions.** God will never leave us content in our sin. NEVER ! Please remember that. NEVER ! If you really think about it, **you wouldn't want Him to.**

'Almost ok,' may mean I have struggled at trying to open doors that God has shut. Many of His answers come in the form of closed doors. If we insist on trying to yank them open again, we can be sure we won't like what we find behind them. Wisdom leaves closed any door that God has shut in His infinite wisdom.

God has made it real easy for each one of us, it's we who complicate it. Trust Him, or don't trust Him. Believe Him, or don't believe Him. Follow Him, or don't follow Him. Your choice.

"Father, strip away from me whatever is blocking
other people's view of You in my life."
-Tim Walter-

FEBRUARY 16

"God where are we going?..."

"Think of what Christ did: He left His heavenly home, in obedience to His Father, came to earth to live and to be one of us. Remember, this was God in human form – Immanuel – God with us. His motives would be misunderstood, Jesus willingly suffered in order to identify with us. His whole purpose and reason for coming was to give everything for us – including His precious blood and life."
-Franklin Graham-

"Follow Me," implies that God knows where He is going and I don't. I need help. That's another reason we aren't 'ok' is that I am going in one direction and God is going in another. (Remember we are supposed to be following Him, not the other way around.)

How can you possibly hear someone calling to you when you are walking away from them? Then we wonder why we haven't heard from God in a while. Duh !

Maybe you have deliberately walked away from Him. Maybe, you played at this 'religion thing' and found it wasn't all it was cracked up to be. Maybe, you had this tremendous hurt in your life and you hold God responsible for it. As hard as you try, you just can't seem to get over it. That big "WHY?" question continues to separate you from God. I think at one time or another, we have all felt that way. We feel like our prayers don't get any higher than the ceiling, much less all the way to heaven. It's possible you don't feel like you are very important to God, that He probably has better things to do than help you. Things like running the universe. But, you know what? He doesn't. His word says, "Come to Me, all of you who are weary and laden down with cares. I will give you rest." Now, does that sound like someone who is too busy for you? Let's take a closer look at that verse. God doesn't just say come, and then not tell you where to come to. He says come to Him. Are you weary? Come. Are you laden down? Come. Do you need rest? Come. What a simple request, but what a hard thing for us to do sometimes.

FEBRUARY 17

Religion or relationship? You decide.

"The agonies of God's Son were incomparable. No one ever suffered
like this Man. Through all of eternity, we will contemplate the
killing of the Son of God and sing, "Worthy is the Lamb that was slain."
-John Piper-

God isn't interested in 'religion.' He wants a **relationship** (a closeness, nearness, connectedness), a **personal relationship** because He is a personal God. The most tender words I have ever read in the Bible are, "**Abba**, Father." It means Daddy. Can you imagine the magnitude of that statement? What is more intimate then God inviting you to call Him, Daddy? Would He tell you to do something that wasn't possible? He invites you to come to Him. When your heart is right, humbled before Him, head is bowed, asking for His help, believe me you are already in His presence. He will never turn away a child of His. In fact, He invites us to climb up into His lap and tell Him what hurts. It is a very safe place to be, I know because I have spent a lot of time there. I guarantee that you will not want to leave...and you don't have to. Think about Abba Father today. All day. It can't help but make you smile. That's unmatched intimacy with the Creator of the universe.

"Everyone else came into the world to live.
Jesus came into the world to die."
-Fulton Sheen-

Dwight L. Moody has said it best, "The loss of a soul! Christ knew what it meant. that is what brought Him from the bosom of the Father, that is what brought Him from the throne, that is what brought Him to Calvary."

February 18

Man's love says, "I'll love you if"...God's love, well, one look at the cross will confirm, to even the hardest heart, how fierce is His love for mankind.

"Christ came down to save us from a fiery hell, and any man who is cast down to hell from here must go in the full blaze of the gospel, and over the mangled body of the Son of God."
-D.L. Moody-

God's love is unconditional. That is very hard for us to understand because we aren't able to love anyone the way God does. Our love always comes with a price tag, an "I'll love you **if**..." or "I'll love you **when**..." We always want something from the other person. We can't love them 'just because,' but God can. I understood God's unconditional love a little better when someone said,

"God's unconditional love always comes with His unconditional acceptance."

Remember the verse, "God **so** loved the world..." It doesn't just say, "God loved the world," no, it says "He **so** loved the world." Well, the great news is that He **so** loved it when it was in a big fat mess. He didn't say "clean up your act first," or "do this or do that and I'll think about loving you." No, God '**sooooo**' loved us, and because of the mess we were all in, explains the rest of the verse... "He so loved the world that He sent His only begotten Son, that whoever believes in Him shall not perish, but shall have everlasting life. The world was in a mess, so God sent His Son. Apparently, the mess was so big, only God could fix it. So, He did. Now, that's something to shout hallelujah about! Have you experienced His unconditional love and His unconditional acceptance? If not, why not? You can this very minute.

February 19

The definition of hopelessness: A very hardened and cold heart that turns its back on perfect love...God's perfect love.

"I wonder how many of us have turned away from Jesus, given up any hope of the spiritual life because we don't fit, because we aren't like everyone else, and because our Christianity seems so different and strange from the rest of the churches. I wonder if we realize how anxious Jesus is to reach out and walk with us arm in arm."
-Michael Yaconelli-

Do you remember, in the beginning of this book I said there were some things that we will **never** have answers to, this side of heaven? Well, this is one of them. Why does God love us so much? I don't know. We sure don't deserve it. But, if I were to guess why, I would say it's because of who He is. He is love. It's not just something He does, it's who He is. Wow! When you go to bed tonight, I hope you will ponder the word "**so**." It's such a small word, almost insignificant and easy to pass right over, but what an impact it can have on your understanding of God's love for you. "God **so** loved the world." The next time your life seems to be in a mess, I hope the word "**so**" will come to mind. Your mess will never be too big for Him to handle.

How about wanting something that you know God doesn't want you to have. Wanting a relationship that God knows will destroy you or your children. Or maybe you want a different job, a bigger house? Maybe, it's just a matter of timing. Maybe there is something you want and God wants to provide it for you; just not now. We all should go by the wisdom of this statement:

If God doesn't want me to have something, then I shouldn't want it either.

If God says to leave something alone, then we would be wise to leave it alone. Walk away and don't look back.

FEBRUARY 20

The best things in life aren't things.

"Because Jesus Christ is a man, He feels what we feel.
Because He is God, He can do something about it."
-Tony Evans-

Maybe you've ignored something you know God has told you to do. Have you turned a deaf ear to Him, on purpose? You might have even fooled yourself into thinking, "Not now, Lord, but I'll do it later." Knowing in your heart you have no intentions of ever doing it. You may fool yourself, but you aren't fooling God. You'll just be "almost ok." It's like being "almost obedient." "Almost obedient" is disobedience, no matter which way you slice it.

Do you have any un-confessed sin in your life? I can guarantee you that you are not ok. Are you compromising with some sin you don't want to give up or won't give up? Sin is such a big enemy in the believer's life and so a whole lot more will be said about it later on. Why? Because it's imperative that if you are going to take God seriously – you must also take sin seriously. Sin got us into the mess we find ourselves in.

Have you heard the good news of the gospel, over and over, and repeatedly rejected it. Maybe, you thought you would wait until some later time. Later may be too late. No one knows when our last day on this earth will be. God planned the day we would all enter this world and the day we would leave it. He has left the choice up to us where we will be spending eternity, after leaving this earth. It is a choice each of us will make, alone. Those who don't know God's love will never be ok. Those who are unsaved will never be even "almost ok"... without Jesus. There will be a lot of "almost ok" people populating hell.

"Discipline entails more than catching a child in the act and punishing him. Far
more important is nurturing his will for the good, which means supporting him
whenever he chooses right over wrong – or, as my mother used to put it,
"winning him for the good."
-Johann Christoph Arnold-

God longs to win us for the good. Bryan Chapell has said, "Divine discipline is God's merciful expression of His love for children who deserve His wrath, but will never receive it." Think about that the next time God disciplines you then smile, because He is loving you. Love without discipline isn't love, it is indifference. God loves us right where we are, but loves us too much to leave us there. He will bring us higher and higher until the day we leave this earth for His home. Our home. Safely home is His goal for you and for me.

FEBRUARY 21

*Why is it that Satan knows better how much
we are worth to God, than we do?*

"Man's sin reached its full horror and its most awful expression at
Calvary. Not only had we disobeyed God's commandments and defied
God's name, but now we were crucifying God's Son."
-Colin Smith-

Do you know your value to God? Do you want to know? The only way to really find out the answer to this question is to go back in time with me, 2000 years ago to the night the Son of God came into this world. The night He came into a world that didn't want Him. The night all of hell trembled at the significance of God becoming a man and spending 33 years among us. His birth had been prophesied hundreds of years before His coming. Immanuel, God with us. Was He received as the King of glory should have been received? Sadly, no, He was not. He was born into a world that didn't know Him and didn't want to. A world that would reject Him, that would eventually mock who He claimed to be, beat Him, spit on Him, and turned their backs on Him. Then they would put Him to death and rejoice because of what they had done. Hanging from a Roman cross, the words still echo down the corridors of time, "Father, forgive them. They don't know what they're doing." Can you imagine if Jesus hadn't said those words? If He hadn't asked God to forgive a world so corrupt and blinded by sin, it didn't realize the magnitude of what it was doing. The world didn't deserve forgiveness, but it got it because Jesus asked, and God is merciful.

"Confession means that we agree with God. We agree that we have sinned.
We agree that **we are responsible for our sins.** And we agree that God has
the right to rid us of this sin."
-Erwin Lutzer-

February 22

"Til He appeared and the soul felt it's worth..."

When I was in grammar school we used to have a Christmas pageant every year for our parents. This was in the 1950's when God hadn't yet been banned from our schools. Isn't it ironic that our kids can't have a Bible in school today, but they can have one in prison? (Think about it. It's a rather sobering thought, isn't it?) Anyhow, back to our Christmas play. We would practice our favorite Christmas songs for weeks until finally we were ready. The words to "O, Holy Night," have been sung by choirs and congregations in churches across our land throughout the years. I wonder if everyone else paid as little attention to the words, as I did? Not until recently, did the words to this song make their way from my head to my heart. What a blessing I have missed all these years, all because of my indifference. What a shame to know the words to a song so well, you no longer have to think about them as you sing. Your heart and your mouth are disconnected. You no longer care about the message behind the words. I will never listen to this song with indifference again. There is one particular line that caused my heart to skip a beat. It was one of those moments you know, that you know, that you know, that God is whispering to you. This was one of those moments for me. He was whispering I love you...

"O, Holy night..."
The stars are brightly shining. It is the night of our dear Savior's birth.
Long lay the world in sin and error pining,

And my favorite line,

<u>til He appeared and the soul felt its worth."</u>

Does your soul know it's worth to God? My worth and yours, is wrapped up in God's Son, coming to earth and dying for our sins.

"A thrill of hope the weary world rejoices,
for yonder breaks a new and glorious morn."

No one can give hope to a dying world like Jesus does. No one. Question is, "Do you know your worth?"

FEBRUARY 23

The value of a life...do you know what it is?

"New life, supernatural life, the abundant life of the
living Christ is imparted to the person who in desperation
'turns from the old, barren, bleak ways of the world to
keep company with Christ."
-W. Phillip Keller-

Until you know Jesus, you will never know how much you are worth to God. It's impossible to know, apart from Him. The moment He shows up in your life, you begin to know how valuable you are to God and begin to understand how much He loves you. The song we talked about yesterday, O Holy Night continues with -

"Fall on your knees..."

    That's exactly what I wanted to do. Fall on my knees, but I was so stunned I just sat there in silence. I don't remember much of the church service after that song was sung. I sat there pondering those words in my mind, asking myself, "Does my soul know its worth?" I sadly came to the conclusion, no. I was too familiar with the definition of 'worthless'; (useless, unimportant, no good, valueless, poor, miserable). That was me, miserable and useless. I guess I had felt worthless most of my life. Sadly, I think most of us do. I never really thought anyone cared, especially God. I'd had many failures in life, the biggest one was losing my marriage and tearing my family apart, I felt like a failure. My family had been my life, my children were now grown and there wasn't much left to my life. In fact, most of the time I felt like half a person, always feeling as if a part of me was missing. It was. Part of my heart had been taken from me in the divorce and it had left a big gaping hole. Until JESUS...
    Is there a hole in your heart? Jesus will fill it with Himself. You will never be the same again.

FEBRUARY 24

Never be content with someone else's opinion of you. Never.

"Use your imagination and do something you've never
done before. God wants you to taste life, to sample all the goodies
He has made available. Venture out to see His creation.
Notice something you've never noticed before.
It's amazing how alive you will feel."
-Michelle McKinney Hammond-

Years ago my life seemed useless and unimportant. I didn't seem to make much of a difference to anyone. Oh, there might be a few who would miss me for a little while if I died, but I figured they'd get over it. This song we have been studying for the last few days told me differently. Suddenly, a verse of scripture came to my mind that says,

"Are not five sparrows sold for two pennies. And yet not one of them
is forgotten or uncared for in the presence of God. But even the
very hairs of your head are numbered. Do not be struck with fear or seized
with alarm; you are of greater worth than many flocks of sparrows."
(Luke 12:6-7 Amplified Bible)

What was my soul worth? Nothing in my eyes, but to God I was His 'treasured child.' Can you imagine going from useless to being treasured, because of a few words in a song that made their way into my heart. Have you any idea what your soul is worth? I hope you will before you finish this book. I hope you will understand the battle that is raging for your soul. All of hell trembled that night the Savior was born. They had a very good reason to shake in their boots. Satan and death were about to be defeated, **forever**. I hope you are beginning to understand the significance of that night. This is a real war and someone is going to win. It's up to you who will win.

February 25

We live in a very dangerous, unpredictable and troubled world...

"My attitude as a saint to sorrow and difficulty is not to ask
that they may be prevented, but to ask that I may preserve the self that God
created me to be through every fire of sorrow. Our Lord received
Himself in the fire of sorrow, He was saved not from the hour, but
out of the hour. If you receive yourself in the fires of sorrow,
God will make you nourishment for other people."
-Oswald Chambers-

What was the state of the world the night Jesus was born in Bethlehem? It was in the same state my heart was in when I heard those beautiful words to the song, O Holy Night, "the night the soul felt its worth." I mean really heard them for the very first time. It was in a big mess and I was in a mess. Both full of sin, living life alone, doing my own thing, longing to be rescued. Not even knowing I needed rescuing. I guess the world that night felt the same way, because only a few even took notice that God had come to earth. And then suddenly hope filled the earth that night...

"The thrill of hope, a weary world rejoices."

And hope has passed through the centuries and flooded many a weary heart, like mine. The shepherds watched in awe as the angels in heaven sang of His birth. "Peace, goodwill to all men," they proclaimed. Has there been peace and goodwill? No, because from that very moment a baby was being born in a manger, Satan and his demons were plotting the death of that baby. They knew exactly how Jesus' birth would change our relationship with God for all eternity. It will change your relationship with God too by whatever it is you decide to be true or untrue about His Son. You will make a choice before this is over. Embrace Him or reject Him.

February 26

The Christian's life is a fight to the bitter end...

"The first time Jesus came to the earth, He came in humility:
born in a stable, raised in a humble home, and working with Joseph
in the carpenter's shop. He came to serve and to give Himself as a ransom.
Not so the second time. When He comes back this time, He'll come to
be served. He won't be coming back to die, but to sweep His enemies right off
the planet. He will be glorified beyond anything on this earth."
-Ken Hutcherson-

We are in a war, a battle of good vs evil. A bitter fight lay ahead and still does to this day. Jesus came to save souls. Satan would do whatever it took to keep Him from accomplishing His purpose. This war has been raging in full force ever since the night our Savior was born. The world had reason to hope once again, and hell knew it. You have reason to hope because of what happened that night, unless, you allow Satan to steal that hope from you.

You probably don't think you're worth very much right now, I didn't either. But I know you will change your mind after we take a trip back to that night..."O holy night." The song speaks of the night that God came to earth as a Man. It was a night that would change the course of history, forever. A night all of hell began to shudder at the glorious sight. What was happening? Satan had been thrown out of Heaven to the earth, after trying to usurp God's authority. The earth belonged to Satan. He is known as the god of this world. Why was God's Son coming here now? All of hell began to tremble at what His coming might mean.

It was a night to fall on your knees because earth had been visited by heaven. "Oh, night divine," the angels sang, proclaiming the birth of the Messiah. There hasn't been a July 4th fireworks display that could out do the scene in the heavens that night. Israel's King had come, and Israel didn't even know it. They were expecting the long awaited King to claim the throne, not come in a manger. The last thing they expected was a King wrapped in swaddling clothes. So, they missed His arrival. Many still do today. Have you?

February 27

The song "O, Holy night" talks of a night..."O' night divine.."

This was a night that changed the world! Heaven came to earth.
This night changed the lives of lepers, of prostitutes, of the hopeless...the poor,
the sick, the lame, the hungry. It changed my life and it can change yours.

Who did God give the message of Christ's birth to? Not to the rich and famous of that day, but apparently to the only ones willing to listen. He proclaimed the good news to lowly shepherds on a hill, busy tending to their flocks. The sky suddenly filled with angelic hosts. Can you imagine how frightened they must have been? I'm sure it got their immediate attention, however. A heavenly chorus burst into song, such as the world has never heard before. Most of us have heard Mendel's "Messiah" and his famous Hallelujah chorus sung and felt that familiar chill up and down our spine, but this night...this night was different. This night was "divine." It was God Himself, bringing heaven to earth. As the song says, "It was the night of our dear Savior's birth." Sin met GRACE and MERCY that night. No one expected it to be wrapped in swaddling clothes. I know I didn't. Maybe that's why people went about their lives as if nothing had happened. It is the same story today. They believe God should have shown up on planet earth, not as a baby but as a warrior ready to take down the Roman empire. They get His first coming mixed up with His second coming. There will be no mistaking who He is when He rides in as King of Kings and Lord of Lords to put down all rebellion. By then it will be too late for the unbeliever. By then the soul will know the real consequences behind choices given to each one of us by free will. God does not force Himself upon anyone. He extends an invitation to us, "Come unto Me." Some will say yes, some will say no. Even though God has called and called, some will still say no to His invitation of life. Instead they choose death. They trade heaven for hell, love for torment, sight for blindness. Where are you today? Have you met the Savior? He gives you your next breath you know. He provides a glimpse into His power every time you look at a sunrise or up at the skies and see His handiwork. The Bible says, "The Heavens declare His glory."

"From the time the world was created, people have seen the earth
and sky and all that God made. They can clearly see His invisible qualities –
His eternal power and divine nature. So they have no excuse whatsoever for not knowing God."
Romans 1: 20

No excuse! Think about that with a sober mind. No excuse. God requires accountability!

FEBRUARY 28

Lost and broken...

"The gospel starts by teaching us that we, as creatures, are absolutely
dependent on God, and that He, as Creator, has an absolute claim on us.
Only when we have learned this can we see what sin is, and only when we see
what sin is can we understand the good news of salvation from sin."
-J.L. Packer-

What was the condition of the world into which JESUS came that night in Bethlehem? It was dark, rebellious and full of sin, much like our world today. It was a world with no hope. This is a key point. The Son of God did not come to a world that " had it all together." No, He came to a lost and broken world. He came to them just like He comes into our lives, if we'll let Him. He doesn't say to us, "Get your life in order, and then I'll come into it." No, He says, "I'll come into it and get it in order for you, because you can't do it on your own." Jesus came in an ordinary way, was placed in a manger instead of a palace. It was heaven that refused to be silent at His birth. the angelic host broke forth in song and got the Shepherds notice. What a sight that must have been. The sky filled with angels singing!

So, what is your soul worth? It is worth the Son of God, the Savior of the world, leaving the glory of heaven and coming to a wicked world, to rid it of sin, once and for all. You and I are worth God's Son dying to save us. How do I know? I know by the nail prints in His Hands. We put them there. You did and I did. We have a God who loved us more than His own life.

"The truth is that there is an invisible world that is just as real
as the visible world. There are vast numbers of angels, both good
and bad – spirits that exist all around us. There are glorious beings
that would take our breath away if we saw them, and there are evil
beings that would horrify us if we could see them."
-Chip Ingram-

FEBRUARY 29

Leap Year

*"What is the only man made thing we will find in heaven?
The nail prints in Jesus' hands and feet."*
-unknown-

*"It is a grave offense even to bind a Roman citizen, a crime
to flog him, almost the act of parricide to put him to death;
what shall I then call crucifying Him? Language worthy
of such an enormity it is impossible to find."*
-Cicero-

Did Jesus have to die? Yes and no. Yes, He had to die if He was going to save us from death. God's Word says, "The soul that sins, it shall die." Death is the consequence of our sinning. Jesus could have chosen not to give His life for us. So, no, He didn't have to die and who would have blamed Him if He didn't. The world was ungrateful and hostile to Him, but He chose to die. He chose to die rather to live without you or me for all eternity. He could have stayed in heaven and let us all get exactly what we deserved for our rebellion and disobedience. Death comes, then certain judgment. The wages of sin is death. We all deserved to die. He died for us. He came so that we might have life. He came to give us eternal life. I call it the "great exchange." He exchanged His death for mine. He exchanged His life for mine. He gave me eternity with Him, instead of hell. He gave me forgiveness instead of the punishment I deserved. He gave me hope when I had none left. What is your hope centered in? Man or God?

MARCH 1

"God accepts us right where we are, but loves us
too much to leave us there."
-unknown-

There is always pain before we are forever set free from something.

"The devil never points out the abundant blessings of God
in your life. The devil always points out what is missing, lacking or negative."
-Charles Stanley-

Why is it that we believe Satan's lie that we are worthless and so easily turn away from God's love? The enemy does everything he can to keep us away from this truth, because he knows the moment we find out how valuable and how much we are loved by God, **it will change our lives.** It will set us free. Can we come to God just as we are? You betcha !!! The good news is He won't leave us like that.

I will never listen to that song, "O Holy Night," the same ever again. I hope you won't either. I can't wait for Christmas!

You need to know all about our enemy, the things he does and the people he uses. Because Satan knows our great worth to God, he will do "whatever it takes," let me repeat that so you don't miss it, **"whatever it takes"** to separate you from God's love. You may not even realize what's happening. He will lie, he will cheat us out of everything good that God has for us. Satan is a LIAR. He is relentless. He is vicious, he will always be back. He may leave you alone for a time. Just long enough for you to believe you are safe from his schemes and trickery. Then he goes in for the kill. He will always be back. He has a heavy arsenal and his aren't just half-hearted attempts to get us off balance. His attacks are intelligent, well thought out plans to devour us and to steal from us, our peace, our joy, our very life. He wants to steal from us our very soul. His are surprise attacks to get us off guard and to keep us off balance. We are his enemy. This is a very sobering truth to realize that we are all his enemy, believer and unbeliever alike. He wants the believer to live a defeated life, doubting God and His love. He wants the unbeliever to never, never, never hear the message of the cross. There is joy and there is hope in the good news. Satan wants to remove all joy and all hope from each one of our lives. He wants to render us powerless. Has he succeeded in your life? I pray not. There is another awesome song, "Victory In Jesus." Learn it! Memorize it! Sing it! for all of hell to hear.

MARCH 2

Learn a great lesson from the kitten and the lion...

"The first step of courage isn't taken in the midst of a battle;
it's taken when you're willing to walk onto the
battlefield and face the unknown."
-Steven Curtis Chapman-

After these last few days, you should know what your soul is worth to Almighty God. Priceless. Are you going to let the enemy get away with his lies that you are worthless? I didn't think so. But, be assured, Satan does not give up without a fight. It's going to be a long, bitter fight to the end. He doesn't care how he takes us down or how long it takes. He just wants to destroy us and our relationship with our Heavenly Father.

How does God want us to see ourselves? There is a picture that has left a lasting imprint on my mind and on my heart. It is a picture of a little kitten looking into a mirror. What does he see? He sees a roaring lion. The kitten sees a fearless, courageous lion. We should do the same. When we look into a mirror we should see Jesus' reflection in us. God's goal for your life and mine is that each and every day we should become more and more like His Son. Satan will do whatever it takes to stop that from happening. He will hide the mirror, he will break the mirror. He will do whatever it takes for you to remain a coward. He doesn't want you to know who you are in Jesus!

The next time you are feeling down and discouraged, remember the little kitten then roar! Yes, God gives roaring lessons also. Sign up today!

"Courage is simply doing what needs to be done
even though you are scared and tired."
-Rick Johnson-

MARCH 3

Learn the lesson of Sin and the Frog...

"As sinfully and culturally defined, pursuing greatness looks like this:
Individuals motivated by self-interest, self-indulgence, and a false
sense of self-sufficiency pursue selfish ambition for the purpose of
self-glorification. Contrast that with the pursuit of true greatness as
biblically defined: Serving others for the glory of God. This is the genuine
expression of humility; this is true greatness as the Savior has defined it."
-C.J. Mahaney-

I once read the following story: Learn the lesson of the frog that can be boiled to death **without any resistance**. Placed in a cool pot of water on a cooking surface, the frog remains content and unsuspecting as the heat beneath him increases. His internal temperature rises with the temperature of the water, until he is boiled alive.

So it is with the sinner. We are unaware that we are even in a fire. We don't feel the heat. Everything seems to be just great. Content, unaware, of what's happening until it is too late. We have this casual view of sin. It won't hurt me. We play with it. We dance around with it. We make excuses for it. We compromise with it. All the while we are being boiled alive and we don't even know it. Satan is so devious, he can be so subtle at times, that we don't even see the flames. Sin by its very nature blinds us to its dangers. Sin is our enemy. It entangles us like a bug caught in a spider's web, struggling to get free. The bug is no longer in control, the spider is.

Most of us think our sin is no big deal. But if you are going to get serious with God, you must get serious with the sin your life, too. Sin has consequences and God punishes sin. Most of us live by the philosophy found in I Corinthians 15:32: "Let's eat, drink and be merry, for tomorrow we die." What is God's response to this kind of lifestyle? Verse 33 He shouts His answer. "Come to your senses and stop sinning." (NLT)

What is the temperature of your life right now? Now that's a sobering question, isn't it? Do you feel like that frog, sitting in the pot of water thinking everything is ok, not realizing, you are what's for dinner? You are offering "no resistance" to the very thing that is about to destroy you.

Remember when I said I sang and laughed all the way to the pigpen? Thinking everything was just fine. When it was about as far from "fine," as anyone could get. Have you ever taken that same trip? You think you're still in control and you're not? Every sin has some kind of door of entrance. The door may be so well camouflaged by the enemy, that you don't recognize it for what it really is: a door to hell. "Have a bite…" and we compromise, just a little. The moment we begin to rationalize our behavior, our sin, we are that much closer to disobedience. That much closer to stepping over the line that God says, "Don't cross over it." We are that much closer to an indifferent and a cold heart. One day you won't recognize the difference between right and wrong, because the line has become so blurred. You begin to see what you want to see. You begin to do what you want to do and the heck with God and with everybody else. You are going to do your own thing. You can never be successful at living with one foot in Heaven and the other on this earth. You're so off balance in both worlds, you are setting yourself up for a fall. God says, "Choose."

MARCH 4

*Sin is like quicksand. You don't realize it's deadly pull
until you find yourself way in over your head.*

"It takes a lot of humility to cry aloud to God in our distress.
And humility before the living God is precisely what we need."
-Bill Gothard-

A favorite quote of mine by Alexander Solzhenitzyn states:

**"We do not err because truth is difficult to see. It is
visible at a glance. We err because this is more comfortable."**

We sin because it will take away the pain we are feeling inside, right now. Even though the pain will intensify later on because of our disobedience, but we want the "quick fix" now, not later. We make sin look good. We re-label sin. We may struggle against it for a little while, and then we give in to it. Sin brings guilt and then that guilt will push us even farther away from God. We are afraid that we have stepped over that line God has said "Don't cross," so many times that there's no turning back now. We are sure that God will reject us even if we do try and come home. Lies. Lies. Lies of the enemy. God has never said. "I will love you if…" There are no conditions put on His kind of love. None. He accepts us just as we are. Trouble is, we feel so bad and hurt so bad, we'll do anything to stop the pain. So we sin more which brings more guilt, so we sin even more…until the day comes we no longer call what we are doing, sin. We are in a very dangerous place. We have crossed the line and we won't like what we find on the other side of it. There is another choice you know. Always remember, life is all about choices. You have a choice to "repent" at any time. It is never too late to turn your back on sin. Never. The enemy will whisper in your ear, "Boy, you've really done it now. God will never forgive you for that." God will always let the choice be yours, even if it's the wrong one. He warns, but He never forces us to do the right thing. It's called "choice or free will." You must choose this day who you will serve. Keep in mind it is an eternal choice. Make sure it is one you can live with, *forever*. There are no do overs.

MARCH 5

What is true repentance from sin?
When I no longer offer excuses to God for my sinful behavior.

"It concerns me when I hear believers speaking of non-believers as the enemy. According to scripture, those who do not believe have been taken captive by Satan to do his will – they are prisoners of war. Nonbelievers aren't the enemy; they are the enemy's captives."
-Greg Laurie-

When we sin we don't want to be around anyone who is living a godly life. They are living a life we should be living. How many of us would go after, what we know is sin, what we know is outside of God's will for our life, if we knew ahead of time the price we would pay? If we knew ahead of time what the consequences will be? Unfortunately, our desires over-whelm our common sense most of the time. Don't fool yourself into thinking there aren't any consequences. Pay day always comes. We conveniently forget "accountability." We forget that God says, "Thou shalt not." Many of us interpret that to be a "suggestion." It is not. If you put that same sentence in our everyday language, it would read, God says, "Don't do that, you'll be sorry!"

Those who choose to live an ungodly lifestyle, those who don't want to live godly, will spend their time finding something wrong with those who do. Somehow, it makes them feel better about themselves. Just the presence of a believer can bring one's heart under heavy conviction.

Proverbs 21:12 says, "The godly learn by watching **RUIN** overtake the wicked.

God is a God of justice. He says what He means and He means what He says. Sin has consequences. If you sin, your life will be ruined. No ifs, ands or buts about it. Ruin will overtake you eventually. A liquor commercial never shows the drunk driver or the fatal accident that kills an innocent family of four. Think about it.

MARCH 6

*God is kind and loving, but sometimes the only way He
can get our attention, or deal with us, can be very **severe**.*

"In the original language of the New Testament, the word
righteousness means "to stay within the lines." These days, no
one is really sure where the lines are or who is supposed to draw them.
But in a world with no lines, how can we make right choices?...Each person
will have to find his or her own lines – and hang on tight to them."
-John Trent-

Usually, the only way change happens in our lives, is not because of some great revelation, but because of the heat God has applied in our lives. It causes pain. It makes us very, very uncomfortable.

Do you want to be successful in life? Then deal with your sin, now. Are there sins you are hiding, or simply refusing to deal with? Are you compromising, even just a little, with something you know doesn't belong in your life? Are you making excuses for your behavior? Are you sitting in a pan of warm water and you look over and wave to the frog sitting in the pan next to you? The flame is getting hotter and hotter and you don't even know it? The hotter you get the easier it becomes to forget God's mercy and His forgiveness.

"Success depends entirely and absolutely on the
immediate blessing and influence of God."
-Jonathan Edwards-

"God's mercies come day by day. They come when we need them – not earlier and not later.
God gives us what we need today. If we needed more, He would give us more. When we need
something else, He will give that as well. Nothing we truly need will ever be withheld from us.
Search your problems, and within them you will discover the well-disguised mercies of God."
-Ray Prichard-

MARCH 7

*God's mercies are new every morning. It's a good thing because
I'm sure I used up yesterday's supply.*

"Mercy is not the ability to no longer feel the pain and
heartache of living in this world. Mercy is knowing that
I am being held through the pain by my Father."
-Angela Thomas-

How many times in our life have we said, "If I had known that would happen, I never would have..." The consequences are never worth the disobedience, and the thrill for the moment is never worth the pain. The pain will always last longer than the thrill. Always.

The Prodigal son chose to walk away from his father and found himself in a pigpen. Oh, I don't think for a moment that's where he thought he was headed. He was looking for a 'good time.' The hog pen can look real pretty at first. Remember that the enemy offers us an "attractive alternative" to God's plan. Even though the pigpen can look like a beautiful place, anything that keeps me out of the presence of God is still a pigpen. There was only one thing keeping that young man in the stinky place he found himself in, and that was his own decision. He could choose to turn around (repent) and go home. The amazing thing is that at the end of that long road home he will find God there, standing with open arms and a tear trickling down His cheek. His son was lost and is now found. They will be tears of joy. God has missed His child while he was away. He wants us all 'safely home.'

"When the Holy Spirit shows us an area that needs repentance, we
must overcome the instinct to defend ourselves. We must silence the
little lawyer who steps out from a dark closet in our minds, pleading,
"My client is not so bad."
-Francis Frangipane-

Real repentance requires real honesty.

MARCH 8

"God, Please, get me out a here!"

"God has never had a people who were at the mercy of circumstances.
His wisdom always anticipates hell's worst and provides for heaven's best.
So it is with high confidence that we may look to Him, notwithstanding
the bleakness of the present scene surrounding us."
-Jack Hayford-

Sadly, some Christians never make it out of the pigpen. They can waste their whole life away there. They refuse to make right choices and instead make "easy" ones. God cannot and does not fellowship with someone living in willful sin. His holiness will not allow Him to. Yet, His mercy will continue to strive with that person who has walked away from Him. His grace will attempt to draw them back to Himself. It begins with a whisper of warning, "Don't do that.." and eventually becomes a shout...a shout of pain. Don't force God to shout at you. It becomes harder and harder to hear Him. Sin is like quicksand, taking you down and down and down until you are way in over your head. The more you struggle to get out the deeper in you sink. There is no way of escape, unless you look up and see the Hand of God reaching down for you. There is no pit in life that His arm of love cannot rescue you from. Jesus reached out His hand to the prostitute and said, "You don't have to live like this anymore. Go and sin no more." He offers the same words of healing to us. "Go and sin no more," are music to the sinner's ears. Do you see His hand reaching out to you this very moment?

Sin is dirt on the soul you will never be able to wash away, but God can, and He will if you will just ask Him. **God can**...two little words that remind us, we don't have to give up. So, Go! and sin no more!

MARCH 9

There is a heavy price tag for walking in God's will, but there is an even greater price to pay for walking away from Him.

"If I started with the mind and will of God, viewing the
rest of my life from that point of view; other details would
fall into place – or at least fall into a different place."
-Phillip Yancy-

Consider Your Ways. That is what God asks us to do. Consider where you are and why you are there. One of the main reasons life turns out to be so hard is because we are struggling to go in one direction while God is trying to get us to go in the other. We are supposed to be following Him.

Consider your ways. Wow! Stop for a moment and consider the impact of those ways. The God of the universe, with much better things to do, is stopping to ask you to take a long, hard, *honest* inventory of your life. Now that's amazing. Will you do it? It is painful sometimes to realize that we are in a mess because of our own bad choices. It is so much easier to blame someone else for our circumstances but if you really want to be set free you will learn to be honest with yourself.

"Psalm 37:4 reads, "Delight yourself in the Lord; and He will
give you the desires of your heart." Delight comes before desire. If
I delight in God, my desire will be to do things according to His
will and to ask according to His will. Too often we try to make
this principle work in reverse; and we lack desire because our
delight is not great enough."
-John Maxwell-

What is it that you desire today? If God granted them to you right now would it bring honor and glory to Him or to you?

MARCH 10

The Tears of Gethsemane...the night before His crucifixion Jesus found Himself all alone in the Garden of Gethsemane with the weight of the sins of the world on His shoulders... He was about to face a slow, deliberate, painful execution.

When you are hurting the most is when you feel like praying the least.

This is when you must pray. A prayerless life renders you powerless. A prayerless life makes it so much easier to simply give up. This is when the thought of giving up must never cross your mind. You are at a major crossroads in life and the choice you make will make the difference between your victory or utter defeat, your breakthrough or destruction. This is where you will either fall to your knees in prayer or you will collapse to your knees because the enemy has won. The choice is yours. The choice is always yours to make. Either way you will end up on your knees.

There is probably no harder place to find yourself in then when God allows you to visit your own private garden of Gethsemane. "Lord, Why am I here?," your heart cries out. The heavens are silent. You begin to sweat, your heart races. Panic is just a breath away. You shake your fists at heaven and with a sob you ask, "God where are you?" The answer? He is in the same place He was when He allowed His own beloved Son, Jesus, the Son of God to face the same bitter experience. Only difference is, His torturous night in the garden, well, He did it for you and for me. He didn't have to go there but He did. Love compelled Him to go there knowing in a few short hours He would be nailed to a cross and give His life for a world that didn't want Him around. A world that didn't want Him interfering with "their plans." It has been said that nails didn't keep Jesus on the cross....love did. How can anyone, without great consequence, turn their backs on love like that? Have you been to the Cross lately? Always remember the price that was paid for your salvation by the Son of God.

MARCH 11

The pain of the Garden of Gethsemane...

"I must pour out my heart in the language which His Spirit
gives me; and more than that, I must trust in the Spirit to speak the
unutterable groanings of my spirit, when my lips cannot actually
express all the emotions of my heart."
-Charles Spurgeon-

Why is the Garden of Gethsemane such a painful place? You may be asking yourself this question. Because in the Garden of Gethsemane we struggle against God's will for our life. What makes it so unbearable? It's because we want God to consider our plan, and HE WILL NOT. There is no negotiating, no bargaining with and no manipulating the God of Heaven. It must be done His way or it won't be done at all. Total surrender is what God is looking for and He will not settle for anything less than just that. You must surrender all. When you do, God wins, but so do you. The battle is over. The fight is over. You can put down the boxing gloves. Healing can begin. It may appear to you that you have chosen the harder path, but time will let you see that though the way may be hard, God traveling with you guarantees your success, your ultimate victory. If you choose instead to walk away from God, to "do your own thing," eventually you will find yourself in the "pigpen of life" just as the Prodigal son did. He thought he was headed for the "good life." He thought life would be good with no accountability to his earthly father or his Heavenly Father. He was going to eat, drink and party. I've been there, have you? One thing he never considered is that the day will come when God's patience runs out on our rebellion and the party is over. You won't like where you find yourself on that day. Far, far away from those you love and lingering at a great distance from a Holy God, spiritually bankrupt, alone and too scared to go home. God gave you what you asked for, independence from Him. It may have seemed like a good choice in the beginning but it was a deadly choice. God says, "Narrow is the road that leads to life and few travel it, but wide is the road that leads to destruction and death and many you will find on that road." Which road are you on? You'd better find out. The Bible says, "There is a way that seems right to a man, it looks good, feels good, but it leads to death." It will not take you where you think you are going. Where are you headed and who is your traveling companion? I pray, for your sake, it is Jesus.

MARCH 12

"God I hurt...I know my child..."

"Regardless of the source of our pain, we must accept that
God knows, God loves and God is at work."
-Charles Stanley-

It is hard for the human mind and heart to understand why God allows suffering. This is where trust and Omnipotence must win out over self and human reasoning. Some questions may never be answered this side of heaven. Why has God taken my loved one? Why has my marriage ended? Why has my child gotten into drugs, and the list goes on and on of human heartache and trials. It doesn't matter the reason we are there, it will hurt and no one escapes. No one. No one in their right mind would ever choose to go there. But knowing that God has led me there is the first step towards victory. When I know He has allowed this trial in my life and knowing He is at my side and will never forsake me helps me to press on. Knowing this, that He will never allow more to fall on my weary shoulders than I can bear. Hanging on to the fact that Gethsemane will not last forever. Being confident there will be an end to the suffering and pain because He says so.

"In the meantime, though misfortune, misery, and trouble
be upon us, we must have this sure confidence in Him that He
will not suffer us to be destroyed either in body or soul, but will
so deal with us, that all things, be they good or evil, shall redound
to our advantage."
-Martin Luther-

MARCH 13

Gethsemane is the one place God teaches us to pray unceasingly.

"Make no mistake, it is intimacy with God
when you are willing to wrestle something out with Him."
-Beth Moore-

What does that mean to pray unceasingly? It means an attitude of the heart that NEVER leaves the presence of God. Prayer is the homesick child calling home. It's okay to struggle in prayer. Jesus did. The moment we get on our knees the enemy comes at us with full force. His fury has no limits. It isn't just a little skirmish, but it is an all-out assault on our mind, will and emotions. Satan lies, "If God really loved you He wouldn't have allowed this in your life," he whispers in your ear. The seed of doubt is planted. Satan continues his assault until he can wear you down because he knows the powers of darkness are paralyzed by even the feeblest of prayers. He despises when the child of God cries out to Him, "Help!" He will keep you off your knees at any cost. There is no such thing as unanswered prayer and the devil knows it. Even during those times you find yourself on your knees and are so hurt you don't even know what to ask anymore. The Holy Spirit intervenes on our behalf at that time. He intercedes with the Father for us. This is just one of the ways the Holy Spirit comforts. He knows we are in a battle for our very soul. His plan for our life is victory!

"You must remember when waging war with the forces
of hell, endurance is the name of the game."
-Rick Renner-

Have you ever hurt so badly, all seemed hopeless, you didn't know what to pray. Then you convinced yourself why bother? Remember you are in a war. We win! So get down on your knees, even if all of heaven seems silent, and no words come. God will answer! The Holy spirit will take our groanings to the Father and all of the angels of heaven will be summoned to act on our behalf, but remember, what will happen if I don't pray? Nothing.Nothing at all.

MARCH 14

*We have a choice to pray and trust or just to pray.
Today, are you expecting God to answer your prayers?*

"Someone has said that when we work, we work; but when we pray, God works. His supernatural strength is available to praying people who are convinced to the core of their beings that he can make a difference."
-Bill Hybels-

A prayerless life will cause you to linger at a distance from God, afraid to approach Him. Why don't we pray? Too busy? Then you've chosen the world over God. Maybe we think we have the answers, or we don't want God to interfere in our life. No one is going to tell me what to do. Maybe we pray but never take the time to listen to His response. A life of sin will cause you not to pray. Nevertheless, the Holy Spirit will continue to convict. You will have to deaden your ears and your heart to His voice until one day you won't be able to hear Him anymore. I can't think of a lonelier place to be. God has given you what you want. He has left you alone, just like you asked Him to.

Whatever things you pray about will reveal your priorities in life. Do I want just 'things'? Do I want God's will for my life? Then I need to get off the fence and take my prayer life very seriously. The heart that truly believes, knows God will answer a heartfelt prayer. It doesn't dictate to God or suggest to Him how He must answer, instead, humbly bows before Him with a desperate need knowing only He can meet it.

"Prayer brings momentum. It lifts the heart above
the challenges of life and gives it a view of
God's resources of victory and hope."
-John Mason-

What is your source of hope? Is it God or something or someone else? Today is there something pressing in your life you need an answer to? Are you still trying to work it out on your own or have you wisely surrendered it to God? I hope by now you have joined the 'Surrender It All Club' and stop wasting your own time and energy on what would be a breeze for God to solve. You will wonder why you waited so long.

MARCH 15

We will all take several trips to the 'Garden of Gethsemane" in our lifetime.

"The heart has been poured out, and now lifted
upon the wings of prayer the message is wafted
up and away through the silent reaches into
space to the Father's Throne."
-John Wright Follette-

The Garden of Gethsemane is a very heart wrenching place where many of life's battles are either won or lost on our knees. It is a place where our Lord fought His greatest battle, sweating great drops of blood for humanity. It is the only place I know to lay your burdens completely down before the Lord. You can lay down the smallest of burdens to the greatest of heartaches, knowing they are safe in His keeping. It is a place you will discover God, who is as real as the air we breathe. You cannot see the air, nor can you see God, but both are vital to our very existence. God will take your broken heart and hold it in His hands, tenderly reshaping and healing. It is a place that when you leave, you will know that you have been in the very presence of God Himself. Jesus ended up all alone in the garden even though he invited His disciples to stay with Him. Instead of keeping company with the Son of God they fell asleep. Are you feeling alone right now? Your friends may desert you, but God will never leave you. So don't be surprised if others desert you in your greatest hour of need. God wants you alone with Himself, just you and Him. No obstacles in the way. When I think back on all the nights I laid my head on my pillow, instead of getting down on my knees, because I was too tired, it makes me want to cry. How many opportunities did I miss to touch another's life...or my own?

"More is accomplished by prayer than by
anything else this world knows."
-Ted Engstrom-

Keep in mind, the most important thing that was accomplished as Jesus struggled that night in the garden of Gethsemane was 'God's will.' He prayed, nevertheless, "Not My will but Thine."
That is the secret, His will. When you want His will at any cost, victory is right around the corner.

MARCH 16

Never let anything keep you off your knees...Never....Never...Never.

"For a long while I was a mistress of the art of
praying for God to change difficult circumstances.
It took years before I learned how to pray for
God to change me in the midst of the
difficult circumstances."
-Karen Burton Mains-

Foolish is the man who lives only for the comfort of today with no thought about tomorrow, foolishly living life as if there were no consequences, no coming judgment. Living a life that questions the very love of God, when even one glance at the Cross shouts how much He does love us. How foolish to take a path through life that leaves God out. Giving God only certain parts of your life when chances are you are withholding the most important parts from Him. You Shout and cheer for your favorite team and never once raise your hands or voice in praise to God. How foolish to go through life hanging on so tightly to "things" it's impossible for God to open your hands and fill them with those things that really matter in life. How sad to know that many of us choose a path that is longer, harder and scarier than God ever intended for us to travel, mostly because we leave Him behind. How foolish to exchange a life of peace and contentment that He offers for a life with no sense of direction, fear, confusion and merely trying to survive day after day. Pride ignores God's warnings and foolishly believes that somehow their life is going to turn out alright. You can have great victory in Gethsemane, but the choice is yours to make.

"Men occasionally stumble over the truth, but most pick
themselves up and hurry off as if nothing had happened."
-Winston Churchill-

When you leave the Garden of Gethsemane, which road will you be on? Is it a road that turns away from God, or the road that takes Him very seriously? Your very eternity rests on the answer to that simple question. God chooses the weak things of this world, not those who are in competition with Him.

MARCH 17

What happens when we ignore the whispers of God?

Oh friend, can't you see we are so much alike
The trials of life cause our vision to dim.
We chose what is easy, not what is right
Until we remember, "It's all about HIM."
When I wait to obey
my heart filled with doubt
I no longer hear His whispers
Sadly, I force Him to shout.
-Cindy Balch-

How does God get our attention? One way is pain. A little pain or a lot of pain it all depends on your response. God is usually gentle at first. He speaks softly to your conscience. "Don't do that...you won't like the results." We ignore Him so He gets a little louder. If we won't listen to His words we force Him to use our circumstances in a way we won't like. There are really only two ways to live one's life... 'For me to live is Christ or for me to live is self.' When He puts us through a trial it is death to self that He is accomplishing. This is why it's so painful. God is taking back control of my life and yours just as it should be.

"Christ's commands were meant to be obeyed. If this is not done,
the accumulation of scripture knowledge only darkens and
hardens and works satisfaction with the pleasure which the
acquisition of knowledge brings, which unfits
us for the Spirit's teaching."
-Andrew Murray-

Growing up and spiritually maturing in Christ, is not an easy task when accomplished on our own. We avoid pain at all costs...God does not. Pain is one of life's greatest teachers and God will use it if we force His hand.

March 18

God calls us first to give up....then to NEVER give up.

"When circumstances in my life might tempt me to panic, feel
terrified, become a nervous wreck, or be filled with dread, I
can choose either to give into those feelings or to trust in God
and present myself to Him to be filled with His peace."
-Elizabeth George-

Give up...then don't give up? That may sound really strange to you, it may even sound contradictory, but that is exactly what He asks of us. He has a plan for your life, a plan that will make you a success. God's definition of success may be different than ours and therein lies the problem and the battle. At some point in time through trial and error on our part He will get us on the same page as He is on. In my own life if Plan A doesn't work, I will try Plan B, then C, D, E, F...you get the point. Eventually, when all goes sour I seek His guidance. In order to bring His plan to fruition He may have to interrupt our plans. At some point, we will be glad He did. As His child we have been bought with a price, the shed blood of Jesus Christ, not so we could continue doing our 'own thing' but to yield our life over to Him and do 'His thing.' I must give up my plan and embrace His then I should NEVER give up until His will is accomplished in my life. Are you continuing to hold onto something you KNOW God has asked you to relinquish? You will never move forward in your Christian life until you have obeyed the last thing God asked you to do. Make a 'declaration of dependence' on the One who gives you and sustains your life.

"Find the gold. Whatever has happened to you in the past,
and whatever is happening in your life right now, look for
the hidden blessing, the lesson to be learned, or the character
trait to be forged. Trust that, since God has allowed these
experiences, somewhere there is gold for you."
-Elizabeth George-

Every Christian should go for the gold! Every circumstance, every trial, every blessing is orchestrated by our Sovereign God. He alone knows the end from the beginning and more important the 'in between.' He can be trusted...with your very life.

MARCH 19

What is true contentment in life?
Answer: God living life WITH me and THROUGH me.

Contentment? How does your life define it? Is it a life with no problems, no heartaches? Where everything is peachy, no hurts, everyone is kind, compassionate, and caring. No, heavens interpretation of contentment is when I can cry out to God, "God I hurt," and He replies, "I know." – and I know that I know that I know in my heart He really does. That's contentment. Where are you today? Do you believe God really loves you and He knows when you are hurting. Do you know at times like that He draws us near to Him. You can crawl up into His lap and He will wrap His everlasting arms around us and wipe away our tears. Do you know a God like that? If you don't then you haven't really met the God of the Bible. The God of the Bible places all your tears in a bottle. He counts the very hairs on your head. Does anyone else do that for you?

> "The reality is that you may not be able to control your environment;
> you may have to deal with sickness, an alcoholic spouse, a teenager on
> drugs, a mother who abandoned you, a father who abused you, a spouse
> who is irresponsible, aging parents, etc. You can, however, control
> your attitude toward your environment. And your attitude
> will greatly influence your behavior."
> -Gary Chapman-

None of us can control our environment. Only God has full reign and knowledge of what will happen next. The choice we do have every minute of every day is to use those obstacles as either stumbling stones or stepping stones. We can let those obstacles take us down or lift us up. Choice is a very powerful thing. Today, reflect on any obstacles you may be facing and ask yourself, "How are they affecting my life?" Keep a thankful heart even when things are going very wrong and look more than hopeless. Isn't that what Romans 8:28 is all about? We know that God will take **whatever circumstance** we are in and turn it for our good and His glory. Now that is something to shout about! God says we don't have to lose our peace. Ever!

He has got your back!

MARCH 20

"Criticism should always leave a person with the feeling he has been helped – not destroyed or belittled."
-unknown-

"To people like you and me, God's word says, "Don't allow sinful kinds of behavior or thoughts to enter your mind, your heart or your relationships. Why? Because these words and actions are, at their core, the very opposite of walking in love. They are neither innocent, nor harmless fun, they are destructive."
-Chip Ingram-

We all grew up reciting the rhyme, "Sticks and stones may hurt my bones, but words can never harm me." What a lie we learned as a child! I think that song is from the devil. Not only do you feel bad from what someone has said to you, now you are supposed to pretend it doesn't hurt when it does. Others say things they shouldn't to us and we have to confess we do the same. How many times have you said something you wish you hadn't? Something you knew hurt someone. In fact, you said it because you *wanted to hurt them*. If we would only realize how much power is in our words we would be wise to think twice before speaking. Words can't be taken back…ever. Once they are out, they are out. There is no big eraser. They can only be forgiven. Forgiven, but maybe never forgotten. So, don't say them. Let God be your avenger. He is very good at it. When we try to avenge ourselves we may feel pretty good for a little while…"Boy, I sure told them didn't I?" And we pound our chest in pride. Until the Holy Spirit steps in to convict…not condemn, but to convict us. "Did you really win?" He says. It is always the wiser path to never let anyone else define who you are. Teach your children who they are in Christ, and He will protect them from the blows of others. He will love them when they think no one else does. He will stand by them when no one else will. He is our shield!

"Unkind words have incredible power to sting."
-Kenneth Boa & Gail Burnett-

MARCH 21

Sometimes God's first response to our prayer is silence.

"The waters which broke down everything else bore up the ark. The more the waters increased the higher the ark was lifted up to heaven."
-Mathew Henry-

God is silent. Those are hard words to understand when life has knocked you down. We get confused. We doubt. Did God even hear me? God's silence can break us if we let it. We pray harder and louder. Silence continues. Then the enemy steps in with his lies. "See, God doesn't care about you. Look at the mess you are in. If He really cared He would do something." But God waits…and waits…and waits. Time is the Christians number one enemy. All kinds of emotions overtake us, fear, doubt, and unbelief step in. I know God has come through for me in the past. Will we continue to trust Him or will we start to doubt, complain and look for another solution for our problem? I always had a Plan B. Now mind you it wasn't God's Plan B it was mine. If I insist, which I did more times than I would like to admit, He gave me over to my plan. I can sum up Plan B in one word…disaster! Over the years God has taught me it is much wiser to wait on Him. He may be silent but He is always WORKING on my problem. He is always involved in my life. He knows what I will face in the future and He is already working on my behalf. The heavens won't always remain silent to our pleas for help. It is the wise Christian who remembers God's answers to prayer may include silence and waiting at the beginning, but it will not last. One day the heavens will break open, God's answer will come thundering down, probably at just the moment you did give up. No need to hang your head. It is harder to trust some days than it is on others. **GOD IS FAITHFUL!** He will teach you that lesson over and over until we finally get it. He does what He says He will do. "I will **NEVER** leave you, neither will I forsake you." Each time we 'hang in there' a little longer, our faith grows and grows until one day it soars!

MARCH 22

It isn't hard living the Christian life...
*It's **IMPOSSIBLE** without God's help.*

"Strength is found in weakness.
Control is found in dependency.
Power is found in surrender."
-Dan Alexander-

Christianity isn't for wimps or the fainthearted. One of these days we all discover that in our own strength we are no match for some of life's problems...but God is. As long as God is on His throne, and I don't know anyone who can remove Him, Satan tried and look what happened to him. These are the paradoxes in life. In weakness I become strong. If I depend on God, He is in control. If I surrender I gain power, His power. This is God's upside down economy. How can this even make sense? God living my life with me. He is the pilot, I am the co-pilot (and not a very good one I might add.) Most of us get this reversed. We want to be the pilot and occasionally and begrudgingly we let Him take over and be the pilot. That usually happens when the storm is so fierce, the skies are darkened, we have lost our way, the plane is bouncing all over the skies, the landing gear is broke, and we have lost all communication with the tower. Sound familiar? It's a good lesson to learn early on, God does not share control with anyone!

"The more we try to gather the control of our lives,
the more everything in our lives falls apart. God
did not create us to control; He created us to
live in agreement with HIM."
-David Edwards-

So next time you reach over to take the steering wheel, don't. The skies are His, the wind is His, the plane is His, and hopefully you are His too.

MARCH 23

Every day of our life we are dependent on God. Some days we are just more convinced of it than others.

"The first step of courage isn't taken in the midst
of the battle; it's taken when you're willing to
walk out onto the battlefield and face the unknown."
-Steven Curtis Chapman-

Unknown to us, but never unknown to God. Some days we are braver and stronger than other days. We can tackle anything life throws at us. Then God sends us a reality check. Usually it is a very sobering or painful reality check. He doesn't want us to spend even one day in pride…"I can do it on my own…I don't need God on this one." Our very next breath on this earth is dependent upon His grace and mercy to give us life. God cares enough to send me pain. It may be I am traveling down the wrong road and He wants to nudge me back on His narrow path. Unfortunately, some of us don't respond to a 'nudge.' We are like Saul of Tarsus who God had to knock off his donkey, blind him and left him on his rump in the middle of the road. God will do whatever it takes if He sees us traveling toward our destruction. Remember that…whatever it takes. And 'whatever' is usually very painful, but it will eventually get my attention. God has many ways to get our attention, don't make it pain.

MARCH 24

You are a walking sermon of what you really believe.

"Courage is simply doing what needs to be done
even though you are scared and tired."
-Rick Johnson-

I read a very famous quote years ago and I have never forgotten it. I don't remember who said it but here it is, "What you **do** speaks so loudly that I can't hear what you are saying." Do your words match up with how you are living your life? If they don't they should. No one listens to a man who says do what I say, not what I do, especially children. Well, if dad or mom does it then it must be okay. So, they drink, they smoke, they party, they lie. Have you ever told your children when they answered the phone to tell the person you aren't home? I have, not realizing I was teaching them it's ok to not tell the truth sometimes, depending on the situation. It's hard to undo something like that with your children, they have very long memories. How about when you go through a trial, do you murmur and complain and throw a pity party and invite all of your friends or do you go somewhere private, get down on your knees and pray for God to get you through this crisis. Is your attitude such that your friends may not even be aware of some heartache in your life?

"Courage is fear that has said its prayers."
-Anne Lamott-

There is a big difference in sharing your heartache with a close friend versus having a perpetual pity party. God desires that we help each other. He does not require us to listen to them tell their story over and over and over without seeking solutions. Some of us like the attention. We want others to feel sorry for us. That road is much easier than making better, harder choices in life. Have you sent invitations to all your friends to attend your pity party or your success party? The choice is always ours to make. If we really want to get whole again, God will move heaven and earth to make sure that happens!

MARCH 25

When you die how much will you leave behind?
Answer: All of it!

"The world is not impressed when Christians get rich and
say thanks to God. They are impressed when God is so
satisfying that we give our riches away for Christ's sake
and count it all gain."
-John Piper-

Yes, we will eventually leave it all behind. You won't find many hearses followed by a U-haul truck. It all stays behind. Many of us approach life as a sophisticated game of Monopoly. We buy we sell, we build houses and hotels, monuments to ourselves. We do our best to outdo and out buy the other guy. We hurt others in the process. We hurt ourselves. And in the end it all goes back in the box. So it is with life - we go into the box too, a simple pine one or a fancy chrome one. Either way, game over, personal gain is passed on to someone else and we must ask ourselves was it all worth it? The time with my children I gave up to get ahead. Did you sacrifice your health? You obtained wealth and then turned around and spent it to get healthy again. Did you ever notice a monopoly board is all about getting ahead in business, there are no vacation spots on the board. No rest and relaxation from the pressures of life. Buy, sell only to learn 'the best things in life aren't things.' As a nurse I have been at the bedside of many who were living their last days on earth and not one of them asked their family to bring them their bank account balance. Neither did they turn on the TV to see what the Dow Jones was for that day. No, time was precious and it was spent talking over memories of the past. Those memories are all the family members have when they walk out of the hospital the day their loved one died. So, while you still can, make some great memories even your grandchildren and great grandchildren will remember you by. Make a video for them. Make one for your own children too. Tell them how proud you are of them, how much you love them. I guarantee they will play it over and over and over again. I know, to this day I do not remember my dad telling me he loved me towards the end of his life. He never said good-bye and he had plenty of time. He knew he was dying. It still hurts. Before you feel sorry for me, I had a mom who told me every day of my life how much she loved me. Wise is the man who invests in what is eternally important, like relationships, family, friends, and people...not things.

MARCH 26

There are two kinds of pain. There is the pain of discipline and the pain of regret. The pain of discipline usually lasts a limited amount of time whereas the pain of regret can last a lifetime.

"We will always experience regret when we live for the moment, and do not weigh our words and deeds *before* we give them life."
-Lisa Bevere-

The pain of discipline and the pain of regret...I have experienced them both. Have you? It is hard to say which one is worse. Wishing you hadn't done the thing you knew to be wrong or regretting the harsh discipline that came from God's hand because you disobeyed. It is a hard lesson to learn that no matter who we are we don't get by with anything. Everything we do has a consequence connected to it whether good or bad. The Bible says don't be a fool, God cannot be mocked, whatever a man sows, that is exactly what he will reap. Problem is we think we are the exception to God's rule. You sow corn, you get corn, you sow discord, it comes right back at you. You gossip, well guess what, someone is going to say some pretty bad things about you. It is a good idea to get into the habit of asking the Lord in the morning, before you start your day, to keep a watch over your mouth. Ask Him to convict you before you sin, and I can guarantee He will stop you in your tracks. You will hear that still, small voice of the Holy Spirit whispering deep down inside you, "Stop it." Question then becomes, will you stop? I wish I could say every time I heard His rebuke, I stopped, but that would be a lie. Sad isn't it? I asked Him to convict me, He did, I brushed it off. Pride kicked in and I kept sinning with my big fat mouth. So, please, please, please listen to Him the first time. You will be so glad you did. You will save yourself a whole lot of heartache. Words, once spoken, are forever.

MARCH 27

This is not a game to God...He is playing for keeps.

The Bible says we were chosen in Him **before** the foundations of the earth! Beth Moore says it like this, "So before God said, "Let there be light." He said, "Let there be Beth Moore." Now insert your own name! WOW! What a way to start your day!

"Long ago and *even before He made the world*, God loved us
and **chose us** in Christ to be holy and without fault in His eyes."
-Ephesians 1:4-

God's plan for you and for me started <u>before</u> He made the earth, the stars, the galaxies! That deserves a Hallelujah! We are not a mistake to God or to our parents. God's plan started long ago. You might say you were a twinkle in God's eye before He even made you. I don't know about you, but this makes me want to jump up and down and sing and shout. It doesn't matter if your own parents gave you up, God will not. He has a plan for you from eternity past and He will fulfill it. When you really stop and think about our own birth you really had nothing to do with it except to show up on planet earth. God chose who our parents would be, what century you would be born in. He decided in His sovereignty whether you would be born to a rich, poor or middle class family. He determined the color of our skin, our nationality and who our relatives would be. (That explains a lot!) There is so much we do not understand and won't this side of heaven.

"If there is one thing I am now absolutely certain
of, it is that no human minds or committees will ever
capture the powerful reality we call God with human
words or formulas or creeds."
-Timothy Johnson-

God is. He always has been. He always will be. Profound thoughts... too marvelous for our understanding. Everything we know has a 'beginning.' God does not. We view everything in our world through the corridors of time. God is outside of time. Amazing! Simply mind boggling is our God!

MARCH 28

"Affliction comes to the believer not to make him sad, but sober; not to make him sorry, but wise. Even as the plow enriches the field so that the seed is multiplied a thousand, o affliction should magnify our joy and increase our spiritual harvest." – Henry Ward Beecher

"So as the lightening cometh out of the east, and shines
even unto the west; so shall the coming of the Son of man be."
-Matthew 24:7-

Sadly, trouble, heartache, and affliction is a part of life. The good news is it won't last forever. It may seem like it will, but Jesus promises us that it will not. There is coming a day when the sorrows of this life will all be over, just a memory of what was. Death will one day lose its grip on us. We will be released from the burden of sin in this life. When Jesus said, "It is finished," He meant, "It is finished." He paid the price for our sins and the sins of the whole world. Thankfully, it doesn't stop there. He rose from the dead giving us the promise of new life in Him. Old things have passed away and Behold, He has made all things new. He came as a baby in a manger, was rejected by a world He had made with His own Hands, and was put to death by evil men. Again, the story does not stop there. HE ROSE FROM THE DEAD, and HE IS COMING AGAIN! All who hear His voice on that day, who hear the trumpet call will rise with Him into everlasting glory. Read how Max Lucado has described that resurrection day when Jesus returns for His own;

"Bodies will push back the dirt and break the surface
of the sea. The earth will tremble, the sky will roar, and
those who do not know Him will shudder. But in that
hour you will not fear, because you know Him."
-Max Lucado-

We need not fear that day if we know Jesus as Savior and as Lord. If you do *not* know Him, there will be nowhere to hide from His wrath. Heaven is real, and real people go there, likewise, hell is real, and real people will go there. Jesus said more about hell than He ever did about heaven. He warns, question is do we believe Him? That baby in a manger, that turned the Roman Empire upside down and inside out, will one day light up the heavens with His return as King of kings and Lord of lords. What a day that will be! Max Lucado goes on to say, "For the Christian, the return of Christ is not a riddle to be solved or a code to be broken, but rather it is a day to be **anticipated**." This is good news for the believer. No matter what happens in our world, we are to keep our eyes fixed and focused on Jesus, never on our circumstances. No man knows the day or the hour of Christ's return. We must live ready!

MARCH 29

*Be kinder than necessary because everyone
you meet is fighting some kind of battle.*

"The Prince of the kings of the earth, the King of glory,
stoops from the throne of His universe, and takes His place
in the workshop of perhaps the meanest village in the land.
How Godlike!"
-John Dawson-

We ALL have problems. It is part of being human. It's how we choose to deal with those problems that really matters. Will I conquer the problem or will it conquer me? Have you ever been down in the dumps and a complete stranger smiled at you and you found your spirits were lifted. You can have that same effect on others. Just a few kind words can change a person's life. "I'm really sorry." "Let me help." "I will pray for you." "I forgive you"...

"When we run out of power to be and to do what we
ought, the Lord has only just begun to supply us with
His strength to live well beyond what we can do on our own."
-Jill Briscoe-

It is far too easy some days to get off track. To forget the important things in life, and get caught up in the truly mundane or the unimportant. We live for the moment and forget there is an eternity that awaits us, a day that we will stand before the God of this universe and give an account of our lives. What we did, what we didn't do, what we should have done...a day of accountability. The world we live in no longer seems to hold people responsible for their actions. Not so with God. We will stand before Him. Excuses will be powerless before His throne. The only thing He will see is whether or not we have accepted His Son as Savior and Lord, or done our own thing. Have we knelt at the foot of the Cross or trampled over it with our rejection and unbelief? Are we washed in the blood of the Lamb who gave His very life for us, or have we chosen to be clothed in our own righteousness which is nothing but filthy rags in His sight?

"Few of us dare to dream of what God might have had
in mind when He made us the unique way that we
are and breathed His life into us."
-Cindi McMenamin-

Live as if your eternity depends on it...because it does.

MARCH 30

Walk away from God and at some point in time you can be guaranteed that the pain will outweigh the pleasure.

"I have no sympathy with the idea that God puts
us behind the blood and saves us, and then leaves
us in Egypt to be under the old taskmaster. I believe
God brings us out of Egypt into the promised land,
and that it is the privilege of every child of God to
be delivered from every foe, from every besetting sin."
-D.L. Moody-

Sin is always fun for a while, but it comes with a very big price tag. It will eventually bankrupt your life. Nothing has changed since the Garden of Eden. Satan said, "Has God really said…? Eve began to doubt, she began to look at the forbidden fruit, she took her eyes off of all the other trees in the garden. Satan pressed in, "Go ahead and eat to your heart's content." Did God really say, "Don't eat it… in the day you do you will surely die." Unfortunately, doubt won. Next thing we know Eve is handing Adam the fruit and saying, "Yum, take a bite honey." Unfortunately he did and the world was plunged into darkness. Man was separated from his God. Adam and Eve's spirit was shut off from communicating with God. They were thrown out of the garden to toil in life and childbirth, some tradeoff that was. It wasn't all about the fruit. It was about DISOBEDIENCE. God said "Don't," and Adam said, "You're not going to tell me what to do." Was a bite from a piece of fruit worth the price the world has paid since their disobedience? God is right," The heart of man is desperately wicked, who can know it?" All sin is disobedience towards God. Do an inventory. Is there something God has put His finger on in your life and you ignore Him? That's disobedience. All you accomplish is to prolong the process and force God to turn the heat up just a little bit hotter until you obey. If you are His child He will not leave you content in your disobedience.

"Sin is the ruin and misery of the soul. It is destructive
in its very nature, and if God should leave it without
restraint, nothing else would be needed to make the soul miserable."
-Jonathan Edwards-

Learn to call sin what it is…sin. Sin is something never to be trifled with. Take it as serious as God takes it. Confess it immediately. Turn from it! Think of it as a destructive fire. As a fire that, unless brought to God's throne of grace, will destroy everything and everyone in its path. It can destroy everything you hold dear. Never believe the enemy's lie that you have committed the unpardonable sin. Unless you have rejected Jesus Christ as Savior and Lord, you may bring everything to Him. He knows all about it anyway. So, confess it and be forgiven! Do not let the sun go down before getting on your knees before the only One who can wash your sins away, forever. Just like the song, you can be washed whiter than snow. Though our sins be like crimson, His blood can make us whiter than snow. Is it time for a heavenly bath?

MARCH 31

"Do not let yourself be deceived...
whatsoever a man sows, that and only that is what he will reap."
-Galatians 6:7-

"One of the reasons that many Christians seem to have no
thrill at being forgiven through the gospel is that they have
not been brokenhearted over their sin. They have not despaired.
They have not wrestled with warranted self-loathing. They
have not grieved over their sin because of its moral repugnance,
but have grieved only because of guilt feelings and threats of hell."
-John Piper-

When a farmer plants corn he doesn't expect to get peas. So why do most of us think that when we sin something good is going to result? The wages of sin is death. Sin brings death to our peace, death to our contentment, to relationships, to our power to be an effective influence in the world for God. Remember, others watch what you do more than what you say. Do you call yourself a Christian, a follower of Christ and then live like the devil? Do you believe yourself to be the 'exception' to God's rule, "The soul that sins it shall die." I know I did for a very long time. Like many others, my response would be, "But, I'm a good person." I was blinded by my own pride. Believing that I knew better than God did, and I wouldn't send someone like me to hell, so therefore He wouldn't either. How wrong I was. God is persistent and I am so grateful He is. One day He tired of my shenanigans (a nicer word for sin), and brought me to a place where I could no longer escape who I really was...a sinner in need of a Savior. That was the worst day of my life and it was the best day of my life. No more games, no more pretending to be someone I was not.

"Dare we make light of that which
brings down the wrath of God."
-Mathew Henry-

For years I made light of sin. Not just of sin, but of my own sin. If I saw others do what I did, I was appalled by their behavior but seemed to justify my own actions. What we refuse to accept in others we accept ourselves doing. Billy Graham has said, "We've tried calling sin "errors" or "mistakes" or "poor judgment," but sin itself has stayed the same." We need to be honest with God. I will leave you today with this last thought to meditate on throughout the day;

"All sin must be wept over; here, in godly sorrow,
or, hereafter in eternal misery."
-Mathew Henry-

If you have a lost loved one or friend, don't stop praying for them. An eternity without Christ is an unimaginable horror with no end...

APRIL 1

God does not give Saturday's grace on Tuesday,
He gives it on Saturday.

"God wants you to experience His grace whether you have faced
your life with courage or with cowardice. Grace is not about
us; it is about God. He will meet you wherever you are to
help you to take the next gutsy step."
-Patsy Clairmont & Traci Mullins-

God will help us take the next gutsy step. That should make you smile. We don't have to face life alone. Have you ever wondered how some people can go through such tragedies and heartache and still praise God? You think to yourself, if that ever happened to me it would destroy me. You find yourself distancing yourself from them just in case 'bad things happening' is 'catchy,' when just the opposite should be true. We should embrace them, find out where that kind of faith and strength comes from. It's from the GRACE that God gives at the time we need it, not before. I used to think there was no way I could make it through life if I lost my mom....and then I did. She had been the rock of my life, my biggest cheerleader. My consistent connection to the God she loved. She was generous to a fault and full of wisdom. My heart hurt so badly but God's grace was there to reassure me she was with HIM and He gave me His grace and peace when I needed it. Not before, but when I needed it. Closing our eyes in this world and opening them to see Jesus, this is death for the Christian. None of us stay on this earth forever. We will all leave, eventually. On my mom's gravesite headstone we wrote, "Safely Home." One day I will join her again. I said 'So long mom' but not goodbye... as she took her last breath and died in my arms. Life doesn't get much harder than that. God does not want us to live our lives in fear of the unknown, fear of what might happen tomorrow, fear that we won't be able to handle it. Maybe, that is why He made sure to tell us that He would never put anything on us that He would come along side and help us carry the burden. Fear paralyzes us. His grace is a gift to us to overcome every fear.

"Always remember that, every time you step out of your
comfort zone, you step into God's comfort zone."
-Mark Cahill-

What is it that you fear? What is keeping you from truly living 'free'? What you refuse to face, you can *never* overcome. Remember, it is the truth that sets us free.

"Fear can be conquered only by
faith, and faith thrives on truth."
-Brendan O'Rourke-

April 2

*"A 'spiritual ache' must be brought to the Cross of Christ
or carried alone until the soul collapses underneath its weight."*
-Cindy Balch-

"Our heavenly Healer often has to hurt us in order to
heal us. We sometimes fail to recognize His mighty love
in this, yet we are firmly held always in the Everlasting arms."
-Elizabeth Elliot-

Give me a toothache anytime compared to a 'spiritual ache' of the heart, of the soul. A toothache will eventually go away, but a spiritual ache can linger and linger. Nothing fills that ache in the spirit but God. We all have heart trouble. Your heart is empty. It yearns for more. It's a heart in want, a heart of sin. It longs to be free. It searches far and wide for answers and finds none. It is a heart that keeps score in life. It sees what it wants to see and does what it wants to do. It says what it pleases. It thinks itself to be free, yet remains blinded by the chains of bondage wrapped tightly around it. It is a heart that cares for only 'self', a heart that looks for any answer other than God. A heart with no answers, no faith, no direction, no light, no truth, hungry for God and doesn't even realize it. It is a heart full of fear and doubt. It's a heart that doesn't know how to sing in prisons or loses its song when tough times come. A heart looking for truth but when presented with the Cross of Christ, looks elsewhere. A heart that is dishonest with God, self and others. It is a heart that refuses over and over to say 'YES' to God, a heart that refuses to make that crucial trip to Calvary where sin and God's grace meet and GRACE WINS! A place where ***whosoever will*** can be washed whiter than snow by the blood of Jesus. It's a heart that makes thousands of decisions over a lifetime except the most important one, Jesus died for my sins, Jesus rose from the dead, Jesus is coming again. He's coming for me is He coming for you?

"Jesus is what makes heaven, heaven."
-John Courson-

Grace and mercy or death and judgment, which one will it be? It's your choice. It always has been your choice.

APRIL 3

❋

Jesus said, "Follow Me..."

"The Shepherd is responsible *for* His sheep, the
sheep are responsible *to* the Shepherd."
-unknown-

Jesus said, "Follow **Me**." It was a command not a suggestion. There is no negotiating, no conditions, no exceptions. He leads, I follow. He will take me places I never dreamed possible. With God, the ride can get pretty wild at times. Life is like my favorite ride at Disneyland, the 'Cars.' The very first time on the ride, I went with my daughter and twin grandsons who were 10 years old at the time. It was their birthday. We started off putt, putting through Radiator town, going around and through mountains. Then the ride broke down. That wasn't part of the plan, it just happened while we were on it. One of my grandsons was scared as we sat in the semi darkness while the other thought this was the greatest. Finally, the ride restarted and we continued to putt putt some more. I thought to myself, this is really boring, why on earth do people stand in line for 3 hours for this. Are they all crazy? Did they forget to take their meds? Then all of a sudden you come to a stop. An ominous feeling of fear overtook me. I quickly wondered why they let old people like me on this ride. I was sure something I didn't like was about to happen. I was right. You are lined up with another car alongside of you, the engines are revving up and the race begins. You go from zero to 90 miles an hour in 5 seconds flat, holding on for dear life, racing around curves and never slowing down, not sure you will live to see the finish line. There's even a camera at the finish line that documents your terror as you cross over. I didn't realize Disney people were that sadistic (kidding of course). Once it was over I wanted to do it again. Now, I'm the crazy one. They let us stay on the ride because of the previous break down. This time, however, I knew what to expect. I braced myself and held on for dear life...again. So, it is with God. Life may be boring and mundane and then all of a sudden you find yourself in a scary place. Hold on, God can be trusted more than a theme park ride can. So enjoy the ride and hold on to Him. Smile! Who knows, God make take your picture at the end and put it on His refrigerator!

April 4

*I asked God to change me...I wish I had the
sense to buckle my seat belt first.*

Growing up in the Lord means you need to
let God remove some undesired attitudes that
hinder your growing in Him.

I was tired of living the way I was living, so I asked God to change me. "Lord, I'm tired of living this way. Please change me into the person You want me to be." Well, faithful as He is, He began the process and I began the kicking and the screaming. "What are you doing, Lord?' I mumbled through the pain, forgetting what I had prayed. So, be prepared if you get up the courage to pray that same prayer because it is one He definitely will answer. His goal is to make us like His Son. It is often a very long, painful process. There is a lot of junk we have to get rid of in our lives. Letting go of some of it is excruciating. The other side of glory, when it is all over, God will see Jesus when he looks at me. Right now He isn't anywhere near done with me. I have a long ways to go, but I am headed in the right direction. Are you?

> "As Christians we should never fear change. We must
> believe in change so long as it is change oriented toward
> godliness. The Christian life is a life of continual change."
> -Jay Adams-

Change is necessary. It is also very painful at times. It involves letting go of something we may hold dear. God in His wisdom sees things in our life that are not good for us. Thankfully, He doesn't show us everything that is wrong with us all at once. No, He is merciful to change us a little bit at a time, otherwise it would be too overwhelming for us. We would become hardened and resentful, and turn back to our old ways. Remember to buckle your seat belt *before* praying for God to change you. That is definitely a prayer He answers.

April 5

"God, I wish I were beautiful...
He replied, "I wish you could see what I see."
-Unknown-

"Shape and height, texture and color determined by
the amazing genes that the Lord has implanted in you
as He designed you in the womb. These were His gifts
to you. Be assured that God liked what He created you to
be, in all your physical features. You are beautiful to Him."
-Pat Warren-

God said, "Go stand in front of the mirror and I will show you what I see when I look at you. I see My reflection. Beauty isn't measured by years, but by character. I see eyes of trust. Trusting Me to take care of you. I see lips that continually praise My name. I see knees that bow before Me in humility, asking for My help. I see a heart that has found its rest in Me. Your prayers are like you calling home. Your feet may remain on earth, but your heart is my home. Your eyes, I see your Father's reflection in them. You have your Father's eyes you know. I see a heart that was once full of rebellion and strife that is now at peace. It is filled with compassion for others. Self is no longer number one." Someday you will understand that beauty is often measured in sorrow and tears, trials and triumphs, gains and losses in life. You wouldn't know how to say kind words to others unless someone had spoken venom against you. You wouldn't understand how important a hug could be unless someone had hugged you at just right the time.

My mom never thought she was pretty, according to the world's standards. In the eyes of her children and grandchildren she was the most beautiful woman in the whole wide world. She was a Proverbs 31 woman full of love for the Lord and it showed every day in her countenance.

We are all one of a kind in God's eyes. I am reminded of the joke: "You're unique alright, when God made you He said, "I'll never do that again."

April 6

"Why me Lord?...why is this happening to me?"

"When God begins to burn, destroy, and purify, the soul
does not perceive that these operations are intended for
its good, but rather supposes the contrary."
-Francois Fenelon-

Trouble comes to us all. Do a quick spiritual check-up: Do you get down in the dumps when trouble comes or do you get down on your knees? I used to spend a lot of time in the dumps, now I spend more time on my knees. God in His Sovereignty sends into each of our lives both good times and bad times. He promises, like no one else can, to make something good come out of even the worst circumstances if we will just trust Him. Trust Him even though I don't understand...especially when I don't understand. When Jesus lay in the tomb after being beaten and crucified, the onlookers thought this was the end of His ministry. The devils in hell danced a jig at His death. When in fact, it was just the beginning of God's plan unfolding! The grave could not hold Him. So when the worst thing happens in your life, the thing you have feared the most, take heart and remember Jesus. He will take this tragedy and turn it into your triumph. He will take your heartache and give you a message of hope and healing the world won't know what to do with it. God does not wring His hands when we get into trouble. He doesn't wonder to Himself, "Now how did that happen?" Our God is all knowing and all powerful. He and He alone can take the worst of circumstances and bring a resurrection morning into our lives. It is never over until He says it's over! He promises that no matter what happens in our life He will always be there. He promises never to leave or forsake us. Never. We can't say that about anyone else in our lives. (My mom came awful close, but even she failed at times.) So, if doubt ever gets you down, read the end of the story again. We win. No matter how many times I read it, we always win! The tomb is still empty and God is still in control! Live by faith not by your feelings. Faith sees and believes God will do exactly what He has promised. Like Job, we can proclaim with confidence. "Even though He slay me, in my flesh I shall see God." AMEN! Now that is something to shout about!

April 7

*Don't keep score in life...**choose** to stay free.*

"The reason we see hypocrisy and fraud and unreality in others is because they are all in our own hearts. The great characteristic of a saint is humility – Yes, all those things and other evils would have been manifested in me but for the grace of God, therefore I have no right to judge."
-Oswald Chambers-

Are you plotting to get even with someone? Stop it! "I can't let them get away with that." Yes, you can, but God won't. He will intervene on your behalf if you will just turn your case over to Him. "Vengeance belongs to Me," says the Lord, "I ***will*** repay." Notice it says He will, not maybe, He will, and it doesn't say He will think about it, but He will repay. Only He has the wisdom and knowledge to accomplish it. Only He knows how much pressure to apply and what is in the person's heart that made them hurt you. I think personally, I would rather have God work it out than me. He is much more compassionate and merciful than I am. Let Him keep score. He is a God of justice. What frustrates us is we ask for justice and then we wait...and wait... and wait some more. It may be swift in some cases, but usually it will take longer than we think it should. But by the time God has vindicated us He has also worked on my heart and life at the same time and the urgency for retribution is gone. One day He will right all of the wrongs in the world, until then throw away your scoreboard. One day you will be glad you did. It's the only way to stay free. Make that choice today. Get on your knees and bring all of your injustices before God and don't get up until you have given them all over to Him, as painful as it might be. He will take care of them for you and free you at the same time. So, let God wipe your slate clean of unforgiveness and then go on and enjoy your day.

"Betrayal by someone you trust is like an earthquake.
The very ground beneath you is suddenly unstable."
-Barbara Bartocci-

God offers us earthquake insurance...Himself. Beth Moore has said, "When God dwells at the center of our lives, peace and contentment will belong to us as surely as we belong to God."

April 8

Standing firm against strong pressure and temptation is never easy, but the alternative is deadly.

"Many a man goes through life hanging his head with shame because he has never discovered the distinction between temptation and sin."
-Henry Drummond-

Temptation is NOT sin. Jesus was tempted by the devil but He did not sin. How many times have we heard, "But *everyone's* doing it." Are they? And just who is '*everybody?*' Often people will 'give in to get along.' Is that even biblical? I don't think so. As a child of God He has put certain boundaries around our lives, not to make it so we can't have any fun, but to protect us. Every alcoholic started with 'just one drink.' Every office affair started with just a simple glance in someone's direction, an innocent (or not so innocent) smile. Every cookie I ate led to eating 10 cookies, even though I had the best of intentions to eat just 'one.' God says flee temptation. Run! Don't stop to consider it, not even for one minute. Run! Once you begin to 'consider' your options you are toast. The enemy has your attention and he will be relentless until you give in to, 'just this once.'

"Let's all wise up. Some of us aren't fighting the fire; we're playing with fire, flirting with the devil. Stop it! Stop it now before all hell literally breaks loose."
-Beth Moore-

When I read this I pictured a scene going on in hell, the demons placing bets as to how long before each of us fell to their tactics. I can see it now. The cookies are on the kitchen counter. One demon laughs, "I'll give her a week." While another hisses, "A week? She didn't last a day last week when I tempted her to buy them at the supermarket!" And so it goes. Another one bites the dust, just don't let it be you. Remember! Temptation is not sin. Sin requires an act of the will that goes against God's will for our life. God wants our life to be in balance. Yes, we can have a cookie or two, but not 12 or 20 without the consequences showing up in the mirror sooner rather than later.

"Brokenness is the shattering of my self-will – the absolute surrender of my will to the will of God. It is saying, "Yes, Lord!" – no resistance, no chaffing, no stubbornness – simply submitting myself to His direction and will in my life."
-Nancy Leigh DeMoss-

As time goes by you will find it is much easier to submit to God than it is to fight against Him.

April 9

Sometimes God gives us the 'GIFT' of desperation.
-Joyce Meyer-

"You can rest in the knowledge that even when bad things happen, God is always there. He is always in charge. Although He may not always deliver in the way you expect, you will find that His grace is more than sufficient."
-Kay Arthur-

Desperation, a gift? "Well, count me out! I have enough problems, thank you very much" you may be saying. Desperation usually means that I have exhausted all of *my* plans and solutions for my troubles and 'all I have left is God.' Isn't that the craziest thing you or I have ever said, "All I have left now is God, guess I'll pray." Wow! All you have left is the Creator of the Universe! The One who holds the oceans in His hands, and at the same time flung the stars in the sky, and named them all. He is the One who counts the exact number of hairs on your head. Now granted that is an easier task for some of us than others. Maybe this desperation thing isn't such a bad thing after all. If God left us alone to our own solutions then we would never know His vast resources for our life. The Bible says, "Call on me in your time of **TROUBLE**, I will hear and I will answer." So, why not call on Him as soon as trouble arrives and maybe, just maybe, we wouldn't get so desperate.

"Oftentimes, the only way for us to know what's in our heart is for God to squeeze it by our circumstances. He already knows, it's we who need to be made aware. This revelation isn't meant to condemn us but to give us the opportunity to humbly ask for His help...and to recognize our dependence upon Him."
-Rebecca Lusignolo-

APRIL 10

God chooses the weak things of this world – never those who are in competition with Him.

"One never accomplishes the will of God by breaking the law of God, violating the principles of God, or ignoring the wisdom of God."
-Andy Stanley-

Don't we all like to think we are strong. We think that we can hold up under anything the enemy throws at us? Super Christian with a big 'S on our cape,' only to find out that with one good attack of the devil we are flailing, off balance doubting and surrendering. Wimpy Christian is more like it. On the night of Jesus birth, God didn't send His angels to the strong religious sect or to the rulers of Jerusalem, but to lowly, common, weak shepherds. What a night that must have been, the angels singing of the glory of God becoming man and dwelling among sinners. Not long after, Herod attempted to kill baby Jesus by his edict that all males under the age of two be slaughtered. God intervened by warning Mary and Joseph to flee to Egypt until it was safe to return. What has God asked you to flee from? Did you obey or did you find yourself right smack dab in the middle of something that you can't handle. God always warns. The question is, 'Do we pay attention to His warnings?' If we insist on our Plan B or C or D then we are in competition with God and His plan for our life. If you want to be self-sufficient in life, God will let you.

"The Lord God Almighty, since before He spoke creation into being, has been orchestrating things to harmoniously converge and culminate in the glory, honor, and worship of His Son, the Lord Jesus Christ. That is why history is His story."
-Preston Parrish-

It is His story, His plan, His beginning, His ending, His in-between...ultimately His glory. Not mine. Not yours. His alone.

APRIL 11

Pay now. Pay later. You will eventually pay.

"The Lord of the universe stands ready to pick up your life
and give it significance, a sense of fulfillment beyond anything
you have ever experienced. Your heart has got eternity in it...and
you will not be fulfilled until you know you are making an eternal
difference with the one life you have.
-Ron Hutchcraft-

Did you hear about the farmer who planted corn and to his surprise got a crop of broccoli instead? Of course you didn't. It doesn't happen. You plant corn you get corn. It's as simple as that. God has made it so easy for us. So when the Bible very clearly says, "Whatsoever a man sows, that is what he will reap", why do we think we are the one exception to the rule? I know I did. I like many others before me and after me find out there are *no exceptions*, usually when it's too late. God means what He says and says what He means. If you plant anger, down the road you will reap a really ugly harvest of anger, bitterness and unforgiveness, but it works for our good too. If we plant kind words, smiles, and love then we will reap good things into our lives. Sometimes we don't reap until years later. By that time we think we have pulled one over on God. If you think that, then all I can say is watch out! There are no crop failures with God. None.

"Until men feel that they owe everything to God, that
they are cherished by His paternal care, and that He is
the author of all of their blessings, so that nothing is to
be looked for away from Him, they will never submit to Him
in voluntary obedience, nay, unless they place their entire
happiness in Him, they will never yield up their
whole selves to Him in truth and sincerity."
-John Calvin-

Instead of spending your life praying for a crop failure, plant the good stuff to begin with and begin with prayer. Then sit back and watch it grow into something that will last throughout all eternity.

APRIL 12

*"It is **impossible** to govern the world without the Bible."*
-George Washington-

"Infinite potentates have raged against this book, and sought to destroy
and uproot it – King Alexander the Great, the princes of Egypt and of Babylon,
the Monarchs of Persia, of Greece, and of Rome, the emperors Julius
and Augustus – but nothing prevailed; they are all gone
and vanished, while the Bible remains."
-Martin Luther-

America's first President said those words, it is impossible to govern without the guidance of God's Holy Word. It may shock some of you. You might have heard others say that America is not a Christian nation and that it was not founded on the principles of the Bible and on the beliefs in the Almighty. To say this is to be ignorant or disingenuous. Maybe you don't agree with the Christian principles, but to say they didn't exist is a lie. This is not the America I grew up in, which was during the 50's and 60's. We never locked our doors, we hopped on our bikes and rode around with friends until the street lights came on and we knew it was time for dinner. We drank from hoses not bottled water. We didn't need metal detectors at our schools. The worse thing I can remember is you couldn't wear patent leathered shoes because some boy might be able to look up your dress. Our individual freedoms are slowly eroding away and most are too busy with everyday life to pay attention. One day Americans will wake up and wonder what has happened to our liberties, our right to be free, our free speech, and it will be too late. Tyranny is fast approaching as our Constitution is ignored and berated as outdated and useless. Law makers now feel free to tell us how big our sodas can be that we drink. Thankfully, that law was eventually overturned. Bad things happen when good people do nothing. The book of Revelation speaks of a one world government one day under the control of the Antichrist. History is slowly marching towards that fulfillment. A one world religion will reign at the same time. The good news is, Jesus promises to take His true church out of this world before His wrath comes upon the whole earth. The tribulation period is 7 years of God's judgment on an unbelieving world. This is what results when man attempts to rule without God. We live in an ever changing, unpredictable world, where anything goes. It is a good day to know you belong to Jesus, a good day indeed. The book of Revelation also says, "We win!" One with God is always a majority.

Whose side are you on?

"Having killed God, the atheist is left with no reason
for being, no morality to espouse, no meaning to life,
and no hope beyond the grave."
-Ravi Zacharias-

April 13

I don't need to keep beating myself up for something I did wrong yesterday.

"When you repent of your sin and are broken before
the Lord, He sees you through every step of the painful
consequences. His mercy, grace, and goodness enable
you to bear it all with hope."
-David Wilkerson-

I don't know about you, but I have gotten very, very good at this. I can beat myself up for days over something I did wrong a week ago, or 20 years ago. Does it do any good? No! so don't waste your time on yesterday. Learn a lesson from it if you must, then *let it go*. Oh, and then, don't do it again. I still laugh at the words I read written by former hockey goalie Jacques Plante when he said, "How would you like a job where if you made a mistake, a big red light goes on and 18,000 people boo?" Why do we continue to beat ourselves up? We forget we are human and we will make mistakes. Some we do on purpose, others out of stupidity. I have found one of the hardest things in life is to forgive myself. I believe, as most of us do, we should be punished, so we punish ourselves in our own minds if someone else doesn't do it. How long do you have to beat yourself up for doing wrong? A week, a month, see how silly it is to hold onto things God says to repent of and then let them go.

"Come boldly into His throne of GRACE – even
when you have sinned and failed. He FORGIVES –
instantly - those who repent with godly sorrow."
-David Wilkerson-

Come boldly? Yes, boldly. Amazing, isn't it. Don't go off in a corner and beat yourself up. Instead, realize you have sinned, you have failed Him, you know you shouldn't have done what you did, then immediately go to His throne of GRACE. If it weren't a throne of GRACE, none of us could come. We couldn't even slither in. God's GRACE is taking me right where I am, and showing me mercy when I really deserve judgment. Jesus' blood has made it all possible. He washes us whiter than snow. He does a better job than any bleach product we could buy. He cleans us up on the inside! He changes our 'want to' so that we don't want to (sin) anymore.

APRIL 14

*A man who is too proud to get on his knees before Almighty God
is probably too proud to hear what He has to say.*
-Unknown-

"*Humble yourself* under the mighty hand of God
and in due time He will lift you up."
1 Peter 5:6

This verse seems to say that either we do the humbling or God will. It appears that if we will do the humbling then God will do the lifting. We have a choice in life to humble ourselves under God's mighty hand or walk proudly on this earth, defying the Living God, seeking status and recognition from man. Humility on the other hand, admits I need help. It means I can't do it on my own and I'm not smart enough. I need God's help desperately. Most of like to think we are self-sufficient and tough as nails, but one good dose of getting humbled by God will cure you of any further delusions that you don't need Him.

"I have more trouble with myself than
with any other man I ever met."
Dwight L. Moody

Saul of Tarsus was a very proud, 'religious to his finger-tips' man. He believed it was his duty to wipe all of the Christians off the face of the map. Everything he was doing was wrong in God's sight, but still Saul did it 'in the name of God.' Arrogantly, he thought he was doing God a favor. Not until God blinded him, knocked him off his high horse and confronted him with his behavior, did he wisely change his tune. When you are blinded, you need help. When you are lying on the ground, you need help up. The story has a happy ending. God changed Saul's name to Paul and used him to write two thirds of the New Testament. No man was used by God as powerfully as Paul was. But it was only after he had a 'come to Jesus' experience. When you start to have proud thoughts, compare your life to Mother Theresa's who dedicated her whole life to helping those who could never help themselves. She lived in the filth and poverty of those she helped. She was willing to go where few others would. Surely, her recompense was in heaven because it certainly wasn't here on this earth. Where is it that God wants you to make a difference in someone's life? Will you go if He asks? It is best to think twice before saying no. Mother Theresa could have lived her life comfortably, but in her heart she knew that she would be miserable anywhere else in the world because God wanted her in Calcutta. Those orphans needed her more than she needed the comforts of life. She gave up the 'comfortable,' for the will of God. I am sure, right now, as she stands in the presence of the God she served so faithfully, she is glad she made the hard choices.

April 15

*"No man should tell another man about hell
unless he can do it with tears in his eyes."*
-Charles H. Spurgeon-

"The main reason we believe in hell is
because Jesus Christ declares that it is so."
-D. James Kennedy-

Hell exists. Jesus said so. That should be enough, but for some people they choose not to believe the Son of God. It is to their own peril. After all, common sense dictates that He knows more about hell than we do. Talking about Hell makes us very uncomfortable, but when you realize that Jesus had more to say about hell then heaven, it is crucial to get the good news of the gospel out to as many as we can as quickly as we can. Hell is a real place and real people will go there. People you know. They may be your friends or your neighbors, maybe even your family member. They may be people who may have sat in a church pew all of their life. They have religion, but they don't have Jesus. These chilling words said by Jesus, "Depart from Me, I never knew you."

"No man can ever enter heaven until he is
first convinced that he deserves hell."
-John Everett-

How will they know unless someone tells them? Jesus said, "Go ye into all of the world, preach the gospel to all men." Maybe you can't go to another continent, but how about inviting your neighbor to church? They may be going through a horrific trial that you know nothing about. Sadly, they are going through it without the Lord. Many a testimony from a saved person stated they were invited time and time again to church by a friend or a neighbor and finally went to shut them up. It was there they came face to face with the risen Lord. Spend the rest of the day, listening to those you meet. They may be telling you about a deep need in their life you might have not heard any other day. Listen closely. We all have our testimony of how the Lord came into our lives. They may be able to dispute what they believe about the Bible, but they cannot explain how radically Jesus moves to change a life. You don't have anything to lose, they have eternity.

"Testimony is showing your scars
and telling how Jesus healed you."
– Warren Walden

APRIL 16

*There is only one thing you have to do to
spend eternity in hell. Nothing.*

"Hell is out of fashion today, but it is not out of business.
Just because we don't like the idea of hell doesn't mean
that it does not exist. Many people say they do not believe in hell,
so hell can't exist. But remember: it doesn't matter what we
believe; it matters what is true."
-Mark Cahill-

"Hell was not made for man, but for the devil and his angels."
-Matthew 25:41-

Every time I hear someone say, "Hell? (they laugh) All my friends will be there (they laugh some more), we will party on!" I cringe inside. Just the opposite is true. The party is over. The music has stopped. Pay day has arrived. The Bible says there will be "weeping and wailing and gnashing of teeth," some party, I tell myself. I used to think hell would be full of a lot of people, finally repentant, sorry for all their bad deeds. Not so. They are where they 'chose' to be. I had a one way ticket to hell, so do you. "Party on!" was my motto too, until I came to my senses. Eat, drink and be merry! Jesus bought my return ticket for me. He changed my final destination the day He was crucified for my sins, the day I repented of my sins and He became my Lord and Savior. Someone once said that, "Nails did not hold Jesus to the cross, love did." I believe that. He did not have to do what He did.

"The safest road to hell is the gradual one – the gentle slope,
soft underfoot, without sudden turnings,
without milestones, without signposts."
C.S. Lewis

No obstacles in your way. Smooth sailing all the way to destruction. Unless, someone intervenes and tells them Jesus is the way. Not one of many ways, but He is THE WAY. He is God's only fire insurance.

April 17

*Denial may protect us from pain,
but it also prevents us from healing.*

"Reorient yourself to new circumstances. Let it hurt
for a while. It will get better. Take your time. Heal
slowly, from the inside out. Learn or relearn how to
tap into the amazing love and healing of Jesus Christ."
-John Splinter-

Relationships will fail. Important relationships will dissolve. Sadly, it is a given in life. It may be because of something you did, or something the other person did. It is only natural to want to make the 'unfamiliar' familiar, again. You can do that by working directly to form new attachments – or you can reach backwards for memories of a time when it was more comfortable for you. This is not likely to be about your continued love for someone you neither respect, trust or admire their behavior anymore. This is about trying to desperately reconstruct a time in which you felt connected and safer. One of the things we do when we're scared to death of the 'new' is that we refocus in on the old. It's harder to say, "I'm scared to death," but know in your heart things have to change and it's so much easier to try to hang onto the past. Most of us aren't very good at 'letting go.' Even though we know it is the *right* thing to do. We need to focus not on the ending but on the new beginning. We need to look at the open door God has provided in front of us, not the door which has been painfully closed. Our future is always as bright as the promises of God and He has promised to heal us everywhere we hurt. To heal us in all the broken places. A heart that longs after God and His will and plan for my life cannot help but become whole again.

"You don't know how God will redeem your life from the pit,
but you must trust that He will. Like the little boy who offered
the loaves and fish to the disciples without knowing how Jesus
would use them, offer your circumstances to the Lord. He knows how
to transform the worst of circumstances into miraculous healing."
-Brendan O'Rourke-

APRIL 18

*Be like Enoch who walked with God, and you will
never have to wonder if you are on the right road.*

"I do not know how near it may be to us; it may be that some
of us will be ushered very soon into the presence of the King. One
gaze at Him will be enough to reward us for all we have had to bear.
Yes, there is peace for the past, grace for the present, and glory for the future."
-D.L.Moody-

What was Enoch's secret? **Every day He walked with God**, until one day God said, "Hmmm, Enoch, it looks like we are closer to my house than yours, I think I'll take you home with Me." And He did. Enoch left the things of this world that day… never to return. When you are traveling with God you are always on the right road. If there are scary giants on the road, God has your back. The giants are afraid of Him. If there are temptations on this road, He will take you by the hand and tell you, "I have a better way, follow Me." If there are sorrows along the way, He will tell you all about that day in Jerusalem, they nailed Him to a cross, not because He had done anything wrong, but because they weren't expecting the Messiah to come as a baby in a a manger. If there is hopelessness along the road, He will show you His empty tomb. If there is pain and loss on this road He will tell you about His home in heaven where one day you will be reunited with those you love, for all eternity. If there is disappointment on this journey with God, He will sadly tell you of the day, when not only His friend Judas betrayed Him but Peter denied that he even knew Him. So, stay on the road with Jesus and don't look back. Max Lucado put it this way, "Cemeteries interrupt the finest families. Retirement finds the best employees. Age withers the strongest bodies. But with change comes the reassuring appreciation of heaven's permanence." With Jesus forever and ever and ever…

APRIL 19

*We take nothing with us when we leave this world,
so why do we keep piling it up?*

"If we give instead of keep, if we invest in the eternal instead
of the temporal, we store up treasures in heaven that will never stop
paying dividends. Whatever treasures we store up here on earth
will be left behind when we leave. Whatever treasures we store up
in heaven will be waiting for us when we arrive."
-Randy Alcorn-

Someone once said, "You will know God really has your mind, heart, soul and spirit when He has your checkbook." Our checkbook reveals so much about us, the good, the bad and the ugly. It reveals what is REALLY important to us. What do you spend your money on? Did you reach out to others who have nothing? They aren't very hard to find. The TV shows us their plight all the time. Trouble is we quickly turn the channel and pretend that will make it all go away. It doesn't. Those kids remain, hungry, sick and unclothed. God will find someone else to help them if you won't. And you miss His blessing He had in store for you, if you had just given a little of that designer coffee money you spend every day on someone who has no food. Invest in the eternal.

I was never really interested in heaven until someone I loved very much went there before she had fully lived her life. My sister was gone at age 31. The day she was buried my brother-in-law died of Leukemia. He was 39. It just never seemed possible, but it happened. Since that time I have lost many of my family members and some of my friends. That happens as we age. What was important way back then loses its luster in the light of the glory that awaits the believer. I think a lot of the joy that Jesus promises us in heaven is when we see our loved ones again after being apart from them for so long. I like to think of it like this: Jesus tells my family in heaven, "Today, Cindy is coming home!" My mom hurries to the Pearly gates waiting for her 'baby's arrival. She is early, but that's because she's my mom. She misses me as much as I miss her. My dad is right behind, my sister and grandmother, aunt and uncles follow. Smiles are stuck on their faces that would put a Cheshire cat to shame! My mom sees me first and knocks over St. Peter to get to me. It has only been two years since my mom left this world, but in my heart it feels like an eternity. God's goal is to get us all 'safely home." O happy day!! My heart is deeply indebted to Jesus for making this day not only possible but a reality.

APRIL 20

Life. I cannot figure it out on my own and neither can you.

"We all want our children to be smart. Unfortunately, people have
largely forgotten that there is a huge difference between intelligence
and wisdom. Intelligence is a measurement of things you know.
Wisdom is your ability to discern right from wrong and make moral
choices. A wise person will follow God. An intelligent person may or may not."
-Sonya Haskins-

Today's newspapers are filled with endless tragedies. You turn on the television and the same sadness is repeated over and over. A shooting, a murder, a traffic accident with fatalities, it's someone you know, children starving, earthquakes, hurricanes. Senseless acts of human depravity and misery.. Then the feelings of hopelessness wash over you. You wish you could do something to change the world, but the task seems so monumental, you turn off your TV and walk away. The nagging thought of , "Why, God?" stays with you throughout the day. You hug your children a little tighter. You call your spouse at work just to hear their voice. How can you explain these sorrows to inquisitive kids who depend on your wisdom at times like these? Answer: You can't, at least never adequately enough to satisfy the human soul. Sin entered man in the Garden of Eden and everything has spiraled down from there. We all make bad choices that affect other's lives, sometimes intentionally, other times out of stupidity. So, how do we respond when life throws us curve balls we can't hit? You focus on God and who He is. You focus on what He is asking you to do. Is there someone on your block that needs help? Help them. Is there a donation you can make to help feed someone else's children? Then make it. Can you buy a gift at Christmas for a child who has parents that are barely able to feed them? Buy it. You CAN change the world. We all can together...until Jesus returns and rights the wrongs of this world. So, don't spend the day sad, go out and find someone to help! It will put a smile on their face and yours. Miracles come in cans! I can...you can...we can all make a difference! Turn your 'can't' into 'cans' and God will redeem them.

"Do not underestimate the role you may play in clearing
the obstacles in someone's spiritual journey."
-Ravi Zacharias-

April 21

There is a line God draws in the sand that we can cross over.

"We receive scars in two ways: What has been done to us
by other people or what has been done through us
by our own mistakes and failures."
-Sharon Jaynes-

Have you ever been stopped at railroad tracks with the clanging of the bell and the wooden barrier starts to drop to make sure you stop! Yet, deep down inside were you ever tempted to chance it? You don't see the train *yet*, your mind says, "I can make it." A little voice deeper down says, "Don't be stupid!" Which voice wins? God's warning or foolish pride? Well, sometimes stupidity wins out. I know, I have been to the railroad tracks a time or two. My version was, "Well, God, everyone else is doing it." Same with the other choices we make in life. God says, "Don't do that...you won't like the result," and just like Adam and Eve, we say, "I got this one God," and you take a big bite of the forbidden fruit. "Yummy," you say. However, the consequences can be devastating. It's like getting broadsided by a train in some cases. Most alcoholics when they took their first drink didn't think, "Gee, I think I'll destroy my life with booze." No, they think they are in control and they are until that moment they aren't anymore. It's years later they see the train coming, the warning signs were ignored. Take home point is this, the consequences can be delayed for a long, long time to where we think we have gotten away with it. No one gets by with sin, no one, but we still try. I do, not as much as I used to, but every now and then stupidity takes over. What has God warned you about lately?

"Very often in times of deep confusion, pain, selfishness,
and anger, we do things that hurt others far more than we can imagine."
-Jay Kessler-

April 22

"One half of all the ills in life come because men are unwilling to sit down quietly for thirty minutes to think through some of the possible consequences of their acts."
– Pascal-

"Sometimes when you are going forward spiritually, you go backwards in the natural because when our natural circumstances don't suit us, we press in spiritually with God."
-Joyce Meyer-

Thirty minutes is such a trivial time in our life to think through what the consequences to our actions might be, but this time is so important. We always seem to focus on the here and now. God focuses on eternity. What is this choice going to do for me *now*? We never ask ourselves, "Will I be happy with this choice 5 years from now?" More importantly, did you ask God what He wants you to do? My answer is no, not when I knew He would say no. What was I thinking? I was thinking, but I wouldn't say it out loud, that I knew better than God, or He was just trying to spoil my fun. It took me YEARS to figure out how really smart God is. He has all of the facts, I don't. I make the same mistakes over and over, and He has been so patient with me to pick me up, brush me off and send me on my way again. Giving me test after test, chance after chance to get it right. I'll tell you one thing I've learned is, you don't flunk God's tests. You get to take them over, and over and over... get the message? He will leave us to make our own choices, but He will not leave us content! Like the Prodigal you will wake up one day and say, "How in the world did I end up here, in the pigpen." Then you have a "Duh!" moment. We finally connect the dots of our actions to our results. If you ask God for His help, the Holy Spirit is very good at helping us connect the dots. The Book of James says we can ask God for wisdom in any situation. Then James says, "But when you ask Him, be sure that you really **expect** Him to answer, for a doubtful mind is as unsettled as a wave of the sea that is driven and tossed by the sea." (James 1:5-6). Are you expecting God to answer your prayers?

APRIL 23

"All men die. Some never live."
-Unknown-

"Though death is a universal human experience, we should
not assume that it is a natural human experience. It is not what
God intended. It is a result of 'the Fall,' of things corrupted from
the way they were meant to be. Death is an enemy because it
runs counter to life. God is life. All that lives comes from the
life-giving Spirit of God. Death is the enemy of life because
it disrupts the life that God intended."
-Albert Hsu-

I am reminded of the famous song, 'I did it my way." Sound familiar? Sounds good doesn't it? "Bless God, no one's going to tell me how to live my life or which rules to follow. I am captain of my ship! Party on!" Trouble is that living life MY way leaves God completely out of the picture. You are at the wheel, God isn't even a passenger anymore, if He ever was. You are on your own, because you chose to be on your own. When the ship starts to sink, and it will sink, you have only yourself to blame. You're following your compass instead of His. He knows where all of the roadblocks of life are and He can steer us safely away from them, if we let Him.

There are two ways to live your life, with Him or without Him. The Bible says, "For me to live is Christ..." Who in their right mind could turn down the Creator of the Universe's help in this life? Unbelievably, many do. I did for a really long time, longer than I care to admit.

Live your life! Not someone else's. Don't live by the pressure of others. In the end it will be you and me standing all alone before Almighty God and give an account for what we did with the life that was given to us. But live it with God's Omnipotent guidance, love, support and wisdom. I believe the theme song of hell will be, "I did it my way."

"Death, and judgment, and eternity are not fancies, but
stern realities. Make time to think about them. Stand still,
and look them in the face. You will be obliged one day to
make time to die, whether you are prepared or not."
-J.C. Ryle-

APRIL 24

All of us have become experts in re-labeling sin.

"Sin has sired a thousand heartaches and broken a
million promises. Your addiction can be traced back
to sin. Your mistrust can be traced back to sin. Bigotry,
robbery, adultery – all because of sin. But in
heaven, all of this will end."
-Max Lucado-

The human race doesn't much like being called a sinner. I know I didn't. But it is true. The Bible declares, "All have sinned and fallen short of the glory of God, there is *no one* righteous, no, not one." (Rom.3:23) Why do we re-label sin? We do it mostly to justify our actions. If we really want to do something and our conscience is telling us it's wrong then we have to put a new label on it. Gossip becomes, "I want to tell you about Mary, you won't believe what happened, of course I'm only telling you this so we can *pray* for her." We listen intently, forgetting that someone who gossips to you will also gossip to another about you. We can justify our bad language. "Well, he made me so mad I had to say something and that's what came out." What is in our heart will eventually come out of our mouth. You may be sitting in your chair reading this, smugly saying, "I'll never do that." Then someone cuts you off on the road or goes through a red light. Or they steal something from you. Best thing we can do for ourselves is call it what it is, SIN. God can then forgive it, but not until then. "If we confess our sin, He is faithful and just to forgive us our sin and to cleanse us from ALL unrighteousness." (I John 1:9) Remember, He is the Savior who takes away the sin of the world, not just yours, but of the world. (1John 2:2) WOW! Now that's amazing. Think back on the worse thing you have ever done. Now, if you have confessed it, Jesus has washed you whiter than snow! Romans 3:24 says, "Yet, **NOW** God in His gracious kindness declares us **NOT GUILTY!** What He said to the woman at the well, He says to you and me, "Go, and sin no more."

"The terrors of the Lord may make us afraid of sin,
but the love of the Lord alone, will make us hate it;
not the flames of hell, but the love of heaven."
-James Thomas Holloway-

April 25

Every obedient child of God is going to be called to wash a lot of stinky feet.

"Then He began to wash the disciples' feet...Peter said to Him, Why? And Jesus replied, "You don't understand why I am doing it; *someday you will.*"
-John 13:4-9-

But I don't want to wash someone's stinky feet. Neither do I, but Jesus did and He tells us to do the same. On the night before He was to be crucified, He laid aside His robe, girded a towel around His waist and proceeded to wash the disciple's dirty, stinky feet. Peter protests! "No, Lord"... and Jesus says to him, if I don't wash you, you can have no part with me. Peter says, "Then wash me all over, Lord." Good old Peter. He has to get his own feet out of his mouth before they can be washed. Been there, done that. Washing feet is a very humbling experience. Jesus knew at the time He was going to ask of His disciples a lot more than washing stinky feet. They would be stoned, persecuted, blasphemed, lied about, shunned, and fear death through most of their ministries on this earth. Jesus didn't say, "Oh you poor guys," no He said, "Forgive them." God's ways are not our ways. In order to wash stinky feet you have to rely on the Lord with everything that is in you. It is more natural to turn away from those who abuse us than to offer to wash their feet. So, get your bucket and soap! A great blessing will follow and Jesus will strengthen you to do the task. Remember, you do it for Him. He is the Master and we are His servants.

"What we call our strong points will become the source
of our most alarming weakness, if they are not tempered
and sanctified by the increasing humility and ever acting
faith, which are among the chief characteristics of a Christian."
-George Edward Jelf-

God has a way of teaching us humility if we refuse to humble ourselves before Him. This usually happens at the worst possible time and may cause us great embarrassment. If you really think about the day you gave your life to Christ it was probably one of the most humble moments of your existence. I don't know anyone who didn't come to Him with empty hands and an even emptier heart. No one said, "Here I am Lord, boy are you lucky to get me." Realizing you are a sinner on your way to hell, seeing yourself as God sees you, maybe for the very first time, shatters every ounce of pride we might have had. Contrast your sin with God's grace to save you and no wonder they call it "amazing' grace. One last thought by Benedict of Nursia; "The way of ascending is humility; the way of descending is pride."

April 26

Even in not choosing, we choose.

"The old sinful nature loves to do evil, which is just the opposite of what the Holy Spirit wants. And the Spirit gives us desires that are opposite from what the sinful nature desires. These two forces are constantly fighting each other, and your choices are *never free from this conflict.*"
Galatians 5:17

The devil would just as soon send you to hell from a church pew as from the gutter. The greatest deception of all, "I am a good person, I go to church." Guess who Jesus had the most trouble with while He was on this earth? The religious! The Pharisees and the Sadducees are the ones who stirred up the people and the Roman government to crucify Him. They had their man made rules and laws for the people to follow, Jesus came with a message of grace, forgiveness and love. They didn't recognize who He was. Some still don't today. They mock and jeer at His name. They try to remove Him from everyday life. The children in schools can no longer pray as they could when I was in grammar school. The Ten Commandments have been removed from the walls and replaced by metal detectors and no one connects the dots.

"God is patient not wanting anyone to perish, but come to repentance." 1 Peter 3:9

If you have had the good news presented to you and you refuse it...you have made a choice. It is a very serious choice to do nothing. What must a man do to be lost? Nothing. Absolutely nothing.

"Men are not sent to hell because they are murderers or liars, they are sent to hell because they are unrighteous."
-David Jeremiah-

God's mercy extends to **whosoever will**. Are you a "whosoever will?" That alone is an amazing statement. King David was a murderer and an adulterer, Paul the apostle was guilty of killing Christians all in the name of God, yet these men were saved. There is hope for us all and that hope is the death, burial and resurrection of Jesus Christ. Without the cross, mankind is eternally lost.

April 27

God never said come boldly to His throne of worthiness –
He said to come boldly to His throne of <u>grace</u>.
-Unknown-

"So, let us come *boldly* to the throne of our gracious God. There we will receive His mercy and
His grace to help us in our time of trouble."
-Hebrews 4:16-

Where do most of us go when trouble strikes? Some go to the liquor cabinet, to the medicine cabinet, others go shopping. I used to go shopping, but I discovered the answers I need in life were never found at the mall. Believe me, I went to most of them and came away with lots of 'stuff' and a very empty heart. The enemy would like us to believe that we are too bad for God to help us now. He lies and tells us, boy you sure blew it. God is done with you. Lies! Lies! Lies! There isn't anything you can do to make God stop loving you or stop pursuing you. The word **boldly** here, just blows me away. Usually, by the time we have really screwed things up so bad, we feel ashamed, not bold. We feel cowardly, stupid for doing what we did, surely not bold. God sees us in Jesus, with confidence as His child, washed by the blood of the Lamb, I can come boldly. No excuses! No blaming the 'other' guy.

"The fact that we are God's people says nothing about
our natures or us. We are God's people only by His grace,
because our natures are entirely too prone to evil and rebellion."
-Mark Dever-

We are prone to evil and rebellion. That is a harsh statement, but very true. We all have a bent away from God, not towards Him. We all want to do our own thing, not His. It's only when He allows our 'own thing' to play out in our lives and the bottom drops out from under us, that we finally come to our senses and cry out to Him. I think the majority of us come to Jesus in the same way, lost, alone and frightened. It is only in Him we have hope for a better life. When you return, it will be as if you never left. God remembers our sins no more.

APRIL 28

*"God knows when His child is too weary to pray
and too weary to take one more step."*

"Come unto Me, all who are weary and heavy laden,
and I will give you rest."
Matthew 11:28

Life can completely overwhelm us at times. It is so much easier to trust God, when it's the other person who is hurting. Have you ever gone to bed at night and *wanted* to pray, but the words just wouldn't come? You hurt so badly inside as if God were scrubbing the bottom of your soul from the inside out. You were at a loss for words. You began to doubt...is God there? Can He hear me? Does He care? Then you eventually cried yourself to sleep only to wake up to the same pain in the morning. God knows all about your pain. He knows what it is that has brought you to despair. He will answer your cries. I am reminded of the woman who cried out to God, "Lord I hurt!" and God replied, "I know my child...I know." And blessed is the soul that 'knows He knows' and waits for His answer.

"You never know how much you believe anything
until its truth or falsehood becomes a matter
of life and death to you."
C.S. Lewis

Grief is real to the Christian and to the unbeliever as well. I had never known real grief in my life until I was twenty seven years old. I was standing at my sister's gravesite, as the bottom completely fell out from under my life. The twenty third Psalm came to life, "Yea, though I walk through the valley of the shadow of death, I will fear no evil..." Young people weren't supposed to die in my world, but she did. I stood there heartbroken, having been raised in a Christian home, dragged to church every Sunday by my mom, knowing about Jesus, but not knowing Him. That all changed. Death hardens some. They turn their back on God and shake their fist at Him. Me, I wept until there were no more tears to cry. God in His mercy had brought me to a place of utter brokenness and then to a place of healing. I learned that day that God uses the circumstances of our life, no matter how hopeless they may seem at the time, to beckon us into the safety of His arms. I climbed up into His arms, and now forty one years later, you can still find me there. Remember, there is always a safe place you can go... your Father's arms. You will never find a safer place.

APRIL 29

Sometimes the Lord calms the storm and sometimes
He simply calms His child in the midst of the storm.
-Unknown-

"As evening came, Jesus said to His disciples, "Let us cross
over to the other side of the lake....but soon a fierce storm arose....
Jesus was sleeping in the back of the boat"
Mark 4: 35-41

The shocking thing about this verse is Jesus *knowingly* sent His disciple's right smack dab into a very threatening storm, while at the same time He promised they would get to the other side... with Him. While Jesus slept in the back of the boat the storm came upon them and the disciples were filled with great fear. The passage says that the waves were so high from the winds that water was filling the boat. These men had spent many hours fishing on this lake, they were very seasoned fisherman, yet they became very afraid. Their biggest mistake was to underestimate exactly who Jesus was. In a panic they wake Jesus up and ask him, "Master, don't you care that we are going to drown?" The Sea of Galilee was well known for its violent, raging, unexpected storms. Jesus spoke to the storm and the seas became calm. Wow! Can you imagine? Even the winds and the seas obey Him. That is a great reminder when you find yourself in the midst of a storm in life. Not the water kind but scary just the same. First lesson; Jesus sent them into a storm. Second lesson; Jesus was with them in the middle of the storm and lesson three; Jesus has full control over your circumstances and His ability to rescue you. The more storms He accompanies you through, the more your trust builds and your certainty that He has the ability to save you. He never said it wouldn't be a rocky trip, but He did say you would safely reach the other side.

"God is so sovereign. He's so much in control that even
when Satan tries to ruin our lives, God takes the weapon
that Satan wants to use to destroy us and turns it into a good thing."
-James MacDonald-

There is no better illustration of this than the crucifixion of Jesus. Satan wanted Him dead and he accomplished just that. It appeared as if God had lost all control. That could not be further from the truth. God's plan had included, all along, that Jesus would die for the sins of the world. If Satan had known this, he would have come up with a different plan. I can only imagine the scene in hell, on that third day when Jesus rose out of the grave triumphant! If Jesus has power over death, we need not fear any place He wants us to go. If Jesus wants you somewhere, He will make sure you get there safely. Never underestimate Jesus' ability to save. Thought for the day: If the winds and the seas and the stars obey Jesus, shouldn't we?

APRIL 30

Nothing in life should be so important to me that it keeps me off my knees.

"Listen to my voice in the morning, Lord. Each morning
I bring my requests to You, Lord and wait **expectantly**."
Psalm 5:3

Pray without ceasing. This is a command not a suggestion. Pray! Pray! Pray! Pray in the morning when you are rested and free from the burdens of the day. Pray when you go to bed at night and leave those burdens in His capable Hands. Pray when you are scared, doubting, confused and by all means pray when you are thankful.

"For Christians, prayer is like breathing. You don't
have to think to breathe because the atmosphere exerts
pressure on your lungs and forces you to breathe. That's why
it is more difficult to hold your breath than it is to breathe.
Similarly, when you are born into the family of God, you
enter into a spiritual atmosphere wherein God's presence
and grace exert pressure, or influence, on your life. Prayer
is the normal response to that pressure."
-John MacArthur-

You cannot get to know someone you don't spend time with. You will never learn to trust God if you don't learn who He is and what He can do. It is doubtful that anyone will ever know the power of a praying mom this side of heaven. I was blessed with having a mother like that. She spent a lot of years on her knees praying for my sisters and me. Some of her prayers weren't answered exactly the way she thought they would, but she never gave up. She persevered with the Lord. The Bible says, "Train up a child in the way he should go and when he is old he will not depart." He may go astray temporarily but he will always come back to that solid foundation God provides to a life that will trust Him.

"Our little ones won't be with us forever. When they are
grown, they won't remember whether they had size one
designer jeans or a solid maple crib. But they will remember,
even subconsciously, whether they were loved and protected."
-Sandra Aldrich-

What better way to protect your children than to pray for them. It is a privilege to lift them up before God's throne of grace and mercy each and every day. The world is an ungodly place and is antagonistic to the things of God. If you will take the time to pray with your children every day before they go out into the world, it will be something their little hearts and minds will never forget.

MAY 1

God doesn't look at what you give, but what you have kept for yourself.

"Bring all the tithes into the storehouse so there will be enough food in my temple. If you do, says the Lord Almighty, I will open up the windows of heaven for you. I will pour out a blessing so great you won't have enough room to take it in. Try it. Let Me prove it to you."
Malachi 3:10

Why is it that a waitress or a waiter gets 15 – 20% and God gets 10%, if that? I shudder when I think that in heaven God may pull out my old checkbook registers and go over them in detail. I'll bet you would too. Crazy thing about this verse is God is actually asking us to test Him in this area. He is saying, "If you will…then He will" Tithing is a privilege, not a burden. It is not easy sometimes, nor is it easy to do it with a joyful heart as He requests. What I have learned though is that if I will start little, it gets easier and easier to open up your pocketbook to Him. Start by giving even a little something, but start. Who in their right mind wouldn't want God to open up the windows of heaven for them and pour out a blessing that boggles the mind?

"The tithe is not an obligation, but a *privilege*
allowing us to have a part in God's work."
-Sandra Aldrich-

I heard said a long time ago, "You can know if God really has you heart and soul, if He has your checkbook." Does He have yours? It isn't easy, there is always something we need or want. There is always an excuse not to give to God.

"The world is not impressed when Christians get rich and
say thanks to God. They are impressed when God is so
satisfying that we give away our riches for Christ's sake and count it gain."
-John Piper-

Money can't buy happiness. Ask the crowd in Hollywood. It can't buy health. Oh, you may be able to afford better healthcare, but in the end, we are all the same. It can't buy peace of mind. Only God can provide that. On the other hand, money can buy food and clothes for the needy. It can buy dental care for the poor. It can buy fresh water for a village that is forced to use dirty river water, just to survive. There are so many hurting people in our world today. Look for them, you will find them, and offer to help where you can. I will do the same.

May 2

*The amount of time you spend reading
your Bible reveals it's real worth to you.*

"Thy Word is a lamp for my feet, and a light for my path."
Psalm 119:105

Is your time with God every day precious to you? His light will make the darkness flee from our lives. Think about walking into a very dark room. You stumble around until you find the light switch. Once you turn the light on all of the darkness disappears. Or remember back to when you were a child and the 'boogie man' was hiding under your bed. Funny that he only came out at night when I was going to sleep. I wasn't afraid of him during the day...in the light. My children know that if a fire broke out in my house, next to saving them and my grandkids, and my cat, (anything that breathes) the first possession I would grab would be my Bible. You may think that is silly, but I have had my Bible over 41 years now, and there are so many precious notes and personal remembrances in it I would be saddened to lose the memories of when I prayed and God answered. Saddened to forget those times I gave up on God at the last minute only to find Him coming through for me after all. Always on time... His time, not mine...but on time. Saddened to lose the pages filled with tear stains as I wrestled with God, or held onto Him with every last ounce of strength I had which at times wasn't much. His Word is living! It is sharper than any two edged sword. It can divide the bone from the marrow. Doctors can't do that, at least none that I know.

"God hung the universe with words. Everything you
will ever see, touch or taste had its genesis in a word
from God. You exist because God spoke."
-Fawn Parish-

God's word gives me the light I need to make it through this dark world. I may not understand what's going on all of the time, but if I stay on His path I will eventually make it safely home.

"I have before me God's word which cannot fail, nor
can the gates of hell prevail against it; thereby will
I remain, though the whole world be against me."
-Martin Luther-

Martin Luther stood on God's word and brought the Protestant Reformation even though many opposed him. He believed God's word said that man was saved by faith alone, not works. He staked his very life on that truth. There are some things in this life we can never compromise, and God's word is one of them.

May 3

*It's a lot easier to go along with God's plan for my life than to
continually struggle with Him, in an attempt to get Him to go along with mine.*

Most men have a plan in life. Live a good life... go to heaven. Work your way to heaven. God's word says just the opposite. Our righteousness is as filthy rags in His sight. Ouch! No one ever answers the question if you have to do good works, how many, and for how long? It's a question they can't answer because it's not true. God says salvation is a GIFT. No man can boast at what Christ has done for us. No man.

> Lewis S. Chafer said, "Anyone can devise a plan by which good
> people go to heaven. Only God can devise a plan whereby
> sinners, which are His enemies, can go to heaven."

God's plan reaches back into eternity past. It was laid before the foundations of the world. Before you or I even existed. Now this may shock you, but sin did not start in the Garden of Eden with Adam and Eve, but in Heaven with Lucifer, angel of God who wanted to dethrone God and take over. He said, "I will...I will...I will" and God said, "Oh no you won't," and he was thrown to the earth where he has deceived man for centuries, "Has God really said...?" In other words, take the fruit from the tree of knowledge of good and evil, enjoy it, "Eat, God isn't telling you the truth . You aren't going to die. If you eat it you will know everything, both good and evil." Well, we all know the bad news. Eve ate and then gave some to Adam and he ate. Their eyes were opened, and they were instantly ashamed of their nakedness." Freedom has its limits. God is in control and has the authority to tell us what we can and cannot do. Some people don't like that. The good news is that God introduced a plan to save man. He would send His only begotten Son into the world as Redeemer and sacrifice for ALL sin. It's best to stick with God's plan for salvation, you won't like where you end up with your plan. I don't think I remember anywhere in the Bible God consulting man's opinion. A young Chinese girl once wrote, "I have known Him all my life, and one day I learned His name." Deep in our hearts we know there is someone above and beyond our understanding. What is His name? Savior, Redeemer, Lord, Prince of Peace, the Son of God, Holy One of Israel. At the Cross good and evil collided and Jesus won.

MAY 4

*A wise person knows that sometimes God will cause us to surrender
in humiliation when His patience has run out on our rebellion.*

God said, "Jonah, Go to the great city of Nineveh to announce my judgment
against them because I have seen how wicked its people are."
Jonah 1:2

The story of Jonah is a very sobering lesson for us all. Run! Run! Run! God told him to go to Nineveh, Jonah said, "No way," he went in the opposite direction and the fight was on. Guess who won? You can't run away from God and get by with it…at least not for long and not without a lot of unnecessary pain. God started out judging the Ninevites and ended up chastising Jonah for his disobedience. Jonah knew the Ninevites were a very evil people. There was no question about that. He hated them, in fact. God was sending him to them to announce His judgment on their evil. Instead Jonah boarded a ship headed for Joppa. God caused a great storm to arise, and the sailors were perplexed, but Jonah was not. He knew God was sending the waves. He told the sailors on board to throw him overboard and the winds would stop. They did and it did. God had a big fish waiting for Jonah that swallowed him up. I like to call this fish the "Motel 6" for the disobedient. Jonah spent 3 days and 3 nights in the belly of this fish, until he finally came to his senses and repented. What did God do? He had the fish spit him out, and again told him to go to Nineveh. After this harrowing attitude adjustment Jonah decided it might be a good idea to go to Nineveh. How many preachers today would give anything to preach God's message to a big city and see them all repent? Not Jonah. The people repented into sackcloth and ashes, but Jonah's anger burned still. Why? He accused God of being "a gracious and compassionate God, slow to anger and filled with unfailing love." Yikes! I think the story didn't end there. I think Jonah had a few more rounds with God and a lot more to learn. Just like us, Jonah surrendered in humiliation, but not before he tried Plan A, B, C and lost. Our God is persistent. The next time He tells you to take a little trip to Nineveh, go. I think you will be glad you did, and along the way a whole lot of people will get blessed by your obedience.

MAY 5

Circumstances are God's attention getters.

"All things work together for good for those who love God
and are called according to His purpose."
Romans 8:28

ALL things will work together, not some things, not a few things, but **all** things. The good the bad and the ugly of life are in His control. He has the power over life and death. Let's take a trip to the tomb of Lazarus. Mary and Martha's brother Lazarus gets very ill and then dies. Even though they sent urgent messages to Jesus that the one he loved was sick, Jesus tarried. He did not immediately come to heal Lazarus. When He did arrive, Martha met Him and said, "Lord, if you had been here our brother would not have died. But even now I know that God will give you whatever You ask.' Jesus told her, "Your brother will rise again." "Yes," Martha said, "when everyone else rises, on resurrection day." Jesus told her, "**I AM** the resurrection and the life. Those who believe in Me, even though they die like everyone else, will live again. They are given eternal life for believing in Me and will never perish. Do you believe this, Martha?" Martha confesses, "Yes, Lord." This is a beautiful story. Martha asked Jesus for a miracle to heal her sick brother and Jesus brought her an even greater miracle, He gave her a resurrection! Can you imagine being at that tomb that day when Jesus proclaimed, "Lazarus, come forth!"...and he did. What was the response of the religious rulers? They determined to put Jesus to death. When Jesus commands us to follow Him it will include death, but it will also include a glorious resurrection one day!

"The valley of the shadow of death holds no darkness for the child
of God. There must be light, else there could be no shadow. Jesus
is the light. He has overcome death."
Dwight L. Moody

MAY 6

*Compromise may take the pressure off of you temporarily,
but in the end you will be a big time loser.*

"They do *not* compromise with evil."
Psalm 119:3

There are some things in life you can't compromise...your principles. You can compromise about where to eat, what to wear, but not what you truly believe. You just can't. Even in Politics.

"Something morally wrong can never be politically right."
Lord Shaftesbury

Children learn more by what you do than by what you say. They can see right through the empty words and promises and know your true character by you doing exactly what you said you would do. Children need role models and they need boundaries to feel safe. If you continually move your moral compass you shake their very foundation. Ralph Waldo Emerson said, "No change of circumstances can repair a defect of character."

An unknown author writes:

If a child lives with criticism,
he learns to condemn.
If a child lives with hostility,
he learns to fight.
If a child lives with fear,
he learns to be apprehensive.
If a child lives with pity,
he learns to feel sorry for himself.
If a child lives with jealousy,
he learns to feel guilty.
If a child lives with encouragement,
he learns to be self-confident.
If a child lives with tolerance,
he learns to be patient.
If a child lives with acceptance,
he learns to love.

If a child lives with approval,
he learns to like himself.
If a child lives with recognition,
he learns to have a goal.

If a child lives with fairness,
he learns what justice is.
If a child lives with honesty,
he learns what truth is.
If a child lives with sincerity,
he learns to have faith in himself and
those around him.
If a child lives with love,
he learns that the world is a
wonderful place to live in.

MAY 7

*I can go with God or I can fight Him. If you are
wise, you will choose to put down the boxing gloves.*

"Don't you realize how kind, tolerant, and patient God is with you? Or don't you care? Can't you see how kind He has been in giving you time to turn from your sin?"
Romans 2:4 (LAB)

God doesn't want to fight you, but He will. The stakes are too high for Him to give up on you. He knows eternity is a very long time. Most of the time, the painful consequences of our own sin will get our attention faster than anything else will. Take the Prodigal Son for instance. He started off living it up! Then his life slowly began to spiral down, and down, until finally it was out of control. He went from the good life to the pigpen. His friends had deserted him, he was hungry and no one would feed him. The only job he could get was slopping with the pigs. He had reached the lowest level in life when he would have settled with eating the pig's food, if he could get there before they did, but even that was a struggle. Culturally, Jewish boys were to have nothing to do with pigs. Their diet excluded pork, yet he found himself right in the middle of the biggest pork fest he had ever seen. Pork chops, bacon, pork roast, all forbidden by Jewish law. This story doesn't end here, thank goodness, and by God's mercy the young lad "came to his senses." This translates into, "Yikes! What am I doing here? Even the servants in my father's house are better off than I am." Out of options, dirty, scared and lonely, he headed back home. His father saw him coming from a long ways away and ran to him. Don't miss this. The father was looking for his return every single day. He even had his binoculars out looking for the lad. If you are lost or someone you love is lost take heart, God has His binoculars out looking for them. He will not give up on them as easily as they give up on themselves. He will eventually bring them to two options, with Him or against Him. We all must choose.

"The flesh is willing to flatter itself, and many
who now give themselves every indulgence, promise
to themselves an easy entrance into life. Thus men
practice mutual deception on each other and
fall asleep (die) in wicked indifference."
-John Calvin-

Are you out of options yet? You will be one day. Jesus says, I AM *the way...*" any other detour in life will be very costly, so go home before it gets too dark and you can't find your way.

MAY 8

*If God doesn't want me to have something
then I shouldn't want it either.*

"The *victorious* invaders then plundered Sodom and Gomorrah and began their long journey
home, taking all the wealth and food with them.
They also *captured Lot*, Abram's nephew who lived in Sodom."
Genesis 2:11-3:23

If you remember the story of Abram and his nephew Lot at all, you already know things didn't end so well for the cities of Sodom and Gomorrah or for Lot's wife. God had so blessed Abram and his family that they needed more land for all their herds. On their journey to find this land they came to a fork in the road, one day. Abram let Lot choose which road he would take. Of course he took the easy road, the path of least resistance. He saw the lush green lands before him and decided this was easy street for him and his family and headed for the city of Sodom. Sadly, he drug his family into his bad choices. He was certainly not expecting the ending to his fairytale life that he got. Been there, done that! Turned out, Lot's compromise cost him more than he ever could have imagined. Lot soon became content to live among the 'ungodly.' The city became so wicked, that God set out to destroy it. Abram intervened on his nephew's behalf once again, but Abram couldn't find even 10 righteous men in the whole city, therefore, God's judgment fell. First God's patience is long-suffering, then His warning, followed swiftly by His anger and wrath. God sent His angels to warn Lot to get out of the city and not look back. The Bible says Lot hesitated, so the Angel grabbed his hand and Lot's two daughters and wife, and they fled the city. "Then, the Lord rained down fire and burning sulfur from the heavens on Sodom and Gomorrah.' (Gen.3:24) God will not leave us content in sin. He will not. We are told to flee, not settle down in the middle of it. Lesson today: If someone is praying for you and you're in the middle of something you shouldn't be, Look out! God always warns, but there is a line we can cross over. It is a line that is there to protect us. Make sure you stay on God's side of that line. Sudden destruction is just on the other side of that line.

MAY 9

*"There is only one thing worse than not
waiting on God - and that is wishing you had."*
-Charles Stanley-

"Be *still* in the presence of the LORD, and *wait patiently* for Him to act.
Psalm 37:7

"I have it all worked out God, now all I need is for you to bless *my plan* and make it happen." We try to help God. Is He impressed? No. In this verse He commands, "Be still in His presence." If that isn't hard enough, He also commands us to be patient. If you know who God is this may be hard but not impossible. If you don't know God's faithfulness and mercy than this will be impossible. Waiting and being quiet about it at the same time goes against our human desire to fix things 'ourselves,' and to complain about them until they are fixed. It requires us to throw out our 'Plan B' and stick with God's Plan A, if we want His blessings. God is not obligated to bless any of my plans or efforts, but if I am willing to wait on Him He does promise a blessing. God is honored by our faith and trust in Him to work things out in our lives. He doesn't want us meddling in His business. I believe He requires our 'stillness' in order for us to be able to hear His voice when He speaks. Proverbs 3:5 promises us..."He will direct our path." I also believe He requires us to be patient because He has a different clock than we do. We are a microwave society that wants 'instant' everything! God works on His own timetable, one we usually don't like. We want Him to speed things up, but He doesn't. He will answer and if you are patient you will not be 'miserable' while you wait. It's your choice, His way or mine. He never promised it would be easy, but in the end so worth the wait.

*"The word trial is defined as a test or examination of
our character. When trials come, we are to receive them
with joy, recognizing a God-given opportunity to identify
those specific character flaws we need to change so
that we may love more purely."*
-Ray and Nancy Kane-

MAY 10

*God knows there are some lessons in life we
can only learn by going through difficulty.*

"Yes, even though I walk through the dark valley of death,
I will not fear, for You are close beside me."
Psalm 23:4

There are some roads in life God never intended for us to travel alone. Death is one of the hardest experiences of life. As humans, we are helpless in its presence. As my own mom slipped from this life into eternity, I held her close in my arms, but death won that day. It always does. At times like this we get our boxing gloves and swing and swing and swing against it to no avail. We cry out to God in our pain. Death will claim whoever it came for. We can hold on tightly to this world, but eventually we all will have to let go. Death's statistics are staggering, one out of one die. That should be very sobering to us all. Yet, many continue to gamble with death. Believers and unbelievers know this verse very well. It is often recited at funerals and will either give you comfort or make you very uncomfortable. A funeral is where we come face to face with the reality of death, other's and our own. No one escapes, no one. You can't wish it away, you can't drive it away, it is relentless but it doesn't have to be scary. It all depends upon your perspective. Jesus has conquered death for all who believe in Him. My mom was one of His, and as she closed her eyes on this earth for the last time, she opened them to Jesus on the 'other side.' The Apostle Paul writes in 1 Corinthians 15:55, "Death is swallowed up in **victory**. O death where is your victory? O death, where is your sting? Victory came in an empty tomb! Death lost its sting the moment Jesus walked out of that tomb and was raised to life. I am reminded of the words to a song, "Because He lives...I can face tomorrow..." I walked out of the hospital that day not hoping I would see my mom again someday, but KNOWING that I would. Christ had won the victory for her...and for me and you. We can now proclaim with Job..."Yet, though He slay me, in my flesh I shall see God."

MAY 11

*God will change your circumstances, but first
He will use your circumstances to change you.*

"As he was nearing Damascus on *his mission*, a brilliant light from heaven suddenly beamed down on him. He fell to the ground and heard a voice saying, "Saul! Saul! Why are you persecuting Me? Who are you, Lord? Saul asked."
-Acts 9:4-5-

What was Saul's mission? As he traveled the road to Damascus his plan was to kill every Christian he could get his hands on, all in the name of 'religion.' He thought he was doing God a favor. God however, had a very different plan. Guess who won? Saul of Tarsus was sincere, but he was sincerely wrong. Saul thought he was doing God's work by killing the followers of Jesus. He was a deeply 'religious' man, whose religion was in opposition to God. Is your religion in opposition to God? Instead of killing Christians, Saul came face to face with the living Christ. He was blinded and then 'knocked off his high horse of religiosity' and humbled before God and man. It turns out this was the best thing that could have ever happened to him. Paul's life was turned upside down and inside out that day but he was a man God used to spread the gospel as no other. This was a mind boggling conversion, but not all conversions are quite so dramatic. I sat alone one night, trying to figure out why my sister had died, turned on Billy Graham and as he preached, I cried. The song "Just as I am," played in the background. There were no fireworks, just tears, no crowds to cheer, nothing to offer God, except a very badly broken heart and just me alone with God. I would never be alone again after that day. That was my trip down the Damascus road. I had rebelled for years against a loving God. Not only my circumstances were changed, but I was too. Fear was exchanged for hope. Has it been an easy journey? No!, No!, No!. Has it been worth it? Yes! Yes! Yes! What will you do when God takes you on a little trip to Damascus? Be ready for an attitude adjustment.

MAY 12

❈

"I remember my mother's prayers and they have always followed me.
They have clung to me all of my life."
-Abraham Lincoln-

"Always be *joyful*. Keep on praying."
1 Thes.5:17

A mother's love is a mighty powerful thing. Why? It is spiritual warfare against an unseen enemy, an enemy who comes to kill, steal and destroy our lives and the lives of our children. Prayer has no boundaries, it can reach to the other side of the world and up to heaven in a nanosecond. It has no limitations. We can ask the impossible of God. In fact, we are encouraged to do just that. It isn't expensive, but it is priceless. A prayerless life has no power.

"Some people think God does not like to be
troubled with our constant coming and asking. The
only way to trouble God is not to come at all."
-D.L.Moody-

Prayer invites the Creator of the Universe to intervene in my life and the lives for whom I am praying. Prayer is a privilege. What else in life gives you instant, unimpeded access to God Almighty? Notice in this verse it says to 'always be joyful then to pray unceasingly. Therefore prayer is never dependent on my circumstances in life.

"Make no decision without prayer."
-Elizabeth George-

I can pray when I am happy, when I am sad. When I am perplexed or simply to thank God for all of His blessings that have come my way. Prayer is one of the most powerful tools a believer has in his war chest. It is meant to be used and often. It is an attitude of the heart to pray unceasingly. No one can walk through life continually muttering prayers to heaven, but a prayerful heart stays in perfect communion with our Father in heaven. It is a soul that never leaves His presence. A heart that is dependent upon Him for everything in life, big or small. It believes His promises and asks for the impossible. Prayer seeks God's counsel and accepts His discipline. Prayer is always answered by God, "Yes, no, or wait - I have something better." Have you been praying for a long time about something or for someone? Well, don't you dare give up now!

MAY 13

God accepts me right where I am, but He
loves me too much to leave me there.

"Beloved, do not be amazed and bewildered at the *fiery* ordeal which is taking
place to test your quality, as though something strange were befalling you."
1 Peter 4:12

Wouldn't it be wonderful if we could just learn life's lessons from a book and be done with it? We all know that it just doesn't happen that way. Jesus said, "My sheep hear my voice and they follow Me." (John 10:3) We have to learn through life's sorrows and trials to discern His voice from the world's noise. We have to listen for that 'still, small voice.' Just as a parent teaches their child how to live, so does God teach us. He is very patient with us. It's not easy to step out in faith the very first time. It's not easy to turn the other cheek, or turn away when someone falsely maligns you. Jesus has to teach us how to be godly in an ungodly world. Life with Him is a process of day by day learning. Sometimes it's a process of falling and getting back up one more time than I have fallen. He will teach us never to give up. Guaranteed in a few years you will look back and see the progress you have made from the time you first turned your life over to Him. I love what Joyce Meyer says, "I'm not where I want to be, but thank God I'm not where I used to be." It's a journey we are on with God. He will take us some places we don't want to go, but He will be with us all the way. He will never let go of our hand. Oh, the lessons we will learn for all eternity. He is a faithful companion! He will see us all the way to the end of our journey on this earth and into eternity. Wow! So, don't lose heart. He will accomplish in each one of us how to be more and more like Him. In this age we live in, I think about what it would be like to take a 'selfie' with Jesus. I imagine one of His arms around my shoulder, and His other hand is over my mouth! One of life's greatest lessons is taming the tongue. What would your selfie look like?

MAY 14

With God there is no way to lose. Without God there is no way to win.

"The fear of the LORD is the beginning of wisdom.
Only fools despise wisdom and discipline."
Proverbs 1:7

The beginning of wisdom starts with acknowledging God. Fear of the Lord requires in this life that we take Him very seriously and that we obey Him. You cannot leave Him out of the equation of life. If you do it will be to your own peril. We are to honor Him, respect Him and thank Him for all He does on our behalf. Where do your world views come from? From friends, relatives, your own wisdom? God is and always will be the 'final' authority on everything. Only He is Omnipotent. He alone holds the power of the universe in His hands. Only He is Omniscient, meaning He holds all knowledge. There is NOTHING that He doesn't know. He knows what you did yesterday, what you did 10 years ago, and He *alone* knows why. He searches our hearts and knows our motives.

There is no wisdom, no insight, no plan
that can succeed against the Lord.
Proverb 21:30

All of our decisions in life should be made in life in light of His Word. Many choose to 'go it alone.' The later cry out to God and blame Him for their circumstances. Wisdom, on the other hand, considers the consequences ahead of time. God doesn't require us to understand everything He does or why He does it. He does require we trust Him with our life. Everything God does, He does in love. Love isn't just something God does it is His very nature. The Bible says, "God is love." Faith or human reasoning? You must choose. Human reasoning will never be able to comprehend Divine Sovereignty or Omniscience. Never.

"Wisdom shouts in the streets. She cries out in the public square."
Proverbs 1:20
The question is, are you listening?

MAY 15

"I know my Redeemer lives..."
-Job 19:25-

*I write these things to you who believe in the name of the Son of God so that you may **KNOW** that you have eternal life...*
-1 John 5:13-

A few women, and a few men, at an empty tomb, turned the world upside down and inside out. Jesus conquered death and the grave for us. Jesus paid a debt He did not owe for me and for you. He was the sinless Son of God. We owed a debt we could not pay. God was very clear in the Garden of Eden, if you eat of the forbidden fruit you shall surely die. The wages of sin is death. It is eternal separation from the One who made us. Adam and Eve didn't die physically right after eating the fruit, but they did die spiritually. The new birth is restoration of our spirit with God's spirit. We all are spiritually separated from a God who would rather die than to live without us.

> "We are all the time coming to the end of things here – the end of the week, the end of the month, the end of the year, the end of school days. It is end, end, end, all the time. But, thank God, He is going to satisfy us with long life; no end to it, an endless life."
> -D.L Moody-

Eternity is a very long time so it is utter foolishness to live for the moment. Take a look at your calendar today. What is it filled with? Live today! Today, you may take your last breath. As you do, will you be thinking, "I wish I would have..." Don't wish, do it now while you still can. I am reminded of a story a man tells of his wife who wanted this special dress. He refused to let her buy it because he didn't want to 'waste' the money. He eventually bought it....but sadly, he bought it to bury her in and lived with that regret the rest of his life.

MAY 16

God doesn't punish mistakes, but He does punish rebellion.

"Foolishness is bound up in the heart of a child, but the rod of
discipline will drive it far from him."
–Proverbs 22:15-

Rebellion seldom ends well. God does not punish us for being human and making mistakes, but He does punish rebellion. This verse tells me there are no 'time outs' with God. His discipline can come slowly after we have worn down His patience with us, or it can come fast and furious. Unfortunately, God's rod and staff come together. The rod is used to discipline us and push us in the right direction. Common sense is learned, it is not something bestowed on us from our parents. The young have no fear, and sometimes no common sense. A small child can walk up to a stove and out of curiosity will put his small hand to the flame. He has to learn that fire burns. That when contained under a saucepan can make some delicious foods, or contained in a fireplace can warm you to the marrow, but if let loose can destroy everything in its path, including a life. A child will run into the street after a ball without any mind to traffic. Just as God teaches us right from wrong, He expects us to do the same for our children and for our grandchildren. Rebellion must be dealt with and God's way is by driving it from the heart. That can be a very painful process. Foolishness is bound up in the heart of a child. It must be driven out by discipline. Love does not let a child do whatever he wants. Love first corrects and then disciplines if needed. When I was in school, almost every child had a reverent fear of their teacher and the Principal. Sadly, that is not the case anymore. Today, parents can be arrested for disciplining their own children. And we wonder why we need metal detectors in school. If we gave the paddle back to the teacher or the Principal and did it God's way I think we wouldn't need those metal detectors anymore. Once we choose to reject God's wisdom and replace it with human reasoning we are on a dangerous path. First we need to teach our children to *fear* God. What does that mean? It means to take Him very seriously. Do you take God seriously? Does your life show it? Be very careful, your children are watching!

MAY 17

*The definition of stupid: Doing the same thing over and
over again and expecting a different result.*
-Unknown-

"Wherever we direct our view, we discover the melancholy
proofs of our depravity; whether we look to ancient or modern
times, to barbarous or civilized nations, to the conduct of the
world around us, or to the monitor within the breast;
whether we read, or hear, or act, or think, or feel, the same
humiliating lesson is thrust upon us."
-William Wilberforce-

Have you ever had the following conversation with God? "It's me again Lord, Yep, I blew it again. I didn't mean to, but I just couldn't seem to help myself. I wouldn't blame You if you turned me away and never listened to another one of my prayers. If you'll forgive me just one more time I promise I will never do it again…" Famous last words, I promise I will never do it again. Those words are usually very sincerely spoken, but it is the naïve heart that believes it can conquer sin on its own without God's help.

Billy Graham comments on sin, "Suppose someone should offer
me a plateful of crumbs after I have eaten a T-bone steak.
I would say, "No, thank you. I am already satisfied." Christian,
that is the secret – you can be so filled with the things
of God that you do not have time for the sinful pleasures of the world."

I know I have tried and tried to overcome temptations on my own, and if you are honest you have too. God doesn't condemn us for being fragile human beings but He does discipline our rebellion. Motive is very important to God. If we knowingly turn from Him, to do something He has said don't do, the hammer will fall. How many times does God have to hit us upside the head before we get it? We must connect the dots in life, for every action there will be a consequence. It is up to us and the way we make choices that will determine if the consequences will be bitter or a blessing. I am accountable to God for my choices and my actions. Choose wisely.

"Knowledge is proud that he has learned so much;
wisdom is humble that he knows no more."
-William Cowper-

Someone once said, "Genius has limits, stupidity does not."

MAY 18

"God, I hurt...I know MY child...I know."

"Of all delusions perhaps none is so great as the thought that our past
has ruined our present, that the evils we have done,
the mistakes we have committed, have
made all further hope impossible."
-Archbishop Goodier-

How should you treat a divorced person; a drug addict; an alcoholic? The same way you would treat a crippled shell of a person. Treat them as the cripple they are and by the grace of God they will not remain that way. I remember the day I dragged myself out of bed to go to a Divorce recovery group. It was a big scary step. I hurt so bad it almost seemed easier to end life than to live with the pain one more day. What they offered me was 'hope.' I had lost ALL hope, not just some, but all. I was a miserable shell of a person. One day at work, a nurse I worked with, asked me a simple question that rocked my world, "You don't smile very much do you?" she said. She was right. I didn't. I didn't want to smile, I didn't want to live. I had spent my whole nursing career in Critical Care helping others heal, and yet I was helpless to save myself.

"There is no medicine like hope, no incentive so great, and no tonic so
powerful, as expectation of something better tomorrow."
G.K Chesterton

I had to *learn* to hope again. I had to learn to *trust* again. I had to learn to *live* again. I needed to be surrounded by those who still believed in hope. They were my strength in those dark days because I had none of my own. I held onto the words by Joyce Meyer, "God can heal you everywhere you hurt." "Everywhere, Lord?" "Yes, everywhere." So, I gave Him all of the broken pieces as best I could. It was a very long process. It took a long time to get me into the mess and it took a long time to repair the mess. Oh, don't get me wrong, God could have healed me in an instant, but that isn't how He works. He has many hard lessons to teach us on this journey with Him.

"When you are saying a situation or a person is hopeless
you are slamming the door in the face of God."
Charles Allen

God had to show me, me. That was the most painful process of all. He stripped away the excuses, the lies, the anger and the bitterness. He did heal me, to the point that one day I was able to help lead the Divorce Recovery group. I saw firsthand what God did for me, and He also did for hundreds of others too, those who were willing to be completely honest with Him. Are you being honest with God? Are you honest with yourself? If you will be then the healing process can begin. God can and will do amazing things.

MAY 19

God's will – exactly what I would do if I had all of the facts.
-Unknown-

Jesus prayed, "Your will be done...not mine."
Matthew 6:10

"God what are you doing!?" "Why did God let this happen to me?" These are age old questions down through the centuries that go unanswered, even to this day. Who can know the mind of God? Who has His wisdom? This is why He often shuts us up to faith and trust.

"The dark threads are as needful in the Weaver's skillful hand
as the threads of gold and silver in the pattern He has planned."
Anonymous –the Divine Weaver

Life hurts. It hurts more when the pain seems so senseless. It is never senseless to God. It hurts when we can't find the answers to the why questions. He allows hurt in our life with a grander purpose than we could ever know. We learn almost nothing about God when life is simple and trouble free, but we learn who we are when the bottom drops out of our life. More importantly we learn who God is and what He can do. His power has no limits. So, when God suddenly pulls the rug out from under us, you can know that something good is coming. Joyce Meyer has said, "The secret to a trial for the child of God is to find the treasure in it." Somewhere, despite the pain and the heartache, you will learn a valuable lesson you could not learn any other way. The key to life is 'not having to know why, but trusting in Him and knowing He is more than sufficient to see you through.'

"Whatever affliction comes in our life, our Lord goes into the valley
with us, leading us by the hand, even carrying us when it is necessary."
Billy Graham

Once you become a child of God, you will NEVER be alone again. Never. Never. Never.

"Given the grace of God, given your knowledge of
God's word, given your present state of sanctification,
given the resources of the Holy Spirit within, there is
no trial into which God calls you that is
beyond your ability to withstand."
-Jay Adams-

MAY 20

*You can gauge the scope of the mission to which God has
called you, by the level of attack mounted against you by the enemy.*

Jesus said, "You shall know the truth
and the truth will set you free."
John 8:32

What has God called you to? Take a moment to pause and think about it. Did it come to you in the form of a desire or maybe a dream you have to accomplish something great? Whatever it is you will have opposition from the enemy. Someone once said, "No enemy can come so near that God is not nearer." Throughout history blood has been shed across continents all in the name of freedom. Freedom is not free. Many have laid down their life to pay for our freedom. The battle for freedom of speech was fought because someone, somewhere, wants to silence others if they don't agree with them.

Archibald Rutledge tells the story that as a young boy he was always catching and caging wild things. He particularly loved the sound of the mockingbird, so he decided to catch one and keep it so he could hear it sing anytime. He found a very young mockingbird and placed it in a cage outside his home. On the second day he saw a mother bird fly to the cage to feed the young bird through the bars. This pleased young Archibald. But the following morning he found the little bird dead. Later, young Arch was talking to the renowned ornithologist Arthur Wayne, who told him, "A mother mockingbird, finding her young in a cage, will sometimes take it poisonous berries. She evidently thinks it better for one she loves to die rather than live in captivity."

Americans hold the same sentiment. "Give me Liberty, or give me death." (Patrick Henry)

"Never in the field of human conflict was so much
owed by so many to so few."
Winston Churchill

Thank a soldier today. He gave up his freedom and time with his family so you can be free to spend time with yours. It's called sacrifice.

MAY 21

❋

Do you want to be happy for a moment? Get revenge!
Do you want to be happy forever? Forgive.

"God designed the human machine to run on Himself. He is the fuel
our spirits were designed to burn...That is why it is no good asking
God to make us happy in our own way without bothering about religion.
God cannot give us happiness apart from Himself, because there is no such thing."
-unknown-

Every one desires to be happy in this life. Happiness is something you have to work at. It doesn't just drop in your lap. Happiness comes from treating others as you would have them treat you. Happiness is always dependent upon our circumstances, whereas joy comes from the Lord. I can be happy one minute, then get a phone call that will put me down in the dumps. My happiness dissolves when my circumstances change. That is not how God intended for us to live. Someone has said, "Happiness is the perfume that you cannot pour without getting a little bit on yourselves."

"The happiness which brings enduring worth to life is not the superficial kind of
happiness that is dependent on circumstances. It is the happiness and contentment that
fills the soul even in the most distressing circumstances and the most bitter
environment. It is the kind of happiness that grins when things go wrong and
smiles through the tears. The happiness for which our souls ache is one
undisturbed by success or failure, one which will root deeply inside us and give
inward relaxation, peace and contentment, no matter what the surface
problems may be. That kind of happiness stands in need of no outward stimulus."
-Billy Graham-

You can buy happiness temporarily for someone, a new shiny car, a big house, but eventually the thrill will die out and you'll be looking for something else to make you happy. It's always something else we seek, when it is God we need to make us happy.
"The reason people find it so hard to be happy is that they
always see the past better than it really was, the present worse
than it is, and the future less resolved than it will be."
-Marcel Pagnol-

You can't buy happiness, health, love or peace. Those are things only God can supply. Seek God, and all of these things you so desire will follow. What are you seeking?

MAY 22

Where God's grace does not keep you from falling down
His mercy will keep you from staying down.

"I am not what I ought to be; I am not what I wish to be;
I am not what I hope to be; but by the GRACE of God
I am what I am."
-John Newton-

A failure is one who does *not* get up that last time he has fallen. Life can be hard some days. So hard you want to pack it all up and give up. How many of God's saints over the years felt discouraged at one time or another? I have been there and I am sure you have too. I have had many a 'faith failure.' We will probably be there a time or two more before this is all over. The good news is the grace of God comes to us when we need it. God does not give Saturday's grace on Tuesday. No, He gives it on Saturday.

"Why do we expect the best from a world steeped in pain?
Continually we find ourselves blinded by reality. Every new
morning offers another chance to admit our inadequacy – once
again for this new day, a chance to accept the bewildering
ecstasy of God's grace. Why is it so difficult to accept such
a love when His grace is the one gift that can
penetrate the messy corners of our world?"
-Bonnie Keen-

If God was willing to send His only Son to this earth to die for us, how much more willing is He help those of us He has saved, to live a life of faith on this earth? God says His grace is sufficient for the child of God. Paul, the Apostle, prayed for God to remove the thorn of flesh from him, God said, "No." Paul prayed again, and God still said, "No." Paul prayed a third time and the answer was still the same. Paul learned to live with that thorn of flesh and sometimes we are asked to do the same. It is the same for us. We can pray for God to remove something in our life that is hard and difficult to handle. Sometimes, in His wisdom, He will remove it. Other times, God in His wisdom, will not remove it. Has His love changed for us because He has not removed the trial? No. Through it we learn to trust Him in the greatest of trials. We learn to no longer lean on ourselves or someone else, but on God alone. Others may desert us when things go wrong, but God never will. God's grace will teach us to be thankful, even when the bottom is dropping out of our lives because Jesus will be there to catch us.

"God doesn't just give us grace, He gives
us Jesus, the Lord of grace."
-Joni Eareckson Tada-

MAY 23

Waiting on God can be one of the hardest trials we ever go through.

"I have tried in my own strength to worry
through, and have merely mentioned my troubles to God.
Now I am going to pray the situation through until I get light."
-Charles M. Alexander-

We must always remember, God promises He will never put any more on us than we are able to bear. He says He will provide a way of escape for the believer. God is the believer's greatest cheer leader. He brings hard and difficult times into our lives to break our will, but He will never break our spirit. He will not so burden us that He does not step in and help to carry the load. Often we can reach the point of despair. God is stretching us and it hurts. He is growing our faith. We moan and we groan, "God if you loved me you would take away this pain." We try to get Him to feel sorry for us, instead He stretches us a little further. We are sure we are going to break, but we do not.

"He has walled me in, and I cannot escape. He has bound me
in heavy chains. And though I cry and shout, he shuts out my prayers.
He has blocked my path with a high stone wall. He has twisted the
road before me with many detours."
-Lamentations 3:7-9

No wonder this book of the Bible is called Lamentations, because it is the cry of a heart deep in despair and without hope. I have been there and it is the loneliest place on earth, there is nowhere to go, nowhere to turn, the heavens are silent and there is no one to help. It appeared as if God had abandoned me. He had not, nor will He ever in the future. Sometimes His silent withdrawal is because of our disobedience. The consequences to disobedience are meant to pierce the heart. They are meant to make us think twice about ever repeating that behavior again. We cry out, we repent, we bargain with God, yet God remains silent. When He has fulfilled His purpose, He will make His presence known once again. I shudder to this day, when I remember how awful I felt in my sin. Sin breaks our fellowship with God as nothing else can. No sin is worth the price of being separated from God.
"Who dares accuse us whom God has chosen for His own? Will God?
No, He is the one who has given us right standing with Himself."
-Romans 8:33-

God will eventually restore us to a right relationship with Him, but before He does, He will teach us the terrible consequences of sinning. It is by His grace that He does not abandon us to ourselves, but restores us to Himself by His grace. No wonder it is called **amazing** grace.

May 24

*It is not always our circumstances that need fixing,
instead it is something deep down inside of us that is broken.*

"Leave the broken, irreversible past in God's hands, and
step out into the invincible future with Him."
-Oswald Chambers

Someone has said, "Loss is always a good place to start over." We all will have to face losing something or someone very near and dear to our hearts. We will experience loss at one time or another in our lives and the question is, "How do we deal with that loss?" We do have choices. We can become angry, resentful towards others and towards God, or we can accept the loss as coming from the hand of an Omniscient God, knowing that He will see me through the pain, sorrow and heartache. The first way will ultimately lead to a defeated life, the second way of 'faith' will lead to a victorious life, though it be the way of suffering and obedience, whether or not I understand the why, is irrelevant to His final purpose for the sorrow. I must learn to trust Him and Him alone in the darkness.

"Seeing that a Pilot steers the ship in which we sail,
who will never allow us to perish even in the midst
of shipwrecks, there is no reason why our minds should
be overwhelmed with fear and overcome with weariness."
-John Calvin-

When you know the Captain of the ship, you don't need to fear the darkness that may lie ahead. God is in control whether or not my circumstances appear as if that is so or not. He has not, nor will He ever, relinquish the reigns of this world to anyone, including Satan, who is called the god of this world. Christians know Satan has been defeated over 2000 years ago at Calvary. Even though defeated, he still makes many an attempt to destroy the child of God, but our eternal destiny was bought and paid for by the precious blood of Jesus Christ. We need not live a defeated life. Earth is not our home, we are heaven bound. The child of God must persevere, though he or she stumble or fall, the fall will never be fatal. God will always be there to pick us up, dust us off, and send us back into the battle.

"If I obey Jesus Christ in the seemingly random circumstances
of life, they become pinholes through which I see the face of God."
-Oswald Chambers-

Obey God in the dark times of life and you cannot lose, disobey and you cannot win. Choose wisely.

MAY 25

❊

*God does not reveal His will to us for our consideration, but for our **obedience**.*

You call me master, and obey Me not;
You call me light, and seek Me not;
You call me way, and walk Me not;
You call me wise, and follow Me not;
You call me fair, and love Me not;
You call me eternal and seek Me not;
You call Me gracious, and trust Me not;
You call me noble, and serve Me not;
You call Me mighty, and honor Me not;
You call me just, and fear Me not;
If I condemn thee, blame Me not.
-In the Cathedral at Lubek, Germany-

What is the measure of your love for the Lord? Jesus said, "If you love me, you will obey Me." Are you quick to obey or do you have to think about it for a long time? Do you have to reason it away if it's not something you want to do?

"I started to read the Book to find out what the ideal
life was, and I found that the only thing worth doing in
this world was to do the will of God; whether that was done
in the pulpit or in the slums, whether it was done in the
college or class-room or on the street, it did not matter at all."
-Henry Drummond-

I can come up with so many reasons and excuses why I shouldn't do what God has told me to do, but in the end they are still 'excuses.' Oswald Chambers has said it best. "The tiniest fragment of obedience and heaven opens up and the profoundest truths of God are yours straight away. God will never reveal more truth about Himself until *you obey* what you know already."

"Choose to love the Lord your God and to obey Him
and to commit yourself to Him, for He is your life."
Deuteronomy 30:20

He is your life. Meditate on that the rest of the day.

MAY 26

*There will come a day when you will go through a trial
so painful you won't be able to find a Bible verse to explain it.
You will either trust God or walk away from Him. Many have walked away.*

The Lord says, "I will rescue those who love Me.
I will protect those who trust in my name.
When they call on Me, I will answer; I will be with
them in trouble. I will rescue them and honor them."

Psalm 91:14-15

What happens to us in a trial? The darkness overwhelms us. We begin to doubt and the more the fire heats up in our life, the greater our pain, the more doubt we have. "Does God love me?" we cry out. The heavens are silent. Trials can be brought on by my disobedience, by someone else's choices that affect my life, or as in Job's case, by Satan. Regardless of the cause, the hardest thing to reconcile is that God has allowed it in my life. He could have stopped it, but He didn't. We try to come up with a plan that will stop the hurting, anything, even compromise. The better plan is to crawl up into God's lap and stay there until the storm has passed. Think of your own child on a stormy night, the rain is falling, the lightening is flashing. You hear the pitter patter of little feet and before you know it they are under the covers with you. Why? Because they need to not only know they are safe, but feel they are safe. You wrap your arms tightly around them and whisper, "Don't be afraid, mommy is here." Soon they are asleep and so are you. Why? Because you know God is watching over you and your child.

Is your life in a tailspin right now? Call on the Lord. He promises to be with us in trouble, not just close by, but *with us*. Best of all He promises to rescue us. Job went through a trial so painful he lost not only his earthly possessions, but also his children were taken from him. Yet his faith may have waivered under the pressure, but in the end he could proclaim, "Even though He slay me, I know that in my flesh I shall see God." Job knew that death was not the end. He endured unto the end. Job had no idea what was happening to him. He had no clue that God had taken down the protective hedges of his life and let Satan in. Satan's mission is to kill, steal and destroy our lives. He takes no prisoners! Despair shouts, "Give up." God whispers, "Hold on!" Good news is God will one day put him in chains and cast him into the lake of fire. Satan doesn't scare God, so he shouldn't scare you either.

"The place where God puts you will not be perfect. Even
Eden was exposed to the possibility of evil. But there is
no better place to be than where God has set you down."

-Colin Smith-

Thought for the day: Bloom where God has planted you.

MAY 27

*It takes two to make a relationship. It only takes **one** to destroy it.*

"Do not be unequally yoked with unbelievers."
-2 Corinthians 6:14-

"It is easier to clean up the physical damage done by
a tornado than the emotional damage caused by a divorce."
-Steve Grissom & Kathy Leonard-

DO NOT be unequally yoked to unbelievers, is a command, not a suggestion. This is sad but true and particularly devastating in marriage. This principle stands firm in all relationships. Business partners should not be unequally yoked. Children and their friends should not be unequally yoked. That's how trouble begins. Two people having a different set of values, a different goal and differing ways to achieve success honestly. One lives in the light of God's presence while the other abides in darkness. It's all about a person's 'will'. One spouse can work diligently to make the marriage work but the other has different plans. In fact, they may already have Plan B, and she is a brunette. Jesus says, "Take My yoke upon you. Let Me teach you, because I am humble and gentle, and you will find rest for your souls. For my yoke fits perfectly, and the burden I give you is light." Matthew 12:28-30. A yoke was a very heavy harness made out of wood that fit over the oxen. It was then attached to whatever it was the oxen were brought in to pull. In my mind's eye, I see a taskmaster over the oxen with a whip pressing them on. Not so, in Jesus case. He tells us he is humble and gentle. He will get down under the load with us if we will let Him. He will give us time for rest if we need it. He will quench our thirst. His burden is light. So, why would anyone want to carry the burden alone? Maybe we would be wise to consider the words of John Baillie:

"Give me a stout heart to bear my own burdens.
Give me a willing heart to bear the burdens of others.
Give me a believing heart to *cast* ALL burdens upon Thee, O Lord."

Remember, the most important relationship we will ever have on this earth is with God. When He sees me, He sees me in His Son, the true burden bearer.

May 28

Giving up is NEVER of God, but letting go is.

"Each time the mystery of suffering touches us personally
and all the cosmic questions arise fresh in our minds, we face
the choice between faith (which accepts) and unbelief (which refuses to accept.)"
-Elisabeth Elliot

God's plan for us always begins with 'surrender.' The harder I hold onto something the more painful it will be for me when I am forced to let go of it. Don't make Him have to force something out of your hand. He is an all wise God. If He doesn't want you to have something or someone in your life then that should be the end of the argument. God is in need of nothing. The cattle on a thousand hills are His. He adds and removes things from our life because of His love. Because He is Omniscient and knows what that 'thing' or that 'someone' will do to us in the end. Anything that becomes more important than God in your life, God has painted a big red bull's eye on it and He is coming after it.

"To 'endure' is the first thing that a child ought to learn,
and that which he will have the most need to know."
-Jean Jacques Rousseau-

Endurance was the Apostle Paul's middle name. He was ship wrecked, stoned and left for dead, beaten, imprisoned and still he shouted from the rooftops every opportunity God gave him that Jesus was the Son of God, born of a virgin, crucified and raised to life and He is coming again! Does knowing Jesus make you want to shout?

MAY 29

*Some of the circumstances in my life are nothing more than a
loving God nudging me in a better direction.*

"..for I have learned, in whatsoever state I am, therewith to be content."
Philippians 4:11

What does discontentment in your life cause you to do? Complain? Drink, do drugs? Go shopping? What fills that empty space in your heart when things aren't going so well? The Apostle Paul did not write about his contentment from a five star hotel…he wrote those words from a dirty, filthy prison. God gave Paul an extraordinary mission. He was to go to the gentiles and present to them the gospel message of Christ. But first, he had to come to a place in his life where the message he was bringing was more important than his own comfort. Paul came to the place where he could be happy having abundance or very little. His contentment was not dependent upon his circumstances. Paul knew the power of God in a person's life to meet them right where they were. The Christians life does not make sense to the world. This is best illustrated in the following story written by A.W. Tozer:

"A real Christian is an odd number, anyway. He feels supreme
love for One he has never seen; talks familiarly every day to someone he
cannot see; expects to go to heaven on the virtue of Another; empties himself
in order to be full; admits he is wrong so he can be declared right; goes down
in order to get up; is strongest when he is weakest; richest when he is poorest and
happy when he is feels the worst. He dies so he can live; forsakes in order to have;
gives away so he can keep; sees the invisible, hears the inaudible, and knows
that which passes knowledge."

Life grinds away at all of us. Question is does it grind you down or does it polish you? God's intent is that we come out of life's experiences, refined as gold.

"The darker the night grows, and the fiercer the storm becomes,
the better we will remember that He of the lake of Galilee came to
them upon the waves in the night when the storm was wildest."
-Charles Spurgeon-

If you are in the middle of a storm and the waves are threatening to pull you down in defeat, look up, the God who commands the sea, is walking towards you with all of the answers you will need. In His other hand is a life preserver.

MAY 30

*The greatest thing a father can do for
his children is to love their mother.*
-Unknown-

"Love is patient and kind. It is not jealous or boastful or proud, or rude. Love does not demand
its own way. Love is not irritable, and it keeps no record of when it has been wronged. It is
never glad at injustice but rejoices whenever the truth wins out. Love never gives up, never
loses faith, is always hopeful, and endures every circumstance. Love will last forever..."
1 Corinthians 13:4-7

Love is not just a 'feeling' we have, but it is something we have to *choose* to do. God's standards are so much higher than ours will ever be. We tend to keep score in life. We have a long laundry lists of ways to get even. God says throw it away. With Him there is no payback, unless He does the paying and His retribution is always done in *love*. Ours is not. We tend to boast about all of our accomplishments. God says let Me be the One to brag about you. I'll put your picture on my refrigerator for all the angels in heaven to see. Love rejoices in truth, we run from it more often than not. Love never gives up, we do. God never gives up on us, no matter what we have done. He knows there can always be something better in our life if we would just give our lives to Him. Love never loses faith. Our foundations are shaken when we are criticized or maligned by others. Love is always hopeful. It sees what our human eyes cannot. Love endures all things. God is sitting on ready to intervene on your behalf if you will leave the consequences with Him and Him alone. Children learn by example better than anything you can tell them. Someone once said, "What you do speaks so loudly, I can't hear what you are saying." Words should always be measured by actions. I can tell you I love you, but do I show it? Do you? Watch out! Your children are watching and listening and it doesn't matter how old they are or you are. Love is eternal. God said, "I have loved you with an everlasting love."

"The heart of a child is the most precious of God's creation.
Never break it. At all costs, never break it."
-Joseph L. Whitten-

MAY 31

I wish I had chosen door # 2...

"Choose this day whom you will serve...as for me
and my house we will serve the Lord."
Joshua 24:15

How many times in life have we either said those words or at least thought them? I have said them many times. "I wish I hadn't done that." Regret fills the heart… "I wish I had of…I wish I would of…I wish I hadn't said that." There comes a time in every one's life we are confronted with our choices. Some will be life changing. Do we follow God or the world? It should be an easy choice, but usually it is not. Conflict starts in our hearts. Inner turmoil takes over. God has brought us to that dreaded red line of His. Will I continue on in my own way and cross the line or will I yield to His wisdom and love.

"We are to find as much bitterness in weeping for
sin as ever we found sweetness in committing it."
-Thomas Watson-

There are two kinds of pain in life. The pain of discipline for those things I did and shouldn't have, and the pain of regret for those things I did and shouldn't have or those things I wish I would have done and didn't. Usually the hurt from discipline, although it may sting, is usually short lived, whereas, the pain of regret can last a lifetime. Some of the choices we make have a higher price tag than others. God's boundaries are meant to keep us safe. It is the wise person who remembers that God is more interested in my holiness than my comfort. The moment I take one step away from Him I am headed for trouble. All of those bad choices we make in life will end up taking us to a place we never intended to go. Choose wisely.

Thought for the day: Do you have wishbone or backbone?

June 1

Heavenly push-ups...

"In the Bible, clouds are always connected with God. Clouds
are those sorrows or sufferings or providences, within or without our
personal lives, which seem to dispute the rule of God. It is by those
very clouds that the spirit of God is teaching us how to walk by faith.
If there were no clouds, we should have no faith."
-Oswald Chambers-

If you can't carry a tune, or your heart is too sorrowful to sing, then try heavenly push-ups. When the burden is too heavy for my shoulders to bear, the Lord says to cast all of my burdens and cares on Him. So, I push them back up to heaven, to the One who is able to sustain me. Jesus calls us to bear one another's burdens, but nowhere does He tell us to hold onto them or to fret and worry over them. In His wisdom He invites us to cast ALL our cares, not just our own, but those we have helped our brother to carry. The more we understand who God is, the better we get at heavenly push-ups. We can choose to hold onto our troubles or we can push them up to the only One who has shoulders strong enough to carry the weight of the world. Pride holds on and thinks it has an answer while faith learns to let go and push! The longer we hold onto our troubles, the more we tend to magnify them out of proportion and the more unsolvable they become. Freedom is found when you get really good at pushing ! So, push!

"Even though you have missed God's plan entirely for years
and years, that plan can still swing into operation the
minute you're ready to step up and step in, with God at your side."
-Tony Evans-

Step up and step in is another way of saying repent. Come to God honestly, open your heart to Him, invite Him in and then sit back and take in all that you have missed being away from Him. Once you are His child, He will never let go of you.

June 2

"If sinners be damned, at least let them leap into hell over our bodies. If they perish, let them perish with our arms about their knees. Let no one go there unwarned and unprayed for."
-Charles Spurgeon-

Has God placed one of these Christians in your path? Someone who has desperately tried to share the truth with you even if it meant risking it all, even your friendship? Maybe, you are married to someone like this. How did you respond to the only message of hope and eternal life that heaven has to offer a dying and lost world? Did you leap over them, still hell bent on living life your own way? Many do, you know. They foolishly tell themselves they still have tomorrow to change their minds. For many, tomorrow will never come. This is why there is such an urgency in God's message, now. Today is the day you can hear God speaking to you, if you will only listen. Can you feel that tug on your heartstrings? That's God. Do you know in your heart there has to be more than what you are experiencing? That's God, too. Tomorrow is promised to no man. As a Critical Care nurse, I have seen a man come into the hospital and his wife walk out a widow. September 11th is another example of the uncertainty of life. Those who lost their loved ones that day, don't you think their day would have been a lot different if they knew that was the last time they would see them this side of heaven? Would they want a do over for the last words spoken that morning? There are lots of days I wish I could get a 'word do over.' Sadly, there is no such thing, but there is forgiveness of others and yourself. None of us could have imagined or anticipated the events of that day. We were all changed forever. Evil came to our shores that day and has never left. Given the world we live in today, with its uncertainty and spontaneous acts of terror, it is stupid to ignore God's truth. Will you? Eternity is always just one heartbeat away.

> "Nothing is so important to man as his own state, nothing is as formidable as his eternity; and thus it is not natural that there should be men indifferent to the loss of their existence and the perils of everlasting suffering."
> -Blaise Pascal-

June 3

"Heroes and cowards all look alike...until the battle begins."

"This is the greatest sight you will ever see. Son of God
and Son of Man, there He hangs, bearing pains
unutterable, the just for the unjust, to bring us to God.
Oh, the glory of that sight!"
-Charles Spurgeon-

No matter where you start out in life, and no matter where you find yourself right at this moment, you will, at some time, take a journey back in time. A journey to a Roman cross, the day the world decided to put the Son of God to death. This is a journey God intends for us all to make. It is a journey that will bring you face to face with truth. What you do with that truth is entirely up to you. You will come face to face with Jesus. You will then have to choose. There were many spectators that day. Imagine yourself as one of them. The crowds were large because it was a Jewish holiday. Most were both tired and excited. There were some just like you and me. There were some who stood at the foot of the cross, staring up into the face of God's Son, mocking and jeering Him. There were some who spit in His face and turned away in disgust. There were others who had spent three years hanging onto every word He said. Which one are you? There were some who encouraged Him to come down from the cross and save Himself...there were others who understood why He couldn't. Some saw a criminal, others saw 'Immanuel,' God with us. There were some who believed and some who will never believe. There are still people like that today. Some were drawn to Him and some turned away. Some who laughed and some who cried. Some who were glad to see Him die and there were others who lost all hope when He did. There were some who heard the words, "It is finished," and gave up, and some who heard those same words and knew it was just the beginning. Some who pierced His side with a spear and some who today, pierce His heart with their rebellion and unbelief. The battle is still raging. You are either for Him or you are against Him. Which one are you? Be careful how you answer. Your eternal destiny depends on it.

JUNE 4

The enemy loves to bring up stuff he knows we can't do anything about.

"Put on the WHOLE armor of God so that you will be able to stand firm
against the strategies and tricks of the devil…"
Ephesians 6:11-18

Most of the things we worry about in life never happen, and the devil knows that, but he wants to steal our joy, make us doubt God and live a defeated life. The Bible says, "The joy of the Lord is our strength." So, if Satan can steal our joy he also gets our strength. God knows that humans are no match for the devil in our human strength so He provides us with His armor. He calls us to battle with the enemy, but not until He has prepared us. Today, we will learn about the *'Belt of truth.'* First God tells us to put on the 'belt of truth.' This is not a suggestion, but a command. Put it on! Truth should be the very foundation of each of our lives. Jesus said, I am the way, not 'a way,' He is the 'only way,' not one of many ways. "He is the way, the truth and the life." Not only do we have to know what we believe, but who we believe. You can sincerely believe the wrong thing and many do. You have to know who God is. He is my protector, my Savior, my fortress, my shield. He holds the whole world in His hands. He gave boundaries to the oceans. His word is truth and His word is the final authority.

"The lies of the devil always have a ring of truth
to them. The best counterfeit is always as
close to the original as possible."
-Charles Stanley-

When there are differing opinions, it doesn't matter what I think or what you think, but what is important is what God says. He makes the rules and we follow them. His word is a lamp to light our path. (Psalm 119:105) A light not only illuminates the way of safety, but it also shows the stumbling stones and obstacles in our way. It guides us and directs us in the way we should go and the way we should not take, all the while protecting us. Most importantly, it drives away darkness. Satan is in no hurry to take us down, he can be very patient. He has lots of time. God's word is sharper than any two-edged sword. It is able to divide the thought and attitudes of our heart (Heb.4:12 LB). His word is not just meant to be heard, but to be *lived*. It alone has the power to change and heal a life.

June 5

Knowledge is knowing the right thing to do. Wisdom is doing it.

"We all want our children to be smart. Unfortunately,
people have largely forgotten that there is a huge
difference between intelligence and wisdom. Intelligence
is a measurement of things you know. Wisdom is your
ability to discern right from wrong and make moral choices.
A wise person will follow God. An intelligent person may or may not."
-Sonya Haskins-

There is a big difference between someone who knows what the right thing to do is but doesn't do it, and someone who knows what is right and chooses to do it. That person is not only walking in wisdom but also in obedience. He does what God says. It doesn't matter if it's convenient at the time, if it is hard, he will do it. The next piece of God's armor He commands us to put on is the *"Breastplate of Righteousness."* For the Roman soldier this breastplate covered his vital organs, especially the heart. God's word says, "Above all else, let the peace of God guard your hearts and your minds. (Phil.4:7 NIV) Out of mouth the heart speaks. Whatever is in your heart will eventually come out of your mouth, so that is why it is virtually impossible to be angry and not have it show. Garbage in. Garbage out. A filthy mouth is then a sure sign of a filthy life. Therefore, it is important to watch what you let into your life. Pornography is one example. Once something is allowed to enter your mind it is almost impossible to get it out…except for God's intervention and healing. A wound to the heart can be fatal. We must protect our hearts. God's word says, "Where your treasure is there will your heart be also. (Matthew 6:21 NIV) What is your treasure and who are you following? We are to put on God's righteousness because we don't have any of our own. In fact, the Bible goes so far as to say our righteousness is as filthy rags in God's sight. (Isa. 64:6 NIV) Righteousness is 'right living' before God. If you want your prayers answered, do what God says. "The prayer of a righteous man is powerful and effective." (James 5:16 NIV) A person's life without Jesus has no hope of ever pleasing God by what he or she does. Put on the breastplate of righteousness!

June 6

This life is all the believer will know of hell.
It is all the unbeliever will know of heaven.

"My peace I give you, not as the world gives you do I give to you. Do not let your hearts be troubled, neither let them be afraid..."
-Jesus – (John 14:27)

"God's peace can break through the bleakest of circumstances, even into those moments when we stare into darkness and the shadow of death."
-Virginia Ann Froehle-

The next piece of armor we put on is to *"shod our feet with the gospel shoes of peace."* The Christian life is an uphill battle, but one day it will be over. Everyone's journey will eventually end. Where you spend eternity is up to you. The Roman soldiers went to battle every day and so does the child of God. I am sure the Romans longed for peace as we do. The Roman soldiers' sandals had studs or nails on the bottom of them. This enabled the soldier to keep from slipping. This armor enables the Christian to keep from backsliding. Firm footing resulted in a firm foundation. The soldier could not be easily knocked down. Likewise, the Christian must have sure footing. He must know what he believes and why he believes it and should be ready, willing and able to share the good news with anyone who asks him about the peace that lies within him. Many unbelievers watch the Christian's life very closely. They are very quick to criticize. They can't help but see there is something very different about them, but may be too afraid or too embarrassed to ask what that something is. It is a peace that they can't explain. A rebellious life has no peace. God will never leave us content in our rebellion or sin. Even a Christian who is disobedient can lose his or her peace. A heart full of peace is one of the greatest indicators that you are in the will of God. Rebellion and peace cannot reside in the same heart. Live in peace or live in turmoil. Which one is it for you? Use peace as a thermometer of your Christian life.

June 7

*You can't make God love you anymore than He
already does and you can't make Him stop loving you.*

One of Satan's greatest lies is "God doesn't love you...anymore." "Look at what you've done...Man, you have blown it now." Our next piece of God's armor today is taking up the *"Shield of Faith"* which is able to stop 'every' fiery dart that the enemy sends our way. In the battle of life, faith is your shield. You must know what you believe. You must know the truth. There is no safety in believing a lie, and Satan's arsenal is full of them.

"Lift up over all the covering, shield of faith, upon
which you can quench all the flaming missiles of the wicked one."
-Ephesian 6:16-

This verse tell us one of the strategies of the enemy in sending fiery darts. What exactly are those fiery darts? First we must define them. They are the lies or the half-truths of Satan. The first one he sent was to Adam and Eve. "Has God really said you can't eat from the tree?" And since the Garden of Eden there have been many variation of that theme, questioning God and His boundaries in our life, His protective boundaries. Can you hear the doubt? "Did God really say that?" "Did He really mean that?" Any thought that causes us to doubt God is a fiery dart straight from the pit of hell itself. A fiery dart, or lie from the enemy, if believed, can send your whole life, or an area of it, up in flames if it finds its target. These darts are aimed at us personally, especially at our weak areas. They are meant to destroy you. Fiery darts like, "Just one drink won't hurt you," or "You're not going to let them get away with that are you?" "You can sleep with your boyfriend, after all you 'love each other,' don't you?" "You've blown it now buddy, God will never forgive you for this one." All lies, sometimes mixed with half-truths, and all meant to destroy. God knows that our thoughts always precede our actions. It is important, therefore, to stop the thought immediately. Don't think about, don't ponder it, reject it at its onset. If you don't, Satan will wear you down. He is relentless. He will continue to send those thoughts (fiery darts) until you go down in defeat, but you do not have to. Not if you do what God says to do and take up the Shield of Faith.

June 8

God's love is the same even when we are walking away from Him.

"Knowing oneself loved by God is not a matter of knowing
God's love. It's not a matter of saying the right words or even
claiming the right beliefs. It's about something that happens on
a level deeper than words and ideas and knowledge and thoughts.
It's something that gets inside one's soul and never leaves."
-Lynne Hybels-

Today's piece of God's armor is the "Helmet of Salvation." The helmet of salvation protects our thinking. Salvation has been given to us as a gift from God. Sometimes, we easily forget that. We find ourselves trying to 'earn' our way to Heaven. When we sin, Satan immediately attacks with things like, "God is so disappointed in you, He doesn't love you anymore, if He ever did." "You should have known better." On and on he goes. Sound familiar? We often think these are our own thoughts, when in reality, they are sent straight from hell by the enemy of our souls flinging fiery darts, left and right. We duck, we weave, anything to keep them from hitting their target. If Satan can make you think you aren't really saved, you will become a powerless Christian. You will then become so entangled in trying to earn your salvation back, that he has defeated you. Salvation was God's gift to you and Satan stole it. He didn't take your salvation if you are a true believer. He only stole your 'assurance' of salvation. You must know who you are in Christ. Notice those two little words, but probably two of the most important words in your Bible, "In Christ." On our own we are defenseless, hopeless, lost sinners. "In Christ," we are children of the living God, covered by the blood of Jesus, and able by His power to stand against the forces of hell. We aren't just secure, we are 'eternally' secure in Christ. Protecting your mind protects your whole person. God wants His children to get used to the smell of gunpowder. Satan's bullets are flying all around us. Every day he has a new batch to send our way. Bullets that cause doubt and render helpless the strongest to the weakest soldier of God. Head wounds are fatal. God knows we are in a battle for our very survival. Good news is, we win!

June 9

God does not promise us an easy journey,
He does, however, promise us a safe one.

Today we put on the last piece of God's armor. God says, "Take up the sword of the Spirit which is the Word of God." This is the only offensive weapon the child of God is given. All others have been defensive weapons. The Roman soldier's sword was a lethal weapon. It was a short, double-edged blade designed for 'close' combat. Don't miss that, 'close' combat. Sometimes the enemy gets so close we can feel him breathing down our necks. Other times, the chill of evil surrounding us can be numbing. Yet, the very moment we speak God's word, "It is written…," the devil must flee. He has no defense against the word of God. But, make no mistake he will be back. In fact, you can count on it. Jesus spent forty days and forty nights in the wilderness, in *close* combat with the devil. What was the weapon He chose? He chose the Word of God. Whatever Satan would tempt Jesus with, Jesus would always respond with, "It is written," and He quoted from God's word. Why? It's because God's word is light and truth. Light drives out darkness and exposes evil for what it really is. Remember the enemy flees at the Word of God. It drives him away. Satan encourages us to keep our sins hidden in darkness. God says bring them out into the light so He can heal them and forgive them. Confess them and be set free. God's armor is meant for the enemy to flee from your presence and His armor will enable the believer to be left standing when the battle is over. Today, and every day stand firm, and stand your ground! Remember we win!

JUNE 10

The great exchange...

"Choose this day, who you are going to serve."
Joshua 24:15 NIV

The Bible is the greatest love story ever told. It requires a decision on your part. God says in Deuteronomy 30:19; " Today, I have given you the choice between life and death, between blessings and curses ...oh that you would choose life." Don't miss that. Choose when? Today! You are serving someone right now, even if it is yourself, so you have to make a choice. You may not have tomorrow. Tomorrow is promised to no man. The uncertainty of life makes the choice that much more important. Whom will you choose? By not choosing you choose. When God asks the question, He even gives us the right answer. Choose life! The moment we choose Him, everything becomes new. I call it the great exchange:

He will exchange...
My wounded heart for His nail scarred
Hands of love.
My filth for His righteousness.
My loneliness for His comfort.
My want for His riches in glory.
My earthly home for streets of gold.
My foolishness for His wisdom.
My unsteadiness for His anchor.
My hatred for His heart of love.
My failures for His success.
My poverty for His riches.
My turmoil for His peace.
My sins for His forgiveness.
My uncertainty for His wisdom.

My despair for His hope.
My sadness for joy unspeakable.
My anger for His gentleness.
My chains for His freedom.
My weakness for His strength.
My heavy heart for His laughter.
My shame for His name.
My rejection for His acceptance.
My dreams for His.
My burdens for His song.
My compromise for His commitment.
My condemnation for His approval.
My hell for His eternity.
This life of sorrow for an eternity of joy.

The great exchange. How crazy do you have to be to continue holding onto those things in life that weigh you down? Those things that separate you from the King of Kings. Where else can you get a deal like this? You can't. He alone offers us life...His life. You have been bought with a price...paid for in red. His blood.

June 11

God have mercy on those who oppose Him.

"Do not be deceived and misled, God will not allow Himself
to be sneered at (scorned, distained or mocked.) For
whatsoever a man sows, that and that only shall he reap."
-Galatians 6:7-

You live a life of rebellion against God, you will one day reap the consequences. Heaven is a real place and real people go there. Hell is a real place and real people go there. There are only two destinations after life, heaven or hell. There is no purgatory, as some religions believe. The Bible is very clear that after death comes judgment. No second chances to get it right. No 'do overs.' Hell is the complete absence of God. I cannot think of a worse place to be then to be eternally separated from love, God's love. God's love provided His Son to die for your sins. God's justice will fall on those who reject such love. For them there is no other cure. It is like being poisoned and then rejecting the cure. Why does judgment come after we die? I believe, it's because of the law of sowing and reaping. "What? you may be asking yourself. Everything we do or say has some consequences to it, good or bad. What we do also affects other people's lives, sometimes with a much greater impact than we could ever have imagined. Again, that impact could be a good thing or a bad thing. For years after our own death, the impact of our lives and the choices *we made* are still being felt by others. God's principle of sowing and reaping can work for us or against us. Some of our choices have immediate results, while others can take years for the effects to be visible. Not until the end will 'everyone's' sowing and reaping be made known. God's holiness demands justice. You cannot live like a devil all of your life and then expect to go to heaven. If that were the case, there would be no reason for repentance. To repent you must turn from sin.

"Oh brethren, above all things shun hypocrisy. If ye
mean to be damned, make up your minds to it, and be
damned like honest men; but do not, I beseech you,
pretend to go to heaven while all the time you are going to hell."
-Charles Spurgeon-

In the end, we will face God for all of our actions. He will allow us to see how we affected someone else's life. Did we harm them, or did we help them. This is why I think parents will have a lot to answer for. It's a day when God will right all wrongs. He will vindicate those who were persecuted or wronged. He is today, watching how I treat my fellow man. He is watching you too.

JUNE 12

❈

"A clever person solves a problem. A wise person avoids it."
-Albert Einstein-

If we are really honest with ourselves, we have gotten ourselves into most of the trouble we experience in life. We make really bad choices. It's like Ready! **Fire!** Aim! We aim after the damage is done. We miss the mark by our foolishness and then blame someone else. We even go so far as to blame God. "God, why did you let this happen to me?" He tried to warn us, but we refused to pay attention. I am so guilty of that. That feeling deep in your gut that says, "Don't do it." We dial it down a notch by ignoring it until we no longer hear it or feel it. We silence the warning bells and then wonder what happened when the bottom falls out of our lives. Exhausted, tired and disappointed we get down on our knees and pray. God is faithful. He will use this experience in life to teach you a valuable lesson about who He is, and who you are not. He is Sovereign, you are not. He is wise, we are foolish, most of the time. He is faithful, we sometimes are. He knows His way is the best way. Period. No ifs, ands, or buts. He knows what the consequences will be to our rebellion, and as any good father, He does not want to see us suffer needlessly. Most of our worry comes from mistrusting God or anger because we don't get our way. Do you know someone who has become so angry at God, they shake their fist in His face, walk away and never look back? They believe themselves to be smarter than He is. When in reality, we don't understand why He allows some hurtful things to happen in our lives or the lives of others.

"My thoughts are not your thoughts, neither are your ways My ways, says the Lord. For as the
heavens are higher than the earth, so are My ways higher than your ways and
My thoughts than your thoughts."
-Isaiah 55:8-9-

This verse kind of puts us in our place doesn't it? There is no way for a human mind to understand God's ways. If we could, He would not be God. He would be just like us, trying to figure things out. His plan was put into place before the world began! He wrote your name in the Book of Life before creation. That is mind boggling. That is one reason He asks us to TRUST Him. Just like a child jumps off a high place into their father's arms, all because that child trusts that their father will catch them, they will be safe. So, it is with God. He asks for our trust. He doesn't force us to trust Him, He asks, we choose. The unknown is known to God. That should calm most of your fears. He knows the beginning from the end and the end from the beginning. Read the Book of Revelation. We win! If you really want to be wowed by God, read where He predicts the future events of the last seven years of mankind's history on this earth before He makes all things new. It will boggle your mind. Just a sample, God says, Iran and Russia will form an alliance and march against Israel to destroy her. Problem is, God also says they will be destroyed on the mountains outside of Israel. (Read Ezekiel Chapters 38 & 39). God's Holy Spirit indwells every believer. He convicts us (*not* condemns) and leads us in the paths we should take. We would do well to heed His still small voice.

"Heaven and earth, all the emperors, kings, and princes of the world, could not raise a fit dwell-
ing-place for God; yet, in a weak human soul, that keeps His word, He willingly resides."
-Martin Luther-

June 13

*You may not have gotten a great start in life
but, you can have a great finish.*

"The wages of sin are the same for the sinner and the saint."
-Judson Cornwall-

It's all up to you how you finish. Sad, but true, but not all Christians live the kind of life God had planned for them. Sometimes, it's downright impossible to tell them apart from the rest of the world. I know, I was one of them. Friends were confused, "You're a what?" translated, "Yikes! you're a Christian? Your life sure doesn't show it." And it didn't. I am a work in progress and so are you if you belong to Jesus. Not all Christians walk in love as they should. Not all Christians walk in obedience to God's word. Not all walk in mercy, compassion or kindness. I'm sure you are saying to yourself right now, "Well, what makes you think they are even Christians?" Only God really knows the heart of each one of us. He is more interested in *why* we do the things we do, and the motive behind our actions, then the action themselves. Why? because it reflects the *true* condition of our heart. It's very different for someone to steal because he or his family is starving versus someone who steals for the thrill of it. None of us have the wisdom to know the deep secret hearts of men. Only God does. His judgments will be fair. He is a just judge.

"The books are balanced in heaven, not here."
Josh Billing
"You cannot judge a man till you know his whole story."
Thomas Fuller

Only God knows our *whole* story. He asks us not to judge, but He does call us to be fruit inspectors, "Therefore you will know them by their fruits. Not everyone who says to Me Lord, Lord, will enter the kingdom of heaven, but he who does the will of My Father, who is in Heaven." Matthew 7:20-21 If you are a child of God your life will show it. It is impossible to stay the same once the Holy Spirit has taken up residence in your heart.

JUNE 14

❖

"Anything you say, can and will be used against you in an argument,
three years from now, twenty years from now."

"Forgiveness. Nothing is more foreign to sinful human nature.
And nothing is more characteristic of divine grace."
-John MacArthur-

This would actually be funny, if it weren't so true. I can remember wrongs done to me forty years ago and I'm sure you can too. I also have no trouble reminding the person, over and over and over again. How many of us keep a 'you done me wrong' list? I know I used to. I don't anymore. God made me throw it away. You can't allow feelings to run your life, unless you love roller coaster rides. It is very dangerous to live by feelings. They cannot be depended on. They change all too frequently. "Today, I like you, however, tomorrow doesn't look too promising." If suddenly, my circumstances took a nose dive, then so did my spirits. God does not have a 'get even' list. If we confess our sins to Him, He promises to remove them as far as the east is from the west and to *remember them no more*. (Isaiah 43:25) If God remembers them no more, how can we? His standard is perfect. His ways are perfect. It's those who don't think they have done anything wrong, therefore, have no need to confess, that are in big trouble! You can live with the weight of your sins on your shoulders or you can be forgiven. Emotions have nothing to do with our salvation. If God says it's true, it's true. The blood of Jesus can wash a sinner white as snow. Meditate on the following verse today:

"As far as the east is from the west, so far has He removed our transgressions from us."
Psalm 103:12

Not only does He promise to "remember them no more" but, to remove them forever.
"Every man has a right to his opinion, but no man has a right to be wrong in his facts."
Bernard Baruch

Start afresh today! How about trading in your 'get even' list for a 'bucket list' instead? Start today doing those things you promised yourself you would do, before you die. Make a new list, a 'No regrets list!'

JUNE 15

✻

What is normal? Answer: It's a cycle on my washing machine.

"We haven't yet dreamed big enough dreams of
what we could mean to one another."
-Larry Crabb-

Aren't there some days you just feel 'silly?' I think those are stress relief days, ordained by God. We live in a pressure cooker world. Sometimes, you just have to escape it. We all have our quirks. All of us are a little off balance in one way or another. But you know what? It's okay. God doesn't expect perfection from any of us. He expects us to be kind to one another. So, today, why not look for someone you can do a good deed for. I'll bet they wouldn't be hard to find. Take your child to the zoo – on a school day! I used to take my kids to Disneyland on their birthdays, even if it was on a school day. In fact, I think they had more fun because they got to play hooky. I even took their friends if their parents would let them. Those were days we built special memories. Bend the rules just a little. If you can have fun, so will your kids. Last week, my daughter took my twin grandsons to the zoo – on a Friday! (Don't tell the school.) All I can say is, "You go girl!" Wish I had been there. That day the baboons and the tigers were more important than math and geography. The wonderful thing that happened that day was the mama baboon brought her baby out for all to watch her nurse him. Even baboons have the sense to make their kids feel pretty special. Time spent together is the real issue here. It didn't have to be the zoo, it could have been anywhere! That day it was confirmed to them, once again, that they were truly loved!

"Children are the anchors that
hold a mother to life."
-Sophocles-

"A baby is God's opinion that the world should go on."
-Unknown-

JUNE 16

'Someday' is not a day of the week.

"Today, if you hear His voice, do not harden your hearts, as happened in the rebellion of Israel
and their provocation and embitterment of Me in the day of testing in the wilderness..."
Hebrews 3:15

Don't we all treat 'someday' as the eight day of the week? I know I have. Sometimes, I still do. The laundry, I'll do it tomorrow...the thank-you cards, I'll send them...just not today. The garage? oh, it can wait. All of these tomorrows finally stack up to become 'someday.' Trouble with 'someday' is it causes us to lose control of our lives, today. The burdens become so heavy, that without God's help to deal with them, we never would. Every day there are things we must do, and things we would like to. Some days, my 'want to' overrides my 'must do.' We live in a 'microwave society.' We want everything now!. We don't want to wait. We don't want to 'earn' what it is we are seeking, we would prefer someone just give it to us. Thomas Jefferson, the third President of the United States, had his 10 rules for living a good life. Here they are:

1. Never put off till tomorrow what you can do today.
2. Never trouble another for what you can do yourself.
3. Never spend your money before you have it.
4. Never buy what you do not want because it is cheap.
5. Prides costs us more than hunger, thirst and cold.
6. Never repent of having eaten too little.
7. Nothing is troublesome that we do willingly.
8. Never let the evils which have never happened cost you pain.
9. Always take things by their smooth handle.
10. When angry, count to ten before you speak, if very angry, count to one hundred.

I would say that President Jefferson was one wise fellow. Don't put stuff off, don't spend money you don't have, think long and hard before you let your anger get the best of you. I think if we practiced these things, our 'tomorrows' would just get better and better.

We leave today with a message from Abraham Lincoln:

"I do the very best I know how – the very best I can; and I mean to
keep doing so until the end. If the end brings me out all right,
what is said against me won't amount to anything.
if the end brings me out wrong, then angels swearing
I was right would make no difference"

Do your best today. Remember right is right, and wrong is wrong. Try your very best not to get them mixed up.

JUNE 17

Our circumstances may change...God does not.

"I Am the Lord your God, I do not change..."
Malachi 3:6

One of the most precious things about our relationship with God is that He does not change. He is forever faithful, forever forgiving, forever compassionate and the list goes on and on. We can count on Him. On the other hand, He can't always count on us. Our emotions sometimes interfere with our reasoning and we can end up being all over the map emotionally. Today I believe, tomorrow I doubt, the next day, well, who knows...I'll have to let you know. God wants us to be as stable as He is. We are all on a journey in this life. Some of us are on our own, but the wise are traveling with God. It can be a very scary, sometimes tearful, sometimes joyful, oftentimes a very lonely journey. Yet, God remains steadfast in our life even on those days when our vision is clouded and we can't see Him or His purposes as clearly as we would like. Fear sometimes blinds us to reality.

"We fear to face some horrible things that once hurt
us, and we stuff it into the black holes of our
unconsciousness where we suppose it won't hurt us.
But it only comes back disguised; it is like a demon
wearing an angel's face. It lays low for a while only
to slug us later, on the sly."
-Lewis Smedes-

We start out with very little faith, but as we learn of Him and travel down some pretty scary roads with God, our faith begins to blossom. Some places I have traveled were because of my own rotten choices. Still He never deserted me. Some days, I walked at His side, and other days He had to drag me to where we were going. He promised to never leave me and He never did. On good days I would have periods of amazing trust and belief, on not so good days there were times of doubt, mistrust and sometimes sheer indifference. There were times when I would have unimaginable glimpses into the heart of God, and dark days when I wondered if He even existed. Thankfully, as the years go by, I can honestly say those dark days have become fewer and fewer. God doesn't have to drag me along quite as much as he used to. I don't kick and scream as much as I used to and I try really hard not to take my hand out of His. When I do, He grabs hold, and never lets it go. He is faithful!

Forever!

"Jesus Christ is always the same, yesterday, today and forever!"
-Hebrews 13:8-

JUNE 18

*Don't let past circumstances be your **excuse** to stay the way you are.*

"From glory to glory..."

Excuses! Excuses! Excuses! I had a whole bag of them and would reach into it whenever the situation presented itself. You have a bag of excuses too, you may not be aware of it, but you do. The most famous excuse is, "The dog ate my homework." How about some others, "I didn't know...", or "I wouldn't have done it if so and so hadn't made me do it." Always loved this one, "It's not my fault." Don't forget, "The devil made me do it." Really? Excuses are just that excuses. They don't deal with reality. They are meant to cast blame away from ourselves. We live in a world today where there is very little accountability for our behavior. I spent many years floating down that old Egyptian river of 'denial.' Not the River Nile, but denial.

"When it comes to accepting the truth about
ourselves, things have not changed much since Adam & Eve."
-Henry Cloud-

The smartest thing we can do it put up the little white flag of surrender. When you realize that God does hold me accountable for my actions and choices, then and only then can I throw away my excuse bag, forever. It's not easy. No one ever said it would be, but the peace you get in return is priceless. Once you choose to live in honesty before God, you will also enjoy an intimacy with Him you may have never known was possible.

"Our 'inner self' doesn't want to dump God entirely,
just keep Him at a comfortable distance."
-Chuck Swindoll-

June 19

Miracles come in cans..."I can"...not "I can't."

"A saint's life is in the hands of God as a bow and arrow in the hands of an archer. God is aiming at something the saint cannot see; He stretches and strains, and every now and again the saint says, I cannot stand any more. But God does not heed; He goes on stretching until His purpose is in sight, then He lets fly."
-Oswald Chambers-

Is your life in the hands of God? If it is, God will begin the repairs necessary, the moment you give your heart and life to Him. C.S. Lewis has said it best, "Imagine yourself as a living house. God comes in to rebuild that house. At first, perhaps, you can understand what He is doing when he is getting the drains right and stopping the leaks in the roof and so on; you knew those jobs needed doing and so you are not surprised. But presently He starts knocking the house about in a way that hurts abominably and does not seem to make any sense. What on earth is He up to? The explanation is that He is building quite a different house from the one you thought of – throwing out a new wing here, putting on an extra floor there, running up towers, making courtyards. You thought you were being made into a decent little cottage; but He is building a palace. He intends to come and live in it Himself."

God has come to live in the heart of every believer. That is a truth that man can hardly fathom, God living in the heart of a man or woman who has surrendered to Him. The Holy Spirit has come to guide and direct us through this life if we will just let Him. God's plan is so inexplicable to the human heart, we don't know the half of it, neither can we fully understand it. We must trust. How glorious God's plan that He sent His only Son, Jesus Christ, who was willing to leave heaven's glory for sinners, give His life as a ransom, paid for our sins, died, was buried in a borrowed grave, and rose again from the dead. He did all of this to give us new life all to save us from the path of destruction that we were once on. Why a borrowed grave? because He didn't plan to be there long. Now that has to make you smile.

"Praise Him for dreaming up such a fantastically innovative, glorious gracious plan whereby you and I can face anything this world can throw at us, not due to our ability, but to His ability through us."
-Bill Gillham-

June 20

What do you do with the swiss cheese moments of life?

"Humility is taught by hardship in the face of obedience.
Humility is tested by the choices we make."
-Tim Burns-

Life is bittersweet at times. There are some very painful times, and then we have some magical moments that make it all worthwhile. Problems happen to each and every one of us. The goal is not to let those problems make 'swiss cheese' out of our lives. Swiss cheese is filled with empty, meaningless holes. There are never any quick fixes to life's problems that are worth anything. Quick fixes are temporary at best. God uses the element of time to change us and to show us how hard life is and how much harder it can get without His presence and His help. He will never leave us content without Him. Never. Misery is when you know that God is dealing with and you run because you know there is something you will have to give up. Contentment in this life can only come when you finally hand over to Him that thing, or things, He is after. You know He's going to get it one way or another. Misery comes from forcing God to take it out of my clenched fists. Something He will do if I force His hand. Our lives are the sum total of our responses to God, whether in obedience or in rebellion. How we respond to God determines much of how our life will go and how He will guide us, either gently or with His rod of correction. Most of us, let how 'we feel' run our lives and influence our decisions. Take chocolate cake for instance. If we ate a piece of chocolate cake and saw that it immediately went to our thighs, if we would have any sense we would give up chocolate cake every night for dessert. Over time, however, we will see not only the chocolate cake, but the potato chips, tacos, hamburgers and ice cream evenly distributed on both thighs and the backside and other places we never knew fat could hide. Lesson: We need to start connecting the dots of life. What we do always has consequences, either good or bad. If we can't get it on our own, I believe God will send someone into our lives that will help us connect the dots. It might not be so fun when they do it. Know this truth, as God helps us to connect the dots, He is loving on us in ways we can only imagine. How do you respond to God when He is after something in your life you don't want to give up? He will make swiss cheese of you if He has to, but He doesn't want to. He would rather you give it up willingly and allow Him to replace it with something spectacular.

JUNE 21

❖

The true measure of a man is what he does when no one is looking...

"I AM the way, I AM the truth, I AM the life."

Are you the same person in secret as you are in public? God wants us to be. God gives specific instructions, not generalities. Follow Me. Listen to Me. Obey Me. Thou shalt. Thou shalt not. Commands, not suggestions and they are all for our protection. Do you follow Him, or tend to wander sometimes? Do you march to different drumbeats, depending on the situation? Some of us are so pig-headed we give God no choice but to bring on the storm. God not only allows, but also sometimes sends trials and hard times. Both can hurt. It is a testimony to God's grace, faithfulness and love that there will be an undeniable difference between the way the child of God gets through the same storm as an unbeliever. Those who are watching will know that there is something awesomely different about you. When sin's consequences start to become a reality in our life, and they will, and when the pain of failure causes such unbearable pain that it causes us to stop and take a long hard look at the path we are traveling, when God has finally got our attention, then and only then, can He begin to change our life and put us back on His path. This is why God doesn't stop the pain right away. Pain is one of life's greatest "attention getters." Not until something hurts badly enough will it cause us to stop and take an inventory of our life and the price that is required of us to follow sin. Sin is very expensive, and pain may be the only way God can get us to listen. So, beware! The moment you hear yourself start to 'rationalize' your behavior, you are headed for trouble with a capital "T." Pain stops us in our tracks more than anything else I know. A wise man learns the lesson from his own pain. If pain brings you closer to God, embrace it, if it takes you farther away from Him, surrender it to Him.

"Be patient and tough; someday this pain will be useful to you."
-Ovid-

June 22

Sometimes there is no other way but 'through.'

"As sure as ever God puts His children into the furnace, He will
be in the furnace with them.
Charles H. Spurgeon

This is best demonstrated in the lives of the three Hebrew children, Shadrach, Meshach and Abednego, who refused to bow down and worship a statue of King Nebuchadnezzar. This enraged the King and he had his strongest men in his kingdom bind the three men and cast them into a burning fiery furnace. The fire was so hot it killed the men who threw the young men into the furnace at the King's command. What happens next borders on the spectacular. When King Nebuchadnezzar looked into the furnace not only did he see four men instead of three, but all were unbound and unhurt. The fourth he proclaimed as a god. The king asks, "Did we not throw three men into the furnace?" He called to the men to come out and called them the servants of the Most High God. These men were miraculously delivered by God. There wasn't even the smell of smoke on them. They would have been obedient unto death. I believe it is because they had determined a head of time to follow God, no matter what it cost them. This isn't always the case that God miraculously delivers us from our enemies. There are still many, in foreign lands, that go to their deaths proclaiming the God of the Bible and His Son Jesus Christ. John the Baptist was beheaded, Peter was crucified upside down. All these men hung on to their faith to the bitter end. As our world changes and God has been taken out of the schools, there is a drive to take Him out of everything in this nation. Job, the most persecuted man of all of history, his words echo down the corridors of time, "Yet though He kill me, I will trust Him." Jesus came to set us free. We are a free nation, and our liberties are slowly being eroded away by ungodly men. We must have determined in our hearts what place does God have in our lives. One day we may shout, as Patrick Henry did, "Give me liberty or give me death."

"Thank you Lord that this has a purpose. You're going to teach me something
of your greatness in this that I would never have known otherwise."
Sandy Edmonson

JUNE 23

Victory is getting up one more time than you have been knocked down...

"This is what I found out about religion: it gives you
courage to make the decisions you must make in a crisis
and the confidence to leave the results to a higher Power.
Only by trust in God can a man carrying responsibility find repose."
-Dwight D. Eisenhower-

"Trials teach us who we are." This was said by the great preacher Charles Spurgeon. No one in their right mind likes trials or wants them in their lives. Unfortunately, Jesus said, "In this world you will have tribulation." Then He tells us to be of good cheer because He has overcome the world. It doesn't get any better than that. What He is telling us is we WIN!

"All things work for good for those who love God. (Romans 8:28) Not
some things or most things but ALL things; so praise Him even in your troubles."
-unknown-

No one suffered as did Jesus. It boggles the mind to think He came into this world to die. His sole purpose was to fulfill the will of God and to die for the sins of the world, for my sins and yours. He was a man of sorrows and yet he still gave His life to ransom us from our sins. He came because there was no other way to save humanity. It took the death of the Son of God to save a lost world and He did it willingly. Always remember that, He did it willingly. No one forced Him. He was not a victim of the Romans or of the Jewish rulers. He was always in control. The Bible says of Him in John 10:17-18, "For this reason the Father loves Me, because I lay down My own life – to take it back again. *No one takes it away from Me.* On the contrary, I lay it down voluntarily. I am authorized and have power to lay it down and I am authorized and have power to take it back again." (AB) Jesus, while hanging on a Roman Cross, looked to the future when we would all be with Him in heaven. It was a price He was willing to pay. We die because we are sinners. Jesus died because He loved us so much He couldn't bear to live without us. He has made heaven our home by His death. On my mother's grave marker are two simple words, "Safely Home." God wants us all safely home, that is why He sent His Son to redeem us from an eternity of hell. He bought back what the devil attempted to steal. Courage comes from knowing who you are in Christ and never forgetting it. As His child He will equip us to face all of life's uncertainty's, not with fear, but with FAITH. Are you headed home? He promises to get you there 'safely' if you are His child. One day we will all be "safely home."

JUNE 24

God's power does not diminish with any turn of events...

I attended a Bible study group for many years at Calvary Church. At one of our luncheons we were asked to find and read something that meant a lot to us. One woman brought something she had written herself about the twenty third Psalm. I have kept a copy of it in my Bible all of these years. First we need to read the 23rd Psalm:

Learning The 23rd Psalm
"The Lord is my Shepherd; I shall not want.
He maketh me to lie down in green pastures; He leadeth me beside the still waters.
He restoreth my soul; He leadeth me in the paths of righteousness for His name's sake.
Yea, though I walk through the valley of the shadow of death, I will fear no evil
for Thou art with me.. Thy rod and thy staff they comfort me.
Thou prepares a table before me in the presence of mine enemies. Thou annointest my head with oil.
My cup runneth over. Surely, goodness and mercy shall follow me all the days of my life
and I will dwell in the house of the Lord forever. - Psalm 23

"I have just walked through the valley of the shadow of death, but I did fear evil. The Lord is my Shepherd, but I did feel want. It is like someone putting a great fortune in the bank for you. If you don't realize it is yours and you don't take it out and use it, you still feel the same wants you always felt. I couldn't lie down in green pastures, I was too busy trying to find my way out of the valley. I didn't have time for still waters, I had too much to worry about. I was too busy watching my enemy to see the table prepared for me. I couldn't take my eyes off the enemy's full cup long enough to observe that mine was overflowing. I was running too fast to realize goodness and mercy following me. I thought the presence I felt behind me was my enemy catching up, so I ran faster until I stumbled and began tumbling toward the cliff of no return. It was then that His rod and staff caught me and pulled me back to safety. Oh, what a relief, what a comfort. Now I take time to enjoy the rhythmic flow of the peaceful still waters. I slow down enough to lie in green pastures and let Him restore my soul. Now I can see the bountiful table, a health giving feast He has prepared for me. I slow down enough to lie in green pastures and let Him restore my soul. Let my enemy have his full cup. Mine is running over. Now I know that when I walked through the valley of the shadow of death, I didn't need to fear for He was with me all the time. Thank God, His mercy and goodness followed me, for now I can truly say, "The Lord is my Shepherd I shall not want and I will dwell in the house of the Lord forever."

-Vivian Langford-

Can I get an AMEN!

JUNE 25

Starting all over again...

"Give unto them beauty for ashes, the oil of joy for mourning,
the garment of praise for the spirit of heaviness."
Isaiah 61:3

A Chinese proverb says, "The man who removes a mountain, begins by carrying away small stones." The more we stand and look at a mountain, or a problem in life, the more overwhelming it will become. Every great accomplishment in life began with a decision to at least try. It isn't important how many times we fall, it's making sure we get up after each fall, especially the last one. We can't do anything about our past, but we can have a brand new finish. God is a God of second, third...a gazillion chances if we promise not to quit and give up. Look at Thomas Edison, the inventor of the light bulb. He lost count how many times he tried, but his secret is he kept going. He used to joke that he knew lots of ways how not to make a light bulb until he finally realized the way to make one. Thank goodness he did or I would be sitting in the dark writing this. Life is hard. God can and will use every experience of our lives to make us whole. He wants us spiritually, emotionally and physically healthy once again. The bad news is, there are no bandaides or quick fixes with God. Healing takes time but He will exchange the ashes of your life for beauty, one day. He will replace your mourning with His oil of joy. Oil is used as a symbol in the Bible for anointing. God is saying He will pour out His oil of joy from your head to your toes if you will hang in there with Him. Last, but not least, this verse in Isaiah promises that God will take that cloak of heaviness off of you one day and replace it with a garment of praise. Where once there was sadness reigning in your life, God will give you a new song. He will give you a song deep within your soul that will praise Him for His deliverance. One day God will right all wrongs, not just some, but all wrongs. The world and you and me will be as God intended before Satan said, "Here, yummy, take a bite." God will get the last word on this earth and before He is done, He will make all things new, us included.

June 26

You are NEVER alone...all you have to do is whisper His name, "Jesus"...

"He heals the brokenhearted and binds up their wounds."
Psalms 147:3

The great preacher, Charles Spurgeon once said, "If He bids us carry a burden, He carries it also" He also said, "If you have a burden on your back, remember prayer, for you shall carry it well if you pray." God is in the healing business. He has been for thousands of years. No one can do it quite like He does. I joke with my son who is a surgeon, "God heals and you collect the money."

If we depended upon man to heal our broken heart, it would remain broken. Where man would have to use crazy glue, God uses His word. He is doing an eternal work in your life, if you will let Him. He does not want us wandering around in the wilderness for even one more day. He wants to bring us to the Promised Land The 'wilderness' is meant to be temporary, but for some of us it has become a permanent dwelling place. The Bible talks about the children of Israel being led out of Egypt by Moses. They were on their way to the Promised Land. God had miraculously intervened in their lives and set them free from the slavery bonds of Pharaoh. You would think that they would have been grateful but they weren't. They murmured, they complained, they were scared. Mostly, they were disobedient. Instead of focusing on the God who had just delivered them from bondage by His divine power, they were focused on their circumstances. This angered God. Oh yes, we can make God angry by our pettiness, our complaining and our ungratefulness, for all He does for us. What happened? Instead of making an 11 day trip from Egypt to the Promised Land it took them almost 40 years! Talk about taking the long way! Don't miss that, it took them 39 years and 11 months and 19 days longer than it should have. Ouch! I have to wonder how a people can be so obstinate, until I look at my own heart. God will deliver us, if we cooperate it will take much less time than if we choose to fight Him every step of the way. Sometimes we all act as if we have no sense at all. We have experienced God's deliverance and then, a few days later, when the next crisis strikes, wonder if He is even exists. Jeremiah says it best:

"The heart is deceitful above all things and
desperately wicked, who can know it."
Jeremiah 19:9 NIV

We all need a heart check-up. Time to make an appointment with the Great Physician.

June 27

Stop worrying...most of it never happens.

Let us continue today with the story of the Israelites in the wilderness. God placed the Israelites in an impossible situation and then provided 'everything' they needed to make a safe journey. They didn't deserve it, but then again neither do we. Now, I don't blame them for being scared. I would have been too. They had just come out of Egypt, having survived the death angel, and here they are up against the Red sea with nowhere to go. The Egyptian army was in hot pursuit behind them, very sorry they had let God's people go. It looks like they hadn't learned any lessons from the last few days, either. Think of the Israelites predicament with impassable water in front of them and the enemy behind them. God put them into a position where they were shut in on all sides and no options. Don't miss this truth, it was who God brought them to this place. Have you ever felt surrounded by the enemy on all sides? Only a miracle could save God's people and that's exactly what God gave them, despite their unbelief. Did they really think God was going to dump them in the desert and leave them to fend for themselves. I'll bet it crossed His mind a time or two. But, it is not God's nature to abandon us, ever, even when we seem to have left all common sense behind.

I'm sure you know the rest of the story. Moses raised his rod, God parted the Red Sea and the Israelites walked across DRY land to safety on the other side. God didn't just do a miracle He did the 'spectacular.' Pharaoh's army still in pursuit was drowned, every last one of them. God will destroy our enemies too, if we will hang in there with Him. I wish I could tell you that everybody lived happily ever after, but I can't. The people still doubted and mistrusted God, He got angry and decided to take them the really LONG way to the promise land so he could teach them a thing or two. It would take them 40 years before they learned. Forty years is a very long time in obedience school. Those who were in unbelief never did make it to the promise land. They died before they reached it. Only their descendants were allowed to enter. What is the lesson to be learned? God will deal with our rebellion and we probably won't like His methods.

June 28

*What causes us more heartache, the things we have done
or the things we failed to do?*

I'm not sure any of us can really answer that question. Both can cause a boatload of heartache and regret and have. If given the opportunity to live our lives over again, what changes would each of us make? If we knew the end of the story, how it would all turn out, I know I would have lived my life much differently. Instead of looking to others or the world to satisfy the deep longings of my heart, I would have gone instead to the Cross of Jesus Christ. There I would have found more love for me than I could ever have grabbed ahold of. There I would have found a Savior willing to give His own life just to save mine. There I would have realized, one day I would be heading home, to God's home, heaven. God desires us to live a balanced and a stable life while on this earth, a life that is not dependent on circumstances.

> "God created us with a need to be fed and filled, yet our
> desires seemingly go unmet. In striving to find fulfillment, our
> longings may swing wildly out of balance into realms of addiction.
> Left unchecked, our misplaced contentment crashes into our
> empty lives as we attempt to fill up on treasures that devastate not
> only our pocketbooks, but also our souls."
> -Marsha Crockett-

If we could have a 'do over,' I don't think any of us would live life trying to accumulate more 'stuff.' I do think we would be kinder, and more understanding to others. I believe we would work harder at making relationships work, instead of packing up our anger and resentment in a suit case, and walking away. We would not have lived life selfishly. We would strive to do God's will instead of our own. We probably would not have fought with God, every time He tried to change something in our life that was wrong. We would have obeyed God, knowing He only had our best interests at heart. The good news is, you can start to do all of those things now. The past is the past. You can't change it, but you can change your future, starting right now. With every repentant heart, God gives us a new 'want to.'

> "If you stay connected to Him, if you draw spiritual nourishment
> from Him, if you allow the power that flows through Him to flow
> through you, nothing will hold you back from reaching the most
> abundant life possible."
> –Bruce Wilkinson-

How can we stay connected to God? Start your day off with Him. Make time for Him early on and the rest of your day will flow. Spend time in His word and in prayer. A prayerless life is a powerless life.

June 29

You're in the army now...

*"Onward Christian soldiers, marching on to war.
With the Cross of Jesus, going on before."
-Sabine Baring-Gould 1869-*

What???? I'm in the army?? If there ever was a place I never wanted to be, it would be in the army. I don't like fighting, I don't like guns and I especially don't like getting up early in the morning. In fact, I think I prefer guns to getting up early. So, you can imagine my surprise when a fellow Christian told me that the day I gave my life to Jesus Christ, I was inducted into the army of God. Involuntarily, I might add. The only thing worse than being inducted into the army is being ignorant of the spiritual battle that is raging in this world of ours and pretending it doesn't exist. Every day of our lives, Satan is trying his best to destroy us. Think of all the families and marriages Satan destroys each and every day. All you have to do is look at divorce statistics, the suicide rate, or the drug and alcohol casualties, to know we have a very dangerous enemy.

*"The devil roams about like a roaring lion,
seeking anyone he can devour."*
1 Peter 5:8 LB

Notice the word 'devour.' What an awful word. Notice the word 'anyone.' That includes you and me, our family, children, and friends. God knows, there are others like me who would not voluntarily enlist, so He does it for us. He does it, not to scare us, but to protect us. War is hell and Christians are at war with hell itself, but first we have to settle the battle between God and ourselves. He never asks, "Shall we do it your way or My way?" Yet, if we were honest with ourselves we do think we should be able to offer up our opinions. Inside each one of us there is just enough rebellion towards God to get us into real trouble. When a serviceman enters the Army, Navy, Airforce or Marines, the first thing he is required to do is 'surrender.' Total surrender! So it is with the Christian soldier, we are no longer in charge, God is. His enemy becomes our enemy. I take my orders from Him now. His battle plan now becomes my battle plan. Good news! It may not seem like it some days, but WE WIN! No matter how many times I read the last page of God's Word, we still WIN!

June 30

When your heart begins to lose hope, it will also begin to lose strength.

"The Lord is my strength and shield. I trust Him with all
of my heart. He helps me, and my heart is filled with joy.
I burst out in songs of thanksgiving."
Psalm 28:7 NLT

What steals our joy? The enemy! We war, not against flesh and blood (other humans), but against rulers, authorities and those mighty powers of darkness (Ephesians 6:12). These are unseen enemies, demons who like Satan were cast out of heaven for defying God. Ever since that day there is a battle that has been raging in the spiritual realm. Satan uses deceit, trickery and half-truths to defeat us. The battle begins in each one of our minds. We must have a plan ahead of time to defeat the devil. He has his strategies in place in order to bring us down. Strategies are well thought out plans. He uses schemes to wreck and ruin our lives and the lives of those we love. He uses trickery to get us going in a direction we never intended to go. Don't pass over that word trickery too fast. It makes us think something is real when it is not. Satan sets a trap for us because he knows each one of our weaknesses. He doesn't bother to tempt us to rob a bank because he knows we will not. He will tempt us to tell a lie, or to spend too much money, buy now, pay later. I know I fell for that one. He will tempt us to take a drink. "Just take one drink, that never hurt anybody," and an alcoholic is born. Whatever opportunity we give the devil, he will take it. In fact, he will pounce on it. His attacks are well thought out and he has been watching our every move. He has been in the deceiving business since Adam and Eve. He successfully deceived one-third of God's angels to follow him. His deception has no limits, no boundaries. If he can get us to tell a lie, a little white lie, we have opened the door for him in our life. Irony of it all, is first Satan tempts us to do wrong and then when we do, he then becomes our accuser. "Look what you've done. Boy, you have really blown it now, God will never forgive you." Lie! Lie! Lie! Our joy is gone if we believe him. Or we can believe God when He says, "If you confess your sins, He is faithful and just to forgive us our sins and to cleanse us from *ALL* unrighteousness.

July 1

Never let a child down that is depending on you. Never.

Let Me Guide A Little Child
Dear Lord, I do not ask
That Thou shouldst give me some high work of Thine,
Some noble calling, or some wondrous task.
Give me a little hand to hold in mine.
Give me a little child to point the way
Over the strange, sweet paths that lead to Thee.
Give me a little voice to teach to pray,
Give me the shining eyes Thy face to see.
The only crown I ask, dear Lord to wear
Is this: That I may teach a little child.
I do not ask that I may ever stand
Among the wise, the worthy, or the great;
I only ask that softly, hand in hand,
A child and I may enter at the Gate.
-unknown-

There is no higher calling in life than that of a parent. It has been said that "The hand that rocks the cradle, rules the world." We will never know the power of a praying mom or dad this side of eternity. I do not know anyone in my life who has prayed for me more than my beloved mother did. No one. She never gave up. She had an uncanny ability to know when her children were in trouble and she would immediately go to Jesus with her heavy heart. That uncanny ability was the power of the Holy Spirit in deep fellowship with her spirit. It hurts my heart to hear some woman say, "I'm just a housewife." There is no higher calling than raising godly children.

"More things are wrought by prayer, than this world dreams of…"
Alfred, Lord Tennyson

Children are a gift from God. Blessed is the man whose quiver is full, says the Bible. God has entrusted to us an awesome blessing and responsibility which we should take very seriously.

"But whoever causes one of these little ones who believe in Me to sin,
it would be better for him to have a large millstone
hung around his neck and to be drowned in the depths of the sea."
Matthew 18:6

July 2

Help if you can...

"To be happy, you must first make others happy."
Swedish Proverb

Pride says, "Well, what about me?" What about you? The secret is finding the balance between the two. God expects us to take care of ourselves, both physically and mentally, so that we may help others. A well-balanced life is spiritual warfare. Satan loves it when we are off balance in life. He does his best to get us to fall. He lies to us, "This is good, so it must be of God." Not always true. Sometimes God takes us by way of the hard path, the one less traveled. Hell sings in glee when we run from God, when we insist on our way, when we try to get rid of the pain in life with medications or alcohol. He even likes it when we try to please others, because he knows we can't always do that and sometimes we shouldn't. The devils dance when we go to bed concentrating on all of our problems instead of God's solutions. They run when we stop to lend a helping hand, because then we are showing God's character to the world when we care for others. Want to know what really makes the devil mad? It's when we love our enemies. He knows the only way we can do that is by the power of God in us. If we will meet another's need, then God will meet ours. The greatest thing about helping someone else is you can't be focused on them and yourself at the same time. Where is your focus?

July 3

Never doubt in the darkness, what God has revealed in the light...

"Who among you fears the Lord and obeys His servant? If such
a man *walks in darkness, without one ray of light*, let them trust
the Lord, let them rely upon their God. But see here, you who
live in your own light and warm yourselves from your
own fires and not from God's; you will live among sorrows."
Isaiah 50:10 LB

This is such a powerful scripture. As Christians, every day we should be walking in the light of God's word, eager to learn more about Him. We discover who He is and all that He promises. Our faith grows and we become strong in the Lord. It is easy walking in the light. Rarely, do we stumble or fall. Then suddenly the lights go out in our life and we are thrust into darkness. If you have never been there as a child of God, just wait, you will. It is a time of uncertainty and doubt. God has veiled Himself from us. We don't know why, we just know we are painfully alone, in reality we really aren't, but we think we are. We cry, "Where are you God?" He is where He has always been. He has not moved, I have, the moment I cast doubt on my God. God wants us so firmly rooted in our faith that what we have learned in His glorious light we *will not forget* when the candle goes out. We are to be unshakeable, no matter how dark it gets. He wants us to know that He will turn the lights on in His due time, not mine. The rest of this scripture speaks about how dangerous it is to light your own fire to get out of the darkness. God says if you live in your own light you will live among sorrows. Our way is usually the worst way out because it is always the easy path. Instead of relying on God's power to deliver us from the darkness we come up with our own plan. Someone has said, "If you do not have clear direction from God or know what to do, do nothing." Trust that He is nearby and will deliver you. When Daniel was thrown into the lion's den he did not go in kicking and screaming, neither did he focus on the lions. His eyes were upon his God the whole time. He didn't sit in a corner of the den, shaking in his boots. No, He knew his God was faithful. God then shut the mouths of the lions and protected Daniel. There were many observers that day, including the King who threw him in the den for refusing to stop worshipping and praying to Jehovah God.

"God delights to increase the faith of His children.
We ought, instead of wanting no trials before victory,
no exercise for patience, to be willing to take them from God's
hand as a means. Trials, obstacles, difficulties, and
sometimes defeats, are the very food of faith."
George Muller

Remember! Daniel was prepared to die rather than stop worshiping God.

JULY 4

Truth can pack a real wallop...

"You shall know the truth, and the truth shall make you *free*."
John 8:32

Who doesn't want to be free? One of the most powerful proclamations Jesus ever made was "I AM the TRUTH..." It wasn't just something He practiced, it was His very nature. He is called the living Word of God. When you meet Him you have come face to face with truth. Truth demands a decision, belief or unbelief. Truth will be attacked and often viciously. It is not a question of 'if' but 'when.' As a soldier in the army of God you must be ready.

"If I profess with the loudest voice and clearest exposition every portion of the truth of God except precisely that little point which the world and the devil are at that moment attacking, I am not confessing Christ, however boldly I may be professing Christ. Where the battle rages, there the loyalty of the soldier is proved; and to be steady on all the battlefield besides, is mere flight and disgrace if he flinches at that point."
Martin Luther

On the battlefield of life, truth is a hard fought battle. Many have opposed God's truth in the past and many still do today. As a Christian you will NEVER fight a battle alone. NEVER. God is with us every step of the way. Our world is changing every day. Right has become wrong and wrong has become right. God addresses this in Isaiah 5:20; "Woe to those who call evil good and good evil, who put darkness for light and light for darkness, who put bitter for sweet and sweet for bitter." "Woe," is a very powerful word. It is a word of judgment on an individual who does these things, There is no escape from 'woe.' What was once viewed in America as unacceptable by society is now not only accepted, but encouraged. What was once done in the back alleys of America is now done on Main Street. The Ten Commandments, which once graced the walls of every school in America, have been taken down one by one because a few found them to be offensive. In its place metal gun detectors have risen. There is a bitter fight raging today to remove the Pledge of Allegiance from the schools. "One nation under God," has become offensive to many. Why? Because if there is a God, then He is *ultimate authority* and man is not free to do whatever he thinks is right. We are held to God's standards not men's. The Ten Commandments were not 'suggestions' they were commands of God for us to follow for our own protection. "Thou shalt not murder" has been removed and recently a devastating shooting and murder of small children took place at Sandyhook Elementary School in Newtown, Connecticut. When we as a nation turn our backs on God and His Word, we are headed for calamity. Evil will be out of control once it is unleashed.

"The face of the Lord is against those who do evil, to cut off the remembrance of them from the earth. When the righteous cry for help, the Lord hears, and delivers them out of *all* their distress and troubles. The Lord is close to the brokenhearted and saves those who are crushed with sorrow for sin and are humbly and thoroughly repentant. Many evils confront the righteous, but the Lord delivers him out of them *ALL*"
Psalms 34:16-19

July 5

*Stop running. There are two people you will
never be able to outrun...God and yourself.*

"The younger son said to his father, "Father *give me* my share of the estate." So, he divided his property between them. Not long after, the younger son got together all that he had and set off for a far country, and there he squandered his wealth in riotous living."
Luke 15:12-14

Have you ever taken a trip to the 'far country? "Where is that? you might be asking. It is anywhere you choose to go and God is not welcome. It is a place of misery. Oh, it may not seem like it at first. The 'far country' could be a mansion in Beverly Hills or it could be in the projects of Chicago. God is not welcome and He knows it. It's a place where Frank Sinatra sang about, a place where, "I did it my way." Sin always looks good at first, but in the end it leads to our destruction. Sin is no respecter of persons. Its consequences are deadly for both rich and poor, young and old, male or female. The 'far country' is where the Prodigal son lived for a while. He said, "Father give me...", that always ends badly when we start our request with 'give me.' His father gave him his inheritance that had been saved for him. It's well to note that this father did not try to stop him. He let him go. His heart was grieved, but he let him go. There are many times in my life I wish God would not have allowed me to make such dumb choices. Yet, He does allow us to choose, whether we chose right or we choose wrong, He allows it to be our decision. The prodigal son wanted it his way, and he got it. He wanted to be captain of his own ship, not realizing it was going to sink one day. He sailed off into the sunset, singing and laughing all the way to the 'far country.' Until one day there was a severe famine. He had left his Father's house, craving independence and the 'good life.' His father gave him his inheritance and didn't stop him. The son had no mind for the future, it was only what he could get out of the here and now. The Bible says 'riotous living' was his desire. He shook off all parental and heavenly authority and went and did his own thing. He had lots of money and lots of friends, at least, until his lots of money was gone and so were his 'friends.' All alone, he found himself broke, tired, hungry and jobless. Finally, he was able to get a job feeding swine. He was so hungry he tried to eat the hogs food, but they would beat him to it. You know you have really hit rock bottom when the swine can outsmart you. Finally, he came to his senses. He longed for home. He thought to himself, even my father's servants are living better than I am, I will arise and go to my father's house and become a servant, I am no longer worthy to be his son. Best decision he ever made and it was made in pain. The great thing about it, we can all go home if we find ourselves in the pigpen like this boy did. All we have to do is come to our senses. The boy's father sees the lad coming down a dirt road from afar off. He doesn't say, "Boy, I'll fix him. I'll teach him what happens when you defy your father." No, his father ran to meet him, and hugged and kissed him. Remember, the boy was dirty and stinky, he smelled more like a pig than a human, but the father didn't care because the boy was his son. What the father did next, defies logic. He threw the biggest party ever! He gave the boy a ring, in those days only given to sons. He gave him a robe and new shoes. He killed the fatted calf and they rejoiced at the boys return. You might be asking, why wasn't he punished? He was, the whole time he was in the far country he felt the sting of the consequences of the life he had chosen 'away from his father.' It's the same with us. God says, "Please, come home, just as you are." He will clean you up and restore you as a son of the Most High God. Wow! That's amazing. Amazing grace. What are you waiting for?

July 6

Pray! Expect an answer...

The answer to your prayer might not be what you had expected, but if you leave the answer to the Lord it will be exactly what you need.

"I asked God for strength that I might achieve;
I was made weak that I might learn humbly to obey.
I asked for help that I might do greater things;
I was given infirmity that I might do better things.
I asked for riches that I might be happy;
I was given poverty that I might be wise.
I asked for all things that I might enjoy life;
I was given life that I might enjoy all things.
I was given nothing I asked for;
But everything that I had hoped for.
Despite myself, my prayers were answered;
I am among all men most richly blessed.
An unknown Confederate Soldier

How many prayers do we pray, not really expecting God to answer? Why bother to pray then if you don't expect an answer? Isn't it time we started believing He will answer? Mary and Martha sent a message to Jesus that their brother Lazarus was very sick. Instead of returning to Bethany, Jesus stayed in the town he was in. It appeared to the sisters that Jesus had not only not answered their prayer to come, but it looked like He ignored them. They asked for healing from a sickness, He was preparing to give them a miracle that bordered on the Spectacular! He gave them something much greater, a resurrection! There was never a question after that whether Jesus had the power to bring a man back to life again. He had done it right before their eyes. There were witnesses that day who were stunned into silence at His power. There were religious rulers who saw His miracles and plotted to put Him to death. So, don't get discouraged when you pray and it seems that the heavens are silent. If they are, it is only temporary. Your miracle is on its way and it might just be wrapped up in the spectacular too.

"I never had any difficulty believing in
miracles, since I experienced the miracle
of a change in my own heart."
Augustine of Hippo

July 7

Why do we believe God can do it for someone else, but not for me?

"He is able to do exceedingly, abundantly, above and beyond anything I could ever think, dream or ask."

Dream the unthinkable! Believe the unimaginable! Think BIG! We have a BIG awesome God who loves to bless His children. You may be saying to yourself, "But, I'm not worthy." and you are right. None of us are worthy, but He blesses us because of who He is, not because of who we are or what we have done. The most magnificent day of a person's life, in my opinion, is the day we realize that Jesus is who He says He is and at that very moment changes our lives and our final destination. People can argue the facts of the Bible over and over and disagree, but no one can explain the transformation of an unbeliever to a believer. Only God can change a heart. How does a drug addict suddenly become clean, a prostitute change her ways, it is by the love of God. His mercy and grace shine down on a life and they are forgiven and changed forever. How can anyone explain the life of Saul of Tarsus who became Paul the Apostle, they cannot apart from God's divine intervention. Saul was a murderer of Christians. He believed in his heart he was doing the will of God. Was he? No, he was deceived by religion. Then one day he met Jesus. His life was never the same. Instead of the pursuer he became the pursued. The religious crowd now wanted to kill him. Eventually, he would die, but not before becoming the Apostle to the gentile world.

Paul's journeys brought the good news to my ancestors and yours. Once alienated from God we were brought into the family of God by God's grace. Paul wanted a relationship with God but was going about it all wrong. God put a stop to it very abruptly one day on the Road to Damascus. If a man's heart is sincerely bent towards God, He will move heaven and earth to save that man.

"God often takes a course for accomplishing His purposes directly contrary to what our narrow views would prescribe. He brings a death upon our feelings, wishes and prospects when He is about to give us the desires of our heart."
-John Newton-

July 8

The thrill of the moment of sin is <u>never</u> worth the pain it brings later.

"The wages of sin is death, but the free gift of God
is eternal life in Jesus Christ our Lord."
Romans 6:23

"Sin is a Trojan horse out of which comes a whole army of troubles."
-Thomas Watson-

The moment we really understand this principle from God's word, we will save ourselves tons of **future** sorrow and pain. There is always a pay day right around the corner. There are consequences to every choice we make in life. Good choices, good life, bad choices, bad life. You cannot defy God's laws by sowing bad seed and expecting a good result, yet many of us do.

"Why is God so extremely severe in dealing with sin? Simply because sin
is a broken law, a broken relationship, a broken fellowship and it produces a broken life."
-Judson Cornwall-

Let's face it. Sin can be fun. However, it is only fun for a while. It would be disingenuous to tell anyone otherwise. Sin can be fun, but the consequences can be deadly. The consequences can last a short time or they can last a lifetime. We are free to sin, but it is God who chooses our consequences and they will be tailor made just for us. We will not like God's answer to us for our rebellion. In fact, the pain from the consequences can readily exceed any pleasure we might have felt during the sinning. God will never leave us happy and satisfied in our sin. NEVER. Sin affects everything around us. Look at Adam and Eve. Their sin devastated the whole world. Their son Cain killed his brother. Can you imagine how Adam and Eve felt when they were told Able was dead, at the hands of his own brother? They had not known what death was except when God killed an animal to make a covering for their shame and nakedness. They came face to face with death in their own family for the very first time, it rocked their world. It has rocked our world ever since. In fact, sin has turned our world upside down and inside out.

"Temptation is not a sin, yielding is."
-Billy Sunday-

We don't want to completely turn our backs on God for fear we may really need Him someday. No, what we attempt to do is keep Him at a safe distance. At least, that's what we think we are doing. How can you possibly think you are keeping God at a safe distance when He is both Omniscient and Omnipotent? He knows all. He is everywhere and He has the power to destroy us in a heartbeat. We are always one heartbeat away from eternity.

JULY 9

"Ouch! God, what are You doing?" Pain will usually get our attention...

"Out of pain and problems have come the sweetest songs,
the most poignant poems, the most gripping stories." -Billy Graham-

What is your story? We all have one. if you are a Christian you have a testimony, or maybe you just have the monies. Our story starts the day we were born and will continue throughout eternity with a brief and temporary interruption called death. We close our eyes on this side of heaven to open them on the other side to the face of God... if you are His child. The pain and suffering we have experienced on this earth will pale in the light of the glory of heaven. Avoiding as much pain as we can is human nature. God, however, does not allow us to avoid all pain.

"We spend our whole lives trying to avoid anything that will hurt or be hard. But there's a better
kind of life – a deeper, more fulfilling kind of life that isn't about avoiding every pain. It's about
finding God faithful and powerful in the midst of whatever thorns He allows." -James MacDonald-

Suffering is just a part of life. We have suffered, we are suffering or suffering is right around the corner or down the road a bit. The good news is suffering never comes to us without an abundance of God's grace right on suffering's heels. The soul cries out to God, "God, I can't stand the pain anymore," God answers, "My grace is sufficient for thee." And so it is, just like it was for the Apostle Paul when he cried out to God three times to remove this thorn in his life that God had allowed. God allowing thorns and other things that cause us great pain is a hard concept for both the believer and the unbeliever to understand, but nevertheless, it is true. It is sometimes easier to understand why we suffer when we have sinned, done something stupid and are merely experiencing the painful results of our disobedience. What's terribly hard to understand is when you have tried to obey God, you have done your very best and yet God has allowed a very difficult trial for you to go through. The unbeliever would say, "There is no God." or "He doesn't care about what's happening to me." The believer on the other hand, would fall on their knees before the KING of kings and LORD of lords and ask for understanding. If none came, trust enters the picture. You cannot trust someone you do not know so trust will never work for the unbeliever. They are left to find an answer on their own. They don't know God, by choice. There is great peace in realizing you don't have all of the answers and you never will. We will have what God reveals to us, nothing more. Everything else is speculation on our part. The believer need never speculate. If his or her questions go unanswered they know the God of the universe who has the answers and will reveal them in His time and according to His wisdom. Some things He will never reveal to us this side of glory. Peace comes with accepting that. Job had no idea why he was suffering so much yet believed and still he could say, "Even though He slay me, yet in my flesh I shall see God."

"Those whom God uses most effectively have been hammered,
filed, and tempered in the furnace of trials and heartaches."
-Charles Swindoll-

Can God be trusted? Well, can He? Do you trust Him sometimes or do you trust Him all of the time? He longs to teach you to trust Him, regardless of your circumstances.

July 10

Run your own life...not others.

"But Jesus did not commit Himself unto them, because He
knew all men, and needed not that any should testify of man;
for He knew what was in man."
John 2:24-25

This is a sobering lesson to learn today. There is a good reason Jesus has told us not to judge others. We are not capable of judging others. Only Jesus knows what is in the heart of a man, I don't, you don't, none of us do and we never will. We cannot judge another man's heart. We may see another man's actions, but we do not know the 'why' behind those actions. On the other hand, we are called to be fruit inspectors of other's lives. Jesus said, "By their fruit you will know them." Jesus has given us a way to tell the make believers from the believers without casting judgment.

"The reason we see hypocrisy and fraud and unreality in others is because
they are all in our own hearts. The great characteristic of a saint is humility –
yes, all those things and other evils would have been manifested in me
but for the grace of God, therefore I have no right to judge."
-Oswald Chambers-

The longer I live, the more I too have come to understand that it is only by God's grace that I survive each and every day. Once I gave my heart to Jesus, He has held my hand and never let go. His grace saved me, and His grace keeps me. He can do the same for you if you will let Him.
He asks us to leave the judgment of the world to Him.

"The coming again of Christ will be a vindication
of the moral order of the universe and a revelation of God's
sovereign purpose in history."
-William Fitch-

July 11

Praise God in everything!

"Let everything that has breath, PRAISE the Lord."
Psalms 150:6

Do you have breath? Then Praise Him! Praise is one of the highest forms of spiritual warfare. Praise Him whether you feel like it or not. Praise Him especially when you want to give up. He will give you strength not to. Praise Him with a heavy heart if you have to and it won't remain heavy for long. Praise is the clearest and most direct means by which you declare your utter dependence on God. You and I can do nothing without Him. Praise causes the enemy to flee and the darkness turns to light. Praise does not depend on emotions. Praise will glorify and magnify God. Praise has the power to place our focus back on God and take it off of our problems. Praise humbles us. There is only one God, and we are not Him. It gives us a clearer view of ourselves, our weaknesses, our need for God to intervene in our lives. Asking for God's help goes against everything within us. It hurts our pride and ego. Praise says, as nothing else can, "I can't do it alone, God I need you." Moreover, Praise honors God. Even if all we can do is say, "Help! Lord", He will hear. The more we get to know Him, the more we realize just how awesome He is. Charles Spurgeon has said it best:

"Look at the very birds on earth – how they shame us!
Dear little creatures, if you watch them when they
are singing, you will sometimes wonder how so much
sound can out of such diminutive bodies.
How they throw their whole selves into the music,
and seem to melt themselves away in song!
How the wing vibrates, the throat pulsates, and every
part of their body rejoices to assist the strain!
This is the way in which we ought to praise God."
Charles Spurgeon

Praise opens up our hearts to heaven itself. It stirs something holy within us to desire to live as we ought, wholly and separated unto Him! It has been said that if a heart is praising, it will be impossible to complain at the same time. Praise establishes our faith on a firm foundation, a foundation that cannot be moved. The greater we see God, the smaller our problems become.

"Praising God is one of the highest and purest
acts of religion. In prayer we act like
men; in praise we act like angels."
Thomas Watson

JULY 12

Be still. Be balanced. So when the ground beneath you shakes, you won't.

Life is all about choices. Good choices produce a good life. Bad choices give us a longing in our heart, a spiritual ache so devastatingly painful it can paralyze us. A tooth ache hurts, but it can eventually be fixed. How do you know if you have a spiritual ache? Read the list below and be honest with yourself: Do you have any of these.

A heart that is empty.
A heart that yearns for more.
A heart that knows there is more.
A heart that is in want.
A heart in sin.
A heart longing to be free.
A heart that looks for an answer, other than God.
A heart that says what it pleases.
A heart that keeps score in life.
A heart that has no time.
A heart that does what it pleases.
A heart that cares only for self.
A heart full of fear and doubt.
A heart that is dishonest with God, others and self.
A heart that has lost its song.
A heart that has forgotten what's important in life.

Do you have any of these symptoms of a 'spiritual ache?' A heart with no answers, no faith, no direction, no light, no truth, hungry for God and you don't even know it? Then there is good news for you. God is just a prayer away. Sitting on ready to help you, but first you must admit you need help. He says, "Call upon Me in your time of trouble, I will hear and I will answer." He will put that song back in your heart once again. He will take away all fear and doubt and replace it with His peace and hope. Our heart is like a jigsaw puzzle and we were born with one big piece missing. He is that piece. Until He comes into your heart you will always feel as if something is missing because it is. His name is JESUS.

July 13

Never give up.
-Winston Churchill-

I read a story years ago where Winston Churchill was invited to speak at a private all-boys school he had attended in his younger years. The school was very excited to have such a famous man coming to speak. The awe and anticipation of his speech was palpable in the air. The day finally arrived. The larger than life, Mr. Churchill was said to have walked up to the podium, looked out into the young faces of his audience, pounded his fist on the podium and very loudly shouted, "Never give up! Never give up! No, never give up.!" He then sat down. Of course the audience was speechless. They had expected a long winded speech from the great man. Instead, he delivered words he had lived by which changed the world. Almost singlehandedly, England with Churchill's help stood its ground against Hitler's invasion. If it weren't for the tenacity and wisdom of Churchill we would all be goose stepping. There is nothing harder than holding on with everything you have and regardless of what comes against you, never giving up. Hold onto truth. Hold onto what you know is the right path regardless of the opposition that is mounted against it. For a man to do nothing is the equivalent of condoning the evil.

> "Not to oppose error, is to approve of it, and not to
> defend truth is to suppress it, and indeed to neglect
> to confound evil men, when we can do it, is no less
> sin than to encourage them."
> Pope Felix III

"It is men, not God, who have produced racks, whips, prisons, slavery, guns, bayonets, and bombs; it is by human avarice or human stupidity, not by the churlishness of nature, that we have poverty and overwork." – C.S. Lewis.

JULY 14

❋

Time doesn't heal. God does, but He uses time.

"Yesterday is history. Tomorrow is a mystery. And today?
Today is a **gift**. That's why we call it the present."
-Babatunde Olatunji-

It has been said that time heals. God is our healer, but He uses time. He rarely does things instantaneously because there are lessons we must learn during the healing process. God's healing always begins on the inside of us. We can fix things up ourselves on the outside, a new hairdo, new clothes, we lose some weight, but these are only temporary. God's changes are permanent. He reaches deep down into the heart and soul of man. When we reach inside, we find empty places we fill with alcohol, sex or drugs, and we remain empty. We will try anything to make the pain go away, anything but facing the truth. God wants to fill us with Himself so we won't have any need for those other things.

"When I was a child, I laughed and wept,
Time crept.
When, as a youth, I dreamed and talked,
Time walked.
When I became a full grown man,
Time ran.
And later, as I older grew.
Time flew.
Soon I shall find, while traveling on,
Time gone.
Will Christ have saved my soul by then?
Inscription on clock Chester Cathedral

Loss is a place to start over, not give up. Don't waste one more second grieving something you can't change or never get back. Let it go! Is it easy? No. Will it be worth it? Yes! God does not want you to be miserable for one more day. Give Him your sorrow and let Him begin to heal you. He is more than ready to heal you and do something new in your life, but first you must let go. Don't waste any more of your life. If you will come to Him with empty hands, He will fill you beyond your wildest imagination.

JULY 15

Nothing to lose...everything to gain.

"For what will it profit a man if he gains the whole world and loses his own soul? Or what would a man give as an exchange for his life?"
Matthew 16:26

Jesus is the One who asked these questions. That puts a whole new importance on it, doesn't it? Are you living with His eternal perspective of life and what follows our time spent here on this earth, or are you living for the here and now? What would you exchange your life for here that is more important than your eternal soul? These are very sobering questions. Jesus made it very clear that we are the ones who choose, not only what we do with our lives, but where we will ultimately spend eternity. We are all eternal beings, whether believer or unbeliever. The difference is spending eternity with Jesus or without Him. So, the real question is what would you trade a relationship with Jesus for in this life?

"He who provides for this life, but takes no care for eternity,
is wise for a moment, but a fool forever."
John Tillotson

The Bible says, "The fool has said in his heart there is no God." The fool who lives his life as if God does not exist is an even bigger fool. It is wise to note that the Holy Scriptures begin with Genesis 1:1, "In the beginning God..." It declares that He is. It makes no argument for His existence.

July 16

Always remember to say thank you. Didn't Jesus heal 10 lepers?

"As He entered a village, there, ten lepers stood at a distance, crying out, "Jesus, Master, have mercy on us!" He looked at them and said, "Go show yourselves to the priests." And as they went their leprosy disappeared. One of them, when he saw that he was healed, came back to Jesus, shouting, "Praise God I am healed!" He fell face down on the ground at Jesus' feet thanking Him for what He had done." This man was a Samaritan. Jesus asked, "Didn't I heal ten men?" Where are the other nine?"
Luke 17:12

Every time I read this scripture about Jesus healing the 10 lepers and *only one* came back to thank Him, I think to myself which leper would I have been? In Jesus day anyone with Leprosy was required to yell, "Unclean!" if they came close to anyone. They were isolated from their own families and friends because of this deadly disease. There was no cure for Leprosy in those days. Unclean, was a warning for others to stay away from the Leper. In today's society we won't even go around anyone with a cold, much less Leprosy, but Jesus did. Jesus answered their cries for mercy. He sent the lepers to the Priest *before they were healed*, so each step they took, they took in faith that He would heal them. As they walked they were healed. Would I have believed He would heal before I saw any evidence of it? I don't know. I wish I did but I can't say for sure. It is a real soul searching question, isn't it? I pray that my faith can be so strong and so sure that when Jesus speaks, I believe and obey whatever He says, whether it makes sense to me or not.

> "I believe that when we are in the midst of even the worst of
> life's storms, our reaction as children of the King should be
> to thank God, for it may be that He allowed the very trauma
> we are going through at the moment for the purpose of preventing
> us from going through storms that might well destroy us or hinder
> us in doing what He has called us to do. That, friends, is a miracle in and of itself."
> -Mac Brunson-

I believe a Christian can know they truly trust God when their first response to trouble is thanksgiving. Only a sincere heart can praise and obey, while it is hurting.

July 17

Hurting people hurt people.

Pain often means something is wrong. Pain in our body tells us we need to see a doctor. Pain in our heart tells us we need to see the Great Physician, God Himself. Do you need to make a doctor's appointment with heaven? We could save ourselves and others a lot of grief and sorrow if we could just understand that 'hurt people, hurt people.' Maybe they do it intentionally, but then on the other hand maybe they don't. Consider the animal that has been physically abused, he will bite, even if approached by a kind and caring person. How easy it is for us, as human beings, if we have a bad day, to come home and take it out on those we love. Harsh words, or deafening silence, slamming of doors or withdrawal. Many of us do not know how to properly handle the disappointments in life. We think life should be fair, but it is not and it will never be.

> "God whispers to us in our pleasures,
> speaks to us in our conscience,
> but shouts to us in our pain.
> It is His megaphone to rouse a deaf world."
> C.S. Lewis

Are we listening? Can you hear the pain of others? When you ask someone how they are, do you listen closely to their response? If you will take the time to really listen to what they are saying, they will tell you exactly what they need. Who doesn't need understanding when they are hurting? It is a wise person who considers that the harsh words spoken by another are because of some trial or sorrow they are experiencing in life. Maybe, they just lost their job, or a child is sick, or a mother has died. We can choose how we respond whether it be in anger or compassion. We can throw fire on the situation by responding with caustic words. It has been asked, "What do you get when you fight fire with fire?" Answer: You get a bigger fire. Words of love and caring can douse any flame. A smile or a kind word has the ability to melt even the hardest of hearts.

July 18

Ready...fire...aim. oops!

"In heaven we shall appear, not in armor, but in robes of glory. But here these
are to be worn night and day; we must walk, work, and sleep in them, or else we
are not true soldiers of Jesus Christ."
-William Gurnall-

Do you ever fire before taking aim? Sounds silly, but it is painfully true. I know I have done exactly that in the past. We pull out our weapon and get ready for a fight before we even receive our marching orders from God. We need to stay in constant contact with headquarters (Heaven) if we are to have any success. We have a real enemy that wants to destroy us. Satan doesn't care how he brings us down, his mission is to bring us down any way he can. Sadly, he is very good at it. He has taken out some of the greatest of saints. Adam and Eve fell for the old apple trick. Have you? Did Satan hold out something before you that looked harmless and oh so good? We figure because it looks innocent it must be from God. We forget that one of Satan's oldest tricks is to disguise himself as an angel of light. What you see is not what you get. Remember that! That can save you a truckload of trouble if you will go to God first and run it by Him. Ask for His wisdom before you step out. Otherwise you will go before God asking for forgiveness, for doing something He never approved of in your life. Ask yourself this question before you step out, "Do I have peace about it." If not, run!

"Sometimes the worst of times are designed by the enemy
to get you to give up on God's clear direction because he
knows of the powerful and wondrous blessings that are ahead."
-Chip Ingram-

Don't be fooled! God will give you clear direction if you ask Him with a sincere heart. After all, He gave Noah very *specific* directions and measurements to build the ark. He will do the same for you. Don't take a bite of the apple before you get down on your knees and ask for wisdom. You will be glad you did. Approach the apple tree if you must with your spiritual armor on, but better yet, stay away from it all together.

"A proper perspective on spiritual warfare is focused on the
power of God, rather than on the ploys of Satan."
-Hank Hanegraaf-

July 19

Rest!

"He makes me to lie down in green pastures…"
-23rd Psalm-

"I owe, I owe, it's off to work I go." Someone has made a clever play on the words of Snow White and her Seven Dwarfs song. How very true it is in today's world. We work, we gather 'stuff', then more 'stuff. We work even harder to get more. Our health suffers and then the extra money we made to buy more 'stuff' now ends up paying our doctor bills. Sometimes, God has to force us to rest and He does. It is wise to note that in the twenty third Psalm God is leading His own and we are following Him. "Follow Me" is a command and it assumes our obedience. He alone knows where the green pastures are and of our great need for them. He will show us the way. He always has our best interests at heart. He knows where the dangers of life lie. To rebel against His leading is to rebel against our own safety. Sometimes, we forget we are to follow Him and not make Him chase after us or drag us. Sheep in the Bible are sorry little creatures. They are not real bright. They tend to wander where they shouldn't and get themselves into trouble. They are completely dependent upon the Shepherd for everything. They are easy prey for their enemies. Maybe, this is why God has likened man to sheep. We too, are quick to wander, to do 'our own thing.' Once we have come to know the Great Shepherd of the sheep, Jesus, we come to know His voice as He calls. He says, "My sheep recognize my voice; I know them and they follow Me. I give them eternal life and they shall never perish" John 10:27. Here, Jesus distinguishes His sheep from others. Some aren't able to hear Him calling, can you? Sometimes the worries of this world try to drown out His voice. We must get alone with Him every day. The more time we spend with Him, the easier it is for us to recognize His voice above all others.

> "If the blind put their hand in God's, they find
> their way more surely than those who see,
> but have not faith or purpose."
> Helen Keller

God has his ways of slowing us down if He has to. Look at the life of Saul of Tarsus. Hearing God's voice for the very first time can be frightening. Before he heard God's voice, he was on a mission to kill all Christians. After God knocked him off his donkey and blinded him, he suddenly became obedient in his stinky circumstances. Saul said, "Who are you, Lord? and Jesus said, "I am Jesus Whom you are persecuting." Trembling scared and now blind, he asked, "Lord what do You want me to do." Saul's name was changed to Paul and he was now on God's mission, no longer on his own. I don't think it is uncommon for believers to feel at some time in their life as if they have been knocked off their donkey, blinded and coming face to face with their risen Lord. Question is, will you stay blinded or see the One who calls?

July 20

Think before you speak...careful! your attitude is showing...

TODAY

"Today I can complain because the weather is rainy or
I can be thankful that the grass is getting watered for free.
Today I can feel sad that I don't have more money or I can be
glad that my finances encourage me to plan my purchases
wisely and guide me away from waste.
Today I can grumble about my health or I can
rejoice that I am alive.
Today I can lament over all that my parents didn't give me
when I was growing up or I can feel grateful that they
allowed me to be born.
Today I can cry because roses have thorns or I
can celebrate that thorns have roses.
Today I can mourn my lack of friends or I can excitedly embark
upon a quest to discover new relationships.
Today I can whine because I have to go to work
or I can shout for joy because I have a job to do.
Today I can complain because I have to go to school or I can
eagerly open my mind and fill it with rich bits of knowledge.
Today I can murmur dejectedly because I have to do housework or
I can feel honored because the Lord has provided shelter for my mind, body and soul.
Today stretches ahead of me, waiting to be shaped. And here I am, the sculptor
who gets to do the shaping.
What today will be like is up to me.
I get to choose what kind of day I will have.
Author unknown

What a privilege God has given us with each new day to impact our world. To make someone else's life a little easier or allow them to make ours a little bit brighter. Others are watching you! Especially unbelievers, so make sure the message you send is heavenly inspired. Your attitude is showing!

"For out of the abundance of the mouth, the heart speaks."
Matthew 12:34

JULY 21

I don't need fixing...not by you anyway.

"Nothing will change in your life without
knowledge of God's Word."
-Joyce Meyer-

There are a lot of broken things in this world, sadly, that includes people. Aren't you glad God doesn't have an old junkyard where he tosses broken people? Instead of tossing them out He offers to not only 'repair' them as only He can do, but to make us brand new. Our lives would be a lot simpler if we could only grasp the idea that it is not our job to fix people, it is God's. We try to change our children, we try to change our spouse, we try to change our friends, and the list goes on and on. Truth of the matter is how are we going to change anyone else when we can't even change ourselves. Oh, some of our fixes can be temporary, but God's are permanent. I may very well 'need fixin' but it is God who will do it, not you. Only He can change us from the inside out. The inside is a place we can't reach. I can't think of anything more miserable than to live with someone who all the time wants to 'fix you.' I love what Joyce Meyer says, "God can heal you everywhere you hurt!" Only He can do that because He knows why you hurt, where you hurt and how long you will hurt. Only He has the wisdom to not only know what the problem is, but to also know the solution. It's at times like these that God teaches us the most, about ourselves and about others. His process may be slow and sometimes very painful but it will be thorough and He will teach us many things along the way. What we think is the problem may not be the problem at all. It could be something entirely different.

"The poor brokenhearted sinner, going into his bedroom, bends his knee, but can only
utter his mournful cry in the language of sighs and tears. Look! that groan has made all
of the harps of heaven thrill with music; that tear has been caught by God, and put
into a vase made especially for tears, to be perpetually preserved."
-Charles Spurgeon-

Does God really save our tears? The answer is yes. Wow! It's hard to imagine a love like that. So the next time sorrow hits and the tears flow imagine the angels of God gathering them up off your pillow and presenting them to the Lord.

"Lord, You number and record my wanderings, put my tears
into Your bottle – are they not in your book? Then shall
my enemies turn back in the day I cry out;
this I know, for God is for me."
Psalm 56:8

Thought for the day.... "God is for me." What does it matter who is against me if the God of the Universe has my back?

July 22

God's silence is not His consent.

"Where we might think of sin as slip-ups or missteps, God views
sin as a godless attitude that leads to godless actions."
-Max Lucado-

Godless actions will always lead to unwanted circumstances and painful results. When God is silent, that does not mean He gives His approval to our actions. I am reminded about the story of an atheist who was a teacher. In his classroom, he decided to conduct an experiment as to whether God really existed or not. In front of his students he taunted and mocked God, "God if you really exist then strike me dead within 3 minutes." The students all held their breaths. Tick, tock, tick, tock… Three minutes passed and nothing had happened. "See," he told his students, "That proves there is no God." Did it? Of course not! All it proved was how patient God is with even the foolish unbeliever. It is never a wise move to tempt God. God does not respond at our command, rather we respond to His. He is not at our beck and call. We are at His. Silly man, to think the universe revolves around him.

"It is better to remain silent and be thought a fool,
then to open one's mouth and remove all doubt."
-Samuel Johnson-

What is one of the differences between a believer and an unbeliever? The believer fears Almighty God, and simply put, the unbeliever does not. Fear, in this sense, means to take God very seriously. To mock God is for puny man to shake his fist at heaven as if what he thinks really matters. The believer knows and accepts that there are some things in life that just aren't fair. Instead of doubting a loving God, he patiently waits in faith for the day when God will right all wrongs, even the score and cause His will to prevail. Where the believer responds in faith when he doesn't understand, the unbeliever responds with doubt and mocking.

Doubt sees the obstacles
Faith sees the way.
Doubt sees the darkest night
Faith sees the day.
Doubt dreads to take a step
Faith soars on high.
Doubt questions, "Who believes?'
Faith answers, "I."
-Author unknown-

July 23

Like any good teacher of children, God uses repetition.

*"I never teach my pupils; I only attempt to
provide the conditions in which they can learn."*
-Albert Einstein-

Teachable moments! Life is full of them. Much like Albert Einstein, God provides us many different conditions in which we can learn what He wants to teach us. If you ever got daring enough to pray and ask God for 'patience,' you quickly found yourself in bumper to bumper traffic with no way of escape or surrounded by irritating people at work who greatly tried the very last ounce of patience you had. In other words, God puts us into certain situations and uses some people to teach us valuable lessons in life. God sometimes puts us in hard places where we couldn't learn any other way. The oyster is a great example. A foreign body of sand enters the oyster and is very irritating to the creature. The oyster secretes a covering over the grain of sand, over and over until it becomes a priceless pearl. What started out as an irritant became a treasure. We all want 'do overs' at one time or another in life. Famous last words of a fool, "I wish I hadn't done that." The good news is not all teachable moments have to be hard. Your child smiles at you for the first time and you realize how awesome God is to allow you to share with Him in His miracle of life. Your toddler takes his first step and through your own learned lessons in life you know he may fall over and over again as he learns, but he will eventually master it. In fact one day he won't settle for just walking anymore he will be running. I love the saying, "A child is God's opinion that the world should go on." Children, as nothing else can, in this life, show us how truly blessed we really are.

"Childhood memories are one of the most reliable explanations
of "why you are the way you are." These memories are like tapes
playing in your head and they combine with the basic life-style you
learned as a child to determine how you will respond to
what happens to you every day."
-Kevin Leman-

July 24

*"Go ahead, make a mistake. The experience may
be costly, then know it will also be priceless."*
-Peter Peterson-

*"The decision to sin always includes the thought that I cannot
really trust God to watch out for my well-being."*
-John Ortberg-

Have you ever wished you could go back in time, undo a bad decision you made? We all do. Even though we learn from making mistakes, at least I hope we do, it is still better not to have made them at all. Every time we go off the rails, it is because we have chosen to disobey God. It is as simple as that. We believe we have a better way, or we just get sick and tired of waiting on God. We talk ourselves right into disobedience. We begin to listen to the lies of Satan. "If God really loved you, He wouldn't let this happen to you." That sounds reasonable doesn't it? Yet, it is a lie straight from hell itself. Bad things happen to good people all the time. Why? Because we are sinners and we live in a sinful world. People hurt us. We hurt people. Sin is a robber. It robs us of every good thing God has for us.

*"Where is the child of God, who has
sinned, and not smarted for it?"*
-James Thomas Holloway-

No one gets by with sin, no one. Sin always comes with a very high price tag. I used to fool myself into thinking I could get away with disobeying God. I soon found out that any pleasure I might have experienced, quickly turned into deep, deep sorrow. The pleasure will never outweigh the pain. Pain is meant to discourage our disobedience. Sometimes it works better than other times. Deep in the heart of a believer, is a war between good vs evil and it will continue to rage until we are called home to glory. The worst kind of sin is the one we think we have overcome. The one we think we have control over when in reality it controls us. I would like to think of myself as a patient person, at least, until I get hung up in traffic and I'm in a big hurry. Well, patience is the last thing that comes out of my mouth. The good news is, God knows we are a work in progress. We should all wear 'still under construction' signs, around each of our necks.

*"Truth hates sin. Grace loves sinners.
Those full of grace and truth do both."*
-Randy Alcorn-

Truth is found in the Word of God. God's word will keep us from sin. Sin will keep us from God's Word. It's as simple as that. If you sin, immediately go to God and seek His forgiveness. He will accept you with open arms, clean you up and send you out to face another day.

July 25

"Lay it down..."

Sometimes it's not the path we are traveling, but the 'load of burdens' we insist on carrying – burdens we *choose* to carry that weigh us down. Jesus says, *"Lay it down."* We were never meant to carry the weight of the world on our shoulders. That is God's job and He does it very well.

> *"Cast thy burden upon the Lord, and*
> *He shall sustain thee."*
> *Psalm 55:22*

What kind of 'unnecessary baggage' are you carrying in life? Cast it on Him. Do you have worries? Lay it down! Are you troubled about a loved one? Lay it down! Do you have sleepless nights? Lay it down! Bills you can't pay? Lay it down! Do you have a wayward child gone astray? Lay it down! A couple of years ago I became very ill. There was absolutely nothing I could do for myself. I lay on the sofa thinking, "I am too sick to work, what am I going to do?" I sent a very simple prayer heavenward to my Savior. I was too weak to do anything else. "Jesus, You know I have bills to pay and I can hardly get off the sofa. I am going to trust you to help me. I am going to believe you are who you say you are and that you will meet all of my needs as you promised." For the first time in a very long time, I literally took God at His word. It wasn't my great faith, I had no other choice. He gave me such a peace in my heart that I didn't worry about it again, I simply focused on getting better. He was faithful! *My illness taught me a BIG lesson!* A lesson I could have learned no other way. WHEN I COULD NOT HELP MYSELF, HE COULD AND HE PROMISED THAT HE WOULD HELP ME IF I WOULD CAST MY CARE COMPLETELY ON HIM. He told me to cast my care on Him, so I did and I held tightly to His promises. He promised that He would sustain me, and He did. He promised me peace. The burden was lifted. Sometimes the greatest prayer we can pray is "Help! Lord!" Now when life overwhelms me I remember back to that time God proved Himself so faithful. It is a good thing to remember how God has proved Himself faithful to us in the past. Just like King David, before he became king, he faced the giant Goliath, knowing God had already helped him kill the bear and the lion. Never forget what God has done for you in the past. It may be all you have to hang on to.

July 26

No enemy can come so near, that God is not nearer.

"When the ways of man are pleasing to the Lord, He makes even
those who hate him to be at peace with him."
Proverbs 16:7

The Bible says our enemy (Satan) has come to steal, kill and destroy, but Jesus came that we might have life, and have it *abundantly*! There is a wonderful story in the Bible that illustrates God's divine protection over us as nothing else can. It is found in II Kings 6:13-17. The prophet Elisha was on the King of Aram's bucket list of things to do before he dies. He sent his troops, which was a great army out to seize Elisha. One morning Elisha's servant arose from his bed and looked out the window and started to hyperventilate. What he saw was troops, horses and chariots everywhere! King Aram's army was about to let the king update his bucket list. The servant cries out to Elisha, prophet of God, "What are we going to do? We are surrounded on all sides." What was Elisha's reply? You would expect him to say, "Oh boy, are we in trouble now!" Instead he told his servant, "Don't be afraid! There are more on our side than on theirs!" The servant looks around and still only sees Elisha and himself. There are still just the two of them. Elisha prayed, "Oh Lord, open his eyes and let him see." God then opened the eyes of the servant and when he looked up, he saw that the hillside around Elisha was filled with horses and chariots of fire. What a spectacular scene that must have been! The servant's fear evaporated and was immediately replaced with awe and wonder when he saw God's mighty heavenly army coming to the rescue. Faith causes us to see what we can't normally see in the natural. Faith will also take the fear from us as nothing else can. God has spiritual resources we can't even fathom or see, until we put on our spiritual glasses and God reveals them to us. Lesson of the day: The problem is your eyesight not God's power! Maybe it's time for an eye exam and time to turn your enemies over to Him.

July 27

"Help, Lord, I think I need an eye check-up."

Don't focus on the gray skies and dark clouds overhead, but focus instead on that small ray of light shining through. That light is 'hope' that tomorrow will be better.

Have you ever been outside lying on the grass looking up at the starry skies, contemplating life and what's it's really all about? You stare into the limitless boundaries of God's universe that is sprinkled with magnificent light. Some of the stars start to twinkle. That is God putting on a spectacular light show just for you. You look at the moon and remember that man has been there, walked on its landscape and safely returned home. You smile and the man in the moon smiles back at you. All is well with the world. Then, out of nowhere, trouble strikes your life. You feel like you've been sucker punched and your world turns upside down and inside out. You return to that same spot that gave you so much comfort, but the stars are gone and the sky is black. Fear and doubt creep up behind you. You want to run, but where to? Then you hear a still small voice of the Shepherd inviting you back to lie on the grass again and look up. As you begin to look up again, God fills your heart with His peace that passes all understanding as He reminds you that the stars are still there in all of their glory. They are only blanketed by a 'temporary' darkness that will pass with time. The universe still spins at His commands. The oceans roar at the sound of His name and the stars are still twinkling and the man in the moon is still smiling. Hope has replaced the fear and awe and God has overcome the darkness. Lesson: LOOK UP! Don't look around you or ahead of you or in back of you, look up and remember:

> The Lord has not turned away from the suffering of the
> one in pain or trouble. He has not hidden His face from him.
> But He has heard his cry for help."
> Psalms 22:24

If you light even the smallest of candles and the darkness will flee. God's word is a lamp unto my feet and a light unto my path. "Twinkle, twinkle little star..."

JULY 28

❊

A man always has two good reasons for the things that he does – a good one and the real one.

"Come now and let us reason *together*, says the LORD. Though your sins are like scarlet, they shall be as white as snow; though they are red like crimson, they shall be like wool. If you are *willing* and *obedient*, you shall eat the good of the land; but if you *refuse* and *rebel*, you will be devoured by the sword. For the mouth of the LORD has spoken it."
-Isaiah 1:18-20-

"I can't believe I did that." "What was I thinking?" "I never should have..." "I wish I had never...." Can you ever remember saying something similar to these? Stupid makes us do a lot of dumb things in this life. Usually it's because of our wrong motive and because we choose to leave God out of the equation. Yet God says, "Come, let us reason this out together..." Instead of coming to Him we decide to try out our own plan first. We reason to ourselves instead of 'with' God that what we are doing maybe wrong, but it will somehow turn out right in the end. Wrong! Wrong! Wrong! God wants to be involved in every aspect of your life. Nothing is too big for Him and nothing is ever too small that He is not concerned how it will affect our life. In the end though, the choice is ours. He will not force you to choose what is right, but as you can see in this scripture, if our choice involves rebelling we will be devoured by the sword. Well, what in the world does that even mean? The sword is God's word, plain and simple. Obey God's word and there is blessing ahead, ignore God's word and you do so at your own peril. To obey means to keep your appointment with God, to 'reason together' when you have a really important choice to make in life.

"He who **knows** to do right but does not do it, to him it is sin."
James 4:17

Someone has once said, "You are always free to change your mind and choose a different future." Free to choose to obey. Free to choose to rebel. Two very different pathways. Two very different results. Two very different lives, so choose wisely! Eat from the good of the land or be devoured by the sword. Seems like a no brainer to me.

July 29

You are a walking sermon of what you believe.

Today, ponder this for a minute or two. Many will NEVER read the Bible, but they are watching you. They are very closely following your life. You are a 'walking' sermon to them especially if you claim to be a child of God, a follower of Jesus. Your words can bring healing or destruction. Your words can be empty or full of power. Years ago a man's handshake was his word. There wasn't any need for long contracts between men. If he shook your hand that meant he would do what he said he would do. His name and honor were at stake. Today, is a different story. Politicians lie to us every single day. They make these big promises until they get elected and then they forget what they promised until the next election and then they suddenly remember again. Telling the truth doesn't always get you elected so the truth is replaced with lies or worse with half-truths. It isn't easy, but honesty is its own defense. Honesty is warfare in this evil world we live in. Honesty is important to God and essential to the child of God.

> When we make good choices even when we are hurting
> we take back ground from the enemy.
> Are you living what you believe or are you someone else on Sunday than you are the rest of the week? How much more important is your life if it is your children watching?
> "Are you more worried about what people think of you, or
> about what God thinks of you? Too many times believers
> worry what others think. However, when we are witnessing
> to people, what is the very worst thing they can do to us?
> They can kill us and send us to Heaven."
> -Mark Cahill-

Thought for the day: Are you more concerned about your reputation with God or your fellow man? Your life will reveal which one you seek after, godliness or worldliness.

July 30

Victory comes when our breaking point becomes our turning point.

Love doesn't live here anymore. This is the cry of many a lonely heart today. A heart with no answers, no faith, no direction, no truth and what little light there was has burned out. A heart that has forgotten what is important in life. Sadder still is this is the result of choice. This kind of pain brought on by neglecting God in your life is the worst kind of pain there is. A toothache can hurt a lot, but once the tooth is pulled the pain disappears.

Love Doesn't Live Here Anymore

Days are gone we laughed and we danced
The music once filled the air.
Silence reigns, no thought for tomorrow
Dreams we no longer share.

Empty days and emptier nights
A shadow is cast by fear.
Once youthful and strong
How quickly the years disappeared.

Where did love go you want to know?
Well, you no longer take time to pray.
A man will reap just what he sows
When he insists on his own way.

Everyone tries to go it alone
No one calls on His name anymore.
Instead of a repentant, forgiving heart
It's more important to keep score.

Busy days and busier lives,
filled with things to do.
Places to go and people to see
Lord, we forgot to make time for You.

Then one day I looked around
"How can this be?" I cried.
I no longer seemed to care
I don't know truth from a lie.

What has made Him walk away?
And why is my heart full of fear?
It's really very simple my friend.
Love no longer lives here.
-Cindy Balch-

Has love grown cold in your life? Is your Bible collecting dust instead of tears? Are you too busy? Do you think you have really good excuses for ignoring your Creator? GOD is LOVE. It is not just something He does but it is who He is. When you turn away from Him in your life, He will stand at the door and keep knocking for you to let Him in. The good news is He is persistent. The bad news is so are some of us. There is a line a person can cross where God stops knocking because you stop listening. You will be the One to walk away but if you ever get so far into the deep pit of life just know that He is always just a whispered prayer away. He died for you – He died to give you eternal life. He lives to show you the way, His way. You don't have to live in darkness unless you choose to. The Bible can only change a life that is willing to take the time to read it.

"I believe in Christianity as I believe the sun has risen, not only because I see it, but because, by it, I see everything else." C.S. Lewis

JULY 31

Pain and sorrow are two of life's greatest teachers.
Pain will get our attention as nothing else can.

I walked a mile with Pleasure
She chatted all the way.
But left me none the wiser
For all she had to say.
I walked a mile with Sorrow
And ne'er a word said she;
But, oh! The things I learned from her
When sorrow walked with me."
-by Robert Hamilton-

Who are you walking with? If you have your hand in the Lord's it won't matter where He leads you. Oh, He may take you some places you'd much rather *not* go, but He will never leave your side. I know this from experience as do many other Christians. Life is a journey. Day by day we walk it alone or choose to walk with Him. We let Him show us the way. Every now and then we may wander off His path, but He will never let us out of His sight. We may feel the sting of the consequences for our wandering, but we will also feel His arms wrapped tightly around us, loving us, reassuring us of His love and care. An old hymn puts sorrow into perspective for us.

God understands your sorrow,
He sees the falling tear,
And whispers, "I AM with thee,"
Then falter not, nor fear.
God understands your heartache,
He knows the bitter pain;
O, trust Him in the darkness,
You cannot trust in vain.
God understands your weakness,
He knows the tempter's power;
And He will walk beside you,
However, dark the hour.
-Oswald Smith 1890-1986
B.D Ackley 1872-1958

AUGUST 1

It's really hard to schedule a crisis these days...

"Fear not, for I have overcome the world."
-Jesus-

Sometimes we see a crisis coming, other times we are completely blindsided. We live in a very unpredictable world these days. Not only is it unpredictable, but it can be downright scary. Terrorism is a threat all over the world. The unthinkable happens when godless nations rule. The world was stunned into silence when the Twin Towers were brought down and 3,000 innocent Americans were murdered. The rise of Russia today threatens our peace and security once again. There are nuclear bombs with lunatics like North Korea's leader holding the button in his hand, doing everything he can to make his missiles capable of reaching America's shores. Iran wants to place their missiles in Venezuela to reach America. Every day the paper or the news seems to be filled with more bad news. Isis marches unafraid across the Middle East, while America keeps silent, but God sees them. A new crisis looms ahead every single day. It's hard not to fear unless you learn to keep your focus where it belongs, on God alone. Have you ever felt like you have lost your way? I have. Have you ever been so overwhelmed with life that you find yourself down on your knees with nothing to say? Many of us have. So, remember this:

"At the point of our desperation <u>God is just beginning to work</u>."
-unknown-

Regardless of what the future holds, if I am a child of the LIVING God then I never need despair. If life ends here on earth, it begins in Heaven. After you read the following poem, close your eyes and imagine with me for just a moment how wonderful it will be to close your eyes forever on this side of Heaven only to open them and see Jesus face to face. Oh my! Can anything be more wonderful than that? I imagine my mom and dad and my sister waiting for my arrival. Until then remember Jesus' words, "I will be with you until the end."

Think of stepping on shore and find it Heaven!
Of taking a hold of a hand and finding it is God's.
Of breathing new air, and finding it celestial air,
Of feeling invigorated, and finding it immortality,
Of passing from storm and tempest to an unbroken calm,
Of waking up, and finding it home!
-Anonymous-

AUGUST 2

God has given us the gift of 'choice.'
"Whosoever calls upon the name of the Lord shall be saved."

He will never take the 'gift of choice' away, but He can and will make us very uncomfortable with our bad choices. So, choose wisely. Another sobering truth is unless we hear the truth, how can we follow it. Someone must tell us. The great commission Jesus gave to his 12 disciples at His ascension was to, "**Go** into ALL the world, tell the world the good news!" Everyone loves good news, don't they? So, why is it often rejected? I know why for years I ran from the truth. It required a decision and a life change I wasn't willing to make. That is, until the bottom literally dropped out of my life and a decision was inevitable. I chose wisely. I chose a God I had spent many years running from. I just knew that if I ever gave my life to Him He would then get me a one way ticket on a boat as a missionary to a place I knew I didn't want to go. I wanted to marry someday, have 2.2 children as the statistics declared, with a little house and a white picket fence and don't forget the dog in the backyard. I wasn't smart enough to realize back then that if the mission field was where God wanted me then that was where I should want to be also. I might have been miserable in Africa somewhere, but I would have been more miserable in my disobedience to God. You never lose when you are in the center of His will. NEVER. One day when I was questioning my life, a friend handed me a note that said, *"God's will: Exactly where I would want to be if I knew what God knew."* So true! The missionaries fulfill the great commission of God, but that does not let us off the hook. We also need to go and tell the good news. I may not be able to travel to China or Africa, but I am determined to send others. I can walk across the street and go tell friends and neighbors. I can tell whomever God places in my path. The following is a poem read by Dr. McGee on his radio program Thru the Bible. It is a sobering poem about what happens when we don't tell the lost about Jesus.

My Friend
My friend I stand in judgment now
And feel you are to blame somehow.
On earth I walked with you day by day
And never did you point the way.
You knew the Lord in truth and glory
But never did you tell the story.
My knowledge then was very dim
You could have led me safe to Him.
Though we lived together here on earth
You never told me of the second birth.
And now I stand this day condemned
Because you failed to mention Him.
You taught me many things that's true
I called you friend and trusted you.
But now I learn that it's too late
And you could have kept me from this fate.
We worked by day and talked by night
And yet you showed me not the light.
You let me live and love and die
You knew I'd never live on high.
Yes, I called you friend in life
And trusted you through joy and strife
And yet on coming to this dreadful end
I cannot now call you my friend.
-Anonymous-

Of course, not everyone we tell will jump up and down and get excited about the good news. Some don't like to be told they are a sinner and may even defriend you. But, they won't go to judgment never having heard the good news that Jesus came to earth, Immanuel, God with us, died on a cross for our sins, rose again and is coming back for us so we can live with Him forever and ever. There will be no parties in hell, only weeping and wailing and gnashing of teeth. (Matthew 8:12) That is one 'party' I think I'll pass on. I'm sure you will too.

AUGUST 3

Be you! Dance to the music you hear not what someone else hears.

"As the ark of the Lord came into the City of David, Michal, Saul's daughter (David's wife), looked out the window and saw King David leaping and dancing before the Lord, and she despised him in her heart. 2 Samuel 6:16-17

Years ago there was a song that went something like this: "You and I travel to the beat of a different drum..." So true! We are all wired differently by our Creator. King David heard the music of victory in bringing the ark back to Jerusalem and his wife Michal not only did not feel the music she looked on in disgust. God punished Michal for her more than stinky attitude by making her childless until her death. Our attitude seems very important to God. Have you ever judged another because they heard the music and you did not? Were you ever irritated because someone fought a major battle in life and celebrated by dancing? Today, I think we call it the 'happy dance.' Wouldn't it be a boring world if we all dressed the same, ate the same thing, combed our hair the same way, drove the same car? Good news flash! It's ok to be 'you!' Dancing can be fun even if you don't know how. When my daughter was about one and a half years old I would put her in a little circular thingy with wheels and she would push herself all around the room. She would bump into all kinds of things along the way, furniture, my shins, but would eventually make it over to my mom's stereo and flip up the button to turn it on. Music would blast and she would begin to dance. She would rock her head to the left then to the right, jumping up and down at the same time to the beat of the music. It didn't matter what was going on around her she was oblivious to everything but the music. She was in a happy place doing the happy dance. We make life so complicated these days by forgetting to listen to the music of life and dance along with it. Fred Astaire, the famous dance partner of Ginger Rogers, put it best when he said,

"I have no desire to prove anything by dancing...I just dance."

Sometimes the music God sends is sad, slow and serious. Sometimes it's so loud it rocks our world, but He always gives us a reason to dance. With Him, we know that all things will work together for our good. Not some things but ALL things. King David danced a dance of victory and so can we if we will just keep our eyes on God. So take a few minutes today and be goofy and dance before the Lord as David did. If you are a child of the living God and have read the book you know that in the end, we win!! Now, that is something to dance about! So, the next time someone you know is doing the 'happy dance,' jump right in and join them. No one likes to dance alone. Dancing is something you can do even if your heart is breaking. So, the next time you see someone dancing, rejoice with them that life is good for them that day. Tomorrow they may not want to dance until you give them a reason 'not to sit this one out.' Don't be a wallflower, be like my daughter and go searching for the music and don't stop until you find it.

AUGUST 4

Some trials and heartaches in life will leave us an entirely
'different' person than we were before the tragedy..

Some trials are designed that way and some leave us different simply because of the way we respond to them. God is continually growing us up, whether we like it or not. He often pinpoints an area in our life that does not please Him, therefore, it has to go. We see Him zeroing in on an area in our life and we hunker down and resist with everything in us. Do we really think that will make Him change His mind? Of course not! The tighter we hold onto something the more painful it will be to eventually let it go. As the years go by I have discovered it is much easier on me to 'let it go' and the sooner the better. God can make us pretty miserable in our circumstances until we beg Him to take the thing we previously wouldn't let go of. Good bye and good riddance. At times like this don't push against God…embrace Him. Let Him make those changes He knows are necessary in our lives. This has been a very hard lesson for me in life. I don't like change. I like things to pretty much stay the same and predictable. Well, the older I got I found out God doesn't do boring. Sometimes He shakes, rattles and rolls things up. If you really stop and think about who He is and what He has done in the past, like taking a few loaves of bread and a couple of fish from a kid and using it to feed over 5,000 hungry people on a hillside their own sardine sandwiches with plenty to spare, then change isn't quite as scary as we may think.

> "Now, to Him who is able to do immeasurably more than all we ask,
> think or imagine, according to His power that is at work within us, to
> Him be glory in the church and in Christ Jesus forever and ever
> through endless ages."
> Ephesians 3:20

Lesson: Dream big dreams for God and then hang on! He longs to bless you! He longs to do more for you than you could ever imagine! In the meantime, life is an adventure that will eventually lead us safely home.

> "Life can only be understood backwards, but it must be lived forward."
> –Soren Kierkegaard-

AUGUST 5

You are free to choose, but you are not free to choose the consequences…God does.

"Choose you this day who ye will serve…
but as for me and my house, we will serve the Lord."
–Joshua 24:15-

There are so many in choices we make every single day of our lives. Some we make automatically and some we really have to think about. The life changing decisions are the ones that are our focus today. We choose what time to get up, what to have for breakfast, whether to exercise or not (ugh), what time to leave for work, will I be late again or will I arrive on time today. Some choices don't seem all that important in the scheme of things and some will change our lives forever. Some decisions will put us on a path we never thought we would end up on and some choices will turn our upside down world right side up again. Look at the drug addict who chooses to go straight, or the husband who chooses to return to his family after walking out on them months before.

*"Looking back, my life seems like one long
obstacle race, with me as its chief obstacle."*
-Jack Parr-

It wasn't just one bad choice, most likely, that got us into the mess we are in but a series of bad choices. Likewise, it will take a series of good choices to undo the damage that has been done. The good news is that God will be right beside you the moment you choose His way. Life may not get easier, but it will get better with God's help. He specializes in helping the helpless. Whoever it was that said, "God helps those who help themselves," is ignorant. It is not in the Bible where most people expect to find it. No, God does just the opposite and helps those who are at the end of their rope, hanging on by a thread, with nowhere else to go. If you think you can fix it yourself, He will let you try. He is always a whispered prayer away. All it takes is a sincere cry of the heart, "Help!" and He will. He is not gleeful when we fail, He wants to be our number one cheerleader in life. He may put up some obstacles in our pathway to make us stronger. He wills that we make the right choice the first time. He is moved by our misery and His compassion to deliver us. He doesn't promise us an easy journey, but He does promise we will arrive safely and on time to our final destination, Heaven…home.

"You are always free to change your mind and choose a different future."
-Richard Bach-

Hindsight is a wonderful thing. I have pondered how many *different* choices I would have made in my life if I had just taken a few minutes, or a few days to consider the consequences of my actions. I was my worst enemy on many occasions. Sometimes out of stupidity and most of the time out of rebellion. I wanted my way. Unfortunately, God let me have my way too many times. Sin comes with a heavy price…it's called consequences. Think long and hard before choosing and I can guarantee you will be glad you did.

AUGUST 6

Placing your self-worth and self-esteem in someone else's hands other than God's... is tragic.

"For I am the *least worthy* of the apostles, who am not fit or deserving to be called an apostle, because I once wronged and pursued and molested the church of God, oppressing it with cruelty and violence. BUT by the GRACE (the unmerited favor and blessing) of God I am what I am..."
-1 Cor. 15:9-10 AMPB-

The interesting thing about this bible verse is that the Apostle Paul is his own accuser. Oh sure, he had others willing to tell him everything that was wrong with his life but here he condemns himself. He knew the depths of sin to which he had fallen, all in the 'name of God.' Sound familiar? How many of God's people have been slaughtered all in the name of God? Paul thought he was doing God's will by killing Christians until that day he met Jesus on the road to Damascus, knocked off his donkey, blinded by a light from Heaven and then heard the voice of the Lord, "Saul, Saul, why are you persecuting Me." "Who are you Lord?" He replied. "I am Jesus"...trembling and astonished he asked, "Lord, what do you want me to do?" The men who were with Paul were unable to speak for terror, hearing a voice, but seeing no one.

Wouldn't you have loved to be there that day as an observer? Saul, a mighty warrior who thinks he was right smack in the middle of God's will finds out he is not even close. How many times have we thought the same thing? Thinking we were doing God's bidding only to find out God wasn't in it at all. What saved Paul from himself and what saves us from ourselves? Six powerful words, "But by the grace of God..." First God showed Saul the 'real' him and then He slowly showed him what he could be and changed his name to Paul. God alone defines our self-worth! No one else, just God. If He thought we were important enough to die on a Cross for to save us from our sins, then we must be worthy in His eyes for no other person on the face of this earth has paid such a price to prove our worth. So, next time you get to feeling unworthy, take a trip back to Calvary where Jesus endured the cross for the "prize that was set before Him." That 'prize' was you and me. I am worthy because He says I am worthy and He should know. This gives 'priceless' new meaning. The gates of hell will NEVER prevail against the church of Jesus Christ.

AUGUST 7

Check your life compass...
are you keeping up with the world or with God?

Did your parents ever tell you to pick your friends wisely? Friends will either bring you down or lift you up.
"True friends don't spend time gazing into each other's eyes. They may show great tenderness towards each other, but they face in the same direction toward common projects, goals – above all, towards a common Lord."
-C.S. Lewis-

Are you following God or are you following your own plan? Do you involve God in your plans or do you just head out and hope that everything will work out and that God will bless your plan? This is how most of us operate. We come up with a plan, execute it and when it all falls to pieces we look up to heaven and ask God, "Why did You let this happen to me?" Let it happen? He was never a part of it from the beginning. He was trying to stop you but you weren't paying attention. We go by our feelings so much so that if it feels right it must be right. Not necessarily so. Feeling have nothing to do with it. What we think is right today may not feel right tomorrow.

"I can hardly recollect a single plan of mine, which I have not since seen reason to be satisfied, that had it taken place in season and circumstances just as I proposed, it would, humanly speaking, have proved my ruin; or at least would have deprived me of the greater good the Lord had designed for me. We judge of things by their present appearances, but **the Lord sees them in their consequences,** if we could do so likewise we should be perfectly of His mind; but as we cannot, it is an unspeakable mercy that He will manage for us, whether we are pleased with His management or not; and it is spoken of as one of His heaviest judgments, when He gives any person or people up to the way of their own hearts, and to walk after their own counsels." -
John Newton-

How often do we come up with a plan and forget or simply disregard any consequences that might result from our choices? Life is hard enough without making unnecessary wrong choices we know will harm us. The moment we leave God out you can take it to the bank, your plan will fail. We need God's wisdom. He alone knows the future. Proverbs 3:5 says, it best, "In all your ways acknowledge Him and He will direct your path." Go to Him and use His map for navigating through life...the Bible. You will also find out how much He loves you.

AUGUST 8

Death doesn't change who we are on this earth, it only changes our location.

"Precious in the sight of the Lord is the death of His saints."
Psalms 116:15

One of the greatest struggles I faced many years ago on the day we buried my sister was that the day was so 'ordinary' to the rest of the world. The sun was shining like it always did. Everything inside of me wanted to shout out to them, "Don't you know what has happened?" Everyone will face the death of a loved one. After death, like it or not we all have a future appointment at the throne of God where He will judge the deeds of man. If you don't know God this will be a very scary day. It will be a day of divine judgment. For those of us who do know the Lord, this will be a day of rewards for the life lived. The majority of us want God to right all of the wrongs done on this earth…other's wrongs not necessarily our own. There is a story I heard told of two of the meanest brothers Texas had ever seen. They cursed, they cheated the town's people, they drank, they even caroused with women. Then one day one of the brothers died. A preacher was summoned by the brother still alive and was offered one million dollars to do his brothers funeral and all he had to do for the money was to call him a 'saint.' Well, the preacher told the brother he thought that was an impossible task but for that kind of money he would think about it. Well, the day came for the funeral and the preacher stood up and told the truth. This man was a drunk, he cursed, he fought, he told lies and he stole from the good people of this town BUT compared to his brother he was a 'saint.'

If you didn't want anything to do with God on the earth while you were alive, dying isn't going to change that. You are who you are and nice words at a funeral aren't going to change anything. Once we die there is no turning back, no 'do overs.' Eternity is set in stone. The most important decision of a person's life is made this side of heaven. There is no purgatory.

"The character wherewith we sink into the grave at death
is the very character wherewith we shall reappear at the resurrection."
-Thomas Chalmers-

God says, "I have set before you, life and death, choose life." He gives us a multiple choice test: A. Choose life or B. Choose death. Then gives us the answer! Choose life! A wise man makes that choice today for he knows tomorrow is promised to no one. Tomorrow will be too late.

AUGUST 9

It is wise to learn this lesson early in life: "I am responsible for my decisions no matter how I 'feel' at the time."

"Be not afraid, only believe."
Mark 5:36

The fickle feelings of faith! The very moment we depend on our 'feelings' we are doomed. Feelings change, sometimes minute to minute, hour to hour, day to day. They can change because of our circumstances. God does not want us to wobble in our faith but stand firm on His promises. Let me ask you a question. If you only prayed when you 'felt' like it what would your prayer life be? For some of us it would be non-existent. Satan is a big discourager. He wants to steal our power and the most effective way he does it is by taking our feelings on a roller coaster ride. Today I trust God...not sure about tomorrow...I want to...but what if God doesn't come through...I better have Plan B... One day I feel like I can slay giants! Just show me where that slingshot and the rocks are. Tomorrow, I may be running away from God just as fast as my two little feet can carry me. Why? I believe it's because God has to grow us up. The more opportunities He creates for us to 'trust' Him the more we see how faithful our God is. Great faith doesn't come overnight.

"Keep your fears to yourself, but share your courage with others."
-Robert Louis Stevenson-

Most of us have to get knocked down a few times, get battered and bruised along the way before we finally believe God is who He says He is and that He will do exactly what He said He would do.

"You gain strength, courage and confidence by every
experience in which you really stop to look fear in the face.
You are able to say to yourself, "I lived through this horror, I can
take the next thing that comes along."...You must do the thing
you think you cannot do."
- Eleanor Roosevelt-

Lesson: Do it afraid if you have to but do it! Someone once said, "A good scare is worth more to a man than good advice."

AUGUST 10

Most of us see only what we want to see…until it rocks our world.

"Courage is the first of human qualities because it is
the quality which guarantees all the others."
-Winston Churchill-

Winston Churchill is the only man who saw Hitler for who he really was and stood up for his beliefs and saved England. Neville Chamberlain, on the other hand, believed Hitler was an honest man who would keep his word. He watched Hitler's tanks rumble through Europe conquering and killing. Churchill saw the truth and had the courage to stand up against the lies. Do you have eye trouble? Do you only see what you want to see? Do you need an eye check-up? I think we all do at some time or another. We see what we want to see in relationships and when they fall apart we wonder what happened. We see what we want to see in Politicians as they tell some big whoppers so they will get elected of how they will do this or that, and when they do get elected, we find they do nothing and have lied, we are stunned. How many serial killers, after their murders were discovered, had their neighbors say, "He seemed like such a nice, quiet boy." The financial experts of today tell us a crisis is coming. They tell us America cannot sustain this 17 trillion dollar debt or pay entitlements forever. We ignore them even though we know what they are saying is true. America today lacks those with courage, courage to stand up and speak up even though it is unpopular before we hit the point of no return.

"God grant me the courage not to give up what I think
is right, even though I think it is hopeless."
-Admiral Chester W. Nimitz-

May God grant us all the discernment to see the truth, do what is right, and to stand up courageously even though the situation may seem hopeless at the time. With God on our side there is no such thing as a hopeless situation.

AUGUST 11

Be honest with what is missing in your life.

"For you say, I am rich; I have prospered and grown wealthy, and
I am in need of *nothing;* and you do not realize and understand that
you are wretched, pitiable, poor, blind and naked."
Revelation 3:17

These are the words of Jesus to the Church at Laodecia, the church of the last days, before Christ returns. These are 'religious' people He is talking about. Theirs is a religion that does not include God. Apparently, man is not getting better as some suppose, but more and more depraved. We are on the brink of a nuclear war with radicals and crazies with their hands on the switch. America sits back where once we were great. God, once upon a time used America, not as the world's police, but to deter evil and restrain it. We no longer see ourselves in that role and soon all hell will literally break loose. God says man is marching towards that great battle Armageddon. If you listen closely, you can hear the hoof beats of the four horsemen of the apocalypse. Without God's intervention, we are hopeless. I suppose Charles Spurgeon said it best. "There is nothing in man by nature apart from God, which is not vile and deceitful. In me (that is, in my flesh) dwells no good thing. If there be anything good in my nature, if I have been transformed by the renewing of my mind, If I am regenerate, if I have passed from death unto life, if I have been taken out of the family of Satan, and adopted into the family of God's dear Son, and if I am now no more an heir of wrath, but a child of heaven, then all these things are of God, and in no sense, and in no degree whatever are they of myself." God describes for us the last battle of man's defiance and the tragic ending for man who has turned his back on a loving, kind forgiving God:

"And they gathered them together at the place which in Hebrew
is called Armageddon. Then the seventh angel emptied out his bowl
into the air, and a mighty voice came out of the sanctuary of heaven
from the throne of God, saying, It is done!"
Revelation 16:16

It is wise to remember that God always warns before judgment comes. Some will heed that warning, most will not. They laugh at the absurdity of it and walk away with a closed heart and eyes that refuse to see. One out of every four verses in the Bible are prophetic. If you really want to know how it all ends, then study the prophets, John (Book of Revelation), Ezekiel, Daniel. One of my favorite books in understanding how it all ends is by Hal Lindsey, 'The Late Great Planet Earth.' God always warns and He also promises to deliver those who will listen to His warnings from the horrors yet to come upon this earth. Make no mistake, they are coming. Which side will you be on?

AUGUST 12

Use the storms of life like an eagle does...to rise above it.

The crazy thing about eagles is, they can see a storm coming from miles away and they don't run from it. Instead they use the winds of the storm to carry them above the turmoil. They time it perfectly and fly directly into the storm and let the winds lift them higher, higher and still higher until they are soaring above the turmoil. Trouble and sorrow is a part of life. A very unwelcome part of life, but nevertheless it is part of being human.

"Believe me, every man has his secret sorrows which the world knows not;
and oftentimes we call a man cold when he is only sad."
-Henry Wadsworth Longfellow-

There is much to be learned from trials in this life. The same Lord who sends us joy also in His Omniscience allows things in our life we would rather avoid altogether. Those who have learned to trust God with the circumstances of their life will tell you that without a doubt, sorrow made them not only stronger, but a better person. Those who are bitter and resentful towards God for allowing bad things to happen, continue on in their bitterness until it affects every part of their lives. Like the eagle, they will use the adversity to rise above their circumstances. They will not avoid the storm, but use it to their advantage to rise above feelings. They will catch a new glimpse of God. They will find out in the sorrow how faithful He is and when the next storm breaks they grab their wings and their raincoat, they already know how to fly. There is no reason to fear anymore, God has brought you through what you feared most.

"There is a joy in sorrow which none but the mourner can know."
-Martin Farquhar Tupper
Have you signed up for God's flight school?

AUGUST 13

Closed doors...if God has closed a door on you, walk away...
if you force it open you will not like what you find.

Most of us take the path of least resistance. Why? It's because it is a lot easier. Thank God we serve a God who will place roadblocks in our path in order to get our attention and to get us to change direction. Remember what we read a few days ago where God knows ahead of time the consequences of our choices. When He stops us it is out of His great love for us. One bad decision can bring years of heartache. What is the best solution to making hard choices in life? Bring it to the Lord. Lay it before Him. Let Him help you make the right decision. We too often make decision based on our feelings when feelings have nothing to do with it.

Martin Luther was once asked,
"Do you *feel* that you are a child of God
this morning?" and he answered, "I cannot say
that I do, but **I know** that I am."

He knew he was a child of God based on God's Word not on how he felt that particular day. It is only at the feet of Jesus can we find the wisdom we need. We can be our own worst enemy when we rely only upon ourselves. Remember God has said that He has a good plan for our life, a plan not to harm us, but to give us hope and a future.

"All the wisdom of the world is childish foolishness
in comparison with the acknowledgment of Christ."
-Martin Luther-

Someone has said, "Knowledge is knowing what to do, and wisdom is doing it." Don't just know what to do, but have the courage to do it. It may not be popular with your friends or loved ones, but if God is guiding you, you can be sure it will be well worth it in the end.

"A man may learn wisdom, even from a foe."
-Aristophanes-

AUGUST 14

"...and forgive us our trespasses as we forgive those who trespass against us."
Psalm 23

FORGIVE!...unforgiveness is like dirt on the soul. It will never wash off on its own.

Forgive! This is not a suggestion. It is a command. Forgive...no ifs ands or buts. No excuses! "But... you don't know what they did to me?" No, I don't but it doesn't matter. God says to forgive them. He doesn't say it will be easy, in fact we all know that it is not easy to forgive. He doesn't say that the person will respond correctly to our forgiveness or that they will change their behavior. They probably won't. What God does say is that it will set you free. He will deal with them in a way only He knows how to. What they have done to you could never be worse than our own sin that put Jesus on the cross. He forgave us so that we can forgive others.

"I can forgive, but I cannot forget," is just another way
of saying, "I will not forgive."
-Henry Ward Beecher-

For the Christian, refusing to forgive, is not an option. Oh, you can do it if you want, but you will always have a heaviness on your soul. Dirt on the soul only God can wash off. We must learn to forgive God's way. Is it easy? Absolutely not! Our human nature wants revenge, we want the other person to PAY for what they did. Someone did pay, Jesus, who had the sins of the world laid upon Himself. He also had the sins of the person you are angry at laid upon His shoulders. If He can forgive them, so can I. It's not a question of if, but a question of when. Until then the heaviness remains on your soul. Unforgiveness is like carrying an anchor around your neck. Who in their right mind would do that?

"If God were not willing to forgive sin.
Heaven would be empty."
-German Proverb-

AUGUST 15

Lord, please don't leave me this way...

That has been the cry of my heart and I am sure it has been the cry of yours at one time or another. Lord, PLEASE don't leave me this way. My heart longs to know you better. I'm scared and I don't know which way to turn. I'm hurt and my heart is badly broken....please don't leave me this way. I am tired, lonely and afraid. Battered and bruised by the world. Wanting to be used by you, but so afraid of what it will cost me. Lord, don't leave me this way. I want to completely surrender to you but fear grips my heart at the thought. Believing that there is nothing You can't do...for others...just not for me. Sometimes my heart is so cold and unfeeling I don't recognize myself. "Lord, please don't leave me this way."

Embrace change. Most of us plead for God to change us and then when He does we fight Him.

"Lord, I don't want to live life looking back anymore. I don't want to live on the outskirts of the Promise Land, I am tired of living in the wilderness. I no longer want to lose hope. Giving up seems the easier path at times. Lord, I ask and plead for you to change me and then when you start I quickly put up the boxing gloves. My heart longs to say those necessary good-byes and to let go of those things which are harming me. I long to draw near to You, to be honest with You but so afraid You will turn me away too. Lord, please don't leave me this way."

There is good news! Thank God, He doesn't leave us in our sin. The moment we surrender our heart to Him, He begins a new work in our life. He makes us a new creation. Old things are gone, and He begins a process that oftentimes defies logic. Only God can take a drunk, a drug addict, a liar, adulterer, murderer, or cheat and turn their life completely around. Only He can change that one way ticket to hell for a seat on the glory train headed for Heaven. If your final destination isn't heaven, get off now and get on your knees before it is too late. He can and will do for you what He has already done for many others who have asked Him. He is a loving, merciful God, not willing that anyone should perish, but all come to repentance.

AUGUST 16

Hold everything in life loosely except God's hand and those you love.

"For me to live **is Christ**...to die is gain."

Great moments in life are often wrapped in 'insignificance.' I call these "God moments." Those moments in life we take for granted may not even be noticed until they are gone. That smile a stranger gave you when your world was falling apart. How about that person who opened the door for you when you had an arm full of groceries and a sick child at home? Was that insignificant? Of course not. No act of kindness is insignificant. How many of our childhood memories we carry with us through life seemed so 'insignificant' at the time. I can still remember my mom holding our dog Jeffey as he slowly left this world. She had three little girls, my sisters and I, at her side, tearful, watching and wondering....and learning. We were too young to understand death and what it meant. I learned a great lesson that day. My mom loved animals and I learned to love them too. My mom took Jeffey to the vet to have him put to sleep, to put him out of his pain, but could not do it. I remember her bringing him back home, walking through the door, no words, no explanation was necessary. I can close my eyes and see her coming through the door to this day. She brought him home and held him until he died. Her actions spoke loudly in her silence. She never said a word. She didn't have to. She taught me never to leave a friend, not even man's best friend. She taught me even a dog deserves kindness, warmth and love right up until the end. I knew that day she would never leave my side either. And she never did. Oh, what lessons my mom taught me that day and she wasn't even aware of the impact that day had on my young life. God was there that day. No one can love like my mom did without God. No one. My mom passed away over two years ago and I held her in my arms as she took her last breath and left this earth. It was a privilege I thank God for every day. She went to be with her LORD that day and one day I will see her again. How do I know? God has promised and He always keeps His promises. Always.

AUGUST 17

The word no...we do not like the word no.

*"It matters little whether we go to foreign lands or stay at home,
as long as we are sure that is where God puts us."*
-Henry Drummond-

God answers prayer in three ways. "Yes, No or Wait, I have something better." We love the 'yes' answer. We do the 'happy dance' when we get our way. We don't like the 'no.' No, can make us depressed for days. We send out invitations to our pity party. Funny thing is, God's 'no' came with as much love as the yes answer comes with. God doesn't make mistakes. He is Omniscient, all knowing. He knows what path a 'yes' answer to a bad request of ours will lead us. We forget with every decision there will be consequences. Good ones or bad ones. If we are wise we will put our future in His hands even when we don't understand, especially when we don't understand. If we turn to our own way, sure that we have a better way than God, the Bible is very clear that, "God opposes the proud but gives grace to the humble."

"It's a bad plan that can't be changed."
-Publilius Syrus-

We must remember who God is in the midst of adversity. The world runs from God when trouble strikes, it shakes its fist at heaven. The believer, on the other hand, climbs up into God's lap and waits out the storm in safety.

"In all trouble you should seek God. You should not set Him over against your troubles, but within them. God can only relieve your troubles if in your anxiety you cling to Him. Trouble should not really be thought of as this thing or that in particular, for our whole life on earth involves trouble; and through the troubles of our earthly pilgrimage we find God."
-Augustine of Hippo-

Adversity is a blessing in disguise. That explains the soul that can say, "I wouldn't trade that experience for anything. In my trouble I found a God who really loves me."

AUGUST 18

*"We do not err because truth is difficult to see. It is visible at a glance.
We err because it is more comfortable."*
-Alexander Solzhenitsyn-

Our society is slowly drifting away from God. Not towards Him. This isn't about 'religion' as some suppose. It's about following God or self. The good news of Jesus Christ, Son of God, giving His life that I may be forgiven is a message that doesn't have to be heard in a church pew. The beauty of the 'good news' is you can be in a coffee shop with a friend, pondering what life is all about or at a funeral of a loved one and the message can reach deep into the soul of anyone who is really searching for the truth. You can be at the beauty shop, talking to a stranger, listening to the TV or the radio and the message will be just as powerful to transform a life. Why? Because behind the message is the message giver, God Himself, and all of heaven is behind Him. God will move heaven and earth to reach even one soul who cries out to Him, no matter where they are, what they have done, no matter what it takes. That is the power of Jesus. Only He can take a ruined life and put the broken pieces back together again. Christians see the world differently than unbelievers do. When the world looked at David it saw a Shepherd boy, but God saw a King! He saw a giant slayer. What does God see when He looks at you. It might surprise you. Did David do everything right all the time? No, in fact just the opposite. He committed adultery, he was guilty of murdering Bathsheba's husband to cover up his sin, but God never gave up on him just like He will never give up on you or me. The greatest love story ever told begins with "For God so loved the world that He gave His only begotten Son that *whosoever* believes on him shall not perish but be saved." I am a '<u>whosoever</u>' are you? So, don't let anyone ever tell you that Christianity isn't all inclusive. Remind them they are either a 'whosoever will' or a 'whosoever won't.'

AUGUST 19

Prepare for tomorrow, but do not presume upon it.

"What's wrong today is wrong tomorrow, and what's right
yesterday is still right today, Rights and wrongs don't change
for one simple reason: God doesn't change. He is truth. He is right."
-Alex McFarland-

I believe in happy endings, but sadly some things, like really bad choices in life just can't be fixed and sometimes can't be undone. Sometimes a poor decision, like sex outside of marriage, can result in an unwanted pregnancy. The good news is that if you will give your life over to the Lord He will make our bad choices work out for our good and His glory. I did not say it wouldn't' be painful at times, but with the Lord now in charge it of your mess it will turn out more than all right. The consequences are what they are. The Bible tells the story of the rich man who had so much wealth he had to build bigger barns to store it. He didn't realize that he would die that very night. Are you into "stuff?" Do you know of any funeral where the hearse was followed by a U-haul truck? Empty we came into this world and empty we will leave. We can however, send some stuff ahead of us. Anything we did in the name of Jesus to help another will be recorded in heaven and then rewarded when we get there. If you have led anyone to Jesus, there will be a crown for you. We only get to heaven by the death, burial and resurrection of Jesus, no other way. It is not by what we do, but by what Jesus has done. It was a completed work. When He spoke those famous words on the cross, "It is finished," our salvation was a done deal, paid for by the blood of Jesus. Any good works will be rewarded but it won't be the reason you are there. Even our closest family and friends may desert us in our times of need but Jesus never will. No matter how bad the situation may seem, it is never hopeless. He can take the broken bits and pieces of our shattered lives and put them back together again better than we could have ever imagine. The choice is ours. Live life doing your own thing or live life doing His thing. When you think of the consequences it becomes an easy decision.

AUGUST 20

NEVER abandon a friend. NEVER.

"Be slow in choosing a friend and even slower in changing."
-Benjamin Franklin-

Today, let's take a look at the Apostle Paul. The first half of his life was lived believing a LIE. He was 'religious' from the top of his head to the bottom of his feet, but he did not know God. He thought he was doing God a favor by wiping out Christians. After Paul had his 'encounter' with Jesus on the Damascus road, his eyes were opened to the truth. I can imagine that Paul's religious 'friends' bailed on him after his conversion from a murderer of Christians to a believer in Christ. It was their loss. Some today would rather hang onto their 'religiosity' than to follow the truth to wherever it may lead. There is nothing in this life quite as precious as a true friend. The following is a story I read a while back and I think it demonstrates true friendship in the worst possible circumstances :

> One could not but be moved by the story of a soldier who asked his officer if he might go out into 'no man's land' between the trenches in World War I and bring in one of his comrades who lay grievously wounded. "You can go," said the officer, "but it's not worth it." Your friend is probably killed, and you will throw your own life away." The determined soldier went anyway. He managed to get to his friend, carry him on his shoulders and bring him back to safety. The officer looked tenderly on the would-be rescuer and said, "I told you son, it wouldn't be worth it. Your friend is dead and you are mortally wounded." "Oh, but it was worth it, sir." "How could it have possibly been worth it?" The soldier replied, "It was worth it because when I reached my friend he was still alive, and he said to me, "Jim, I knew you would come."

"No greater love has a man than this, that he would be willing to lay down his life for a friend."
-John 15:13-

Are you a friend that can be counted on in troublesome times?

AUGUST 21

NEVER tell a child his or her dreams are silly. NEVER.

So the story goes:
A little boy was working hard drawing a picture. His father was intrigued and asked him, "Son what are you doing?" The little boy replied matter of factly, "Daddy I am drawing a picture of God." His father said, "Son, you can't do that, no one knows what God looks like." The little boy undeterred simply looked at his father with confidence and said, "They will when I get done."

This little boy would not be detoured from attempting the impossible. Discouragement was not a word in his vocabulary. Much like Thomas Edison who failed hundreds of times before the light bulb gave its light. Think about the teacher who told Albert Einstein he would be a failure! Yikes! I wouldn't want to be him or her. It makes me stop and think who I may have discouraged over the years from doing great things. I pray no one.

"We should seize every opportunity to give encouragement.
Encouragement is oxygen to the soul. The days are always
dark enough. There is no need for us to emphasize the fact
by spreading further gloom.
-George M. Adams-

Someone has said, "Failure is the line of least persistence." Failure is easy, don't start, don't even try. No one ever fails unless they quit trying. If your child has a dream, do everything you can to help it come true. I love the 'Make A Wish Foundation,' they make dreams come true for kids who otherwise would die with their dreams unfulfilled. Same with St. Jude's Children's Hospital. Their parents don't have the money needed for their medical bills. These kids suffer from some of the greatest diseases known to man, yet still find hope and dream of a future that is pain free and disease free. They were doomed to death until St. Jude's stepped in. Do you have a dream? You should. If you don't, then go see if you can make someone else's dream come true today.

AUGUST 22

*Listen to your conscience. It is the one thing that
will still hurt when everything else feels 'good.'*

"All the worldly goods which I so carefully gathered, would
I now give for a good conscience, which I so carelessly neglected."
-Lewis Bayly-

"But, it felt so right!" "Everybody is doing it!" That is *not* your conscience speaking, that is your fickle feelings making themselves known. "I knew I shouldn't have done it." That is your conscience! Feelings usually get us into a heap of trouble just as much as ignoring your conscience can. God has equipped us all with a built in radar system to detect right from wrong. He calls it your conscience. The greatest thing a parent can do for a child is guide them and help them to keep their conscience 'finely tuned.' I remember myself, as a young 'foolish' woman wanting to do something I knew was wrong and thinking to myself, "Oh, I know that would break my mom's heart if I did it." Did that stop me? Sadly, it didn't, not every time. Life is process of victories and defeats. How often have I been pushed to the mat, taking the 10 count of defeat when **God suddenly steps in**. He picks me up, brushes me off, pats my head and sends me out for another round at life. Sometimes I win and sometimes, well not so much, but He keeps me in the game. My favorite story in the Bible is the Prodigal Son. Took his dad's money, partied it all away, ended up broke and friendless and the only job he could get was feeding the pigs. In other words, his choices put him right smack dab in the pig pen of life. He wasted his life and squandered away his future or so he thought. Good news is, God knew where he was the whole time. One day the kid's conscience kicked in and he came to his senses! My father's servants are better off than I am I will return home and be my father's servant, can't be his son anymore because of how much I have sinned. So, he swallowed his pride, made a life changing decision and he headed home. His father saw him from afar off and ran to his wayward son, hugged him though he was stinky and smelly and called for his servants to throw him the biggest party the town had ever seen. My son, which was lost, has returned home. That's what a conscience touched by the hand of God will do, it will get us going back in the right direction and eventually get us safely home. First He cleans us up then all heaven celebrates when one sinner repents.

Thought for the day: Pray for God to step in to your life. You will never be sorry He did. Is there a life changing decision you need to make? Please, don't leave God out, go to Him first.

AUGUST 23

*Usually, the first thing that happens to us in the
midst of a trial is an 'attitude' adjustment.*

"God often comforts us, not by changing the circumstances of our lives, but by changing our attitude towards our circumstances."
-S.H.B. Masterman-

"Woe is me." "Poor, pitiful me!" Sound familiar? Someone once said, "If you look for things to make you feel hurt, miserable, wretched and unnecessary, then you are almost *certain* to find them." I know I did and more times then I care to admit. I have learned that sometimes life stinks so I just have to get over it. Here's another tip, life isn't fair either, so get over that one too and you will be a lot happier. If you have to have a 'pity party' then make sure it is a quick one and don't invite a lot of people. If you have a terrible, insurmountable injustice done to you then do what God says to do:

"Anyone who wants justice, let him ask of the LORD."

God is our vindicator and He is very good at it. We don't get by with hurting someone else. We may think we do, but in the end God always has a payday. Crazy thing is sometimes we can't connect the dots when we treat someone bad, think we got by with it, then months later someone does the same thing to us. We cry out,"Why me?" It took me years to figure this one out. I think the Bible calls it reaping what you have been sowing. You plant corn, you get corn. You plant unforgiveness, you get it right back at you. Farmers know that your crop doesn't come in right away. They plant the seed, <u>wait a very long time</u> for it to sprout and then finally they reap more than they have sown and later than they have sown. That's great news if its corn you want, but not so great if you get a stinky crop of hatred, bitterness and unforgiveness. Some crops do take longer than others. Weeds on the one hand, pop right up, when least expected and in the darndest places. They are very hard to get rid of just like some of our sins. I would plant sin and then expect something wonderful to spring up! We forget that sin is a deceiver and it promises us one thing and delivers something totally different. We compromise on a relationship, do things we know we shouldn't and when the results come in we are shocked. I have to smile here remembering the words of my 28 year old, single daughter, "Mom, I think I'm pregnant." Through her tears I heard, "I don't know how it happened." After I got over the shock and stopped hyperventilating, I did some explaining to her about the boy bees and the girl bees (she already knew the story). Let me say right here, she really did it up good. Another conversation a few months later was, "Mom, it's twins." After I fainted, I became a real believer in 'you reap what you sow and MORE than you sow.' My twin grandsons will soon be twelve and they are the best thing that has ever happened to me. Has it been easy, heck no! Has it been worth it? Yes, yes and yes! I love this grandma stuff! P.S. I now have three grandsons!

AUGUST 24

Good intentions are just that, good intentions.

"There is a way that seems right unto a man, but it ends in death."
-Proverbs 14:12-

What's the old saying by Samuel Johnson? "The road to hell is paved with good intentions." I've been on that road, have you? In fact, at times I am still on it. I have had good intentions to clean my garage out for the last 15 years! It never quite gets done. Why? Because I have good intentions and that's all I have. I lack the will and determination and back bone to make up my mind to do the dirty task that awaits me. I would rather 'dream' about a clean garage and what it would be like if I could actually get my car in it. Instead, I sit at my computer doing what I love to do, write! The garage will have to wait. What's another 15 years anyhow?

"To the rich man, Lazarus was part of the landscape. If ever he did notice him,
it never struck him that Lazarus had anything to do with him. He was simply unaware
of his presence, or, if he was aware of it, he had no sense of responsibility for it. A man
may well be condemned, not for doing something, but for doing nothing."
-William Barclay-

As I grow older, the world is changing. There are more 'indifferent' people today than ever. Everyone is doing their own thing. Electronics have taken over our society. We don't talk to each other anymore, at least not without a cell phone. We are indifferent to what's happening in the world but up to date on Facebook. The same can be said during World War II when Hitler marched across Europe.

"In Germany, they first came for the Communists, and I didn't speak up
because I wasn't a Communist. Then they came for the Jews, and I didn't speak
up because I wasn't a Jew. Then they came for the trade unionists, and I didn't speak
up because I wasn't a trade unionist. Then they came for the Catholics, and I didn't speak
up because I wasn't a Catholic. Then they came for me – and
by that time there was no nobody left to speak up."
-Martin Niemoller – German Lutheran pastor speaking about the Holocaust-

AUGUST 25

Be very careful what you ask for. You might just get it.

"Keep thy heart with all diligence; for out
of it flow the issues of life."
-Proverbs 4:23-

What you pray for reveals the condition of your heart. How much you pray reveals how seriously you take God. How long you are willing to pray for the same thing over and over again reveals how dedicated you are to changing lives and futures and how much you really believe that God answers prayer. The older you get the more you realize how blessed you are that God did not answer some of your prayers the way you wanted. Can I get an Amen to that! Only God knows where some of us would be if He had answered our prayers the way we wanted and not according to His infinite wisdom. So, maybe today would be a good time to go to God and thank Him for all the times He told you no. He always has something better for us when He says no to our requests. Keep your heart soft and pliable before Him. Place no conditions on God. Do not allow your heart to be hardened. It is so easy to think we know what's best for us when we really don't. We get angry with God and with others when we don't get our way. How foolish to think I know more than an all knowing God.

"The worst prison would be a closed heart."
Pope John Paul II

Trust your heart to its Maker. Charles Parhurst has said, "The heart has eyes the brain knows nothing about." The heart has discernment our fickle feelings do not have. Yes, people will let us down but believe in them anyway. Some really need for someone to believe in them. Keep on praying. Prayer is an attitude of the heart. It is the privilege of being able to talk to God all day long whether you are driving by a homeless person you can pray for or watching the late night news where the world appears to be coming apart at the seams. Pray! Pray! Pray! A prayer unuttered changes nothing but a prayer prayed can turn the world right side up again. Learn to pray always, start with a very short prayer, "Help!" if you have to, but seek God and you will find Him. He promises that you will.

AUGUST 26

What really defines us is how we rise once we have fallen.

*"The quickest way to get back on your
feet, is to get down on your knees."*
-Samuel M. Shoemaker-

The following is a very sobering account of President Lincoln's rise to the White House:

Failed in business in 1831
Defeated for legislature in 1832
Second failure in business in 1833
Suffered a nervous breakdown in 1836
Defeated for Speaker in 1838
Defeated for Elector in 1840
Defeated for Congress in 1843
Defeated for Senate in 1855
Defeated for Vice President in 1856
Defeated for Senate in 1858
Elected PRESIDENT in 1860

Aren't we glad this amazing man NEVER gave up. For 29 years he fell, got up, fell, got up, fell and rose to the presidency. Slavery was ended by his influence and perseverance. The Gettysburg address is one of the most profound speeches ever given based on, "ALL men are created equal." Our rights come from our Creator, not the government and we all have the right of the pursuit of happiness, it is never guaranteed, but we can pursue it and our personal choices determine the outcome. Have you fallen? Then get back up. Refuse to stay down, refuse to be defeated. Robert Louis Stevenson defines success: "The man is a success who has lived well, laughed often and loved much; who has gained the respect of intelligent men and the love of children; who has filled his niche and accomplished his task; who leaves the world a better place than he found it, whether by an improved poppy, a perfect poem or a rescued soul; who never lacked appreciation of earth's beauty or failed to express it; who looked for the best in others and gave the best he had.

Words to live by: Work hard; Love always; Laugh often; Don't ever give up just find another way. Be kind to everyone. I think Jesus said it best when He said, "Love one another as I have loved you."

AUGUST 27

Don't ever lose the 'awe' of life.
The saddest, emptiest life is one that no longer marvels at the things of God.

The birth of a baby becomes ho hum...until you lose one. A parent becomes a nag...until they are gone. A child becomes a pest...until they grow up and leave home. Life is lived or it is tolerated. We can be joyous or in survival mode. Too many of us choose survival over really, truly living the life Jesus died to give us. We hold on to the bad things that have happened instead of embracing the good. Let them go now!

"Happiness is good health and a bad memory."
-unknown-

Sometimes we just need to be reminded how awesome God is and how spectacular is the world He has created for us.
Here are some amazing facts you may not know:

- The Milky Way galaxy is whirling rapidly, spinning our sun and all its other stars at around 100 million km per hour.
- A day in Mercury lasts approximately as long as 59 days on earth.
- The Sun travels around the galaxy once every 200 million years – a journey of 100,000 light years.
- There may be a huge black hole in the very middle of the most of the galaxies.
- The Universe is probably about 15 billion years old, but the estimations vary.
- Matter spiraling into a black hole is torn apart and glows so brightly that it creates the brightest objects in the universe – quasars.
- The very furthest galaxies are spreading away from us at more than 90% of the speed of light.
- The Universe was once thought to be with working out the age of the Universe is that there are stars in our galaxy which are thought to be 14 to 18 billion years old – older than the estimated age of the Universe. So, either the stars must be younger, or the Universe older. everything that could ever exist, but recent theories about inflation (e.g. Big Bang) suggest our universe may be just one of countless bubbles of space time.
- The Universe may have neither a center nor an edge, because according to Einstein's theory of relativity, gravity bends all of space time around into an endless curve.

and my favorite

- If you fell into a black hole, you would stretch like spaghetti.
(Taken from website amazing spacefacts.com)

Don't ever lose the awe of life. If you start to - then I recommend you google amazing facts about the Universe like I did. I am still laughing at the spaghetti thing. I have decided to stay away from black holes. Remember it is God's universe. He made it for us to live and enjoy life and Him. So, go do it! and go tell someone else to stay away from black holes today.

AUGUST 28

*Criticism doesn't work unless it leaves you a **'better'** person not a **'bitter'** one.*

"If you listen to *constructive* criticism, you will be at home among the wise. If you reject criticism, you only harm yourself; but if you listen to correction, you grow in understanding."
-Proverbs 15-31-32

Who was it that said, " I love being criticized." That would be no one! We all have been the brunt of someone else's slanderous tongue. Have you ever walked away from someone's scathing remarks of you but they said they were "only trying to help?" The Bible makes it very clear there is a type of criticism which is ok. It is 'constructive' criticism and we can learn from this. Its only intention is to 'help' the other person not 'harm' them as most criticism does. Constructive means to 'build up,' so if you can't say something to someone that will make them a better person than it is wise to keep your mouth shut. How many parents have yelled at their child, "I wish you were like your brother!" They do not know the harm they are doing to the child. God didn't make him 'like his brother.' He made him unique and one of a kind. That's pretty special if you ask me. We are all wired differently. Sometimes that wiring may go a little crazy but it can be fixed. God says we are wonderfully and fearfully made. Even that child you are trying to bully by your words.

"What's done to children, they will do to society."
-Dr Karl Menninger-

Words have great power to hurt. They also have great power to heal. I am reminded of a story I heard a long time ago of a first grade class where the teacher was checking the hearing of every child. As each child came up she would whisper into their ear individually, "Say the word cat." and they would repeat it. One child in particular was going through a very rough time at home and the teacher knew it, so when the child's turn came, the teacher bent down and whispered, "I wish you were my little girl." That is one of those 'priceless' moments of life that little girl NEVER forgot. She was valued, maybe for the first time in her young life. She had significance. God does the same for us. When we look up at the stars on a dark night, He whispers, "I turned them on tonight just for you." When we stand on the seashore and mighty waves roar, God whispers, "I can take care of you, Trust Me." When you lose something precious, and suddenly you find it, God whispers, "I love you, everything that is important to you is important to Me." So today, for heaven's sake and yours, "Watch what you say!"

"He has the right to criticize who has the heart to help."
-Abraham Lincoln-

AUGUST 29

You may forget with whom you laughed, but you will never forget with whom you cried.
– Arab proverb-

"A friend is always loyal, and a brother
is born to help in time of need."
Proverbs 17:17

Voltaire once said, "Tears are the silent language of grief." There are tears of sadness and then there are tears of grief. Standing at my mother's gravesite were tears of grief for what I had lost. But they were not tears of hopelessness. I knew she was with her Savior and that I would see her again one day. No one can take her place. To this day, the thought will cross my mind to go to the phone and call her... and then sadly I remember... I can't. I wish God had telephones in heaven because I know my mom would answer if I called. She was my rock here on this earth. She spent my growing up years telling me about Jesus and the rest of the years talking to Jesus about me. Asking Him to protect, guide and keep me. I have tried to do the same for my children and my grandbabies. I want them to know every day of their lives they are covered in prayer. It's a big bad world out there. I hope you had a mother like mine, but if you didn't you can be that kind of a mother yourself.

"A real friend is one who will tell you of your faults and follies
in prosperity and assist with his hand and heart in adversity."
-unknown-

Landrum Bolling wrote, "The chances are that you will never be elected President of the country, write the great American novel, make a million dollars, stop pollution and racial conflict, or save the world. However valid it may be to work at any of these noble goals, there is another one of higher priority – to be an effective parent." Be that someone! Believe in your kids and more importantly – let them know it.

AUGUST 30

Help others. Let your interest in others break the tragedy in your own life.

"Do unto others as you would have them do unto you."
-Jesus-

Change your focus! Stop thinking about your three best friends, "me 'myself', "I" and start thinking of others. There are so many broken hearts in this world, it is very easy to find someone you can help. You don't always need money to help someone. Often times all you need is a smile or a kind word to change someone's day from bad to good. Funny, how smiles are contagious. Someone smiles at you, your spirits are lifted so you then smile at someone else, then they smile at someone and on and on. No telling how many lives you can change with a simple smile or an encouraging word. Try it today. Practice in the mirror before you leave your house and I guarantee you will be smiling as you walk out the door. You might even be laughing. Someone wise once said,

'Don't fight against God's will, instead lean into it.'

God's will does not include pity parties, yet we all have them. The secret to life is keeping them shorter and shorter with each passing year. If you don't you will eventually find out no one wants to come to them anymore. No one except someone else who wants to tell you how much worse their problems are than yours. At first there may be a lot of your friends and then there will be just you. You and your cat. Even he might walk away if you complain enough.

AUGUST 31

Got a broken heart? Give it to God.

"The Christian's faith isn't a leap into the dark. It is a well-placed
trust in the Light of the world, Jesus."
-Ravi Zacharias-

I have shared this before but it is worth repeating. I simply love what Joyce Meyers says, "God can heal you **everywhere** you hurt." Everywhere! I wrote it in big letters in the front of my Bible so I would never forget. Right beside it I wrote, I must give Him all of the pieces! One day I did just that. I was tempted to hold back some of them thinking I could probably fix this one on my own, but remembering how many times God showed me I could not, I handed that one over too. Remember these words when light turns to darkness and you can't seem to find your way.

'He is still.
He is watching.
He will act.'

Always remember this about God. He may be still and it may seem that He is uncaring. You cry out to God, but the heavens are silent. The devil whispers, God doesn't care about you anymore. You have really done it this time. He is through with you!" That is a lie straight from hell. He watches over you, even when He takes you to a hard place in life, especially when He takes you to a hard place. He will <u>never</u> forsake you. Then when the trouble He has allowed in your life has accomplished its purpose, He will act. This holds true even when we get ourselves into a real mess. He will not leave us there unless we chose to stay out of stubbornness. Funny thing is, I have learned in life is that God can and will make you very uncomfortable in your sin until you beg Him to help. We are His children and He won't leave us in the pigpen forever. Like the Prodigal son who one day came to his senses and said "I will go to my father's house," and so must we. As believers we can be a terrible testimony to others when we are in rebellion against God.

"Reality may not be pleasant, but no problem was ever
solved, no goal ever reached without looking at the
situation squarely with no editing or reframing."
-John Townsend-

September 1

Let go. Learn from your mistakes in the past, do not dwell on them and do not hold on to them.

"This is the victory that over cometh the world, even our faith."
1 John 5:4

It requires a great deal of faith to walk away from something you wanted so badly. To forgive yourself for a mistake that may have changed the course of your life or worse, someone else's. To turn away from getting even with someone for the wrong they did to you. It's a choice we all have, to leave it with God who promises to make all things right, or to seek vengeance on our own. If we do the later, it will never turn out good. It may make us feel good for a time, but it won't last. How many words have we all said that we wish we could take back. Same with our actions. I have done many things I regret. I have had things done and said to me that nearly destroyed me if it weren't for God... He says, "Vengeance is mine my child, <u>I WILL</u> repay." I have discovered He is much better at it then I am. I tend to make things much worse when I try to fix them. He may not repay as soon as I think He should and He may not do it the way I want Him to. Only He has all of the facts to do it the right way. I don't have the wisdom to know why people hurt people as they do. I do know that, hurt people, hurt people. They are wounded somewhere deep down in their soul that causes them to wound others. Only God can reach deep down into the heart of a man. How do I know? Because I have hurt others I loved. Sometimes God gave me a good whacking and other times He reached down, put His arms around me and held me close. He doesn't excuse our rebellion, He holds us accountable but only He knows what it will take to get rid of the bad behavior without destroying the person. When the world saw Saul of Tarsus, they saw a murderer of Christians, God saw what he would become, Paul the Apostle. The greatest Apostle the world would ever see. His life was a living testimony to the GREATNESS of our God. Only He can turn a murderer into one of the greatest teachers of the Word of God. What did it cost him? His life. A price he was more than willing to pay for all God had done for him. Lesson: Never give up praying for anyone! If God can save the Apostle Paul then others will be a piece of cake for Him. I am sure Paul's mother never gave up praying for him.

September 2

Some people want to be used...others want to use.

"But he that is the greatest among you shall be your servant.
And whosoever shall exalt himself shall be abased; and he that
shall humble himself shall be exalted."
Matthew 23:11-12

Which one are you, a taker or a giver? This may be a very painful revelation but be honest with yourself. I have been both and by the grace of Jesus I am learning to give. It isn't always easy. In fact, sometimes it is very hard. My feelings don't always catch up with what is the right thing to do. If I think the person 'doesn't deserve' my kindness then it's a harder decision for me to be kind. If I can remind myself that I don't deserve God's kindness but He lavishes it on me anyhow, then I swallow my pride and help the person. God does not let us off the hook simply because we don't want to. He can make us pretty miserable in our self-righteousness until we have a change of heart. It is easier to do what He says the first time He says it. Not only does it help the person who is in need but it also places us into a position where God can bless us. God wants to bless us and He can when our character matches His own.

"In Christianity, men gain righteousness only by confessing
their unrighteousness and being covered by Christ's merit.
Every other religion is man working his way to God.
Christianity is God working His way to men."
-Randy Alcorn-

Isn't it good news that we can't get to heaven on our own merit? It is Jesus who made it possible, and Him alone. When He said, "It is finished," He meant it is finished! He has done it all. That is why God calls salvation a 'gift.' No one is ever required to 'work' for a gift.

September 3

Bad choices get us into messes and only good choices will get us out.

"...choose you this day whom you will serve...but as for me and my house, we will serve the Lord."
Joshua 24:15

Today's question is who are you serving? God? Yourself? Money? Our life is a sum total of all the choices we have made in life. To not make a choice is to make a choice. I think indifference sickens God. Can you imagine being indifferent to Almighty God. What if He were indifferent to us and our plight? When the time comes to make a choice, and you don't make it...you have still made a choice. To do nothing is a choice. To walk away from a problem and hope it goes away is a choice. To ignore what you should do is a choice. Anything that is outside of the will of God is not only a waste of time, but it is futile. We are on our own when we leave God out of the equation. The good news is when we make a choice to do right, to obey God, to live right and to love others, we have all the power of heaven behind us. Most of us have wasted more years than we would like to admit by the bad decisions we have made. It is never too late to start over. It doesn't matter if you had a bad start in life...God will see that the ending is spectacular! The great evangelist Bill Graham said;

"God does not call us to be successful, but to be obedient."
Always remember: It's not hard to live the Christian life...it is impossible, without Jesus.
Adding a little humor: John Wayne said, "Life is hard; It's harder if you're stupid."

God gave us each life to bring Him glory. Someone said, "What you are is God's gift to you, what you become is your gift to God." With all of my heart I don't want to be ashamed of the way I have lived my life on this earth. My mom used to tell me that when she went to heaven she wanted to hear her Savior say, "Well done, thy good and faithful servant." All these years later, I now know why.

September 4

Your life will be measured by what you reap, but it will be determined by what you sow.

New beginnings are often disguised as painful endings -unknown-

Every action has a result. We sow...then we reap its consequences, whether good or bad. If a farmer plants corn, he does not expect to get turnips as his crop. He expects corn. If we hurt someone, how is it that we think something good will come out of it? It won't and it never can. If I climb to the top of the Empire State building and jump off because I think it would be a cool thing to do, well, I think you get the picture. What seems good to us, and we expect it to all turn out good, will not, if it defies any of God's principles. If we lie, cheat or steal we may end up in jail. We reap what we sow. It is so much better as a Christian to sow good seeds during your lifetime. Love the undeserved, feed those who are hungry and God will make sure you have enough food. Be kind to a child. You may be the only one they have who treats them right. The definition of stupidity is, "Doing the same thing over and over and expecting a different result." Yet, we all do it, in relationships, especially. We think the person is going to 'change.' Oh, they will, they will get much worse. God has many warnings in the Bible especially about our behavior and how we treat others. He pretty much summed them all up into one verse, "Do unto others as you would have them do unto you." Do you want someone to lie to you? I didn't think so. Do you want them to cheat you? Of course not!

"Get rid of all bitterness, rage and anger, brawling and slander, along with every form of malice."
Ephesians 4:31

God honors godly behavior and godly behavior honors God. Many people do not go to church but they do watch Christians very closely. Do they live the life they profess? These same people may never pick up a Bible. You may be the only scriptures they read. Our lives should reflect our relationship with God. We should reflect the same grace, mercy and forgiveness He has extended to us. Does it? We are not perfect, that is for sure, but when we do fall, we can say we are sorry and admit we fell short of God's plan for our lives. My sister was going through a very tough time once, and her unbelieving friend knew it. She watched very closely to see how my sister responded to her trials and mistreatment. She never said a word to her, but she watched, and watched for a long time. What she saw eventually brought her to the Lord. She knew my sister's strength had to have come from God. There was no other earthly explanation. Many Christians are lukewarm in their faith. They disregard God in everything they do. One has to wonder if they really are Christians or just church goers. This is why some say all Christians are hypocrites. Sadly, they don't live out what they believe. People can spot a phony a mile away. Sometimes, we are. Sometimes we don't live up to Christ's standards of living. God changes us, but the process can be very slow at times. It takes a moment in time to leave the world behind and give your life to Jesus, but it takes a lifetime for Jesus to get the world out of us. We have many lessons to learn as Christians. Some lessons take longer than others, but once learned will be jewels in our crown of adversity.

"The church is a society of sinners – the only society in the world in which membership is based upon the single qualification that the candidate shall be unworthy of membership."
-Charles C. Morrison-
"The church is the great lost and found department." –Robert Short-

September 5

TRUTH...feelings have nothing to do with it.

Truth is truth no matter how I feel. Truth is what God says it is. There is an old hymn called '*What Will You Do With Jesus?*' That is the question of the ages. Every one of us, at some time in our life, must ask ourselves that question. I believe at some time in a person's life God will shut you up to a Cross and a Savior who gave His life that you might live. You will come face to face with Jesus and will be required to make the most important decision of your entire life. Today let's ponder the words of this old hymn:

"What will you do with Jesus my friend?
Neutral you cannot be.
Someday your heart will be asking, oh friend,
What will He do with me?"

After reading that last line it sends a shiver down my spine. What will He do with me? What will He do with you?

"...man is destined to die once, and after that face judgment."
Hebrews 9:27

Jesus is the judge of all of the universe. One day we will all stand before His throne and give an account for our life, the good, the bad and the ugly. For Christians, it will be a time for rewards or for anything done in the flesh to be burned up. Salvation is a **'gift'** of God, paid for by the precious blood of Jesus. Don't ever think you can earn God's favor. He says you cannot. John Newton knew that when he penned the memorable words to the beloved song Amazing Grace;

"Amazing grace, how sweet the sound, that saved a **wretch** like me."

What did John Newton do to be saved? Nothing. Jesus did it all. Why did he call himself a wretch? Because he was an alcoholic who ran a slave trade business until one day God got a hold of his heart. It is natural for us to think we can 'work' for our salvation, to do something for God to *earn* eternal life. It puffs up our pride. It sounds good, but it is not truth found in the Bible. Our righteousness is as filthy rags in His sight. Does that sound like there is anything we can do to undo our years of sinning? What is God's answer? Jesus crucified. This was God's plan, not mans and that is why it is shunned by many even today. Every other religion of the world, **except** Christianity, makes you **earn** your way to heaven. Those religions say, do,do,do. Jesus says, "Done!" "It is finished!" Tonight when you go to bed, rest your head on His pillow of grace. Grace is God giving us what we don't deserve, mercy is God not giving us what we do deserve.

"Tomorrow's history has already been written. At the
Name of JESUS **every** knee shall bow."
E. Kauffman

This excites me, does it excite you to bow before the KING of kings and LORD of lords? If not you have some heart trouble you need to deal with now.

September 6

Truth is usually the last thing we want to hear.
"Truth is the thread that separates true spirituality from false
spirituality. Spirituality does not give relevance to life;
rather, truth gives relevance to spirituality."
-Ravi Zacharias-

Does God's truth change with time? No. He is the same yesterday, today and forever. He changes not! He is the only One we can really rely on.

"Trust in yourself and you are doomed to disappointment; trust in your
friends and they will die and leave you; trust in money and you may have
it taken from you; trust in reputation and some slanderous tongue may
blast it; but trust in God, and you are never to be confounded in time or eternity."
D.L.Moody

Someone once said, "The man who trusts God is a man who can be trusted." Why is that? Every believer has the Holy Spirit living within them. One of the Holy Spirit's duties is to hold us accountable. He reveals truth to us and then expects us to live by that truth. Unbelievers have no such lie detector living in them. Take the case of Pilate, the Roman Emperor, who when Jesus was brought before him to be put to death, asked Jesus, "What is truth." Did he hold his breath with anticipation of what Jesus would say? No, unbelievably, he walked away before Jesus could respond. He didn't want to know the truth. He only wanted to sound deep and philosophical, not realizing that it was the embodiment of truth standing before him. When we walk away from truth we walk towards deception. Truth is painful sometimes. It may require us to act, to change some behavior we have that does not please God. Some of life's most painful moments come when we face the truth about something in us we have tried to hide for years. The moment we give our hearts to Jesus, He begins to transform us, to make us new creatures. We trade all of those lies for His truth.

"Sometimes truth is costly, but not nearly
as costly as deception."
-Beth Moore-

September 7

Believe in miracles. Each miracle begins with a need.

"We are surrounded by the many miracles
of life, and yet we fail to recognize them."
-Tim Hansel-

Do you have a need today? Our God is still in the miracle business. I love the story of Mary, Martha and Lazarus. They were all friends of Jesus so it was natural for Mary and Martha to send for him when Lazarus became deathly ill. They had a great need. They had seen Jesus heal so many others they were sure He would come and do the same for them. He did not. The Bible says that when Jesus heard the news, instead of rushing to them, He tarried in the town He was in. If you think you can figure God out and what He will do, forget about it. This story is the best illustration of God going above and beyond our request, to give us something greater. Mary and Martha asked Jesus for a healing but Jesus gave them a resurrection! How breath-taking to have been there and see Lazarus come out of the tomb at Jesus' command! Almost every sermon I have heard on this story they make sure to point out that Jesus called Lazarus by name otherwise all of the graves would have emptied out at His command to "Come forth." With those words, new hope was given to the world. Jesus had power over life and death. Their mourning turned into joy! Ask God for a miracle but then let Him answer it His way.

"God knows where every particle of the handful of dust has
gone: He has marked in His book the wandering of every one
of its atoms. He has death so open before His view, that He
can bring all these together, bone to bone, and clothe them with
the very flesh that robed them in the days of yore, and make them live again."
-Charles Spurgeon-

God has triumphed over death and the grave! Death is no longer the end but a glorious new beginning for the child of God.

September 8

Prayer is a privilege, never to be neglected.

"Don't pray to escape trouble. Don't pray to be comfortable in
your emotions. Pray to do the will of God in every situation.
Nothing else is worth praying for."
-John Wesley-

Fear more than anything else can drive us to our knees. A tragedy hits and all of a sudden our world is suddenly shaken to the core. Someone has said, "When your knees are knocking, it might help to kneel on them." Prayer should never be our last resort, but for some it often is. They feel compelled to try everything else first and when that fails they go to God. I know. I myself have done exactly that. Over the years I have learned to go to God FIRST. Unfortunately, I learned this the hard way like most of us. I had more faith in what I could get done then what God could do. Go to Him at the onslaught of trouble and it will save you a lot of heartache in the end. We can choose to carry the burden alone or to give it to God.

"Bending our knees in prayer keeps us from breaking
under the load."
-unknown-

"Fret not!" That is a command from God. Our greatest enemy to prayer is Satan. The moment he sees us start to pray he hinders us any way he can. the telephone will ring, the doorbell will ring, the kids need something right now! It is imperative to pick a time of day to spend with God all by yourself, a time and a place where you and He will conduct today's business. Satan may hinder your prayer but if you will be consistent then prayer will hinder Satan. Press on! Do not give up! I have prayers I have prayed for over 40 years. I continue to pray them because I still believe God will answer. I don't need to know the reason why He hasn't answered them yet but I will not give up! If God has promised something then don't give up! The answer will come. The tough part is leaving the answer up to God as to when He will answer and living in obedience to Him. Rebellion will not get your prayers answered. What God sends will be better than what you have asked for.

"Because of this I say to you, whatever you ask for when you pray,
have faith that you will receive it. Then you will get it."
Mark 11:24

September 9

Your prayer can touch anyone, anywhere in the world, at any time and even more miraculous, it can reach up to the very throne of God.

"When all other courses of action have been eliminated,
When we stand on the edge of the abyss, when we approach
God with empty hands and an aching heart, then
We draw close to the true heart of prayer."
-Jerry Sittser-

Prayer is an **amazing gift** from God. It is an awesome privilege. Think about it…at any moment, anywhere on this earth, no matter what you are doing you can have an instant audience with the King of Kings, and Lord of Lords. Just ponder that thought for a few minutes. If you call on His name, He hears. He is never too busy. Never. Who else do you know that will respond so readily to the cries of your heart? Who else do you know who has the answers to your problem before you even ask?

"Don't pray to escape trouble. Don't pray to be comfortable in your
emotions. Pray to do the will of God in every situation.
Nothing else is worth praying for."
Samuel Shoemaker

The battle stance for the Christian is chin up and knees down.
Do you wonder about prayer? Do you wonder if God really hears YOUR prayer? I think at some point we all do. We have doubts, but then God will show us how foolish our doubting was when He answers with something spectacular…something that only He can do.

Here is a poem worth reading -
Why Wonder?
If radio's slim fingers can pluck a melody from the night
and toss it over a continent or sea;
If the petaled white notes of a violin are blown
across a mountain or a city's din;
If songs like crimson roses are culled from the thin blue air;
Why should mortals wonder that God hears and answers prayer?"
-Ethel Romig Fuller-

It can absolutely boggle the mind when you think about millions of prayers going up before the throne of God in multiple languages all at the same time and He hears each one of us individually. God meets us where we are and commits to take us where He wants us to be. While at the same time He is counting and knows the number of hairs on each of our heads and the number of grains of sand in the whole world. Wow!

September 10

Truth stands the test of time; lies are soon exposed.
-Proverbs 12:19-

"Telling lies about others is as harmful as hitting them with an ax, wounding them with a sword, or shooting them with a sharp arrow."
-Proverbs 25:18-

God apparently takes lying very seriously. Can you imagine hitting someone with an ax? Can you imagine readying your bow and arrow, taking aim and shooting the arrow at someone's intentionally? "I would never do that," you may be saying to yourself right now. Well, the bad news is, we all have done just that when we chose to tell a lie about someone. Only God knows the real damage a lie will do, how many lives it will affect, including the life of the one telling the lie. The Book of Proverbs is filled with wisdom regarding 'lying.' The bottom line is don't do it! If you knew your lie would be exposed one day, would you still tell it? I didn't think so. It sure makes you stop and pause how something we all can do very easily and with a straight face, can be so devastating. I still can't get over the whole ax, lie thing. Some have mastered the skill so much they are worthy of an Academy award for their performance. Politicians have a head start on all of us. How many promises are made that are never intended to be honored? Those are lies, and you can throw in deceit along with it. A lie may get us what we want, it may even get us out of a tight spot or two, but it will only be a temporary fix according to God's word. Truth on the other hand, will stand forever it may not be popular, it isn't easy, but it will be honored by God. Jesus said I AM the way, I AM the TRUTH, and I AM the life. We honor our Savior when we tell the truth regardless of the consequences.

"No man has a good enough memory to make a successful liar."
-Abraham Lincoln-

SEPTEMBER 11

Enjoy today…Life's wake-up calls are reminders of our frailty.

Your telephone rings and it is the police, "There has been an accident…" or, it is the doctor calling you about your test results, "I have some bad news…" Life goes spinning out of control in a heartbeat. If 9/11 and Katrina taught us anything it was surely how frail we are. Life is but a vapor. It passes before we know it. The following is a poem I wrote after the 9/11 attacks shook the world. It is my tribute to all who died that day and to their courageous families: It is lengthy so I hope you will read to the end because America is in a very dangerous place today.

The Day America Fell
By Cindy Balch

Lord, where were You?
Through my tears I cannot see.
The day America fell humbly before You, the day she fell down to her knees.
Lord, where were you? The day those towers fell?
When peace gave way to chaos our lives a fiery hell.
Lord, where were You? The day America wept
As the whole world watched in horror The nation You'd once protected. The nation you had kept.
The nation You had greatly blessed beyond our wildest dreams
Now flounders, reels in uncertainty to know the whys of these tragic things.
Lord, where were You? It seems You've left us on our own
Is it because for years we've shouted for You to leave us alone?
We took You out of our schools and lives and out of our daily conversation
As we willingly turned our backs on You began the downfall of this great nation.
Together as a people, now seeking the God we had denied
Believing we didn't need You choosing instead a life of lies.
Looking down from heaven You must have grieved over our fate
You sent us warning after warning and then it was too late.
Now America faces uncertain times as she never has before
Our complacency now bravery as our nation prepares for war.
When tragedy hit our nation, on that dreadful day
The children in our schools were forbidden by our own laws to pray.
This speaks to how far we have fallen from the God we once held dear
This sadly explains why peace and trust have now been replaced by fear.

Yet three crosses rise midst the rubble of a Savior and two thieves
He's the reason America has fallen… has fallen humbly to her knees.
And because of pride and arrogance the heavens seem silent now
Still hope rises … I see my Savior…a crown of thorns on His bleeding brow.

What made us think we could live without Him when He came to set us free
Does it have to take a tragedy like this to open eyes too blind to see?
What evil is imagined that spits and mocks at God
That hangs Him on a tree to die and beats Him with a rod.
Who's to say which are the more guilty, those who put Him on the cross
Or those who daily profane His name or ignore Him at all costs.

Then call on Him to help them when they've nowhere else to go
Forgetting that a man will always reap exactly what he sows.

We've accepted things we shouldn't have, compromising our beliefs
Exchanging a life of freedom for one of bondage & of grief.
We all did those things which seemed right in our own eyes.
But God gives second chances to those who'll turn from compromise.
Is this what happens Lord, when Your protective hedge comes down?
No shot was fired, roaring engines of planes brought buildings toppling down
Yet as these towers fell another scene played across our land
To give their lives so others might live...brave heroes took a stand
They ran into burning buildings armed only with hearts of love
Their only weapons arms of strength directed by heaven above.
Now America finds herself fighting to gain the world's respect
Not only a war on terror but a war of years of neglect.
What makes a hero a hero? Has strangely been redefined
A hero is someone who stays with a friend not willing to leave them behind.
Though all around them was falling and nothing to see but flames
These brave men became 'great men' that day...the day the terrorists came.
For freedom isn't really free, the price is very high
For since our nation was founded, good men have had to die.
Now we too walk through the valley of death where others before us have trod
Because people no longer mattered and everything came before God.
From Normandy to Vietnam across the seas to Desert Storm
Our flag has flown in majesty though tattered, blood stained and torn
You think your freedom had no price because it wasn't you who paid
But just ask those who sacrificed their sons who now in caskets lay.
Whether or not we are called to fight or to stay behind to pray
We all have to answer the unspoken call that came to us that day
Our lives will never be the same it's a new world in which we live
How true the patriots cry of the past to regret having only one life to give
We've been called to defend our country as never done before
For the battlefield's not in distant lands but has come to America's shores.
They tried to divide our nation to set us sailing on a sea of despair
But they didn't count on our courage and strength when we look to our God in prayer.
How can they dare to say they serve the very same God as we
When all they know is violence & death they'll never know what it means to be free.
Let the whole world know across the globe from sea to shining to sea
Our stars and stripes will forever fly for freedom and liberty.

Each American must now take a stand though the way at times is unclear
And we know that victory may only come after the shedding of many tears.
God has called us all to battle giving to each of us our part
And through it all He joins them both...joy and sorrow in the same heart.

Yes, America may have fallen from the turmoil without and within
But if she fixes her eyes on the Lord
America will rise again.
For in America there still remains courage in every heart that beats
And those who advance on their knees in prayer
Will never face defeat.
The young, the old, rich or poor, yellow, black or white
Though some be called to give their life
Their blood is precious in His sight.
For at the foot of the cross of Christ we are all sinners before His eyes
It was the cross that brought Heaven's King to earth... for our sins is why He died.
We cannot trust our feelings for they change from day to day
But His Word changes not He always will be
The Truth, the Life and the Way.
And though our hearts may tell us God's distant from the sorrows brought our way
Yet all heaven is at our disposal the moment God's people kneel to pray.
So release your doubts and all your fears to the One who cannot fail
His faithfulness His righteousness His justice in the end will prevail
Yea, though we walk through the valley of death we have no cause to fear
He promises never to leave His own, His angels are ever near.
Guarding and protecting though the battle has just begun
But for those of us who know the Lord the battle has already been won.

Old glory waves as a warning for all the world to see
America will answer the call to fight. Americans will die to stay free.
So as we walk through our darkest hour reach out and take His hand
Cradled in His arms of love
In the arms of the great "I AM"
Listen closely to the bells of freedom as across our land they ring
We serve Jehovah, Almighty God
Lord of Lords and King of Kings.
And though through my tears, my sorrow and pain it is hard for me to see
That God sometimes can only get our attention by bringing us to our knees.

So now I know where you were Lord, the day America fell
Lifting her up giving her strength to fight against all the forces of hell.
And now when life overwhelms me and I'm sinking in despair
I will fall on my knees and whisper Your name
And wait silently for you there...
No trial or sorrow is wasted. God speaks loudest in our pain
He's not forgotten those who died that day

Victory will come it will be won in remembrance of each of their names.

Therefore, I lay no conditions On God for He knows better than I what I need
Instead I bow my head and my heart seeking His will and plan for me.

And when the lights of this world fade low and finally grow dim
I'll close my eyes on this side of life but I'll open them up to Him.

And when I think I'm not important to Him in the midst of this world of strife
I humbly remember when He stopped all He was doing
In that moment He gave me life.

Embraced now in the arms of Jesus no longer bothered by earthly things
Casting my cares and leaving them there
Safe in the arms of my King.

Now strong where I once was broken. Seeing where I once was unable to see.
Yes, strong in the broken places from the changes He's made in me.
And though this journey through life is hard I do not face it alone
He takes my hand He leads the way
Only He knows the road that leads me home.
Looking forward to that day in the future though I may not know when or how
When at the name of Jesus Christ all heaven and earth shall bow.
And though there are many with heavy hearts, hearts with unbearable sorrow
Our hope lies in Him the God of today who is also the God of tomorrow.

Yet still in my human frailty... "Lord, I'm scared", I whisper low...
He pulls me close in His arms of love
"Be still my child, I KNOW".

September 12

What do you get when you fight fire with fire?
Answer: You get a bigger fire.

Wisdom says, put down the matches. Walk away if you have to. Learn to pick your battles. Some fights just aren't worth it. Some are.

"**Avoiding** a fight is a mark of honor;
only fools insist on quarreling."
Proverbs 20:3

The Bible has a lot to say about the tongue. It is small, but can inflict incredible damage. "A tiny spark can set a great forest on fire. And the tongue is a flame." When we were young and vulnerable chances are someone said words to us we have never forgotten. Kids taunting one another, calling each other names. Too young to understand the damage they were inflicting. It is time for a heart check. The Bible says, "Out of the heart the mouth speaks." We all have heart trouble proven by the things we say or have said.

Martin Luther has said, ""He (Jesus) sighed," Mark 7:34. This sigh was not drawn from Christ on account of the single tongue and ear of this poor man, but it is a common sigh over all tongues and ears. Our beloved Lord saw full well what an amount of suffering and sorrow would be occasioned by tongues and ears. For the greatest mischief which has been inflicted on Christianity has not risen from tyrants (with persecution, murder and pride against the Word), but from that little bit of flesh which abides between the jaws. This it is which inflicts the greatest injury upon the Kingdom of God."

Lesson: You don't have to say everything you are thinking.
"Why does the tongue have such devastating power? Because
it speaks the thoughts and feelings of the heart, and our
hearts are naturally proud and willing to strike out at others."
-Bill Gothard-

You have a choice to reign in your own tongue or God will let you suffer the consequences. Thought for the day: Think before you speak! Is what you are about to say really necessary? Will it build up someone or tear them down? If it is the latter, hold your tongue. You will be glad you did and so will God.

September 13

Failure never has to be the end of the story.

"Falling down doesn't make you a failure, staying down does."
-unknown-

There is a question we need to ask ourselves, "The last time you failed, did you stop trying because you failed – or did you fail because you stopped trying?" Successes are built on failure. How many times did Thomas Edison fail at discovering electricity? Hundreds of times, but it did not stop him. Can you imagine this world without electricity? God is not a champion of failure, but He is opposed to those who live their lives as though He doesn't exist. It is impossible to succeed without God. Oh, you may have fancy cars, stocks and bonds, grandiose houses and a big bank account, but your heart will be bankrupt. Think about the rich man in the bible who one day surveyed all of his possessions and decided he had so many of them he needed to build bigger barns to hold them all. Most of the world would applaud him, but not God. He called him a fool. Yes, a fool, because he had his priorities out of order. He thought he had years and years to enjoy his 'stuff', he was so wrong, he only had the rest of that day.

God said to him, "You fool, this very night your life will be required
of you and all of the things that you have prepared, whose will they be?"
Luke 12:20.

Are you climbing the ladder of success? At what expense to you or your loved ones? Someone has said, "A person interrupts and endangers his climb up the ladder of success when he stops to pat himself on the back." Any success can only be measured by what you had to give up to reach it. Did you neglect your family, lose friends along the way, lose your integrity or time with your own children? One minister has said, "One day you may wake up and find your ladder of success is leaning against the wrong wall," against a very lonely wall. King Solomon had it all and then some. At the end he said it was all futile. How does God define success? "What does the Lord require of you but to do justly, and to love kindness and mercy, and walk humbly *with* your God." Micah 6:8. He invites us to walk with Him. Wow! What an invitation. We all try many different ways to please God or just ignore Him until the bottom drops out from under us. God's way is clear, be just to people, be kind and merciful at all times and walk humbly with God. Note to self: walk humbly with God, not behind Him, not in front of Him, but stay at His side as hand in hand He leads the way to a successful life on this earth. Humility means I need God every minute of every day, left on my own I will fail. It's not hard to live the Christian life...it is **impossible** without HIM.

September 14

The greatest stealer of time is bad choices.

"The greatest judgment which God Himself can, in this present
life inflict upon a man, is to leave him in the hand of his own boasted free will."
-Augustus Toplady-

Richard Bach has said, "You're always free to change your mind and choose a different future." The moment we stop making bad choices and start to make good choices, our life will turn around. It may take some time but the principle is very simple. Good choices – good life, bad choices – bad life. We choose. We can't blame it on someone else, though many do and that is why their life never changes.

"...choose you this day whom ye will serve...but as for me
and my house we will serve the Lord."
-Joshua 25:15-

Choice: Serve God. Don't serve God. Why do we insist on making it so difficult? It's because we all want our own way with *no consequences*. There is no such thing. Reality check! Every choice has its own consequences. We want to be able to live our lives any way we think is right and have God bless our plan. Unfortunately, it doesn't work like that. Our lives are a sum total of all the choices we have made over the years whether good or bad. Sometimes, I wish God hadn't given us a free will, and then I realize He would have had to make us robots, without the ability to think and choose for ourselves. God says He has a 'good' plan for lives. Without Him, the only plan we have is what we can come up with. His plan for us is founded on His Omniscience. He knows my life and yours from beginning to end. He declared the day we would be born and He will declare the day it all comes to an end. Will it be a glorious finale or a tragic ending, it is up to us. God's plan involves Him showing us the way, directing our path. It may not be easy at times, in fact, I can almost guarantee you some days it will scare the living daylights out of you. Trouble comes to both the Christian and the unbeliever. The difference is the Christian will NEVER walk through trials alone. God will never leave our side.

September 15

*Stop complaining...
Instead whisper a thank you or sing a hallelujah!*

It is impossible to complain and praise at the same time. Both are a choice. How should we react to any situation?

> "He that is down needs fear no fall,
> He that is low no pride;
> He that is humble ever shall
> Have God to be his guide.
> I am content with what I have,
> Little be it or much;
> And, Lord contentment will I crave,
> Because Thou savest such.
> Fulness to such a burden is
> That go on pilgrimage:
> Here little, and hereafter bliss,
> Is best from age to age."
> -John Bunyan-

Go ahead and give it a try. Try to complain and praise God at the same time. You can't do it. They just don't mix. The Bible says that God inhabits the praises of His people. When we praise and worship Him He draws very near to us. Not only does praise bring us close to God but it drives the devil away. Satan was once the Angel of worship in heaven. He led the heavenly choir until one day he decided he wanted to be the one worshiped. God threw him out of heaven! Worship is the attitude of the heart towards a loving, Omniscient God.

> "It is the nature of God, so terribly pure that it destroys all that is
> not pure as fire, which demands like purity in our worship. He will
> have purity. It is not that the fire will burn us if we do not worship
> this; but that the fire will burn us until we worship thus."
> -George MacDonald-

There is power in praise. Worship is at the center of every human being. The only difference between believers and unbelievers is who we worship, God or self.

September 16

*The very moment we make a 'deliberate' decision to reject God,
our lives will begin to spiral down and out of control.*

Remember the Prodigal son was headed for a
good time, yet he ended up in the pigpen.

This has been true in my own life and it will ring true in yours. The longer I live I realize just how important our choices are and how those I have made in the past have affected my life. If I were a preacher I would spend at least 6 months telling my congregation especially the young about the story in the Bible of the Prodigal son. I like to call this story, "A boy and his Pig." It is both a story of defeat and triumph, stupidity and revelation, pride and humiliation, abundance and lack, but most importantly it is a story of the unconditional love of a father for his son. It is a story of God's unmeasured love for us. It is a story of a God who will pursue each one of us to the ends of the earth. He watches daily for our return to Him. He is a God who will never give up on you unless you force His hand by rejecting His **only** solution to sin, His beloved Son, Jesus Christ.

"God cannot give us happiness apart from Himself,
because there is no such thing."
-C.S.Lewis-

The Prodigal son thought he could find happiness in the far country. What is the far country? Any place God is not. He talked his father into giving him his inheritance early and off he went. The boy lived it up with riotous living. Anyone that tells someone that sin is not fun, hasn't been to the far country. Problem is, it's only fun for a while. It never lasts. His money ran out and so did his friends. He found himself broke, lonely and hungry. There was a great famine in the land and so he couldn't even get a job until one man gave him a job of feeding his swine. For a Jewish boy, he couldn't sink any lower than this. He even tried to steal the hogs food, but they wouldn't let him. His mind wandered to his memories of home, a warm bed, plenty of food, people who loved him. I love this part of the story, HE CAME TO HIS SENSES! What does it take to bring us to our senses? In this story the father represents God. If we want to walk away from Him, He will let us. Please don't miss that. He will let you. I know. I did. I too ended up in the pigpen of life. God can make us so uncomfortable in our sin it will drive us back to Him. The boy headed home, prepared to live his days out in his father's house as a servant instead of as a son. As he was close to home His father saw him from a distance and RAN to him. This boy was stinky, smelling like pigs but his father didn't care, He grabbed him and hugged him. What he did next will boggle your mind. He threw him a party! He didn't lecture the boy on what he had done wrong. I think the boy already knew. Too fresh in his mind were the consequences of his choices. God will welcome you that way too the moment you come to your senses. It is your choice to stay in the pigpen or head home. God is waiting for you.

September 17

*The LORD moves **very decisively** against sin.*

That is both a very scary thought and a very comforting one. It's scary if I am the one doing the sinning, comforting if someone has hurt me and I want God to make it all right. The word 'decisively' says a great deal about God's nature. He will not tolerate sin in His universe. The day is coming when He will rid the world of sin once and for all. What a glorious day that will be. The fact that God is decisive means He has a deliberate plan He is following. Nothing can stop Him. Nothing! Jesus is at the very center of God's plan. Foolish men write and pass laws to remove God and prayer from schools. Someone very accurately stated that as long there were tests and quizzes in school there would be prayer.

> "If we confess our sins to Him, He is faithful and just to forgive us
> our sins and to cleanse us from all unrighteousess."
> -1 John 1:9-

When we confess our sins, we agree 100% with what God says about sin and our rebellious behavior, anything short of that is not confession or repentance. We don't make excuses, we don't try to justify our action, we call it what God calls it, sin. The Bible says that "God is light and there is no darkness in Him at all. So we are lying to ourselves if we say we have fellowship with God but go on living in spiritual darkness." (1 John 1:5) Learn to move very decisively away from sin. Stay away from it, don't flirt with it, don't linger anywhere near it or it will take you down.

September 18

*The prodigal son's journey was never
measured by miles, but in misery.*
-Unknown-

Misery…I think every Christian knows exactly what this means. Before Jesus, our journey was measured by a few good times with lots of misery and guilt the rest of the time. After accepting Jesus and turning our lives over to Him, our lives can be measured in joy, no matter what our circumstances. Someone once said, "Our worst day with Jesus is still better than our best day without Him." It doesn't matter how many miles we are away from Jesus, what matters most is the emptiness that is brought into our lives because we have turned our back on Him. Thank God, He never turns His back on us. The Holy Spirit continually draws us back to Him. Sometimes, all it takes is a gentle reminder that we shouldn't be doing that and sometimes God has to pull the carpet right out from under us to get our attention. The big question today is, "Do you want your life measured in misery? Do you want to be a sheep, whose nature it is to wander away from his Shepherd?" If you are one of His, He will bring you back to His fold one way or another. How He does it is up to your response to His gentle tugging at your heart strings. If that doesn't work, He will turn up the heat. Foolish is the person who wrestles with God to get his own way. Just the mere fact that you have to wrestle with Him should be a good indicator it is not His will for you.

I don't know about you but I am tired of misery, guilt, shame and fighting a losing battle when instead I can rest in His arms, safe and protected. This is His invitation to 'whosoever will';

"Come unto Me all you who are weary and carry heavy burdens and I will give you rest."
-Matthew 11:28-

Unfortunately, I think there are a lot more whosoever wont's than whosoever wills. Which one are you? It is your choice.

Thought for the day: Nothing weighs more than unconfessed sin. Nothing.

September 19

*God's judgment is neutral...
it is measured by which side you are found on.*

"We are interested in death but
we rarely speak of judgment."
-Martyn Lloyd-Jones-

What is God's measurement? It is perfection! Do we measure up on our own merits? Absolutely not, that is why He sent Jesus, His 'sinless' Son, who was willing to pay the price for our sins. It only takes one sin to keep you from heaven and it only takes one death, Jesus' death to get you into heaven. It is His blood that cleanses us from all of our unrighteousness. You may be asking, "How can blood wash me whiter than snow?" Because it is the blood of God's only Son shed for you and for me that wipes our slate clean as if we have never sinned. You will never find a better deal than that. The wages of sin is death. The **gift** of God is eternal life. You cannot earn a '**gift**', you simply reach out and take it. No amount of 'good deeds' will get you into heaven. No matter how many you do. Many think God has a scale in heaven and puts our good deeds on one side and our bad deeds on another and if the scale tips to the good side then we are okay. That may sound good but you won't find that anywhere in the Bible. We all fall short of the glory of God according to His word. When Jesus, the 'sinless' Son of God died on the cross He said, **"It is finished!"** What is finished? the payment for sin that a Holy God would now accept. There is no other way to Heaven, but by Jesus. He says, "I AM the way, the truth and the life, NO man comes to the Father but by ME." No man. Case closed! You either come by accepting His payment for your sin or you are lost without Him. You may not like it, but it doesn't change anything. We all think we can do better, strive harder, but in the end we still fall short. Jesus paid for ALL of my sins, past, present and future. That does not mean that there won't be consequences if I sin on this earth. It means, I confess my sins, and He is faithful and just to forgive me and to cleanse me. It's all about what He did 2000 years ago, not how good I can be. Not how good you can be. God says our righteousness (good deeds) is like filthy rags in His sight. Have you ever had a yucky thought and you wondered where in the world did that come from? It came from a sinful heart. The only One who can tip the scale all the way to the side of righteousness is Jesus. If you still think you can 'work' your way to heaven then answer this one question; "Why did God send His Son to this earth and then allow the Romans to crucify Him?" Want the answer? He came to die. He paid a debt He did not owe to pay a debt we could not pay. Hallelujah what a Savior!

"The final judgment will be done to display and
glorify the righteousness of God."
-Jonathan Edwards-

September 20

With God there is no such thing as an 'ordinary' day.

"We may not be able to choose our temperament, our native
intelligence, or our physical appearance, but we do get to choose our attitude."
-John Maxwell-

Most days seem very 'ordinary' until you start looking for God in them. Did you get a great parking spot? Did a much needed check arrive in the mail just in time? Did an old friend call? Was it someone you have been thinking about lately but haven't talked to in years? That is God. Some will say God isn't really interested in the little things of our life. Not true! He is interested in every aspect of our lives.

"The steps of the godly are directed by the Lord.
He delights *in every detail* of their lives."
Psalm 37:23

It is us who limits Him. Did a stranger smile at you and once again made you believe there are still good people in this world? Have you ever looked up at the sky only to see the most beautiful sunrise you have ever seen? God painted that for you this morning, and His finger swept along the skies with a magnificent sunset this evening so your day would end with a tiny glimpse into eternity. If this side of heaven is so beautiful think what the real thing must be like. God whispers to us throughout the day, but are we listening? Unfortunately, for most of us the answer is no. It is a choice we have to make at the beginning of each and every day. Today, go out of your way to look for God's tiny little messages of love throughout your day. You will be astounded at how much He wants to be in your everyday life, not just when trouble comes.

September 21

Do you have an insurmountable problem?
Plead your case before a loving, Sovereign God...then leave it with Him.

"Acquitting the guilty and condemning the innocent –
the Lord detests them both."
Proverbs 17:15

We have all been wronged and treated unjustly in this life. God knows this. What He also knows is each man's heart. We do not. We don't know why a man does what He does, what his real motives are, we can only guess, and guessing is not good enough. This is why God alone is the judge of the earth. We are to walk in love regardless of what has been done to us. We have a higher standard than the world has who seeks vengeance and retaliation when wronged.

"I am not sure exactly what heaven will be like, but I do know that
when we die and it comes time for God to judge us, He will not ask,
"How many good things have you done in your life?" rather He will ask,
"How much love did you put into what you did?"
-Mother Teresa-

How can anyone argue with Mother Teresa whose whole life was spent in the dirtiest slums on the face of this earth, loving the world's most rejected and undesirable? Any time we desire to get even with someone who has wronged us, it would do us well, to look at Jesus hanging on the cross, not for anything He did, but solely for the sins you and I have committed. He was sinless. He was perfect. Yet, He was spit on, lied about, accused of sins He wasn't capable of committing, yet the bible said as He stood before His accusers He opened not His mouth. He trusted God to judge them and so should we. We deserved death, Jesus gave us life. We deserved hell yet He prepared a place in heaven for us to live with Him forever! He is our example. No one says it will be easy. Admitting you're wrong, saying you're sorry, or forgiving someone without seeking revenge are some of the hardest lessons a Christian will ever do. God says He will help us to do just that and He promises to heal our hearts from all of the hurts of this life. We won't get a better deal anywhere else. So, the next time someone hurts you, PRAY! Pray for them, pray for yourself and let God be God. He has also promised to right all wrongs on this earth. What a glorious day that will be! Psalm 37: 7 "Be still in the presence of the Lord and wait patiently for Him to act."

September 22

The Christian walk is progressive, there is <u>never</u> a 'quick fix.'

A baby learning to walk, falls and may feel pain,
but even a baby gets back up and tries again.

"Shake it off!" Have you ever heard those words yelled to someone at a sporting event after taking a hard knock? I have heard it many times and it was usually a parent, who knew from experience, the best way is to get back up after being knocked down and then shake it off. Some things are easier to shake off than others. As we walk, we may stumble, we may take two steps forward and three back, then three steps forward and two back, but we have to keep getting up over and over again. Sometimes we make great progress, big leaps forward and sometimes Satan throws us a curve ball in life and we swing and strike out. We may get knocked down for a while, but God never intends for us to stay down.

"He who limps is still walking."
-Stanislaw J. Lec-

    I heard someone once say, "If you are going to fall, fall forward, that way you are always making progress." Augustine of Hippo gives some good advice to us all, "In all trouble you should seek God. You should not set Him over against your troubles, but within them, God can only relieve your troubles if you, in your anxiety, cling to Him. Trouble should not really be thought of as this thing or that in particular, for our whole life on earth involves trouble; and through the troubles of our earthly pilgrimage we find God."
    Seek God in your trouble and you will find Him. You cannot change what has happened in the past even if you spend your time in regret and worry. Let it go. God is already in our tomorrows.

September 23

*"His compassions NEVER fail.
His mercies are NEW every morning"*
-Lamentations 3:23-

"The value of compassion cannot be over-emphasized. Anyone can criticize. It takes a true believer to be compassionate. No greater burden can be borne by an individual than to know no one cares or understands."
-Arthur H. Stainback

God's mercies are new every morning. Wow! That means He never runs out. Every day we get a new start. We need it because most of us used up yesterday's supply. I love what Mary Ellen Edmunds said, "Do unto others if they *never* ever do unto you. Don't just give kindness to those who deserve it but be kind to everyone. No act of kindness is ever wasted, it will come back to you in ways you never imagined. Who needs our kindness the most? It is those who are hurting. Why is it that we are the cruelest to those we love, those we take for granted?

"Jesus said the entire Old Testament hangs on two commands. Love God and love the person next to you. (Matthew 22:34-40). How can you love the person next to you and not open your heart to him? How can you open your heart without letting yourself be vulnerable? Peter wrote, "Above all, love each other deeply." (1 Peter 4:8)

Do you know how God determines whether or not, we who call ourselves Christians, love Him or not? He says, "Those who love Me, will OBEY Me. Is your life a life of obedience? Do you love God by His standards, or yours?

September 24

*"Those who really know God are no longer cowards!
It strips the fear right out of your life."*
-Joyce Meyer-

What does a coward look like? What does a courageous person look like? They are both ordinary people just like you and me. Ordinary, that is, until life deals them a blow and rocks their world or puts them into a dangerous situation that forces a decision. Sometimes, it's a decision between life and death. Life's pressure is what proves what we are made of. Do we run from the danger or stop and take a stand? A coward has no principles by which they live. Some things in life can be compromised and then there are others that we cannot compromise no matter the cost. The fearless know the difference. Cowards compromise throughout their whole lives, whatever suits their purpose for the moment that is what they do.

"Fear can keep a man out of danger, but courage will support him in it."
-Thomas Fuller-

Joshua had some big shoes to fill following Moses as leader and proved himself to be a man of courage.
"Only be strong and very courageous, being careful to do according to all the law which Moses my servant commanded you; turn not from it to the right hand or to the left, that you may have good success wherever you go." –Joshua 1:7-

The story of Meriam Yehya Ibrahim is a true study in courage. She refused to recant her Christian faith and was the thrown into a Sudanese prison with her toddler child. She was then convicted of apostasy and was sentenced to death by a Sudanese court. Do you think she counted the cost? The court also convicted her of adultery and sentenced her to 100 lashes because her marriage to a Christian man is considered void under Sharia law. When faced with all of these charges how did she respond? Fearlessly she replied, "I am a Christian and I will remain a Christian." If things weren't bad enough for her, she gave birth while in this dirty, filthy prison. Both of her children lived in a small cell with her. She refused to denounce her Christianity. As I followed this story on the news, I had to hang my head in shame as I pondered what my reaction would have been to the same circumstances. She never lost hope. Eventually, with public pressure, she was released. Yet, after her release she was taken captive once again. Did she question God? No. She was released once again and brought to the United States where she told her story. Want to know what a real hero looks like, read her story! It will both humble you and amaze you by her courage and God's faithfulness.

"It is better to live one day as a lion than a hundred years as a sheep." -Italian Proverb-

SEPTEMBER 25

Instead of demanding to know...God whispers, **"TRUST ME."**

"Reasoning is the greatest enemy faith has; it never comes to the aid of spiritual things, but – more frequently than not – struggles against the divine Word, treating with contempt all that emanates from God."
-Martin Luther-

Of course God asks us to use our common sense, but when we think a problem to death to the point of confusion we have gone too far. God is not the author of confusion but of love, power and a sound mind. We are called upon to trust many times throughout our day. We sit in a chair without first testing its strength because we trust it will hold us. Trusting God sometimes will require every bit of faith we can muster up. God puts us in a situation where we are helpless to do anything about our circumstances, then He says, "Trust Me." If you are anything like me, you immediately come up with Plan B, C,D, E, F and all the way to Z if need be. Trouble is, if God is teaching us to trust Him and Him alone, none of those plans will work. We can save ourselves a boatload of trouble by surrendering to Him before going to Plan B.

"Father God, grant me eyes to see Your hand at work and a heart to trust Your ways. Even as I long for quick action and a short cut through my trials, cause faith to rise within me to recognize that Your "scenic route" answers are for my best and Your glory."
-Rebecca Luisignolo-

We can 'think' problems to death, so much so, we talk ourselves right out of faith. God where are You? Don't you love me, Lord? We get confused, we make excuses instead of simply admitting that we don't know why, but God does. God longs for our trust. There are so many things in this life we will never understand this side of heaven. Things we were never meant to understand. We don't understand how electricity works but it doesn't stop us from using it. God's ways are high above our ways. We all will suffer losses that we can't explain.

"Trusting God trumps understanding God. The train will have long left the station and left us on the platform if we determine to ride only with full understanding. Life will have passed us by. I'm choosing to trust the conductor and the track He has laid down for me."
-Terry Esau-

You will never fully trust someone you don't know that is why it is so important to read God's Word and get to know Him. It is His love letter to us. We learn the true heart of God when we view life through His eyes. Those eyes are focused on Jesus Christ, His only Son, giving His life for a lost world. It's easy to trust a God who would rather die than live without me for all eternity. If you will take the time to listen, you will hear Him whisper, "I love you," over and over again.

SEPTEMBER 26

*God wants to be involved in **every** decision of your life.*

No one learns to make right decisions
without being free to make wrong ones.

Do you have a big decision to make in your life? Then before the sun sets you should be down on your knees seeking wisdom only God can give, the sooner the better. If your present day circumstances seem to be at their very worst then please consider the following story by Viktor Frankl:

> "We who lived in concentration camps can remember the men who
> walked through the huts comforting others, giving away their last
> piece of bread. They may have been few in number, but they offer
> sufficient proof that everything can be taken away from a man but
> one thing: the last of the human freedoms – to choose one's attitude
> in any given set of circumstances, to choose one's own way."

Even in the very worst of situations, when your very life and existence is threatened by evil, this story tells us we can still make good choices. These men entered into eternity by offering to someone else their bread so they could live one more day, even though they would forfeit their own lives. There is really no distinction between our 'big or little' requests we petition God for. To Him, who rules the universe, who holds the oceans in the palm of His hand, our requests are all small. That does not mean to diminish their importance to God or to us. He loves us. The question has often been asked, "Is there anything too hard for God?" Of course not! We are His children and He longs to bless us. I like to think that in the morning when I curl up on the sofa with my Bible, my daily devotional, a pen and a notebook, that God smiles and turns to the angels and says, "Hold all my calls, I'll be with my child for a little while, she needs Me." I believe I am that important to Him! I know in reality He does not have to hold all His calls because He is Omniscient (all knowing) and He hears the prayers of His people around the world, some with much greater needs than my own. God has a way of making me feel special when I am alone with Him. During that time I spend with Him I have His full attention. We enter a place where we can shut the world's noise and its problems out. It's just me and my Savior. My problems seem less burdensome in the light of His presence. We all make a conscious decision every day to spend time with God or tackle the day on our own. I have tried it both ways, only one way works. There are many 'paths' that we can take in a day, God says, "If you will trust me I will direct your path, I will make sure you find the right one for you." The Psalmist King David spoke of 'hungering and thirsting after God,' every morning I try to get a better glimpse of what that really means.

September 27

*Blessed are those whose names are written in **the Lamb's book of life**.*

"God was reconciling the world to Himself in Christ, not counting
men's sins against them. And He has committed to us the message of reconciliation."
2 Cor.5:19

Question for today: "Is your name written in the Lamb's Book of Life?" You can be sure you know. How can you be so sure, you may be asking? I am sure because I believe what God says. He says that we may KNOW **now**, not just when we die, but now, that we have eternal life. The one thing that is certain about life is that one day we will leave it. We don't pick that day any more than we pick the day we are born. God controls life and death and the details of our life.

"I write this to you who **BELIEVE** in the name of the Son of God,
that you may **KNOW** (with settled and absolute knowledge)
that you (already) have ETERNAL life."
I John 5:13

This is written to believers! So, if you haven't accepted Jesus Christ as Savior and Lord of your life, then you have no assurance what the future holds for you. Only believer's names are written in the Lamb's book of life. God alone knows the length of our days upon this earth.

"You watched me as I was being formed in utter seclusion, as I was woven together in the dark of the womb. You saw me before I was born. Every day of my life was recorded in your book.
Every moment laid out before a single day had passed."
Psalm 139:15-16

Someone once said, "The nearer the time comes for our departure from this life, the greater our regret for wasting so much of it. Our view of death depends on how we have lived. Some people can die old at forty or die young at eighty."

September 28

Man's list says, "Do, do, do...God says. "Done!"

Work! Work! Work! Do! Do! Do! Get up again tomorrow and do the same thing all over again. God wants us to be successful, but never at the expense of our relationship with Him or others. The Bible says the devil came to steal, kill and destroy, but Jesus came that we might have life, and have it abundantly, until it overflows! Is your life overflowing or are you drowning in a sea of worry? Then it's time to take an honest inventory. If you can't make it an honest one then don't waste your time. Truth is what sets us free. It's truth about ourselves, not truth about others. Wisely choose a goal for which you are willing to exchange a piece of your life for it.

"He who provides for this life, but takes no care for eternity,
is wise for a moment, but a fool forever."
-John Tillotson-

Satan doesn't care how good or noble your intentions are as long as he can keep you focused on tomorrow. I had a friend of mine who I had known since junior high school. She had cancer and ended up in a nursing home. I kept putting off calling her, telling myself I will do it tomorrow. I let too many tomorrows pass until tomorrow turned out to be too late. She passed away one night. This time I regretted what I failed to do. Tomorrow isn't promised to any of us. I think the 9/11 attacks on the twin towers that 'normal' morning proves that we can't count on tomorrow coming. Those people woke up that morning, just another day at work, instead ended in one of America's greatest tragedies and loss of life. How many times did the words "I'm sorry" go unsaid? How many failed to stop and kiss their loved one as they ran out the door that morning, afraid they would be late for work. They had no way of knowing eternity was just a few hours away. Make today count, live it as if it is your last, because it might be.

September 29

With the CROSS before me and the world behind me...there is no turning back.

"Before the foundation of the world was laid, God,
in His divine sovereignty, planned to send His own
Son to the cross to be our Savior."
-Anne Graham Lotz-

Success can be defined in many ways. For some of us it's defined by how much money we have in the bank. For others it can be how educated you are or what kind of car you drive. Christians should measure success differently than the world does. Why? because God measures success differently than the world does. Paul the Apostle was beaten many times with rods, almost to the point of death and thrown in prison more times than he could count. He was driven out of town after he declared the good news of the gospel to them. Would anyone in their right minds say that he was a failure! Absolutely not! Paul wrote the majority of the New Testament and today the Bible is still the best sold book in all of the world. One has to wonder why Paul was treated so badly for bringing the greatest news the world has ever heard, our sins forgiven, a fresh new start, a relationship with the Creator of the Universe and an eternal home in Heaven. And my favorite is that God promises I will one day see my mom again. She will one day hold me in her arms and never let go. Everything she told me about Jesus will become a reality. Who are you longing to see again? What is success to you? Paul defined it as doing God's will. Paul went from a murderer of Christians to the greatest Apostle the world has ever seen. His obedience to the Lord eventually cost him his life. Satan attacked Paul and then attacked him again and again until he was finally put to death. The lesson to learn is Paul NEVER gave up. He kept pressing on despite his circumstances. In his own words when his life was coming to a close he said, "I have fought the good fight." Following Jesus comes with a high price tag, but not following Him comes with an even greater price to pay. I am reminded of the young high school student Cassie Bernall, at Columbine High School who while looking down the barrel of a shotgun was asked do you believe in God? She didn't hesitate even knowing her answer would end in her death. She was killed for her faith. We live in a very scary world today never believing that anyone in the United States would ever suffer such a fate, but it did happen and with the hatred for Christians growing around the world and sadly in our own country, it may happen again. What will you do? Would you give your life rather than deny the Lord? Can you say with conviction that you have fought the good fight of faith?

September 30

Do you know what confuses unbelievers the most?
A believer that says one thing and does another.

"What you do speaks so loudly I can't hear what you are saying!"
-unknown-

Does your mouth and your actions line up? If our actions do not line up with what we are saying, we are living a lie. We deceive ourselves. I think this is why God defines our love for Him by our obedience to Him.

God says, "If you really love Me you will obey Me."
John 14:15

If we love God we will actually follow Him wherever He leads. Now that can scare many of us half to death. What if God wants me to go to Africa to help heal the sick and spread the good news? Simply put then that is where I belong and that is where God's blessings for me will be found. God can give us peaceful hearts in the midst of some of the worse circumstances known to man. Sometimes He leads us through some very scary places. We are called to obedience whether or not we understand what God is doing. He requires us to trust Him, no excuses, no "let me think about it," He requires immediate trust. Ponder the following circumstances of the Apostle Peter:

"And when they brought them, they set them before the high council.
And the high priest asked them saying, "Did we not strictly command
you not to teach in His (Jesus) name? And look, you have filled
Jerusalem with your doctrine, and intend to bring this man's blood on us."
But Peter and the apostles answered and said: "We ought to obey God rather than men."
Acts 5:27-29

That is a profound statement, "We ought to obey God rather than men." They were being led by the Holy Spirit to get the good news out to anyone who would hear and believe. They knew this might not end well and that there was a good possibility they could end up in prison again, but they chose obedience to prison. If you teach this to your children at a very young age it will save them and you a lot of heartache in the future where well- meaning friends try to pressure them to 'join the crowd.' They say, "Everyone is doing it!" That still doesn't make something right that is wrong, no matter how many people are 'doing it.' Lesson: Compromise and you lose.

"A good name is rather to be chosen than great
riches, and loving favor than silver and gold."
Proverbs 22:1

October 1

What are you willing to compromise that you know to be right?

"A Christian is just as much under obligation to obey
God's will in the most secular of his daily businesses as
he is in his closet or at the communion table."
A.A. Hodge

Daniel the prophet was a great man of God who refused to compromise his beliefs. When Jerusalem fell he was captured and brought to Babylon, as a slave, to serve King Nebuchadnezzar's every whim and desire. Because Daniel was found to have possessed such great wisdom he was invited to eat at the King's table and the customs of the Babylonians was different from the requirements of God for the Jewish people. Daniel could have just gone along with the crowd, but instead he took a stand.

"But Daniel **determined in his heart** not to
defile himself by eating the king's rich and dainty food
or by drinking the wine which he drank; therefore he requested
of the chief of eunuchs that he might be allowed not to defile himself."
Daniel 1:8

Now, you would think the King got angry at Daniels request, and that the Eunuch told on him and he was thrown into prison never be heard from again. Yet, that is not what happened. The scripture says, "Daniel *determined in his heart not to defile himself.*" The heart is the best place to determine what is right for out of the heart flows the issues of life. What is in our heart eventually comes out. Daniel's mind was set long before this incident that he would follow God and not defile himself. He did not just possess head knowledge alone, but he had 'heart' knowledge too. So, what were the consequences? God steps in:

"Now God made Daniel to find **favor, compassion**
and **loving kindness** with the chief of the eunuchs."
Daniel 1:9

This is a God thing. Instead of facing discipline, Daniel found favor, compassion and loving kindness with this stranger in a foreign land. Wow! Obey God and He can cause others to like you and shower favor over you. Now this isn't the end of Daniel's story he was tested many more times and one testing got him thrown into a den of very hungry lions! He would have perished had it not been for God. The Lord shut the mouths of the lions and Daniel was set free once again to do God's work. God will never forsake us, never! He isn't afraid of lions and doesn't want you to be either.

October 2

Your children will follow your lead...

"The home marks a child for life."
-Howard Hendricks-

How many of us now that we are getting older do something goofy, then nervously laugh and say "Oh my gosh! I am just like my mother! That would be funny, but it really depends on what kind of a mother you had. If you want to get really depressed today, read about the Proverbs 31 woman. She is God's model woman. She is like WONDER woman! No joke, she does it all. She toils from dawn to dusk (ugh), she makes her own clothes, she can be trusted, she buys and sells, she extends a helping hand to the poor, and opens her arms to the needy. Wow! Must I go one? She gets up at dawn and prepares meals for her household, and this is the only part I like, she plan's the day's work for her servants. Someone to clean my house! If all that wasn't enough, she is clothed with strength and dignity and kindness rules her life. She has no fear of the future. Now you may not have had a mom like her, she would have been a very tough act to follow, but you did see your mother as a role model, good or bad. We all learn from our parents and our children will learn from us.

If you bow down, if you give up, they will too. If you show them the way to Jesus they will follow, maybe not at first, but they will eventually follow Him. If you reject Jesus, chances are they will too.

"You call me master, and obey me not;
You call me light, and seek me not;
You call me the way, and walk me not;
You call me wise, and follow me not;
You call me fair, and love me not'
You call me rich, and ask me not;
You call me eternal, and seek me not;
You call me gracious, and trust me not;
You call me noble, and serve me not;
You call me mighty, and honor me not;
You call me just, and fear me not;
If I condemn thee, blame me not.
In the Cathedral at Lubek, Germany

OCTOBER 3

"Obey God and leave all of the consequences to Him." –Charles Stanley-

"Character may be manifested in the great moments, but it is made in the small ones."
-Phillip Brooks-

Obeying God requires an abundance of character, faith and love. What does love have to do with obedience? Jesus says in John 14:15 : "If you love Me, you will obey Me." Character is who we are when we are alone, and no one is watching. If a man goes out of town on business alone, what does he watch on the hotel room TV? When no one is watching, do you stay true to your beliefs and your conscience or do you reason with yourself, "Just this once, nobody will know." God knows, that should be enough. Faith is required in obedience because we don't always understand what is happening, we don't know what *will* happen, so it requires great courage at those times. To be successful in this life we must obey the Word of God. There is great power in what God says to us. Obedience is not an option, it is a command.

"You may as well quit reading and hearing the Word of God,
and give it to the devil, if you do not desire to live according to it."
-Martin Luther-

How seriously we take God's word is the extent to which we will obey Him. God requires our whole life be dedicated to Him, not just the bits and pieces that we choose to relinquish to Him for a time. It is all or nothing. Just like the Ten Commandments are just that, commands, not suggestions, so too is obedience to the God we profess to love. He may ask us to do something we find very hard and uncomfortable to do. It may be He will ask us to do something we would rather die than do. Obedience isn't always pleasant, but the fruits of it far outweigh the discomfort. We would do good to take a lesson from the angels:

"If two angels were to receive at the same moment a commission from God, one to go down to earth's grandest empire, the other to go sweep the streets of its meanest village, it would be a matter of entire indifference to each which service fell to his lot, the post of ruler or the post of scavenger; for the joy of the angels lies only in obedience to God's will, and with equal joy they would lift a Lazarus in his rags to Abraham's bosom, or be a chariot of fire to carry Elijah home."
-John Newton-

Obedience should never be questioned - it should be followed, regardless of the consequences. Often we are asked to obey with no idea what the outcome will be. It may cost us more than we ever expected but it will always be blessed by God. It is always an act of faith. Faith in a God who would never ask you to do something unless He also provided everything you would need to accomplish it. Moses didn't want to lead the Israelites out of Egypt. He wanted God to find someone else. God said no. Looking back at the story we see, though times were very difficult for them, God provided more than enough for Israelites survival. Yes, they murmured and complained during the process, just as we often do, but they were eventually set free to worship their God. They were no longer in bondage, no longer slaves to an ungodly ruler. God desires to set us free also, but it requires obedience.

"Do not merely listen to the Word, and so deceive yourselves. DO what it says." James 1:22

October 4

Your convictions will be tested!

Someone has said, "Be careful not to re-label sin. Call it what God calls it." How often are we tempted to say, "Just this one time won't hurt anything." Yes, it will. Or, "Everybody is doing it so it must be ok." No, it is not if God says otherwise. "What can it hurt?" The problem with sin is even though you think it won't matter, it will. God promises consequences to all of our actions, the good, the bad and the ugly, like it or not. We all love the good things that happen when we do what's right. Most of us hate the bad consequences that come with bad decisions. We try to explain our circumstances away. "If God really loved me He wouldn't have let this happen to me." Sounds good but it is a big fat lie of the enemy. God does love you and me. He has warned us ahead of time what He expects from us. The Sermon on the Mount, the Ten Commandments were given to help us live right and to help us make right decisions. Sometimes God will put up big obstacles in our lives to keep us from doing the wrong thing. I don't know about you but I got pretty good at jumping over those barriers only to find out they were put there for my protection. The hardest consequences to bear are those that could have and should have been prevented. That's where the famous 'shoulda, woulda's' came from. They are friends with 'if only ida.' "I shoulda listened to my parents." "If only I woulda read the Bible." "If only ida done what I was supposed to." We all have a conscience that speaks to us all day long. Bells go off in our heads and we ignore the warnings. Sad thing is the more you ignore them the quieter they become until they don't even bother you anymore. Many kids grew up in Christian homes and once they left the nest they turned off their alarm system. I tried it too for a while. They did what they wanted to do without anyone interfering, especially God, who blessed us with a conscience that says, "Don't do that!" I was one of those kids. I knew right from wrong, unfortunately wrong was a lot more fun. At least for a while or so I told myself. There isn't any sin worth the price we pay afterwards. Once you make a decision to follow God, to have a daily minute by minute relationship with Him, Satan steps in to make sure it doesn't happen. Your convictions will be tested to see if they are real or not. Many followers of Jesus leave when persecution comes and then there are people like Stephen, the first recorded martyr in the Bible. As he was being stoned to death for his faith, he looked up to heaven and saw the Lord looking down on him smiling His approval for his faithfulness and perseverance.

> "Nothing less than an unconditional surrender
> could ever be a fitting response to Calvary."
> -John Flavel-

Which way will you go when persecution comes? Will you turn your back on God or will you turn to Him regardless of the outcome? Just something to ponder today because trouble is already just right around the corner.

October 5

*Be still and **KNOW**!*
Not be still and wonder, or be still and guess, but BE STILL AND **KNOW**.

The Bible says, "You number and record my wanderings; put my tears into Your bottle – are they not in Your book?" What an awesome God. Think about the tears you have cried over the years and **KNOW** that God has kept track of every single one of them. Likewise, every time we have wandered from Him to do our own thing, He has kept track of those journeys. Those journeys we have taken so we don't have to face the truth about ourselves as God sees us without Him. God is Holy. God is also love. These aren't just things He does, they are who He is, they are His very nature. Most of us forget that God's holiness requires Him to judge sin. Something we all are, sinners. We have this goofy notion that because of His love He will just turn the other way and let us slip into Heaven through the back door. One glance at God's Son hanging on a cross for you and for me will squash that notion. God's holiness required a payment for sin, God's Son agreed to pay it before the foundations of the world.

> "Knowledge without repentance will
> be but a torch to light men to hell."
> -Thomas Watson-

Wow! There is no other payment to satisfy God's wrath against sin than Calvary where His Holy, sinless Son became sin for us, He who knew no sin. We aren't going to enter Heaven through the back door, but carried up to Heaven's gates by God's angels.

> "The knowledge of God without that of our wretchedness creates
> pride. The knowledge of our wretchedness without that of God creates despair.
> The knowledge of Jesus Christ is the middle way, because of Him we find
> both God and our wretchedness."
> -Blaise Pascal-

OCTOBER 6

Unshakable faith...

"How PRECIOUS are Your thoughts about me, O God! They are innumerable! I can't even count them; they outnumber the grains of sand! When I awake in the morning, You are still with me."
Psalm 139:17-18

Today, spend your time meditating on this verse. God not only thinks about me every single day, all day, His thoughts about me are innumerable. So many, they can't even be counted! They outnumber the grains of sand! Wow! After reading this verse how could any of us ever say again, "God doesn't care about me." We can't. Hallelujah! We can't. Now add to that He even counts the number of hairs on our head, and now we got some real shouting and praising to do! You might be saying to yourself, "I don't know how to meditate." Oh, yes you do. Think how many times you have meditated over a problem. You thought about it, rolled it over in your mind, tried to think of a solution. You even stayed awake at night trying to find an answer. Well, God's word is a lot better to meditate on because you will learn how faithful He is and that He can solve those problems that keep you up. I remember in one of my Bible study groups a woman told me, "When you go to bed tonight, give God all of your problems. He is going to be up anyway."

When trouble strikes your life unexpectedly, one of the greatest things you can do is to quote God's word out loud. There is great power in the Word of God. It is sharper than any two edged sword able to divide the soul and the spirit of man. Now, that is power!

"When you meditate, imagine that Jesus Christ is about to talk
to you about the most important thing in the world.
Give Him your complete attention."
-F. Fenelon-

October 7

God causes ALL things to work together for our good and His glory.
-Romans 8:28-

"I have learned to hold everything loosely because
it hurts when God pries my fingers from it."
-Corrie ten Boom-

All things are working together. Wow! Many a weary soul has rested their head on this comforting verse at night and fallen to sleep in the arms of their Lord. Notice that this verse doesn't say some things, but ALL things He will work out for our good. For the Christian, God will turn the most awful circumstances in our lives into a beautiful testimony of His love, kindness, mercy and forgiveness. Corrie ten Boom was an amazing woman with an amazing story. She was held in the Nazi concentration camps in Germany and watched as the soldiers killed her parents and her sister.

I think her act of forgiveness is one of the most magnificent stories ever told. She was ministering in a Church on the subject of forgiveness, telling her nightmare of living in a concentration camp. After she spoke, a man came up to her and as she looked into his eyes, she realized this was the soldier who killed her family. It was a face she vowed never to forget. He extended his hand out to her saying how sorry he was for what he had done. God had convicted him of his evil and he was seeking forgiveness from Corrie. As she tells the story, she just stood there, for what seemed like an eternity. How could she forgive such a man? Why would God even ask her to? But she knew God was. This is a time where our beliefs are tested and are we willing to live out those things we believe. Eventually, she reached out and took his hand. She was set free! As I read her story, I pondered whether or not I could ever have forgiven a man responsible for the deaths of my family. I came to conclude that only an abundant measure of grace poured out at that very moment from God, made it possible. As the saying goes, God gives Saturday's grace on Saturday, not on Tuesday. He is always on time! Whatever HE calls us to, He will provide the necessary tools to accomplish the task. Grace and mercy make forgiveness possible. To forgive is to set a prisoner free, only to find that prisoner is you.

"Afflictions are the steps to heaven."
-Elizabeth Seton-

October 8

QUIET trust...

"Sometimes God calms the storm, and sometimes He allows the storm to rage, and instead quiets His child in the storm.

Quiet trust? Yes. Remaining silent in a storm of life is not our usual response, fear is. A quiet spirit, that means no matter how hard the winds blow, the waves roar, God is still in control. He gives the oceans its boundaries. He holds back the four winds when it suits His purposes. If He has allowed a storm in your life, He promises to be right there with you. Listen to the prophet Isaiah;
"When you pass through the waters, I will be with you, and through
the rivers, they will not overwhelm you. When you walk through the
fire, you will not be burned or scorched, nor will the flame kindle upon you."
-Isaiah 43:2

What a promise! The waters will not drown you, nor will the rivers. The fire won't burn you, in fact, it won't even scorch you. What great news. We will pass through not stay in the calamity. It sounds like the 23rd Psalm. When you pass through the valley of the shadow of death, we need not fear. So, let's sum this up, neither the flood waters, raging fire or death can hurt the child of God. God promises us a safe journey, not necessarily a smooth one, but a safe one. We are called as Christians to 'endure.' Like a soldier in battle, our focus is on our Commander, not on the enemy. We fight with God's weapons, not our own. His weapons are spiritual because we fight an unseen enemy. Have you ever seen a demon? Me neither and I don't want to. God's Word says this His weapons, "They are mighty unto God to the pulling down of strongholds." Christ lives in us and His strength is available to His child. I love what the Apostle Paul said at the end of his life, "I have fought the good fight. I have finished the race, I have kept the faith. Finally, there is laid up for me a crown of righteousness, which the Lord, who is the righteous judge, will give to me on that day." (2 Timothy 4:7-8). Paul finished the race, will you? He fought a good fight. How are you doing against the enemy? Paul always kept the big picture in mind. Heaven was just one heartbeat away. Are you focused on today or eternity? It will make a difference how you live each day. God know where all of the detours, the uphill battles, the breaks in the road are. We do not. We need Him as our constant running companion. Don't leave home without Him.

"There is no little enemy."
-Benjamin Franklin-

October 9

The unbelieving world watches us very closely, ready to condemn.

"There is therefore <u>NOW</u>, NO CONDEMNATION for those which are in Christ Jesus."
Romans 8:1

So, you have a choice to believe God or believe what the world says about you. Have you ever been asked, after doing something wrong, "And you call yourself a Christian?" I'll bet you might have even had that thought yourself after doing something you knew was wrong, but you went ahead and did it anyway. I know I have. News Flash! Christians are not perfect just forgiven. The world is so quick to condemn a Christian who has failed to live up to the name. God says come to Him as you are. He will clean us up and for some of us, it can be a very long process. We will never be perfect on this earth. We will always do things wrong, just not as many as we did before we met the Savior. He takes us as we are, renews our minds and makes us to be like Him. It can be a very painful process sometimes. We walk away from sin and some of our friends don't understand the new choices we are making, so they walk away from us. Our life changes will begin to convict them.

"They persecuted Me (Jesus), they will persecute you also."
-John 15:20-

Have you ever had someone laugh at you when you tried to share your faith with them? Have you ever had someone go ballistic when you mention the name, Jesus? It hurts deeply, right to the very core of what your life is all about. The hardest people to reach are those who knew you **before** you gave your life to the Lord. They saw you partying, cussing, drinking, stealing, gossiping…and the list goes on and on. You try to tell them Jesus has changed you. They laugh some more. You finally walk away, head down, saddened by your failure. Unable to reach others with the good news. You ask yourself, "Why isn't the good news, good news to them?" They are living in darkness. God's light has not yet opened their eyes to His truth. Remember back, what you were like before God reached down through all the muck and mire and saved you? We too were once living in darkness. Satan's job is to keep us from the light, to discourage us from sharing our faith with anyone else. He has people laugh, sneer, and ridicule us so we won't attempt to reach anyone else. He wants us so discouraged so that we will keep our faith to ourselves from now on. He doesn't want you to remember that is how they treated Jesus 2000 years ago and He was the Son of God. He turned the world of His day upside down and inside out so much so the 'religious' leaders plotted to kill Him and not only Him but His followers like Paul, Peter and John. Don't miss that. It was those who claimed to have **religion**, to have an inside tract to God, that stirred up the people to 'crucify Him.'

"The greatest proof of Christianity for others is not how far a man can logically analyze his reasons for believing, but how far in practice he will stake his life on his belief."
-T.S. Elliot-

People see God every day, they just don't recognize Him.

October 10

*If we can be shaken, we cast doubt on our God
and His ability to sustain us.*

"The Christian ideal has not been tried and found wanting. It has
been found difficult and left untried."
-G.K. Chesterton-

When persecution hit the early church, many walked away. Being told you are a sinner on your way to hell unless you repent and turn to God, was not a very popular message in those days. In fact, it's not real popular today either. It brings out the worst in people who don't want to be held accountable for their actions. They want to live life as they please.

"Seeing that a Pilot steers the ship in which we sail, who will never
allow us to perish even in the midst of shipwrecks, there is no reason
why our minds should be overwhelmed
with fear and overcome with weariness."
-John Calvin-

God says, even in the midst of adversity we will make it to the shore, safely to the other side. That shore may be the banks of eternity, but we will make it. There have been martyrs throughout history who died for their Christian faith. I believe if you could talk to them today, they would say it was all worth it. Especially knowing what they know now. Standing in His presence we will one day wonder why on earth we ever doubted Him. God's word is powerful, listen to what Martin Luther has to say, "I simply taught, preached, wrote God's word: otherwise I did nothing. And then, while I slept, or drank Wittenberg beer with my friend Philip or my friend Amsdorf, the word so greatly wakened the papacy that no prince or emperor ever inflicted such damage upon it. I did nothing. The word did it all." Be faithful to pray and tell others about Jesus and God will be faithful and do the rest. It may not happen overnight but it will happen. Be on guard. Satan will ramp up his attacks when we pray, especially for the salvation of others.

"There are few children of God who do not often find the season
of prayer a season of conflict. The devil has a special rage against
us when he sees us on our knees."
-J.C. Ryle

Thought for the day: "Satan dreads nothing but prayer." –Samuel Chadwick- You want to change someone's life eternally? PRAY! If battle ensues, so be it! If God be for me what does it matter who is against me?

October 11

Conviction requires unshakeable confidence in the promises of God.

"Christianity is one beggar telling another beggar where he found bread."
-D.T. Niles-

Our world is changing every day. Sadly, Christians are not only being persecuted all over the world for their beliefs, but they are also being driven from their homes and sometimes put to death. Many times these evil acts are done by 'religious' persecutors who do not know the God of the Bible. Living today as a Christian requires strength, conviction, determination and God's help. Evil is increasing in the world. Many now believe a lie. What used to be wrong is now right, what used to be right is now wrong. Our own history books are being rewritten. This changing world of ours could be real scary if God hadn't warned us about what the end times would be like. Matthew 24 describes the world that is coming. Deception will be the greatest sign that it is here.

"When principles that run against your deepest convictions begin to win the day, then battle is your calling, and peace has become sin; you must, at the price of dearest peace, lay your convictions bare before friend and enemy, with all the fire of your faith."
-Abraham Kuyper-

Someone once said, "Evil will triumph when good men do nothing." Well, years ago when I was growing up, the Ten Commandments hung on the walls of the classroom. At Christmas time we sang Christmas Carols in the classroom. The manger scene was humbly displayed. Then a woman named Madeline Murray O'Hare decided to change this. She was an atheist, a very determined atheist. Good men did nothing and she succeeded. What has replaced Bibles in the schools? Answer: Metal detectors. Children are screened for guns before entering the school. "Thou shalt not kill," goes unread, the Ten Commandments that once hung as a reminder to acceptable human behavior has been discarded into the trash along with morality. Children pick up guns instead of God's word and the results are disastrous.

"This know also, that in the last days **perilous** times shall come. For people will be lovers of themselves and money. They will be boastful and proud. Scoffing at God, disobedient to their parents, and ungrateful. They will consider nothing sacred. They will be unloving and unforgiving; they will slander others and have no self-control; they will be cruel and have no interest in what is good."
II Timothy 3:1-3

Perilous times are upon us and they are going to get much worse. Children bringing guns to school to massacre their classmates or snipers gunning down policemen as they walk out of the police station. What the schools no longer allow must be taught at home. We as Christians are never without hope. Ponder these words of Charles Stanley, "If you are a child of God whose heart's desire is to see God glorified in you, *adversity will not put you down for the count*. There will be those initial moments of shock and confusion. But the man or woman who has perspective on this life and the life to come will always emerge victorious."

October 12

On my knees...the most powerful position in all the world.

"Prayer is not to inform God, but to give man a sight of his misery;
to humble his heart, to excite his desire, to inflame his faith, to animate
his hope, to raise his soul from earth to heaven."
-Adam Clarke-

Getting on my knees reflects a will that is bent towards God, away from self and has a humbled heart that is in total submission to Him. It reflects my great need for Him and my utter dependence on Him. We will fight many battles over the course of our lifetime. If we are wise, the battle will begin on our knees and end the same way.

"Never be ashamed of a scar. It simply means
you were stronger than whatever tried to hurt you."
-Unknown-

A scar says that you have healed in a particular area of your life. We all bear the scars of life. Broken hearts, crumpled egos, failed plans. Someone has said, "A wise man is one who has finally discovered that there are some questions to which nobody has the answer." That is a hard pill to swallow for a lot of us. We want to know 'why' things happen, unfortunately, God sometimes says, "You don't need to know you only need to trust that I know and I will take care of you."

"Remember it is the very time for faith to work when sight ceases.
The greater the difficulties for faith; as long as there remain certain
natural prospects, faith does not get on even as easily as where natural prospects fail."
-George Mueller-

We are more inclined to try to solve our own problems when they seem small. In our ignorance we leave the 'big problems' in our life to God. There is nothing big to God. The giant problem is as easy for Him as an easy problem. He says to cast **all** of our cares on Him, big, small or medium size. He will shoulder them for us. We have a choice, carry the burden ourselves or cast them on Him. Maybe we should use Abraham as our example who 'Under hopeless circumstances, hoped on in God." The example has been given if you were riding in a wagon with runaway horses you knew you could not get under control, yet you were sitting right next to someone who could, what would you do? With any common sense at all, you would immediately give the reigns over. A life of sin is like those runaway horses. Sin cannot be controlled. It will eventually control us and death and destruction are right down the road. Which road are you on? Is there a sin in your life you refuse to let go of? You will never reign in those wild horses until you turn over the reigns to Jesus. Today is a new day and it would be a good time to scoot over and let God do the driving from now on. If you do you will end up safely home. He promises. Live responsibly today and trust Him for tomorrow, He is already there.

OCTOBER 13

Inconsistency will erode away at your child's foundation.

"Our goal is not that children be happy, fulfilled, and successful. Granted, we may desire these things for them. But our highest objective should be that our children would repent from their sins, put their trust in Jesus Christ, and reflect the gospel to the world around them."
-Carolyn Mahaney-

A consistent life lived before God does not yield, does not compromise on principles. It is not double-minded. It's a life that does not stop praying regardless of the circumstances. It does not give up. It does not say one thing and do another. Your children are watching and learning through your actions how to deal with a crisis, how to deal with prosperity, how to deal with rude, unfriendly people, how to deal with tragedies and, just as important, how to deal with success. They will one day mirror your actions. If you retaliate with harsh words so will they. If you respond instead with kindness, so will they. Suffering for doing what is right is one of the most valuable lessons a child can learn from you. Are you going to TRUST God to do what's right for you, not just some of the time but all of the time? If you do, when the bottom drops out of your child's life they will get on their knees and go to God first because they saw how faithful God was to their mom or dad.

"The enemy attacks hard and fiercely when our life is out of balance."
-unknown-

When trouble strikes do you go to God first? Are you willing to get on your knees in front of your children? Some would call this weakness, others would call this wisdom. God looks down with compassion on His child who has reached out to Him for help.

Thought for the day: "You can kill us but you cannot hurt us." – Justin Martyr Wow! What a statement. To be so sure of the goodness and faithfulness of God that you can say even in death, "I know that my Redeemer lives and that in my flesh I shall see God." (-Book of Job-)

October 14

God has a purpose for even the darkest of times in our life.

"God, how am I going to do this? You're not
<u>WE</u> are going to do this together."
-unknown-

You don't have to go it alone! That is such wonderful news. When left on our own we simply seem to make a bigger mess of things. Where do we go? The Bible is not only clear as to where we can go, who will be there, but also what our attitude should be when we go and what can we expect;

"Seeing that we have a great high priest....**JESUS**, the Son of God
let us hold fast to our profession. Let us therefore come **BOLDLY** to the
throne of **GRACE** that we may obtain **MERCY**, and find grace to help in TIME OF NEED."
-Hebrews 4:14-16-

If you aren't jumping for joy after reading that promise of God then you definitely need to read it again, and again until you are either jumping or shouting Hallelujah!. This passage is saying come BOLDLY to God who sits on His throne. Boldness requires a great deal of confidence on the part of the believer. How can a Christian be that confident when they are coming before the very Creator of the Universe, the judge of all men? The answer is simple, it is because of Jesus. God is holy and nothing unholy can enter His presence. Nothing. We have been washed by the blood of the Lamb and we take on His righteousness, therefore we come in His righteousness, we do not come in our own. God calls man's righteousness as filthy rags in His sight. A confident believer comes to his heavenly Father **believing** God will hear and will answer. If you don't believe God will work on your behalf then you won't come boldly, but with distrust, trepidation and fear. We are coming to His throne of grace (undeserving favor). Not to His throne of judgment and condemnation. We do not deserve grace. Maybe that is why it so hard for us to believe in God's grace for ourselves. We know what we deserve but God looks at the cross and sees you there, washed in the blood of the Lamb and exchanges judgment for grace. He doesn't stop there. He pours out His mercy on us too. Grace is God giving me what I don't deserve and mercy is God not giving me what I do deserve. What else am I going to find at God's throne of grace but **HELP** in my time of need. We all deserve punishment and yet God offers to help us through our tough times. Jesus provides the access to God's throne for us. He will take our imperfect requests, sift them through His will for our life and in return we receive grace abounding. Hallelujah! He hears and He answers.

October 15

Never underestimate the power of your life to affect another's.

A kind word, a hug, a smile...even a joke!

"Laughter removes all barriers. When people are laughing together, there are no age differences, no racial barriers, and no economic distictions. It is just people enjoying their existence."
-Bruce Bickel & Stan Jantz-

Today we can be a little lighthearted than usual. We all need to laugh and smile and to forget our troubles, if just for a moment. So, here are a few bible jokes I received from someone on the internet. Unfortunately, I do not know who authored them:
- What kind of motor vehicles are in the Bible?
  Answer: Jehovah drove Adam out of the garden in a Fury! David's Triumph was heard throughout the land, Also the Apostle's probably drove a Honda because they were all in one Accord.
- Who was the greatest comedian in the Bible?
  Answer: Samson. He brought the house down.
- What kind of a man was Boaz before he married Ruth?
  Answer: Ruthless.
- What do they call Pastors in Germany?
  Answer: German Shepherds.
- Who was the greatest financier in the Bible?
  Answer: Pharaoh's daughter. She went down to the Bank of the Nile and drew out a little prophet.
  And finally my favorite:
- What excuse did Adam give to his children as to why they no longer lived in the Garden of Eden?
  Answer: Your mother ate us out of house and home.

Some are pretty silly, I know, but they can start the day off with a smile instead of dreading what lies ahead. Mark Twain once said, "The human race has one effective weapon, and that is laughter."

It is ok to laugh. God knows many of our days are filled with worry and trials that burden us down. So, on the good days, laugh and make someone else laugh. Laugh at your yourself sometimes, everyone else does. Laugh, giggle, be silly every once in a while. Tickle your children. Chase them around the house for fun, not because you are mad at them. Have a make-up day with your young daughter. Let her wear your lipstick and your other war paint, let her style your hair. She won't be young for long so do it now.

My favorite thing to do when my children were young was to put notes in their lunch boxes to remind them how much they were loved. I am sure it made them smile at least once that day. Laughter and smiles are not only contagious but very powerful. It can suddenly change your attitude from sour to happy, or from despair to hope. Hang out with those who make you laugh. There isn't enough time in life to hang out with those who bring you down. The Bible says that little children were drawn to Jesus. Why? I think because he played with them, laughed with them, and let them know it was ok to be a kid and have fun. Sometimes you just got to laugh at life. As I write this, I am icing my poor old knee while at the same time sitting on a heating pad for my poor old back, writing to people who may never read a word I say while waiting for the auto shop to tell me how much the repairs on my car will be Ha!. Life is good!

"A good laugh is sunshine in a house." -Willaim Makepeace Thackeray-

October 16

Even in the darkest of times, we are walking towards the light.

"If you want to be happy, *be*."
-Alexei Tolstoy-

Sounds so very simple, doesn't it? Be happy. He is right you know. Your happiness doesn't come from others and it doesn't come from your circumstances. It comes from you and how you see your world. How you see God depends on the light of God's word. Before we were saved we were in darkness, but since Jesus is the light of the world, the darkness fades a little more each and every day. The closer we draw to Him, the darkness flees in His presence. Someone has said, "A man who views the world the same at fifty as he did at twenty has wasted 30 years." Trials make us grow. Ponder these words:

"Number one, God has brought me here. It is by His will that I am in this place. In that fact I will rest. Number two, He will keep me here in His love and give me grace to behave as His child. Number three, He will make the trial a blessing, teaching me lessons He intends for me to learn and working in me the grace He means to bestow. Number four, in His good time He can bring me out again. How and when, He knows. So, let me say I am here."
-Andrew Murray-

God put me there, He keeps me there, He is working on me there, and He will take me out of there when His will is accomplished and I have grown in my faith and trust Him just a little more with each passing day. He knows exactly when to end my trial and how long to wait until the next one.

Yes, there are very hard times in life, times when the world brings us to our knees, but I think it would be at those very times that God would say, "Stay down there (on your knees) and talk to me. Tell Me what's troubling you." Jesus said, "Be of good cheer, I have overcome the world." He did that for us, not for Himself. God says we are more than conquerors in this life! More than a conqueror is one who knows he will **WIN** the battle **BEFORE** it ever begins. We conquer through Him who loved us. He strengthens us, guides us, and brings us through even the darkest of times. He knows the way even when we don't. I need not fear.

"He that is down needs fear no fall,
He that is low no pride;
He that is humble ever shall
Have God to be his guide.
I am content with what I have,
Little be it or much;
And Lord, contentment still I crave,
Because Thou savest such.
Fulness to such a burden is
That go on pilgrimage:
Here little, and hereafter bliss,
Is best from age to age."
-John Bunyon-

October 17

Is yours a life out of focus?

"Jesus gives us real eyes, so that we can see where the 'real' lies."
-Michael Mc Inerney-

Need an eye check-up? Having trouble focusing? Focus on GOD. Don't look back, don't look ahead, look up and for goodness sake, do not ever give up! Excuses will guarantee failure.

"A man can fail many times but it doesn't mean he is a
failure, until he begins to blame others."
-unknown-

What is the best way to get your life in focus once again? Get on your knees and seek out His guidance and wisdom. This big old scary world appears at times to be spinning out of control but to the child of the living God we know everything is right on time according to God's timetable.

"Failure doesn't mean you are a failure;
it does mean you haven't yet succeeded.
Failure doesn't mean that you have
accomplished nothing;
it does mean that you have learned something.
Failure doesn't mean that you have been a fool;
it does mean that you have a lot of faith.
Failure doesn't mean that you have been disgraced;
it does mean that you were willing to try.
Failure doesn't mean you don't have it;
it does mean that you have to do something in a different way.
Failure doesn't mean you are inferior;
it does mean you are not perfect.
Failure doesn't mean that you have wasted your life;
it does mean that you have a reason to start afresh.
Failure doesn't mean you should give up;
it does mean you must try harder.
Failure doesn't mean you will never make it;
it does mean it will take a little longer,
Failure doesn't mean God has abandoned you;
it does mean God has a better way."
-unknown-

Benjamin Franklin said, "I haven't failed. I have found 1000 ways that don't work." Those who stop trying are guaranteed to fail.

OCTOBER 18

Be available to God every day to be used by Him.

"Even if I knew that tomorrow the world would go to
pieces, I would still plant my apple tree."
-Martin Luther-

There are so many hurting people in our world today, people with no answers, no faith, no direction, no light and no truth. They call themselves happy and fulfilled when deep down inside they are uncertain of their own existence, which can only be defined by God, and fearful of the future because they do not know the One who holds tomorrow in the palm of His hands.

"The next moment is as much beyond our grasp, and as much in God's care,
as that a hundred years away. Care for the next minute is just as foolish as care
for a day in the next thousand years. In neither can we do anything,
in both GOD is doing everything."
-C.S. Lewis-

Are you in a hard place today? Is hope dwindling? Look at the contrast between Jesus and Adam, both spending time in 'a garden.'

"Jesus was in a garden, not of delights as the first Adam
in which he destroyed himself and the whole human
race, but in one of agony, in which he *saved* the whole human race."
-Blaise Pascal-

It matters less where you are than whom you are with. One experience in a garden brought destruction and the other brought life back to a dying, lost world. One listened to those fateful words, "Yum, take a bite." and they did. The other paid with His life because of those words and the consequences of them. Wherever you are today, if you are with Jesus, you will be okay. It may be a hard journey and may last longer than you want it to, but if He walks with you, you will be like His disciples who got into a boat expecting good weather, experienced a terrifying storm, met Jesus in the middle of the storm and made it safely to shore. Though for the day: Row, row, row your boat...never mind the dark clouds overhead.

October 19

*"Lord, why do I believe you will do these things
for everyone else but not for me?"*

"Who has tried to make you feel ignorant and foolish and oh, so,
naive for taking God at His word? Whoever it is and whatever approach
that person is using, the temptation to doubt God's Word is as old
as Creation and comes straight from that old serpent, the Devil."
-Anne Graham Lotz-

We have two choices. Believe God or believe Satan. Who do you believe? It will determine your success or your failure in life. Many a life has been ruined by lies straight from hell. Yes, straight from hell. The Devil tries to tell us we are failures and will never amount to anything. He tells us we are losers. He follows that up with, "No one will ever love you. You will be alone the rest of your life." His next punch is right in the gut, he says, "Why don't you just end it all, check out of life." Many have listened to him. God says a failure is someone who gives up. As long as God is in His heaven, the human soul has hope. It is never over until God says it is over. If we really knew who God was and what He can do, we would never doubt again. Never. John the Baptist doubted, but it didn't last long. As he sat in a stinky, smelly prison, he asked the disciples to go ask Jesus if He really was who He claimed to be. Jesus' reply was based on who He was and what He has done. He has made the lame to walk, the mute to talk and praise Him, and the blind to see. He took 10 Lepers, condemned by their disease to a lifetime of isolation, cleansed them and sent them out back to their families. Who else can do that? No one but God. Trust brings faith and more faith. Doubt brings misery and confusion. Take an inventory of your life today. Do you spend more time in doubt and unbelief than you do in faith? If you are His child, you need not doubt. Our God is faithful to the end.

*"The key to understanding faith is understanding what
it is anchored in. It is not based on our own wisdom or knowledge but in Christ."*
-Steven Curtis Chapman-

Who is your anchor that holds you to life?

October 20

The world can have a profound influence on us, but only if we let it.

We all live *in* the world, but we do not have to let the world get into us. As children of God we are sojourners on this earth, it is not our home. God has set every Christian apart for His glory and to do His will. God's will runs contrary to the plans and schemes of the god of this world, Satan, and so begins the battle between good and evil here on earth.

> "Worldliness is an accepted part of our way of life. Our religious mood is social instead of spiritual. We have lost the art of worship. We are not producing saints. Our models are successful businessmen, celebrated athletes and theatrical personalities. We carry on our religious activities after the methods of the modern advertiser."
> -A.W.Tozer-

Tozer was born in 1897 and died of a heart attack only six months before President John F. Kennedy in 1963. His tombstone simply reads, "A man of God." Now that is an understatement if I ever heard one. Though undereducated by the 'world's standards, he was one of the greatest of preachers and writers of his time and even today. If he thought the 1960's to be decadent what would he think of the state of the world today? Surely, he would think Armageddon must be right around the corner. He might be right. Tozer walked with his God for over 50 years and left some of the greatest books on Christianity the world would ever see. He was a man who **did not compromise** God's word. He surrendered himself to God and bids that we do the same. Listen to his warning:

> "The reason why many are still troubled, still seeking, still making little progress is because they haven't yet come to the end of themselves. We're still trying to give orders, and interfering with God's work within us."

As long as you or I are still driving the car and have refused to give God the steering wheel, you are running your own life. You make stops God would never approve of and go places that grieve Him. If we would simply let Him lead He would take us places we never could have imagined. It would be better than any roller coaster ride on the face of this earth. It might be as scary sometimes, but we will come through it. "God wants the whole person and He will not rest until He gets us in entirety. No part of the man will do." –Tozer-

God's all or nothing principle: He gave all to us and expects no less in return. Total surrender.

October 21

In the center of God's will is the safest place on earth.

"Inside the will of God there is no failure. Outside
the will of God there can be no success."
-Benard Edinger-

God's will, may not be the most popular place at the time, but it will always be the safest place, no matter what is happening all around us. Think of Moses being put into a basket on the Nile River by his mother. Yes, his sister followed along at a distance, but if a crocodile had seen the basket there would have been no rescuing of the Jewish nation, no parting of the Red Sea and certainly no movie starring Charlton Heston. The point is, God made sure the crocodiles stayed far away. He had a great plan for Moses' life that would be fulfilled and it didn't include crocodiles. Moses was alone floating down that river or was he? God in His sovereignty had His eye on that basket until Pharaoh's daughter told her maidservant to fetch it out of the water. The rest was history. What are we supposed to do when there is no one to help and we feel alone and abandoned?

"Would you like me to tell you what supported me through all the years
of exile among a people whose language I could not understand, and whose
attitude towards me was always uncertain and often hostile? It was this, "Lo, I AM with you
always, even unto the end of the world." On these words I staked <u>everything</u>, and
they NEVER failed."
-David Livingstone-

This was a man who had nothing but the Word of the living God to rely upon. He chose to believe God when He said, "I will never abandon you." Livingstone was a Scottish physician and one of the greatest of African missionaries, an explorer and antislavery advocate the world has ever known. He was a man of great courage. Someone has wisely said, "The will of God will never take you where the grace of God cannot keep you." God's faithfulness is never dependent on where we are, it is blind to our circumstances, it is solely dependent on who God is. He cannot be anything other than faithful.

October 22

God's will... exactly what I would do if I had ALL of the facts.

"It is true that wicked men do many things contrary to God's will;
but so great is His wisdom and power, that all things which seem
adverse to His purpose do still tend towards those just and good ends
and issues which he Himself has foreknown."
-Augustine-

Is there a time in your life you can think back to where you begged God to answer your prayer, and then thanked Him days or years later for *not* answering it. I know I have. Lord knows where I would be today if He had answered yes to what I asked Him for. God is Omniscient. There isn't anything He doesn't know. He is the only One who can predict the future with 100% accuracy. His prophets have predicted hundreds of years ago just how this world would come to a close with the battle of Armageddon. I think the books of prophecy in the Bible have cemented my faith more than anything else, except God's love and mercy. It helps me to trust Him who is already present in my tomorrow. It helps me to submit my will to His safe keeping. Life is very hard sometimes. There is a constant struggle within each of us to do what is right.

"Have you not found it hard to be good? Hard to keep from saying
something naughty that you wanted to say? Very hard to keep down
the angry feeling, even if you did not say the angry word? Hard to do
the right thing, because you did not at all like doing it, and quite impossible to
make yourself wish to do it? You asked God to help you do it, and He did help
you; but did you ever think of asking Him to make you like doing it?
Now, this is just what is meant by God's "working in you to will." It means
that He can and will undertake the very thing which you cannot manage. He can and will
take your will, and work it for you; making you want to do just what He wants you to do;
making you like the very things that He likes, and hate just what He hates. It is always
easy to do what we like doing; so, when we have given up our will to Him, and asked
Him to work it for us, it makes everything easy. For we shall want to "do according
to His good pleasure," and we shall be very happy in it; because trying to please Him will
not be fighting against our own wills, when God has taken them and is working them for us.
Do you not see what happy days are before you if you will only take God at His word about
this? Only try Him, and you will see! Tell Him that you cannot manage your will yourself, and
that now you will give it up to Him, and trust Him, from now, not only to work in you to do,
but to work in you to will also, "according to His good pleasure."
Take my will and make it Thine;
It shall be no longer mine.
Take my heart, it is Thine own;
It shall be Thy royal throne."
-Frances Ridley Havergal-

October 23

"I did it MY way."

"I AM the way, the truth and the life." -Jesus-

That song, "I Did It My Way," sung by Frank Sinatra, sends shivers up and down my spine and that is not a good thing. I am fearful for anyone who lives that kind of lifestyle, leaving God out while they do their 'own thing' and then expect it all to turn out great. It won't because it can't. We are bent towards sin. It is the path of least resistance. All our 'friends' are on that path. No one likes to travel on a lonely road. The path to destruction is wide and many are on it, says the Bible. While the path that leads to righteousness is a lonely, narrow path and few there be on it. It's so much easier to go along with the crowd than to listen to God. If you are busy partying and living it up, you make it harder and harder to hear from God, until at some point He is silent. Warnings have been ignored. Make no mistake, God always warns when disaster or judgment is imminent.

We choose the direction we take so why are we surprised to find ourselves in a mess? Is my way really the best way? Probably not, but we all try it first at least until we get knocked down a time or two. Some of us come to our senses sooner than others. I must admit it did take me longer than it should have. It took the death of my sister to stop me in my tracks, take an honest survey of my life and fall on my knees in repentance and forgiveness. Here are W. Tozer's "Rules for Self Discovery:" Ask yourself these questions to determine where you are in life.

1. What do I want most?
2. What do I think about most?
3. How do I spend my money?
4. What do I do in my leisure time?
5. What kind of company do I enjoy?
6. Who and what do I admire?
7. What do I laugh at?

These are very revealing 'life' questions aren't they? Do you laugh at dirty jokes, do you even let them be told in your presence? Why would your friends think it would be okay to tell filthy stuff like that to you? I think you need new friends. God desires for you to come up higher. Who do you admire, a famous football player that abuses his wife or men like Billy Graham? What do I want most in life? Money? Fame? A new car, new house? Or do I want what God wants for me. To seek His kingdom and righteousness and to live as though you were already there? God has given us each a free will. Until we come to the Lord we spend that will doing things that make us happy, not others, doing things that benefit us, not sacrificing for another human being. Those choices will determine where you spend eternity my friend, with Him or without Him. Choose wisely. I haven't found anything offered in this life that can even come close to what Jesus offers me. Nothing. What He offers is a 'forever' thing. What the world offers is temporary on this earth, but the consequences will be eternal death. God offers eternal life with Him, at His home forever, and ever and ever. It is your choice. You alone determine how it all ends.

October 24

*The Lord **frustrates** the plans of the ungodly."*
Psalms 146:10

The plans of the ungodly will not work out
because God will not let them work out.

Frustration is something we all feel at one time or another. A dictionary search defines '**frustrates**' as: 1. To prevent someone from accomplishing a purpose or fulfilling a desire; thwart. 2. To cause feeling of discouragement, annoyance, or lack of fulfillment in. 3. To prevent from coming to fruition or fulfillment, render ineffectual. Why would God frustrate the plans of the ungodly? My answer is love. He is not willing that any should perish, but that all come to repentance. God warns us in many ways, one of them I think is by frustrating our plans that will eventually harm us. Unfortunately, there is such a thing as a 'hardened heart' towards the things of God and that no matter how many road blocks God uses in an attempt to stop us, we persist. We are going to do what we want. Romans 2 tells us about those who God 'gives over to their own desires.' That is so frightening to me. God backs off and says, "Ok, you are on your own." Have at it, but be assured it will not end well for you. God says, "Don't." You say. "Leave me alone, you're not going to tell me what to do." So He does. The spiral into hell begins. I can't think of a scarier scenario than being abandoned to myself.

"A man's worst difficulties begin when he is able to do as he likes."
-Thomas Huxley-

The good news is God is still in the saving business and he can use the worst of our circumstances, as he did with the Apostle Paul to reach someone else teetering on the brink of disaster. We can empathize with someone else's plight when we have been there ourselves and saved by the mighty arm of God reaching down into our mess and pulling us out the moment we call on Him. God thwarted Paul's plans to kill Christian's and he will frustrate your plans as well. Paul, through his experiences wrote some of the greatest letters of warning in the Bible to those who would listen. Are you listening?

October 25

Don't be surprised when others don't understand your Christian values, but never give into theirs. Never.

"The lies of the devil always have a ring of truth to them. The best counterfeit is always as close to the original as possible." -Charles Stanley-

This life will require each one of us to be courageous during our lives and usually at a very inconvenient moment in time. We will be called to take a stand for what we believe in, despite the consequences. Our world is constantly changing. When I was a child growing up in the 50's and 60's we said the Pledge of Allegiance to our flag every morning before beginning our day. Today's children are not allowed to. It might offend someone. Prayers were offered in school, now today a child will be suspended from school or expelled for praying. The Word of God is banned from graduation ceremonies. We used to have Christmas plays put on by the students every Christmas in my grammar school. We sang Christmas carol's that mentioned the names of Jesus and God. We sang of Jesus' virgin birth and death. When we got bored with class we could always study the Ten Commandments that hung on the classroom wall. Today, these things are deemed politically incorrect and outdated. Can you imagine saying God is outdated. I think someone forgot to tell Him. He could probably use a good laugh. God's truths are not offensive and the ten commandments are for our protection. They are commands, not suggestions. What has now taken their place is condoms and birth control pills, with no questions asked, guns in school, metal detectors at the front of the school, kids attacking their teachers, or threatening them with cell phone videos. You can no longer discipline a child at school and we wonder why the youth of today are so violent and selfish, with language that would make a long-shore man blush. Sadly, America has been asleep and allowed these things to creep into our schools just like we did when Madeline Murray O'Hair campaigned *without any opposition*, to remove Bible reading from the schools in 1963. In 1962 a Supreme Court ruled against prayer in the schools. I believe that one act, by one woman, began the decadent decline of this nation. What followed was the free sex, love & drugs generation, sadly, my generation. No boundaries, do your own thing, anything goes, and no respect for authority. It did not end well for O'Hair, in 1995 she was kidnapped, murdered and mutilated along with her son and granddaughter. My generation of liberal thinkers are the ones now in power in the government and what a mess we find ourselves in today. The next generation believes that hard working Americans should now pay not only for their abortions, but for their birth control pills. There is no fear of God anymore. No fear of consequences. No acceptance of personal responsibility.

"Today, classic theological liberalism is no longer the Church's main threat. As we enter a post-Christian world, one driven by consumer culture and the entertainment industry, we face more basic challenges, such as radical devaluation of human life."
-David Neff-

One point two million (1.2 million) babies die every year from abortions. Over 50 million babies have lost their lives since the passing of Roe vs Wade. Abortion leaves one dead and one wounded. American's against abortion has increased in number over the last decade. When you consider the act of abortion stops a beating heart, a heart with a *different blood type* than the mother. It is no wonder many are coming to their senses. If there is a cause out there you believe strongly about, join it and make a difference. Had we not kept silent in the 1960's, I believe we would be living in a much different world today. The church is being silenced. It is an insidious move to cripple the church in society. We must speak out while we still can.

October 26

*The greatest daily challenge for every believer
is in keeping Jesus Lord of our life.*
-unknown-

"Perhaps our place is not at the center of the universe.
God does not exist to make a big deal out of us. We exist
to make a big deal out of Him. It's not about you. It's
not about me. It's all about Him."
-Max Lucado-

Accepting Jesus as Savior is just the beginning of the Christian life. We must then make Him Lord over our lives. We must hand over control of our lives to Him who is Omnipotent and Omniscient. We do not have the wisdom, nor can we ever, to survive the attacks of the enemy. Sometimes they are brutal. Sometimes the attacks are so subtle you think they are from you. You believe them to be your own thoughts. We are in the battle of our life whether we want to be or not. We were enlisted into the army of God the moment we said yes to Jesus. Always remember the enemy is out to kill, steal and destroy us. That is not someone you want to mess with. This is someone you want to immediately turn over to God and let Him fight your battles for you.

"The deceit, the lie of the devil consists of this, that he wishes to make
man believe that he can live without the Word of God."
-Dietrich Bonhoeffer-

John of the Cross said, "The devil fears a soul united to God as much as he fears God himself." The best way to unite your spirit with the Spirit of the living God is by reading His Word. Not only read it, but do what it says. The Bible says that "Fear of God is the beginning of all wisdom." What does it mean to fear God? It means to take Him very seriously. He does not play games. He plays for keeps. To our annoyance, He often works very slowly and methodically to work out His plan. He is always working. It may seem like He doesn't care at times, or has lost interest in us, which can never happen by the way, but instead He works in the shadows sometimes, putting all the pieces of His plan right where they should be to accomplish His purpose.

"God never hurries. There are no deadlines against which He
must work. Only to know this is to quiet our spirits and relax our nerves."
-A.W.Tozer-

When we realize who God is, that we are on His schedule, not our own, He has no deadlines like we do, no watch to check. He is never late and seldom early with His answers. When we realize His answers come on time, we can rest and trust Him to do what is right for us. We live in an 'I want it now' society. A microwave society of instant everything! If you want peace you will have to learn to wait and not complain. Not easy but doable and necessary to live in peace.

October 27

As we grow spiritually, so should our sensitivity to sin.

"The devil is a better theologian than any of us and is a devil still."
-A.W. Tozer-

Satan goes to church every Sunday. He also knows God's Word better than any of us ever could. That may surprise you, but he doesn't have to hang out in bars. He already has that crowd right where he wants them, with ruined, hopeless lives, and no way out but death. It's the 'religious' crowd he is after. He wants the individual that has one foot in heaven and one foot in the world. He wants the 'lukewarm' church goer to stay lukewarm. Jesus didn't have anything good to say to those who are lukewarm towards God and Satan knows it.

"So, because you are lukewarm and neither cold nor hot,
I (Jesus) will spit you out of My mouth!"
Revelation 3:16

Lukewarm people, have no time for God. They can take Him or leave Him. He will not be taken half-heartedly. You are either with Him or against Him. Incredibly, other stuff is more important to them than where they will spend eternity, at least for now. They attend church to make themselves feel good, not because they want a relationship with God but because it is 'expected' of them. It may be something their parents did so they do too. God doesn't look at your church attendance, but at your heart. King David was an adulterer, a murderer of Uriah, Bathsheba's husband, and yet God calls him a man after His own heart. Why? because he repented! Luke warmers don't feel they have anything to repent for. Their sin 'barometer' is broken and they don't plan on getting it fixed anytime soon. Sin should break our hearts as it does God's. It is an awful thing and has caused the pain and misery we see all around us, in our world today. There was a time in my own life I called sin by other names, not what it really was. I am so glad that God did not give up on me and leave me in my deceit, but continued to pursue me and shed His light on my dark life. Question for the day: Do you have a personal relationship with God and Jesus Christ or are you just going through the motions on Sunday? If so, you might as well stay home and watch football. The Holy Spirit was sent into the world to convict sinners, not condemn, but convict. We have all sinned. He draws us to God, but sometimes we are so stubborn it will take a tragedy to alter our course of destruction. Don't think for one minute God won't shake up your life if it will save your soul. There are millions of us who will testify to the fact that He will do just that. Don't make tragedy your catalyst for turning to God, instead make His deep love for you the reason.

October 28

Be honest with God. ALWAYS.

"If we confess our sins, He is faithful and just to forgive us our sins and to cleanse us from ALL unrighteousness." I John 1:9

The question today is, "Do you sugar coat your sin?" I think we all have at one time or another. Especially to our parents, we tell half-truths so it doesn't sound quite so bad what we did. It's hard to call sin what it is, rebellion against a Holy God. A little lie here, a little deceit there, we tell ourselves doesn't really matter. It matters to God. Most of us when confronted with sin answer back, "I am a good person." Let's take the "good person" test. I will give my answers, you give yours. Have you ever lied? Yes. Have you ever stolen something? Yes. Okay, if you answered yes to both these questions, we are both in big trouble. God's word says, liars and thieves cannot enter into the Kingdom of God. I want to go to heaven and I'm sure you do too so what are we going to do? Nothing! Why? Jesus did it all for us.

"However many and however great and burdensome your sins may be, with God there is greater mercy." -Tikhon of Zadonsk-

If we don't realize how bad sin is, and if we don't see sin as God sees sin we are deceiving ourselves. Paster Chuck Smith has said, "Oh, how horrible our sins look when they are committed by someone else!" Isn't that the truth. When we do it it doesn't seem to be as bad as when someone else does it.

"Sin goes in a disguise, and thence is welcome; like Judas, it kisses and kills; like Joab, it salutes and slays." -George Swinnock-

We don't want to sin, but we do. It takes the power of the Holy Spirit working in our lives to change our very nature. We may still sin as Christians, but we are no longer happy in our sin, as we were before. Our heart is bent towards God and pleasing Him, not towards hurting His heart and destroying our fellowship with Him. Thomas Watson has said, "The pleasure of sin is soon gone, but the sting long remains." How true! The sting comes from the consequences of our ungodly behavior. There will always be consequences. God says, "Don't do that." We say, "Don't tell me what to do." Then we cry out to God, "Why did you let this happen?" He didn't, but it's a lot easier to blame someone else than to take responsibility for our own actions.

"All human sin seems so much worse in its consequences than in its intentions."
-Reinhold Niebuhr-

There is good news! Jesus paid the penalty for our sins by His death on the cross. He has set us free from the penalty of sin! When we confess our sins and ask forgiveness, we are taking personal responsibility and God cleanses us and forgives us. His mercies are NEW every morning. Every day He gives us a brand new start. Every day! That is worth shouting Hallelujah!

October 29

*Just because our circumstances appear to be
against us, does not mean that God is against us.*

"Circumstances are constantly affecting us and their purpose is to produce
our sanctification, pleasant circumstances and unpleasant circumstances. We
should therefore be observant and always watching for lessons, seeking and asking questions."
-Dr. Martyn Lloyd-Jones-

Please don't take this the wrong way because I include myself, but most of us don't realize how screwed up we really are. Sin does that. It is the great deceiver. I saw a sign in a Psychiatrist's office at the hospital I worked at that said "What is normal? Answer: It is a cycle on my washing machine." None of us apparently are 'normal.' We each have our own set of hang ups or issues in life. Our own private sins. Many of us are pretty efficient at pretending things are okay when they are not. Sometimes, I think I deserved an academy award for my performance. Pretending that someone's harsh angry words uttered years ago haven't had an impact on our lives. Sometimes we are too proud for own britches. Pride keeps us from asking for the help we desperately need. In ignorance we blame God for where we are in life, when really we are where we are because of some really bad choices we made.

"Great is His faithfulness; His mercies begin afresh each day."
Lamentations 3:23

That is an incredible verse so hold on tightly to it. God's mercies are <u>new every single day</u>. If we use up yesterday's supply, He provides us with a whole new batch every morning. His supply of mercy and kindness towards us is never ending. Does God allow some circumstances we find ourselves in? Yes, But He also promises to be with us in those circumstances and to see us through them. Even those circumstances we bring on ourselves by poor choices.

"People who cover their sins will not prosper. But if they
confess and forsake them, they will receive mercy."
Proverbs 28:13

Whatever place you find yourself in today, make sure that your conscience is clear before God and that there are no unconfessed sins in your life or areas of disobedience. Then do as Proverbs 16:3 says, "Commit our way unto the Lord, and your plans will succeed." I would add that you should pray about everything! Nothing in our lives is insignificant to God especially those things worthy of praying about.

"Pray when you don't feel like it; pray when you feel
like it; pray until you feel like it. Then pray until you get an answer."
-Unknown-

October 30

Great moments in life are often wrapped in the 'insignificant.'

"At strategic moments God again and again manifested Himself to men by miracles so they had outward, confirming evidence that the words they heard from God's servants were true."
-Billy Graham-

I think we may have touched on this subject of 'insignificant' moments in life earlier in the year, but it is a very important one and worth repeating. Most of life is unremarkable, mundane filled with a few exciting events in between. We go to work, we go home, we go to sleep. We get up the next morning and repeat the same process. Day after day, month after month finds us in a rut and no way to escape it. What is wrong? It is our attitude! What is mundane about a great meal when half of the world goes to bed hungry and millions die every day from starvation, many of them children? How about that hot shower you took this morning. Some have to bathe in filthy rivers and end up with dysentery. How about going to your refrigerator and pressing a button and fresh water fills your cup, is that taken for granted? Others across the world walk for miles for drinkable water *every day* of their lives. There is no faucet to turn on or off. My heart hurts when I think back on all of the daily conversations I had with my mom on the phone. Now they are cherished memories, sadly realized and appreciated only after her death. Those fancy shoes you wore to work today probably could have fed a hundred children in a third world country for months. I am reminded of the young boy in the Bible who presented Jesus with a couple loaves of bread and a few fish. Seems insignificant doesn't it. Yet, Jesus took those meager items and fed the multitude with a little boys lunch consisting of a few sardines and a few loaves of bread. Jesus turned those into more than 5,000 sardine sandwiches for the hungry crowd. Sometimes what seems insignificant to us is God's avenue to performing a miracle in someone's life. I dare say that any child presented with shoes, who previously had no shoes would count that as a miracle. Do you have a few sardines you can give to Jesus and watch what He does with them. Give what you can, what is insignificant to you can change another's life.

OCTOBER 31

"When you pray, if you have ANYTHING against ANYONE…"

"Lord, how many times shall I forgive my brother when he sins
against me? Up to seven times?
Jesus answered, "I tell you, not seven times but seventy times seven times."
Matthew 18:21-22

Forgiveness is not an option, it is a command. Forgive! Peter Marshall tells why forgiveness is so important to the believer. "If you hug to yourself any resentment against somebody else, you destroy the bridge by which God would come to you." Forgiving someone who has harmed and hurt you is not easy. No one has said it is, but it always the right thing to do. When you think about how many times God forgives you over and over again it should make forgiving others easier. God never tells us, "Well, you have gone and done it now. You have done that at least 30 times and you keep telling Me you will never do it again, so don't expect Me to forgive you again." Aren't we glad God doesn't treat us the way we insist on treating others? Not only does He forgive, but He no longer remembers our sin. The Bible says God places our sins as far as the East is from the West and remembers them no more.

"Forgiveness is *not an emotion*…Forgiveness is an *act of the will*
and the will can function regardless of the temperature of the heart."
-Corrie ten Boom-

I always used to think 'forgiving' was an emotion. It is not. The anger we experience because of the wrong done to us is an emotion, a very powerful one, so powerful many of us choose not to forgive. We must remember to forgive is an act of the will. It is a choice. God knows that when we forgive, it sets us free, not the one we are forgiving. We think because we forgive someone, we are letting them off the hook. We are, in a way. It lets them off our hook, but not God's. He will deal with them as He sees fit. That part is not our business. The only business we are in is to obey and forgive. Some of the greatest words ever spoken were done by Jesus while hanging on a cross. "Father, forgive them, they don't know what they are doing." I often wonder what would have happened to them if Jesus hadn't prayed that prayer. What they did, they did in ignorance, just like we do and others do sometimes. Only God knows the heart and the motive behind the cruel act. Only He has the wisdom to deal with those who wrong us. He very clearly says, "Vengeance is mine, I will repay", says the Lord. Vengeance? Yikes! If we are the one who wronged someone then those can be some scary words, if we are the one who was wronged, we are probably saying to ourselves, "Yes! Go get them Lord ! Make them pay!" God alone knows how to fairly deal with not only our sin, but the sins of others as well. He is the only One who has the wisdom. When we try to get even with someone we will make a mess of things. We will make things worse so give it to God instead. He will make it right. He promises, and He always keeps His promises.

NOVEMBER 1

*Humility requires that I accept
God's rightful authority over my life.*

"All authority in heaven and earth has been given to Me."
Matthew 28:18

Humbling oneself is not an easy task. We somehow look at humility as a weakness instead of what it really is, power under control. All authority in heaven and earth was given to Jesus! That is a lot of authority. Not only that, but the Bible says about Jesus, "The people were all so amazed that they asked each other, "What is this? A new teaching – and with authority! He even gives orders to evil spirits and they obey Him." (Mark 1:27) Wouldn't you have loved to have been there that day He cast out demons from those poor souls who had been possessed for years? One frightful example is the demoniac, who was possessed by a "legion' of demons for we are many," said the demon to Jesus. Jesus commanded the demons to come out. He didn't suggest it. He didn't get a committee together to see what the best approach would be. With all the authority of heaven behind Him he commanded it and it was so. Even the demons recognized Jesus as they begged him to send 'them' into a herd of swine nearby. Jesus permitted this to happen and immediately the herd of hogs, numbering over 2000, ran headlong down a steep slope into the sea and were drowned in the sea. This scared the living daylights out of the hog feeders and they ran away. The people had heard about what Jesus had done and they looked intently on the demoniac. He is described in Mark 5:15 as "sitting there, clothed and in his right mind." The people were seized with alarm and struck with fear! That is a very strange response to Jesus' setting this man free. You would think they would have 'celebrated' Him. The New Living Translation says in verse 17, "and the crowd began pleading with Jesus to go away and leave them alone." It seems the swine business was much more important to the town than their fellow human being inhabited by demons. The man who had been possessed was apparently the only one in the town with any common sense, he begged Jesus to take him with Him. Jesus told him instead to go home and tell his family, "how much the Lord has done for you and had sympathy for you and mercy on you." The man did that and more! He went and publically proclaimed all that Jesus had done. "The people were astonished and marveled." When was the last time you were astonished or marveled at what Jesus has done for you? Next time, shout it from the rooftops.

November 2

"It is beyond dispute that some awareness of God exists in the human mind by natural instinct, since God Himself has given everyone some idea of Him so that no one can plead ignorance."
-John Calvin-

"For the truth of God is known to them instinctively. God has put this knowledge in their hearts. From the time the world was created people have seen the earth and sky and all that God made. They can clearly see His invisible qualities – His eternal power and divine nature. So they have no excuse whatsoever for not knowing God."
Romans 1:19-20

There is NO excuse for NOT knowing God. We all have an awareness that God exists. When we look around us, we see a world of order and intricate detail, unmatched power and awesome beauty. We can count on the sun coming up each morning and going down in the evening. We know that if we defy gravity and jump off a building, well, that will be the last time we do. We have seen the hidden power in atomic and nuclear bombs unleashed. Those are the material things, how about the spiritual. We have felt the power of His love. We have seen a miracle in the birth of a baby. We have seen the dedication of a soldier who selflessly jumps on a grenade to save his buddies. We have felt the bond between a human and his dog or cat. We have felt our hearts rip in two at the sight of starving children. God is real. He exists. In fact, the Bible begins with Genesis 1:1, "In the beginning God..." God makes a powerful statement. He does not go on to defend it, you either accept it or you don't. Unbelievably, many don't. Atheists spend their whole life trying to prove God doesn't exist. Why would that matter to them if they don't believe He is real. Who are they trying to convince, themselves? Maybe so, because if they are wrong they will be held accountable for a godless, selfish life lived. A life that has denied truth. People in Christopher Columbus' day used to think the earth was flat. They were sincere in their beliefs - but sincerely wrong. The fact they were wrong probably didn't matter much in terms of the eternal, but if you are wrong about God's existence then you are wrong about almost everything, including where you will spend eternity. Not to mention the lie told to millions of children their great, great grandfather was a monkey and before that we came from a pool of swamp water. Which is harder to believe, that lie, or the truth that God has made each and every one of us. He proclaims in Psalms 139 how He knit us together in the womb of our mother? Trouble is the fact that God made and loves them can't be taught in our public schools anymore, but coming from a swamp can. Is there any wonder why America is in decline? The Ten Commandments were taken down from the school walls and metal detectors put up to catch students with guns. One has to wonder why they find the Ten Commandments so offensive to some, is it because there is accountability in the very first Commandment which says "You shall have no other gods before Me." That is a declarative statement. God says, I exist, I have no equal, put no one in your life ahead of me. Period.

NOVEMBER 3

Obedience is never a mistake.

"Do not merely listen to the Word, and so deceive yourselves. *DO what it says*."
James 1:22

"Do what it says" is a command, not a suggestion. It requires action on our part. Benjamin Franklin has said, "How many observe Christ's birthday! How few, His precepts! O! tis easier to keep holidays than commandments." We seem to follow what Jesus says when it benefits us, if it doesn't cost too much, or make us too uncomfortable. That is not obedience. Partial obedience is still disobedience. The day we gave our hearts to the Lord, we enlisted in His army. We are soldiers in the army of the living God. He orders, we obey!

"No man is a successful commander who has not first learned to obey."
-Chinese Proverb-

Obedience means I relinquish my will to God. It is no longer what I want, but what He commands. God has chosen the weak things of this world to confound the wise. God used Moses to come against Pharaoh! (Exodus Chapters 7-8) Do you think Moses was scared? I do. He did his best to talk God out of using him. I believe he thought that God had chosen the wrong person for the task of freeing the Jewish nation from slavery. God wanted them to be free to worship Him. Did God choose the wrong man? No. The Lord never left Moses on his own not for even one minute. Moses could not have freed the people on his own and God knew that. He gave Moses the strength to go before Pharaoh and demand that he "Let my people go." What was Pharaoh's response? He laughed at Moses. I don't think God thought it was funny. What could a man equipped with a rod and a staff do to the mighty kingdom of the Egyptians? Moses brought down plague after plague from Heaven against these people, and instead of bringing the Pharaoh to his knees, he hardened his heart against God. From a rod that turned into a snake, to frogs that filled the land, rivers that turned to blood, Pharaohs heart remained hard and stubborn. Great deception filled that land. Pharaoh's magicians and sorcerers copied every plague that Moses did, all except the last two. Ten plagues, sent by God, came against the Egyptians. Finally, gnats filled the land and the magicians were unable to duplicate this plague. They believed these plagues were sent by God, but Pharaoh still hardened his heart. After repeated warning, Pharaoh refused to let God's people go. His stubborn heart brought great suffering upon his people. The last plague was the killing of the firstborn of every man and woman in the land. This would bring down any thinking, reasonable man to his knees. Moses told the Israelites, place sacrificial blood on the doorposts of your houses and the 'death angel' will pass over, and spare your firstborns. Those who were 'obedient,' their first born sons lived, those who disobeyed, buried their firstborn. The Israelites were freed and took with them great plunder. You would think this was the end of the story but Pharaoh made one last attempt to kill the Israelites. Pharaoh and his mighty army pursued them one more time. Guess he thought after losing his son in death there wasn't much else to lose. He was so wrong. God miraculously opened the Red Sea for the Israelites and they passed on dry land. The Egyptians followed and were drowned, including Pharaoh, as God closed the sea on them. Thought for the day: Did you ever think that others would become a believer if they could see a miracle? How many warnings does it take for you to obey God?

November 4

Delayed obedience is disobedience.

"The goal of discipline is restoration-
never condemnation."
-Unknown-

We are always free to choose a better future. We may have had a rough start in life, but it is no excuse for ending that way. At any moment we can choose a different path. We can change the course of our life instantly, the moment we chose to obey God. Andrew Murray says it best, "God has no pleasure in afflicting us, but He will not keep back even the most painful chastisement if He can, but thereby guide His beloved child to come home and abide in His beloved Son." But isn't God a God of love? Yes, but many forget that He is also a God of justice. You cannot separate the two. It is impossible for Him to turn His back on our sins. Sin always comes with a price tag. Usually, a very high price tag! It will cost us more than we ever dreamed possible for a sin that really wasn't worth it in the end. "I wish I hadn't done that," has become the mantra of the sorrowful sinner. God wishes we hadn't done it too. He does not like disciplining His children, but He will. I have been disciplined so harshly, that I had a major life change. I learned the hard way that God does not mess around. This is not a game to Him. The stakes are high and He plays for keeps. Eternity! We ignore sin to our own peril. Selfishness and pride lead us to do things we know to be wrong. Deception is Satan's number one tool in his warfare against believers.

"Sin is like the poison of the Mamba snake. It is exceedingly deadly. It kills.
Every sin if permitted will become imperious in its demands and every lust
will aim at its maximum expression. Sin is like the devil, its originator. It
is limitless in its capacity for evil."
-Erroll Hulse-

November 5

Faint not! If God calls you to do something,
He will also empower you to do it and supply all
that you need for victory.

"The enemy shall come at me one way
and shall flee before me seven ways."
Deuteronomy 28:7

When you are about to faint what do you do? You find something to lean against...so lean against God. A powerful life is a well-balanced life. A well-balanced life is one of the highest forms of spiritual warfare against Satan, who strives to knock us down so we never get back up again. He wants to destroy us. Not just wound us, but destroy us and our testimony of what God has done in our lives. One of his main weapons is deceit. Let's consider some of the things in life that cause us to stumble. We can get off balance in life when something we really want is missing in our life. We go to great lengths to find it, buy it or steal it. We deceive ourselves into believing something we thing "is good" must be of God. We can destroy others in our path if we want it bad enough. Running away from something in our life will also cause us to get off balance. It's hard to face some circumstances in life, hard to deal with some people or relationships, so we run. Just like Jonah, he ran away from home, but he was really running away from God. Is there something God has told you to do and instead you went the other direction? Remember the Book of a Jonah, if you run from God you can be guaranteed it will not end well. Jonah ran, God went in pursuit of Jonah and guess who won? Not Jonah! Running got Jonah tossed into a storm that threatened his life and the lives of others, eventually swallowed up and spit out by a very big fish. Not listening to God will get us out of balance. Jonah ended up doing what God had told him to do in the first place, before he ran. That is just a royal waste of time. So is insisting on our own way. God did not create us to have our own way, but to seek His will. If you do that, God's promise in Deuteronomy that even though your enemy comes at you one way, He will cause your enemies to flee before you seven ways. In other words, God will scatter your enemies. You won't have to take down your enemies, God will do it for you. Another common behavior that will knock us down in life is to try to constantly please other people, especially at the expense of your own emotional health. That is an impossible task. I know. Sometimes, this is our feeble attempt to bring peace to a volcanic situation. For years I attempted to be a peacemaker. That's how I controlled my own little world. Appease everybody. No strife, no problems. It didn't work, except to teach me it didn't work. If someone acts badly, let them suffer the consequences of their behavior. That may be very hard to do, especially with our children, but with no consequences there will be no change in behavior. Peace in a balanced life comes from allowing God to meet my needs. If I try to meet them, I not only lose my peace, but I develop a restless spirit because I am fighting against the Holy Spirit's work and protection in my life.

Thought for the day: The moment we step out of God's will, we step into Divine discipline. You will find yourself saying, "Ouch," a lot.

NOVEMBER 6

When I cannot stand, He will bear me in His arms.

I think a favorite story of many Christians is, "Footprints in the Sand." The author tells of walking through the toughest trials of her life in which she thinks she walked alone. She begins by dreaming she was walking on the beach with her Lord, where there were two sets of footprints. As life got harder and harder the second set of footprints seemed to disappear. Here is her story -

> One night I dreamed a dream.
> As I was walking along the beach with my Lord.
> Across the dark sky flashed scenes from my life.
> For each scene, I noticed two sets of footprints in the sand,
> One belonging to me and one to my Lord.
> After the last scene of my life flashed before me,
> I looked back at the footprints in the sand.
> I noticed that at many times along the path of my life,
> especially at the very lowest and saddest times,
> there was only one set of footprints.
> This really troubled me, so I asked the Lord about it.
> "Lord, you said once I decided to follow you,
> You'd walk with me all the way.
> But I noticed that during the saddest and most troublesome times of my life,
> there was only one set of footprints.
> I don't understand why, when I needed You the most, You would leave me."
> He whispered, "My precious child, I love you and will never leave you
> Never, ever, during your trials and testings
> When you saw only one set of footprints,
> It was then that I carried you."
> -Mary Stevenson-

If you have been a Christian for any length of time you have probably experienced some very lonely times in your walk with God. The heavens were silent, your prayers seemed to bounce off the ceiling and come back and smack you upside the head. Where was God? You felt so all alone but you weren't. God is growing us up. When things are going our way it is easy to believe in God. In hard times we have two choices: pull away from God in doubt and unbelief or press in as hard as you can to a God who has promised never to leave you. Your circumstances may tell your emotions one thing while God's word and promises tell you something else. Who are you going to believe?

> "There is a deep peace that grows out of illness and loneliness and a sense of failure. God cannot get close when everything is delightful. He seems to need these darker hours, these empty-hearted hours, to mean the most to people.
> -Frank C. Laubach-

November 7

Don't cry because something is over...smile because it happened.

"The Bible never belittles disappointment, but it does
add one key word: temporary. What we feel now, we will not always feel."
-Philip Yancy-

Can you remember the last time you did something really stupid? You knew better, but you did it anyway. Unsure of the outcome, but you didn't care! Challenged by a 'friend' to do something dangerous? I think we have all been on that roller coaster of life and miraculously survived so far. So, why do we get back in line and buy another ticket? I think the simple answer is that too many times we live by our 'emotions.' Our fickle emotions, that one day would tell you to get on the ride and the next day would ask you, "Are you crazy?" Emotions are up one day and the next day down in despair and guilt. The thrill for the moment will never last as long as the pain does. It is a 'choice' to buy that ticket. We can't blame it on anyone else when we crash and burn. Like a roller coaster, someone else is in control. If I have a heart in rebellion to God, the roller coaster ride won't be near as fun as you think it will be. A friend offers you some drugs to try. You say no, he persists until he talks you into it. Peer pressure is a powerful tool of the enemy. As a critical care nurse I once took care of a beautiful young 19 year old girl in her first year of college. She went to a party where someone offered her 'ecstacy.' "Try it, just this once won't hurt." It not only hurt her, it killed her. She was a straight A student, a smart girl who made a very bad choice, a choice that left two devastated parents with many unanswered questions, as they stood at the gravesite of their daughter. You see, we can ride that roller coaster of life alone, or we can take someone else with us. It can be your own private sin, or you can drag someone else down with you. While on the coaster you never know where you are or where you are going next. Is there a dangerous curve ahead? There is a warning in the Bible that if anyone causes a child to sin, it would be better if they had a millstone wrapped around their neck and tossed into the sea. Next time you are looking for a little fun and get in line for another ticket you would be wise to consider how much will this really cost me? Eventually, the next ride you take will be the reality train.

November 8

Life can suddenly become very 'unfunny.'

"The wages of sin is *death, but the gift of God is eternal life*."
-Romans 6:23-

Sin entangles us. It's a lot like a bug that gets caught in a spider web. He didn't mean to. He failed to see the trap that was set for him. He can't free himself even if he wanted to. He is no longer in control, the spider is. The spider has a plan as does our enemy, Satan. Throughout the night the spider slowly and meticulously spins and weaves his web. If someone knocks it down, he starts all over again. He will not be deterred.

"Never underestimate the internal price you pay for sin. The weight of guilt
is enormous and bitterness and depression settle uncomfortably in your soul
as you try to suppress the conviction of the Holy Spirit."
-Unknown-

Every sin has a door of entrance. Once entered, it is difficult to escape. The bug struggles and struggles to free himself, all to no avail. He just gets stuck even more. His latter state, is far worse than the first. Yet, he continues to struggle. He tries to put up a fight to no avail. His enemy is greater and smarter than he is. The power of sin over a believer died on the cross with Jesus. He paid the price. We are free if we choose to be. We no longer have to live rebellious lives. We no longer have to be defeated over and over by the devil.

"It has been correctly said that the ground is level at the
foot of the cross. We all come as needy sinners; we all
come with the same need for the pardon that God alone can give us."
-Erwin Lutzer-

Did you ever believe the lie of the enemy that you had sinned too much or too badly to ever be accepted by God into heaven? Well, good news is, God is looking for sinners to save, not those who think they have it all together. Satan has had thousands of years of practice deceiving sinners. He has taken down many of God's saints, but you don't have to fall for his lies anymore. Charles Spurgeon has said, "Because you own yourself to be a sinner I would encourage you to believe that grace is ordained for such as you are." Erwin Lutzer goes on to say, "As sinners, we all have a God-sized problem. Thankfully, there is a God sized solution." JESUS.

November 9

I am learning to lay it down...in <u>silence</u>.

"Let those who will to walk away from you because
of the Lord, let them leave."
I John 2:19

Lay down what? My hurts, my fears, revenge, toxic relationships, and the list goes on and on... Opening up your hands and letting go of whatever God has asked you to let go of is one of life's most painful experiences. You may lose friends who don't like your beliefs in Christianity. Doing it in silence, without complaining or murmuring, is near impossible without God's help. Remember, whatever He asks you to do, He will supply whatever it is you need to do it. Why is it so hard to let go of some things? We don't like to relinquish control of our lives. We want to be in charge of what's in our life or out of it. To some of us, depending on the circumstances, it means we are a failure. Sometimes, letting go means we can no longer 'get even' with someone. That especially hurts when we think or know that we didn't deserve their bad treatment. What benefit is it to me to lay my hurts, burdens and cares down? To lay them down in silence means the battle is over, God has won, but so have I because I obeyed! Victory comes when I can let go without complaining because I want His will, more than I want my own. I have settled my case in heaven and know that God knows better than I do what I need. "But Lord," means I am still holding onto to little part of my hurt when He wants it all. Healing can't come until you give Him it all. I would ask you this – "What better place to lay your burdens than at the foot of the cross of the One who died for you? Laying it down means I exchange what I think is good for me for His very best for me. There are some things that no longer belong in our life and some people. If you are willing to define 'love' the way God defines love, you can easily lay down toxic relationships that are unhealthy, ungodly, and causing you unnecessary pain and heartache. I need to stop trying to make happen, what God never intended to happen. Once I lay it down, facing the truth and allowing God's wisdom to reign in my life, His healing will begin. So, let go and see what God can do. You will be amazed and wonder why you didn't do it sooner.

November 10

The journey is too great for thee...
1 Kings 19:7

"One of the best kept secrets in Christianity is that God accepts us. True, He can't stand our sinful acts, but He loves us. He doesn't have us on a performance-based acceptance, He has us on a Jesus-based acceptance."
-Bill Gillham-

We were not meant to journey through this life alone. Many of us make the mistake of trying. We don't want anyone telling us how to live our lives. That is exactly what the Bible does, it tells us how to live. It is God's blueprint for a successful life. So, why do millions think they can succeed when they ignore the only true instruction book given to man by God? When things go bad, they blame God. "Why did God let this happen to me?" they cry. They don't realize 'bad choices' are the reason our life ends up in the pits. When things go good, though, we are quick to take the credit. Life experiences teach us many lessons in life we could learn no other way. Trials will bring out the real me and a lot of other ugly stuff. I may think I am a patient person, until I get in the grocery checkout line and the clerk is new, it's her first day alone, then she runs out of register tape, then she needs a price check. This is a reality check of where I think I am and where I really am. Thank God He slowly shows us the real us and doesn't reveal it all at once. If He did we wouldn't be able to get out of bed in the morning, we would feel so bad about ourselves. He slowly reveals stuff and teaches us what needs to change and stands by us in the process. God is our best cheerleader in life. Trials reveal God's love for us. If He didn't care He would just leave us to our own destruction. The fact that He doesn't speaks volumes about His loving kindness and mercy in our lives.

"Be not afraid of those trials which God may see fit to send upon thee. It is with the wind and the storm of tribulation that God, in the garner of the soul, separates the true wheat from the chaff. Always remember, therefore, that God comes to thee in thy sorrows as really as in thy joys. He lays low and He builds up. Thou wilt find thyself far from perfection if thou dost not find God in everything."
– Miguel de Molinos-

Learn to look for God even in the worst of circumstances. Just like behind the rainclouds, lies the sun. It hasn't gone away, there is just something temporarily blocking it. The sun will shine again and when it does it will seem brighter than before. Our vision will improve in the trial and we will see God clearer.

"Frame your picture of God based on who He really is, not through the lenses of your circumstances."
-Tim Burns-

November 11

If God doesn't want me to have something then I shouldn't want it either.

"There is no fear of God before their eyes."
Romans 3:18

Today we are going to take a look at the world through God's eyes. The eyes of God search the earth to and fro continually. What does He find? The Bible says that God even knows when a tiny sparrow falls from a tree, so much more is His care for us. Jesus, the Son of God, His eyes looked into Peter's eyes, the disciple who had betrayed that he even knew Jesus. Not once, not twice but three times. What did he see? He saw a man who would cry tears of repentance after committing such a sin. His eyes looked into Judas' eyes, a man who betrayed Him for 30pieces of silver, who betrayed the Lord of Glory for a pittance of money. Jesus looked into the eyes of an adulterer. What did He see? He saw a life filled with years of rejection and worthlessness. A life He could dramatically change with just a few words. Jesus looked into the eyes of 10 lepers, and remarkably He saw a heart of ingratitude in 9 of those lepers. He healed all ten of them and only one returned to thank Him…only one. (Luke 17: 11-21) Looking into Mary Magdalene's eyes He saw eyes of hope where there had been no hope for years. She longed to get out of the life of prostitution, only the touch of Jesus on her life made that possible. Jesus looked into the eyes of Satan full of evil, out in the wilderness while he tested our Lord and was defeated. Jesus looked into the eyes of Pilate and found only contempt and indifference towards the things of God. Nicodemus, the Pharisee had eyes that questioned all he had learned about God up until he met Jesus. Who else did Jesus look at with His eyes of compassion? Here is a list. See if you can find yourself in any of them mentioned. Men on the Road to Emmaus – eyes of sadness and despair because Jesus had been crucified on a cross by Roman soldiers. Jonah – eyes of rebellion. Prodigal son – eyes of rebellion and regret. Daniel – eyes of faith and fearlessness as he faced the hungry lion's and was about to become supper for them. Beggar – eyes of want, despair and hopelessness. What does Jesus see when He looks into your eyes? If you are hopeless, He can bring you hope. If you are questioning – He can give you the answers to life you need because He is the answer. At the beginning of today's reading I wrote the statement "If God doesn't want me to have something then I shouldn't want it either." Seeking after ungodly things is what brings us to a life of rebellion, sadness, despair and hopelessness. Jesus can change all of that if you will let Him. Say yes to Him today and then stop trying to make happen something that God never intended to happen. Then when He looks at you He will see eyes filled with everlasting joy and love for Him. We will be with Jesus for all eternity.

NOVEMBER 12

Faith is NEVER learned in comfortable surroundings.

Make a 'declaration of *dependence*' on Jesus!
One day you will be glad you did.

It is natural for man to make a declaration of independence, but what we really need is a declaration of dependence on God Himself. He says, "Without Me you can do nothing!" Nothing means nothing! Your very next breath is dependent upon the goodness and kindness of God. Tomorrow is promised to no man. We all are just one heartbeat away from eternity.

> "Do not be satisfied with as much Christianity
> as will ease your conscience."
> J.B. Stoney

It is sorrow that shows our dependence upon God as nothing else can. William Booth, founder of the Salvation Army in 1878, describes the day his wife told him she had cancer.

> "I was stunned. I felt as if the whole world were coming
> to a standstill. Opposite me on the wall was a picture of
> Christ on the cross. I thought I could understand it as never
> before. My wife talked to me like a heroine, like an angel
> to me. I could only kneel with her and try to pray."

Sorrow can bring us to our knees, or to our knees before the throne of God. A Chinese proverb says, "A day of sorrow is longer than a month of joy." Anyone who has been told very bad news would agree with that statement. I can still remember the day my mom called me to tell me my older sister had passed away. She was only 31, I was 27. That was over 40 years ago but I still remember the awful pain and confusion I experienced that day and many days after. It turned my whole world upside down and inside out. God used her death as a catalyst to bring me to Himself. The night before her funeral, I was sitting alone on my sofa, watching a Billy Graham crusade on TV. I found myself weeping uncontrollably. My life was a mess and I could no longer deny it. It was then I got down on my knees and gave my life to Jesus. I have never regretted my decision that night. Yes, it has been a bumpy ride some days, and my walk with God was more like He had to drag me some days. Other days, have been filled with unspeakable joy. I think those days are God's gift to us to show us just a tiny glimpse of what heaven will be like for us. Faith is never learned in comfortable surroundings, but no matter how dark it gets, God will shine His light on His child and show them the way through.

NOVEMBER 13

When there is a matter that requires urgent prayer...
PRAY until you BELIEVE God will answer.

Never am I required to stand on my own strength. Never.

Joseph Caryl has said, "Affliction does not hit the saint of God by chance, but by His direction...It is not only the grace of God, but the glory of the believer, when he can stand and take affliction *quietly*." How many of us take affliction quietly? Not many. We shout to the world we are in pain, and lots of it. We tell our family, we tell our neighbors, we tell just about anyone that will listen until they won't. We do not like to suffer in silence, especially when we are sure we haven't done anything to deserve this trial. We try everything we know to make the situation go away and to no avail. We cry, we beg, we plead with God to remove it and He will as soon as it has accomplished its purpose in our life. God directs our troubles just as He does every other aspect of our life.

"Can God? This question wounds and hurts God. God can. This will clear up many a problem. It will bring you through many a difficulty in your life."
-Andrew Murray-

Can God be limited? We act as if He can, by our unbelief. Well, let's see. God made a donkey speak to Balaam. He made a hand, with no body attached to it, write on a wall a very disturbing message of destruction. The Bible says, if man won't praise God, He will make the rocks and mountains to cry out. He parted the Red Sea and millions walked across it without getting wet. Then He closed the Sea and drowned Pharaoh and his army. At Jericho God made the walls come tumbling down after men marched around it then blew their trumpets. That's a really crazy war strategy if you ask me. Fortunately, God didn't need my help taking the walls down. Our God is amazing. We cannot put Him in a box. We are finite beings and incapable of thinking in infinite terms. My mind is still boggled at the fact that the earth is orbiting the sun at approximately 67,108 miles per hour. The sun is 93 million miles away. Wow! Remember the three Hebrew children, Shadrach, Meshach and Abednego who were thrown 'bound' into the fiery furnace because of their refusal to worship any other god than Jehovah? (Daniel Chapter 3). King Nebuchadnezzar looked into the fiery furnace and saw four men instead of just the three he had thrown in there. He was baffled and blurted out, " There are four men in there. Did we not throw just three in? The fourth is like the Son of Man." Not only were there four, but the hands and feet of the three were loosed by the fourth, the Lord Himself. Keep in mind victory for these young men began '**before**' they were thrown into the fire. They had determined in their hearts to worship God alone no matter the consequences and He delivered them from a very painful, fiery death. Victory **in** the fire, Jesus was right by their side. Victory **after** the fire, God was glorified and the Bible says when they came out of the furnace 'they didn't even smell like smoke.' Are you in a fiery furnace right now? Are flames licking at your faith? Call on the Lord. Maybe in God's eyes the only place He can remove whatever has you bound is in the midst of the flames. God is faithful. He doesn't prove His promises to us sitting in a nice little comfy church pew, but instead in the midst of the fire. Thought for the day: "There is a day you will go into the furnace, but there is also a day you will come out. Will you smell like smoke?"

November 14

*"The beginning of anxiety is the end of faith, and
the beginning of true faith is the end of anxiety"*
-George Mueller-

Even a caged bird will still sing to his owner.
-Unknown-

Don't be anxious for anything! Anxiety comes from wanting my way more than I want God's. Are you pursuing God or are you pursuing 'stuff?' Someone has said, "If you exchange your pursuit of God and your time alone with Him for the pursuit of 'stuff' you may find yourself better off, but not a better man." When a child of God gets down on his or her knees in humility before God asking for His help, all of Heaven shouts Hallelujah!

"In my prosperity I said, "This is forever, nothing can stop me
now...then Lord You turned Your face away from me and cut
me off from your river of blessings. Suddenly, my courage was gone.
I was terrified and panic stricken."
Psalm 30: 6-7

In verses six and seven, we see arrogance beyond belief. Then the Lord turns away and shuts off the spicket of His blessings, and the man falls apart. He started out trusting in God, then trusted in himself, then in verse eight, he comes to his senses and cries to the Lord, "Help!"

"I cried out to You, O Lord.."
verse 8

Our pride tends to inflate when things are going good, we take credit for our prosperity. Our pride suddenly deflates when God withdraws His blessings and we realize just how dependent on Him we really are. This man went from prideful to a fool to a beggar in 3 verses. In verse 10 he is begging for mercy and in verse 11 declaring God's goodness, "You have turned my mourning into joyful dancing!" Earthly security is uncertain but God is not. Put your trust in Him. He will not let you down. It ended well for the Psalmist. How will it end for you?

"Pride is: Having a stronger desire to do
my will than God's."
-Neil Anderson & Charles Mylander-

November 15

"As thy days so shall thy strength be."

"In the world you will have tribulation and trials, but be of good
cheer (take courage). For I (Jesus) have overcome the world."
John 16:33

The world's kids today worship at the feet of the super heroes in the movie theaters across America. Batman, Superman, Captain America are all make believe and yet it is a billion dollar industry! We all love good guys who overcome evil with good. Unlike these super heroes, our God is not make believe and He has already won the battle against **ALL** evil. So, we really can take courage.

"The way to grow strong in Christ is to become weak in yourself. Instead of a red,
white and blue costume, our God is clothed in power."
-C.H. Spurgeon-

We must look at life as Martin Luther did, "Even if I knew that tomorrow the world would go to pieces, I would still plant my apple tree." Now that is hope! We live in uncertain days as never before. Recently the news showed a man, just fired from his job, went back to his work, and killed the first person he came in contact with. He then used his knife to behead her. This is unprecedented, a grandmother, beheaded in the United States of America. The man had radical Islamic videos all over his website yet, outrageously, some want to call this workplace violence. We need God more and more each day because it appears He seems to be lowering His hedge of protection over America due to our indifference towards Him.

"The great thing is to be found at one's post as a child of God,
living each day as though it were our last, but planning as
though our world might last a hundred years."
-C.S. Lewis-

God is with us today and will be there for us tomorrow. As history marches on, God's plan is revealed more and more each day. If He is for us then we need not fear what tomorrow may hold for us. We already know we win so hold onto that truth when life gets tough.

"He that fears not the future may enjoy the present."
-Thomas Fuller-

"The reality is it is impossible to distinguish evil from good unless one has
an infinite point that is absolutely good. The infinite reference point for
distinguishing good from evil can be found only in the person of God,
for God alone can exhaust the definition of "absolutely good."
-Norman Geisler-

November 16

Don't be surprised if your answer to prayer comes in 'closed' doors.

"More things are wrought by prayer than the world dreams of."
-Tennyson-

The story of your life will be the story of your prayers and their answers. When in doubt, PRAY! Prayers that are unasked, are prayers never answered. Do you remember Peter and the others in a Roman jail? Did they lament and feel sorry for themselves? Absolutely not! What they did would seem crazy by anyone's standards, everyone except to the Christian. They prayed and they sang songs. They worshipped God from a prison! Now doesn't that just strike you as certifiably nuts? Yet, prayer and singing swung open the doors and set them free. Their songs opened the doors of the jail cell better than any tools passed to them in a cake could have. The Soviet Union fell because of prayer and because of a godly man, President Reagan, who drew his wisdom from God and ended the cold war against Russia in 1994. Today, God's word is allowed into Russia and has set many free and changed many lives by its power. Our nation is trying to get rid of God while Russia now embraces Him, at least until Putin puts an end to it. The following is a quote from one of the Soviet Union's greatest critics, who was expelled from his own country:

> "If I were asked today to formulate as concisely as possible the
> main cause of the ruinous revolution that swallowed up some
> 60 million of our people, I could not put it more accurately than
> to repeat: "Men had forgotten God; that is why all this has happened."
> -Alexander Solzhenitsyn-

God's word is powerful. It has the ability to bring down governments and their ungodly leaders. The strength of our country has always been in its faith in God and His principles for living. The further away we get from God, will destroy this nation from within, never mind those from without,, with their nuclear bombs that want to annihilate us. We will destroy ourselves by our apathy and indifference to Almighty God. As the Bible disappears, so will our liberties. The Bible says, "Blessed is the nation whose God is the Lord." The opposite is also true. Cursed is the nation that turns its back on God. The good news is, one generation, devoted to God can change that and put us back into God's good graces. God can change the condition of the human heart which will change the destiny of a nation. One heart at a time, to save a nation.

November 17

"God does not comfort us to make us comfortable, but to make us comforters.
–Dr. J.H. Jowett-

"To ease another's heartache is to forget one's own."
-Abraham Lincoln-

Trials are a part of life for us all. No one escapes. It is not the trial that defines us but how we handle the trial that will make the biggest impact on our life and others. What is our attitude in times of hardship? Do we throw a pity party and invite all of our friends, or do we see this as coming from the loving Hand of God? Others are watching us, especially unbelievers. They want to know if your faith is real. Trials will reveal just that. It's easy to have a good attitude when things are going great, but hard to maintain that smile when your heart is breaking. Where you go for comfort reveals a lot about your faith or lack of it. Do you go to friends who don't have any more answers than you do, or do you go to God? C.H. Spurgeon, one of the world's greatest preachers, suggests we go to the Cross for comfort:

"We ourselves know by experience that there is no place for comfort like the cross. It is a tree stripped of all foliage, and apparently dead; yet we sit under its shadow with great delight; and its fruit is sweet unto our taste."

Spurgeon also says, "It will greatly comfort you if you can see God's hand in both your losses and your crosses." If I see God in just my blessings I have only half the picture. God is also in my troubles. Some we bring on ourselves, some are caused by others in our life, but all of them are sifted through God's loving hand of Sovereignty and Omniscience. When I went through a divorce it was the most painful experience I have ever had, except the deaths of my family members. I didn't think I would ever heal from the hurt and the pain. It took a long time, but eventually God put the pieces of my life back together again. I painfully learned it takes two to make a relationship work and only one to destroy it. Both have to be willing. I then was able to help lead a Divorce Recovery group for 3 years. I was able to comfort those because God had comforted me and made me a comforter in the process of my healing. Eventually, I was able to see God's marvelous hand through my tears. There are recovery groups out there for alcoholics, sex addicts, drug addicts, you can be set free if you make a choice to get help. It was the hardest thing I did walking into a divorce class because I felt like such a loser. Thank God I didn't stay that way and neither should you. Admit you need help then victory is just a phone call away. Make that call right now!

(divorcerecovery.com)

November 18

Will I really trust Him...no matter what?

The following is a contrast of what we feel, say and what God has promised in His Word:
I say: "It's impossible."
God says: "All things are possible. (Luke 18:27)
I say: "I'm too tired."
God says: "I will give you rest."(Matthew 11:28-30)
I say: "Nobody really loves me."
God says: "I love you." (John 3:16)
I say: "I can't go on."
God says: "My grace is sufficient for you." (II Corinthians 12:9)
I say: "I can't figure things out."
God says: "I will direct your steps." (Proverbs 3:5-6
I say: "I can't do it."
God says: "You can do all things through Christ." (Philippians 4:13)
I say: "I'm not able."
God says: "I AM able. ((II Corinthians 9:8)
I say: "It's not worth it."
God says: "It will be worth it. (Romans 8:28)
I say: "I can't forgive myself."
God says: "I forgive you." (I John 1:9)
I say: "I can't manage."
God says: "I will supply all your needs." (Philippians 4:19)
I say: "I'm afraid."
God says: "I have not given you a spirit of fear." (II Timothy 1:7)
I say: "I'm always worried and frustrated."
God says: "Cast ALL of your cares on Me."
I say: "I don't have enough faith."
God says: I have given everyone a measure of faith." (Romans 12:3)
I say: "I'm not smart enough."
God says: I will give you wisdom." (I Corinthians 1:30)
I say: "I feel all alone."
God says: "I will NEVER leave you or forsake you. (Hebrews 13:5)
-author unknown-

These verses pretty much cover everything from fear to wisdom for a situation, from faith to forgiveness. Jesus' death on the cross paid it ALL for us. We need not fear, He will supply everything we need in this life not to just get by but to be more than a conqueror! If you are feeling down and out read this list over and over as many times as it takes to get you back on your feet again. Remember, do not go by your feelings but by every word that proceeds out of the mouth of God. Feelings are fickle. God is not. He will be your Rock of Gibraltar.

November 19

Be still...God speaks when there is no inward storm.

"Although the world is full of suffering, it is
full also of the overcoming of it."
-Helen Keller-

Helen Keller was an overcomer of her blindness. God calls us to be overcomers too. How do we overcome? Simple answer is to surrender to God! Put down the boxing gloves, the moment you do the war is over. We who were once alienated and hostile towards God, He now calls His child, the moment we give our lives and future to Him. There is no longer a plan B. It is God's plan for my life from that moment forward. We no longer seek our own way but His. He knows the path we are on and where it will lead, what obstacles we face and what enemy lurks on that pathway. We have now signed up to be a soldier in the army of the living God. He becomes the One in charge of everything. We take our orders from Him, not from others or from well-meaning friends. I am now under His protection and His care. He knows where all of the land mines are on the battlefield of life. Sometimes we will need just light artillery, other times we must get the big guns out. Our enemy's mission is to seek and destroy and left alone, we are no match for Satan. He has been doing warfare against Christians for thousands of years, and has been very successful at it. He roams upon the earth looking for someone to devour and destroy. Satan does not give up his territory without a huge fight. Some battles will last longer than others. It depends on what is at stake. The enemy will try to take you out with one punch. If he can't he will try and try again until he does or God stops him. A prolonged siege attack is meant to wear the saint of God down, to weaken the soldier. Job was attacked from all sides, including accusations from his wife and closest friends, but though discouraged at times, he never gave up the fight even when those who should have stood with him, didn't. Neither should we. Job went through more than we could ever dream of going through. Satan was allowed into Job's life after God purposely let down His hedge of protection at Satan's request. We know from God's word why He allowed this attack on Job's life, but Job did not know why yet he remained faithful, refusing to curse God and die as his wife suggested. Satan made an accusation to God against Job, "Does he fear You for nothing? You have blessed his socks off. Let me at him and he will curse you." That is a paraphrase, of course, but you get the picture. Satan could do whatever he wanted to Job with the exception that he could not take Job's life. He took his cattle, his sheep, even his children's lives, he gave him sores all over his body, turned all of his friends and wife against him and still Job said, "Naked I came into the world and naked I will leave, blessed is the name of the Lord." Is your faith that strong? Well, neither is mine. I have been through some really tough times but nothing like that. The Bible says that God will only put on us what we are able to bear. What I learn from this story is that despite his horrible circumstances, Job refused to walk away from God even when it appeared God had walked away from Job, but he knew better. God is faithful and in the end He restored to Job more than he had lost. Thought for the day: Next time you want to give up on God, don't!

November 20

God gets his greatest victories out of apparent defeats.

"Spiritual victory comes only to those
who are prepared for battle."
-Unknown-

Many times in the Bible it 'appears' that God's people were facing the jaws of defeat and destruction. The greatest apparent victory of God's enemy was really God's greatest victory. The sky had blackened in the town of Jerusalem 2000 years ago. There had been a great earthquake, as the Son of God hung there on a cross made by men. It was meant to be a slow and tortuous death, and it was. The criminal was suffocated to death, eventually being unable to take a breath in or out, as their body became weaker and weaker. They had plucked His beard out and beaten Him to a bloody pulp. He was almost unrecognizable. The crown of thorns on His head was placed there to mock Him, a sign overhead read, "Jesus, King of the Jews." His blood spilled to the ground with each heartbeat from the wounds in His hands, feet and side. His mother overwhelmed with grief, as were His followers, stood close by. A crowd that earlier yelled, "Crucify Him!" now looks on as spectators at a football game. Others stared in disbelief, "We thought He had come from God." No one really understood what was happening that day except Jesus. His followers had fled, denied that they even knew Him. God Himself turned His back on His Son. His words echoed across the land, "Father, why have You forsaken Me?" "Father forgive them, they do not know what they are doing." Then came those final words of clarity, "It is FINISHED!" Satan and his minions were now jumping with glee at the death of Jesus, claiming victory. The Pharisees were doing the 'happy dance' around the cross, in all of their piety. That victory would be short lived for not only Satan, but for the enemies of Jesus as well. They still did not quite understand what had just taken place, but they would get a rude awakening just three days later as Jesus rose triumphantly from the dead and left a borrowed tomb, empty. Circumstances made it seem like the enemy had won, when in reality Satan suffered the greatest defeat of his miserable existence. Jesus came to set mankind free and He did just that. Our sin required a death penalty from us all. Jesus took our sins upon Himself and declared us 'not guilty,' if we would turn to Him in repentance and forgiveness. Have you called upon the Savior? If not, why not? Today is a good day to accept His forgiveness and start over again.

November 21

"I walked a mile with pleasure;
She chatted all the way;
But left me none the wiser
For all she had to say.
I walked a mile with sorrow;
And ne'er a word said she;
But, oh, the things I learned from her,
When sorrow walked with me."
-Robert Browning Hamilton-

It takes real sorrow to expose one's true soul.

We never realize how truly blessed we are until that blessing is taken from us. Sadly, all of us take a lot of things for granted. I received an email once that read, "God loves the saint and the sinner but the sinner positions himself so that he is unable to experience God's love because of his rebellion and disobedient life."(-unknown-) Sinners often believe God has abandoned them, when just the opposite is true. We have walked away from Him, not Him from us and still He pursues us. That is love at its finest. It is much like the little child who has been warned over and over yet still follows that ball out into the street, out into danger. There is no reason for any of us to face life alone. Problem is God makes the rules and many of us don't like that. We want to run out into the street and hope it turns out okay. Sometimes it does, sometimes it doesn't. Rebellion is a time stealer. There is no blessing in rebellion, only chastisement and pain which quickly leads to regret.

"Regret for time wasted can become a power of good
in the time that remains, if we will only stop the waste and
the idle, useless regretting."
-Arthur Brisbane-

November 22

"I shall NOT be moved!"
Acts 20:24

"Radical faith doesn't mean that you are not afraid. Radical
Faith just means that you are willing to act despite your fears."
-Chip Ingram-

Radical faith - What does that mean to you? I think radical faith is when I can believe that God is already answering my prayer before I even have time to get down on my knees and pray it. He sends out His mighty angels to fulfill my request. It means that my faith is never dependent upon my circumstances. It is holding tightly to each and every promise of God and never letting go. If God said it then He will do it. Faith isn't something you talk yourself into.

"Faith is believing right here with your head
No matter how your heart feels."
-Beth Moore-

It is never based on emotions but on an all knowing God who has never failed. He has never lost a battle. He has never lost even one soul that is dependent on Him to save them. Faith is a gift of God. The more we believe, the more God proves Himself, faithful, and the more my faith grows. Faith is never blind, no never, it is always anchored in Omnipotence. Faith reaches its fullness the moment I am willing to sacrifice my life for it. Death has no power over the child of God. Faith is learned by studying the Word of God.

"Faith is not generated by a kind of repetitious self-hypnosis;
rather, it is strengthened through a knowledge of the One in whom
it is placed, and that kind of knowledge comes through studying
God's Word and through experiences with Him as we go through life."
-Charles Ryrie-

One of the greatest displays of faith in the Bible is the account of Daniel in the Lion's den. I don't think Daniel was the least bit afraid of the lions. He was more afraid of not believing God could deliver him. I also believe that Daniel got a good night's sleep that night. Do you believe that God will shut the mouths of the lion's for you? If not, why not? He does not respect one human above another. What God will do for one of His children, He will do for all. God does not have favorites, He has 'intimates.' We are as close to God as we choose to be. If you want to crawl up into His lap, you can. If you want to keep your distance from God you can do that too. Sin always stands between God and ourselves. It is up to us how close we draw near to God or how far away we go. It is not God who has not moved, it is us.

November 23

God always sends His staff with His rod.

"Sin would have very few takers if
the consequences were immediate."
-unknown-.

"Thy rod and Thy staff they comfort me." (Psalm 23) How can that be? The rod is an instrument of discipline, how can that bring comfort? The staff can comfort as a tool to lean on when the road gets hard to travel. The Bible says that God disciplines those He loves. He chastises those who are His own. The Christian has not lost the power to sin, but through the power of the Holy Spirit he has lost his desire. What used to be fun as an unbeliever, no longer is. No power on earth can make a man sin if he doesn't want to. He chooses to, not has to. If he does sin, God's rod will bring him back into line with God's will. His rod discourages a man to rebel.

"The rule that governs my life is this: Anything that
dims my vision of Christ, or takes away my taste for Bible
study, or cramps my prayer life, or makes Christian work difficult,
is wrong for me, and I must, as a Christian, turn away from it."
-J. Wilbur Chapman-

If sin's consequences struck us the moment we sinned, we would get the message real fast. If we could connect the dots between our actions and its consequences that quickly, there would be a lot less sinning, myself included. Just like touching the flame on a stove. It only takes one try at it to convince us it is hot and will burn. However, sin's power is in its ability to lure us, entice us then ensnare us. It promises something good and delivers pain and suffering instead.

"If the aspect of this world now dazzles your eyes, the last
day will cure you of this folly, but it will be too late."
-John Calvin-

Sins lure is much like the fisherman who places a worm on the end of his hook. The fish dances around the hook all the time thinking, "Yum," until he bites. It is too late then. How many of Satan's hooks have we bit at, only to find out it wasn't so yummy, after all. In fact, the pain far outweighed any pleasure.

"The tendency to sin gathers force with every new commission.
So the battle goes on in every one of us. We must either
overcome sin, or it will overcome us; we must decide."
-D.L.Moody-

Like everything else in life, sin is a choice.

NOVEMBER 24

Want to excel at spiritual warfare? Learn to praise Him and give thanks in the darkest moments of life.

I have learned that one of the best things I can do when the bottom drops out of my life is to tell God, "I don't like this Lord, it seems unfair, but I CHOOSE to trust you in this." I thank Him for working in my life as only He can do. Do I hurt? Yes. Do I want it to end? Yes. Is it hard to praise Him through tears? Yes! This goes against our nature. We want to cry, throw things, call our friends and invite them to our pity party. We want others to feel sorry for us. All those things will only prolong our pain. They won't help us to feel any better, in fact, they can make us feel worse. It is okay to cry and grieve over a loss. Eventually, you have to let go of the pain so it doesn't ruin your life. Trusting God is a mighty form of spiritual warfare. The devil wants us to doubt. He throws everything he has at us to get us to turn away from God.

> "The times when you and I can't trace his hand of purpose, we must trust His heart of love!"
> -Anne Graham Lotz-

Even faith the size of a mustard seed can accomplish great things. Look how many mustard trees one seed can produce. Even the smallest of faith can whack the devil upside the head. Just be cautious, he will be back with a bigger arsenal. So, you show up to the fight with JESUS. The devil doesn't fight fair, so don't you either! God's Word says; "God is an ever present help, in time of trouble."

NOVEMBER 25

God often waits for <u>me</u>.

"But those who wait upon the Lord will find new strength. They
will fly high on the wings as eagles. They will run and not
grow weary. They will walk and not faint."
Isaiah 40:31

Yikes! I thought I was waiting on Him. No, He is waiting on us most of the time. Sometimes, He will require us to let go of something, before He will fulfill our request. It might be an attitude we need adjusted before answering our prayer. Whether or not we are waiting on God or He is waiting on us, the circumstances can create a storm in our life of great intensity. This storm will test our faith, our strength, our endurance, and our views of life. Storms of great intensity may cause us to question the very foundations of our life, godly principles that have previously anchored us. Do I really trust God? Does God really love me? Will He see me through this? The very truths of our life are tested, not in the good times, but when the bottom falls out, when we find ourselves alone, with no hope and nothing to anchor us. We drift on a sea of confusion with no land in sight. While we waver, toss and turn in the waves, it would do us well to look up and learn from the eagle. An eagle has the uncanny ability of knowing when a storm is brewing. We too may have an alarm going off within us, trouble is on the way. Sometimes, the Holy Spirit will warn us ahead of time. The eagle is not threatened by the storm but instead he uses it to lift himself up and out of harm's way. He uses the very wind that threatens his survival. As the storm builds and builds, the eagle patiently waits and watches for just the right moment. When that moment comes he uses the winds to lift him up, up and away, far above the storm and out of danger. He does not fight the wind instead he rides the winds of the storm to his own advantage. What a picture for the believer. We too, should never fear the storm but look up to the heavens, to our God who watches over us. Our focus should be on our God who controls the winds and the storms of life. God controls the strength of the storm, the length of the storm in our life and the intensity of the storm. It's time to take flying lessons! You will be glad you did. God will have you soaring with the eagles before you know it.

NOVEMBER 26

*The sting of my circumstances will lessen
more and more as I realize He has allowed this to happen.*

Are you worried? Fearful of what may happen? Burdened down with the troubles of today? Are worries weighing you down? Listen to this beautiful story:

> "I walked slowly out on the beach. A few yards below the high-water mark, I stopped and read the words again: WRITE YOUR WORRIES ON THE SAND. I let the paper blow away and picked up a fragment of shell. Kneeling there under the vault of the sky, I wrote several words, one above the other. Then I walked away, and I did not look back. I had written my troubles on the sand. The tide was coming in."
> -Arthur Gordon-

Oh, the wisdom in this simple story. Write your troubles in the sand, then walk away from them and let God do the rest. He will send the tide to carry them to His throne of grace. Yes, it is very difficult to walk away from our problems. We try to reason them out in our human frailty. We think that if we think about them long enough, we will come up with a solution. Sometimes, the solution is to give them to God. Do what you can and He will do the rest:

> "Sometimes we grieve over what God requires us to give up, but patience will prove that what He gives in return is a far greater blessing than we could have ever imagined."
> -unknown-

What has God asked you to give up? It is only in His wisdom that He has asked. If there was any other way, He would not have made such a request of you. I have found a lot of peace knowing that when calamity strikes my life, it is because God has allowed it. Don't miss that. God has allowed it. Satan has no power that God could not reign in. God allows it. That was so hard for me to accept initially, but once you realize that every trouble is sifted through His hands of love before it reaches you, it will help sustain you. Whatever God requires of us, He promises to provide everything we will need to accomplish it. Just as he told the disciples to get into the boat, knowing they would get caught in a raging storm, still Jesus promised they would make it safely to the other side. They did and so will we.

> "God could not make a world in which we are free and at the same time guarantee that everyone would choose Him. So the world is broken and bad things happen. But God promises that He will be with those who love Him. He will bring us through the fire, and we will come forth as gold."
> -James MacDonald-

November 27

*God doesn't tell us to come **boldly** to His throne of **worthiness**,
because we are not worthy, but to His throne of **GRACE**.*

If God's blessings depended on our worthiness we would all be in big trouble. We are sinners, we have sinned against God, we deserve nothing but His wrath and punishment, yet what He offers us as believers is an invitation to come boldly to His throne of grace and mercy will be waiting for us. That is simply amazing! We are not worthy, so let's settle that issue now. When you think about how the Old Testament saints and the New Testament saints revered God, they fell on their faces in God's presence. They didn't try to plead their case before Him, and they didn't try to make excuses for their behavior. No, they fell on their faces before Him. John, the author of the Book of Revelation, in the opening chapters, we find down on His face before the presence of Jesus, yet, the Lord touched his shoulder, told him not to be afraid and to get up. Wow! is all I can say about that. Just wow! Oh, to be touched by Jesus like that.

"Let us then, fearlessly and confidently and **boldly** draw near
to the throne of **grace** (the throne of God's unmerited favor to us sinners),
that we may receive **mercy** (for our failures) and find grace to **help** in good
time for every need (Appropriate help, well-timed help, coming just when we need it."
Hebrews 4:16 (Amplified Bible)

Wow again! This verse is inviting sinners to come boldly to God's throne of grace. It says we can find help for our problems there. It doesn't limit us and it doesn't exclude even those troubles we brought on ourselves by our bad decisions or the decisions of others. We can bring it <u>all</u>. This verse is so incredible. Let me ask you a question, "Without this verse does the thought of approaching God's throne with boldness even dare to cross your mind?" Mine either. I would have hidden somewhere far from Him and prayed His judgment wouldn't be too bad and that I could live to see another sunrise. Seriously, God knows how frail we are and how His children want to do what is right but sometimes fall very short of the perfection God requires. That's why we aren't invited to God's throne of worthiness, because we aren't worthy but we do qualify for His grace because of what a loving and forgiving God we serve. His love for us lifts us up, brushes us off, forgives us, sends us back out into the world to try again. He doesn't give up on us, so we shouldn't either. I think this is what God meant when He wrote in John 3:16, "For God *so* loved the world...not just loved, but *so* loved, that He gave us His most precious gift...Jesus. That deserves a wow and a hallelujah!

NOVEMBER 28

*When you can no longer stand, He will hold you in His arms.
He will keep you safe.*

"The harder the trial, the closer He moves toward you. Are you
feeling crushed today? He is rushing toward you to stand beside you and help you."
-James MacDonald-

There is a lot of pain in this world and we all experience it. Have you ever felt so overwhelmed at times, you could no longer stand? So discouraged with life, you withdraw from it. We are prone to withdraw from friends, family, anything that may bring us more pain. Have you ever had days where you open your eyes in the morning and you want to turn off the alarm, pull the covers back up over your head and not come out until the world was a safer, kinder place? I know I have. In fact, one night there was an earthquake in my city, which was a rather rare occurrence. I opened my eyes to the shake, rattle and rolling around me. I normally would have jumped out of bed, made it to a doorway in 3 seconds flat, but not on this particular night. I wanted to die. So much pain in my life for too long, I didn't care if they found me buried in the rubble the next day. I was done with the pain. I was totally in despair, with no hope of it ever ending. A divorce or death of a loved one can do that to you. In my own strength I was no match for the trial I was going through. The next morning, I went to work and a good friend asked me if I felt the earthquake. "Yes," I muttered, sorry I was still living and breathing. "What did you do?" she asked excitedly. I responded truthfully, "Nothing, but wait for the house to come tumbling down on me." She exclaimed, "Girl, you are depressed!" I thought to myself, "duh!" I finally realized with sudden clarity, I needed help and it took an earthquake, for crying out loud. Next question was where to find it? I had been a Christian for many years, by this time, but I was mad at God for my life, for my circumstances, for everything including there being no world peace! So goofy, now that I look back on it, but my feelings of despair were **real** and were devastating my life. So, that Sunday, I forced myself to go to Church again. All the way there I told the Lord, "I am going to sit in the back pew as far back as I can and please don't let anyone want to shake my hand or talk to me because I might just slap them." I wasn't into cheery people. He was faithful, they didn't. I went back the next week. Gradually, the Lord healed my broken heart. I learned one lesson, sometimes words aren't necessary and all a person really needs is a smile. A smile that says, things will get better. A smile that says, you are important enough to me, that when I pass you I will not ignore you but let you know you are worth my attention. Warning! If someone looks depressed and you come at them with a cheery word, it is best to stay at least one good arm length away. Just sayin…

NOVEMBER 29

Never move from what you know to be right.

"Sinful unregenerate people will do evil things- it is their nature to do so – and laws will never change that." -Douglas Bennett-

Someone wise once said, You cannot legislate morality." Our world is a world of compromise. Everywhere we turn. As I write this, this is an important election year. There will be more compromising of politician's beliefs and more lies told this year than at any other time. The joke is often told, "How can you tell when a politician is lying?" Answer: His lips are moving. The American people have lost faith in our government and for good reason. They no longer tell the truth, no longer govern by the Constitution of the United States, they have done everything they can to remove God from government, schools and our everyday lives all in the name of political correctness. Funny thing is I don't think God is into political correctness.

I believe God laughs when He sees a well-known movie star, standing on the beach, with arms outstretched proclaiming that she is god!" That makes me want to laugh too at the absurdity of it all. One good wave and she would be lying on her back, covered with seaweed, muttering weakly, "I am god." When people reject the only true God, they must replace Him with something else to fill the void. That something might be drugs, alcohol, sex, golf or working too much. It might just be 'stuff' that takes God's place. A bigger house, a bigger car, the biggest flat screen TV on the block! As far back as time goes, men have been replacing God with something or other, especially self! It is no longer about Him, it is all about me. We make up our own ideas of what is and what He is not instead of reading the Bible which reveals Him to man.

"Because when they **knew** God, they glorified Him not as God, neither was thankful, but became vain (useless) in their imaginations, and their foolish heart was darkened, professing themselves to be wise, they became fools."
Romans 1:21

It takes a wild imagination to call yourself God, and not immediately fall on your face laughing. Sadly, some are very serious. There is a whole religion that believes this. These people are raising the next generation. Yikes! Some are looking at God as their fire insurance, just enough God in their lives to keep them out of the fiery furnace, hell. To quote a famous commercial phrase, "That's not how this works, it's not how any of this works." The easiest area to compromise in are the 'gray' areas. We aren't really sure what the right thing to do is and even though our conscience is telling us no, don't do it, we really, really want to, so we do. Trouble is when you start to give in to the small things, it get easier and easier to compromise the big things too. If God sent immediate consequences for our actions I am convinced that compromise would no longer be much of a problem for the church. There would be no time to think about, "Should I or shouldn't I?" we would be too busy nursing our wounds. We linger around sin, hoping we won't catch it, just as Lot lingered around Sodom, even though the angels told him to leave, destruction was just minutes away. Make a list today of things you will **not** compromise on no matter what. Then teach them to your children. We live in a world that may one day force us to choose.

November 30

Singing will give strength to even the weariest soul.

"God has a meaning in each blow of His chisel, each incision of His knife. He knows the way that He takes." -F.B.Meyer-

The Book of Psalms is one of the greatest books to go to when troubles are overwhelming you. King David wrote many of the psalms and they were put to music. How powerful to sing the Word of God. Many of the old hymns of the church came directly from the Bible. "How Great Thou Art," is one of my favorite hymns. I attend a church where the music is upbeat and it lifts my spirits. It is an awesome thing praising God with a multitude of other believers. It is also a precious thing, singing the old hymns, which calm my soul and gives me peace. The Billy Graham Crusades always end with the song, 'Just As I Am,' and no matter how many times I hear that song, it convicts me of the price Jesus paid for my sins. One time, shortly after my sister's death, I did what the song bids, I came, 'just as I am,' and I have never regretted a moment of that decision. Here are the words by Charlotte Elliott, written in 1836, she was an invalid, in the poorest of health. She wrote these words to aid the children of the poorest of clergy, of which her own brother was one. The song did much more than that. it is still changing lives today:

"Just as I am! Without one plea,
But that Thy blood was shed for me.
And that Thou bidd'st me come to Thee,
O Lamb of God, I come, I come!"

Have you come to Him? Without one plea, no excuses, no blame. It's only possible by the blood of Jesus shed for us on the cross. The song continues:

"Just as I am! Tho tossed about
With many a conflict, many a doubt,
With fears within and foes without,
O Lamb of God, I come, I come!"

You don't have to have all the answers before coming, you can be up to your eyeballs in doubt and fears, but you need to come. He invites you, just as you are. What great news is that? I don't have to get cleaned up or make believe I am worthy of this kind of love, before coming, He will do all of that for me after I come. More good news:

"Just as I am! Thou wilt receive,
Wilt welcome, pardon, cleanse, relieve;
Because Thy promise I believe,
O Lamb of God, I come, I come!"

We come simply by faith. We believe the One with nail pierced hands. He then pardons us, cleanses us and relieves us of all guilt and sin. The soul that is praising God like this can never be down in the dumps. If you will praise Him, He will lift you up! So, sing!

DECEMBER 1

Singing can open prison doors...
Acts 16:25

The disciples sang when they were thrown in prison. They sang
until God sent an earthquake, that broke open the prison doors.

Today, we will be touching on the subject of waiting on God. That is a very sore subject for many Christians, myself included. At the get go, we need to establish the fact that God is NEVER late, He usually isn't early, and He is always on time. ALWAYS on time. Let me remind you it is His time, not ours. We may be sweating bullets before He arrives. We get ourselves so worked up sometimes we decide to solve our own problem, our way. We convince ourselves God didn't hear us or just doesn't care. We reason ourselves right out of obedience, sometimes from fear.

"Our hearts are much distressed and burdened, so we go to
prayer and maybe spend much time pouring out our petitions
before the throne. And too many times we get up immediately,
rush out of His presence and often try to answer the
prayer by some efforts of our own."
-John wright Follette-

Big mistake! The moment we take matters into our own hands and leave God out, a disaster is just on the horizon. We fuss and fume as we wait but all it does is frustrate us. It does nothing to change the outcome. If God's answer to our prayer request is to 'wait,' then that is exactly what we will do, like it or not. All the tears in the world won't get God to answer your prayer or mine any sooner. Anger won't change God's mind. He is not going to say, "Oh my, my child is angry, maybe I better answer a little sooner." That is not going to happen. Waiting requires patience. So, the irony of it all is God is teaching us two lessons when we pray. He will teach us not only how to wait but how to do it patiently.

"Patience is the virtue that transforms an angry tongue. Patience
takes time to hesitate and evaluate. It rejects anger as sin. True
patience finds its strength in an unflinching focus on God and
an unconditional love toward those who have hurt us."
-Joseph Stowell-

Keep an unflinching focus on God. Sometimes, that is easier said than done. It depends on how badly we really want something. If it is really important to us, my focus is on the object. If our desire is for something small, then it will be much easier to focus on God. Our God is a good God. He always has our best interest at heart. How many things have we prayed for in the past, and once received, was no big deal. The thrill was gone. If God had answered some of my prayers the way I wanted Him to and when I wanted Him to, I would be in some big trouble. I bet you would be too. We need to learn to trust Him to know what is best for us and to do it at the perfect time.

DECEMBER 2

Trust. Love. Hope. Pray. Rest. Keep Praying.

Today we will be touching on a Christian's everyday life. Most days aren't filled with a lot of excitement, although they certainly can be. We can get so caught up in the everyday 'ho hum!' of life we forget who God is or what Jesus has done for us. It is imperative for the believer to spend time every single day in God's Word. Here is a simple list to help us remember some of the things we will learn by staying in God's Word:

- I have God's individual attention the moment I call on Him.
- What's important to me is important to Him.
- I will learn what is important to Him should be important to me.
- God promises us evil will not last forever.
- If I ever doubt God's love for me, I look at the cross.
- God knows what I need before I even ask Him.
- Take seriously those things God takes seriously.
- Don't take lightly your sin and don't make excuses for it.
- Suffer without quitting or giving up.
- There is an end to all suffering, eventually.
- Repent immediately when you sin.
- Treat everyone with kindness, you don't know the battles they are facing.
- God will give me what I need, not what I want.
- Some people have no one to pray for them, but me.
- I can put a 1,000 demons to flight with my prayer, but with two other buddies we can put 10,000 to flight!
- Relationships are built and maintained by spending time together.
- Some things I ask God for just aren't good for me.
- He promises to meet my every need.
- Every sin has a door of entrance.
- I can cast all of my cares on Him, not just some of them, but all of them.
- I am not in control, He is.
- It is God's job to run the Universe, not mine. He does not need my help.
- God does not reveal His will to me for my consideration but for obedience.
- A short cut to obedience may seem like an easier path, but it will turn out to be a long one.
- Life is a battlefield. There is a real enemy that seeks to destroy me.
- Don't try to reason my way through problems. Trust Him to see me through.
- Don't just ask God for little things when He longs to do big things in my life.
- Stop pretending to be someone I am not.
- There are some things in life we cannot compromise!
- Pray and expect an answer.
- Don't try to understand everything that happens.
- Don't forget there really is a hell. Tell as many as you can.

- What I do speaks louder than any sermon I could preach.
- Forgive! It will set you free and pull down any barriers to God's blessings in my life.
- Your plan for my life always begins with my surrender.
- We can change the world!

There are so many blessings and promises in the Word of God. It is His love letter to a dying world and so few read it. I hope this list will help to encourage you to meet God every morning in the same place, same time. You will be blessed, even if it is just for a few minutes, you will be so encouraged those few minutes will turn into a half hour...an hour...who knows, you may teach others His word one day.

December 3

Let us sing Hallelujah in anticipation!
– C.H. Spurgeon-

"As far as God is concerned, the time to stand is the darkest moment.
It is when everything seems hopeless, when there appears no
way out, when God alone can deliver."
-David Wilkerson-

Anticipation! What a great word. It is a word that makes life somehow seem more worthwhile. It is a word of hope. Things can change. When we lose hope, we lose our desire to live. As long as God is on His throne, we will always have hope. I try to imagine how the children of Israel felt as they left Egypt after years of slavery. There must have been some celebration until, at least until they reached the Red Sea. Pharaoh's army was after them again! Theirs was a short lived victory, or so it seemed. Did they really think, after seeing God's miraculous deliverance of them, that the Red Sea could hinder a God who had just brought plague upon plague on the Egyptians? Talk about little faith! Unfortunately, I think I might have been right beside them wringing my hands, "Oh, God, What are we going to do?" I would have loved to have been there that day when God did the spectacular for them. It would have been so awesome that day to see the Red Sea part for them, so much so they walked across on dry land. Millions of them witnessed God's miraculous power that day.

"You never know how much you really believe anything until
it's truth or falsehood becomes a matter of life and death to you."
-C.S. Lewis-

This was a matter of life and death to the Israelites. Did they anticipate God's help? It sure doesn't sound like it. What does it take for us to believe God? We need to learn who He is. We need to stay in His word until we are convinced He is who He says He is. You will never trust someone you don't know and you shouldn't. God invites us to learn of Him, to make big requests of Him. To be specific in those requests, because then you will know it is God who answered them. Anticipate! It really is a great word, isn't it? I think it is a word God loves for us to use.

December 4

The gardener continues to prune because He expects something good.
John 15:2

To pray unceasingly means your heart never leaves the presence of God.

A LETTER TO GOD

Dear God

It's me again, Lord. I was just wondering how many other moms are on their knees this morning. Especially single moms. Tears in their eyes, hearts breaking in two. Circumstances that seem beyond impossible and no hope to be found amongst the diapers and dirty dishes. I've sure been there Lord, vision dimmed and on the verge of a faith failure. Well, honestly....another faith failure. Why is it so hard sometimes? Why do I so easily forget that You have everything under control? Trusting You should be so easy...sometimes it is so hard.

I realized this morning Lord that being a mom and a grandmother isn't hard...it's impossible... without Your help.

I realized too this morning, Lord, that the hardest thing a mother has to endure on this earth isn't labor pains, isn't dirty diapers, or snotty noses or even snottier attitudes, but it's watching your children turn their backs on You, hijacked by the lies of this world. Some days it looks like the enemy is winning. We seem to have lost our fear and reverence for You. No one seems to take You seriously anymore.

What Lord? What a man sows he will reap? Yes, sin sure seems to be fun for a while, but how painful in the end. I remember the time I...oh, never mind, we both know how that ended. Our children walk away to do their own thing and then when the bottom falls out they expect You to rescue them.

What Lord? I did the same thing? Oh yeah, right, I did. I chose a much harder path through life than You ever intended for me to take. I remember You teaching me that. I remember too not to make pain the only way for You can get my attention.

What's that Lord? A choice? Yes, I know they have a choice that only they can make, but I was praying they would choose wisely. All those years of Sunday school have to mean something.

What? Yeah, I know they have to learn that the best things in life aren't things. Sometimes that takes a long time. We usually don't get it until we have lots of stuff and then realize how empty our lives and our hearts really are. I saw on the news today another famous actor called it quits. Took his own life. He looked like he had the world by the tail. Guess, he didn't after all.

What? It took You one day to get the children of Israel out of Egypt and a lifetime to get Egypt out of them. It's so hard sometimes, trying not to keep up with the Joneses.

Why do You put up with us Lord? "Love. I love you. I love your children too. Never forget that. They belonged to Me first, still do."

I know Lord, there is so much at stake here. Eternity is a very long time. I miss my mom so much, Lord. Will you give her a big hug and kiss for me and tell her to look for my kitty, Harley. It was so hard losing him too, he was my pal for 17 years. It helps me to think of him sitting in my mom's lap.

She loved animals. Me too. Will you let me know when it's the right time to get another kitty friend, when my heart is healed? Life really hurts right now, Lord.

What Lord? Don't give up? I'm trying not to. You're right, "It is what it is until it isn't." Help me to accept where You have me right this moment until You change things.

Christmas season is over Lord, but You know what? Wise men still seek You, don't they?

I'll see you again tomorrow, Lord, same time same place...and oh yeah...thanks. Thanks for loving me so much You would rather die than live without me... no one has ever loved me like You do. Thank you for Your mercies that are new every morning. I can blow it one day and the next day You will give me another chance and another and another. Wow...Amazing grace...God You are amazing. See you tomorrow Lord...

-Cindy Balch-

December 5

"Safely home..."

Mom, as long as I can remember, I remember loving you...

Almost three years ago today my mom left this earth to be with her Lord and Savior, Jesus Christ. She often looked forward to that day, especially towards the end when both her mind and body failed her. This poem is my tribute to a wonderful, kind, caring woman, that I had the privilege of calling mom. She is now 'safely home.'

Her Hands
by Cindy Balch

*I've experienced trials, sorrow and pain
Hurts and losses I can't explain.
I've been through things I don't understand
But one thing I know is why my mother has hands.*

*Her hands held truth when the way was unclear
God used her hands to wipe away my tears.
Hands that never turned me away
Hands that guided me back to what God had to say.*

*Whenever I needed a hug from above
God used my mom and her hands of love.
Those hands would draw me ever so near.
Those hands would show me I had nothing to fear.*

*She bore my sorrows, she shared my strife
She shouldered the burdens of my life.
Hands that knelt at night to pray
Hands that kissed my hurts away.*

*Hands that picked me up off the ground
Hands that turned my life around.
Hands connected to a heart of love
Hands that touched the face of God.*

*Hands that led me to the cross
Hands that never counted the cost.
Hands that showed me how to live
Hands that always knew how to give.
Hands that were always quick to defend
Hands that always sought to mend.*

One hand holding onto mine
The other held His hand divine.
Though life got weary and troublesome
She never let go of either one.
Hands that were gentle yet always strong
Hands that taught me right from wrong.

Hands that held our dog and cried
Hands that stroked him as he died.
Hands that tried to give a reason why
To the three little girls standing by her side.

Hands that tried to teach me things.
Hands that sought to give me wings.
Hands of courage, hands of strength
Hands that would go to any length.

Hand's that disciplined in love.
Hands washed by the Savior's blood.
Hands that tried to reach the lost
To spread the gospel at any cost.

Hands that held loosely the things of this world
But hands that held tightly to her little girls.
Hands of mercy, hands of time
Hands that would never let go of mine.

Hands that fought a world of gloom
Hands that pointed to an empty tomb.
Hands that knew her Savior cared
Hands always lifting those she loved in prayer.

Hands that held her Bible close
Of all her possessions loving His Word the most.

Hands that selflessly gave and gave
Hands that never threatened to walk away.
Hands that forgave when I pierced her heart
Hands always giving me a fresh new start.
Hands that clapped louder than other parents it seemed
Hands that never kept me from following my dreams.

Hands that held sunshine on days of rain
Hands longing for heaven and freedom from pain.
Hands that taught me to love His Word
Hands that proclaimed that Jesus is Lord.

Hands without answers sometimes for her kids
But hands that could point us to the One who did.
Hands that will sadly someday be gone
But will never be forgotten but live on and on.

Hands that will one day welcome my own
When my journey ends and heaven becomes home.
Hands that I'll see again one day
Where she will wipe my last tear away.

I pray that one day the time will come
My kids will say mom's hands are just like Mum's.
Hands of comfort without end
Hands of my mom.....a child's best friend.

Yes, I have passed through many sorrows and pain
Hurts and losses I can't explain
But this I do know and I do understand
God touched my life through my mother's hands.

From my heart to yours Mom...I love you...and thanks.
Cindy

December 6

The giants in life are but God's opportunities, disguised.

"And all this assembly shall know that the Lord saves not with sword and spear; for the battle is the Lord's, and He will give you into our hands."
I Samuel 17:47

How better to prove God's love, power and faithfulness than to put His child up against the biggest, baddest, scariest, dude in town? That's exactly who Goliath was. The whole army of Israel was scared to death of him. Goliath would come out every day and taunt the army of Israel with death threats. One day, David had heard enough and decided to take action. First he spoke to the giant exactly what was about to happen to him;

"You come to me with a sword, a spear and a javelin, but I come to you in the name of the Lord of hosts, the God of the ranks of Israel, Whom you have defied. This day the Lord will deliver you into my hand, and I will smite you and cut off your head." (I Samuel 17:40-46)

Cut off his head today! The Bible says that Goliath was outraged that his adversary was nothing more than an 'adolescent.' This teaches us it doesn't matter how old or how young you are, you can be victorious fighting God's battles. David at his young age was more courageous than all of the army of Israel. One with God is a majority, always remember that. If God is on your side it does not matter who is against you.

King Saul decided David should wear his armor into battle, but it turned out to be too cumbersome. Some battles are not won easily, but this one was. David picked up his slingshot and five smooth stones and *ran quickly to the battle line.* (vs.48) Yes, I said he ran towards Goliath, not away from him. He placed the rock in his slingshot, pulled back, released it and watched it fly and hit Goliath smack dab in the forehead. He watched as the big giant toppled over. David was not afraid because God had given him victory over a lion and a bear in the past. So, to David, this was a piece of cake. What kind of giants are you facing in your life today? Are you running away from them? You don't need to. If God calls you to fight a giant then look around, somewhere God will have placed a slingshot and some rocks for you. Our enemies are Gods enemies and God's enemies are our enemies. Why did David stand against Goliath? ..."that all may know there is a God in Israel." By the way, the reason why David picked up five stones instead of just one is, scholars believe Goliath may have had four brothers and David was ready to take them all on. (vs 46). David knew who God was and he wanted these Philistines to know too. I think they got the message that day. As Christians we bear the name of Christ. We are to honor His name at all costs. David could have died in this battle, but he did not. He was faithful to God, and God was faithful to him. Good to remember next time a giant enters your life that God is the biggest, baddest, scariest One in town.

"When people see how courageous and optimistic you are during your troubled times, they will be drawn to Christ."
-Josh Mc Dowell & Bob Hostetler-

December 7

Covet to be alone with God every single day, if only for a few minutes.

"The enemy will not see you vanish into God's company without an effort to reclaim you."
C.S. Lewis

Have you ever sat down to pray only to have your children have a crisis of some sort, or the phone rings, maybe someone's at your door? Satan does not want you to spend time with God and he certainly does not want you praying. The moment you get down on your knees the battle intensifies. Satan turns the heat up a notch or two. One of his best strategies, has worked for thousands of years, is to bring 'trouble,' and as much of it as he possibly can. He also tries to bring it at the most inopportune time to the child of God.

"The devil loves to fish in troubled waters." -John Trapp-

If we are too busy dealing with problems then we have no time to pray. God says that is the time you must pray. You must take the time, otherwise you will face defeat. Prayer keeps trouble away and trouble keeps prayer away. When praying is the hardest it is the most important. We must develop perseverance as a praying Christian. You may scare the devil off today, but you can be sure he will be back tomorrow and the next day, and the next. Martin Luther King has said, "It is still one of the tragedies of human history that the 'children of darkness' are frequently more determined and zealous than the children of light." Some of the greatest men in history have been prayer warriors. Read what they have to say about the importance of prayer in a believer's life:

- "Prayer opens the heart to God, and it is the means by which the soul, though empty, is filled with God." –John Bunyan-
- "Thou art not a Christian that art not a praying person." –John Bunyan
- The great battles, the battles that decide our destiny and the destiny of generations of yet unborn, are not fought on public platforms, but in the lonely hours of the night and in moments of agony." —Samuel Logan Brengle-
- "Prayer is weakness leaning on Omnipotence." W.S. Bowden
- "Pray as if everything depended upon your prayer." –William Booth-
- "Pray not for crutches, but for wings." –Phillips Brooks-

And finally the words of Henry Ward Beecher, "Prayer covers the whole of a man's life. There is no thought, feeling, yearning or desire, however low, trifling, or vulgar we may deem it, which, if it affects our real interest or happiness, we may not lay before God and be sure of sympathy. His nature is such that our often coming does not tire Him. The whole burden of the whole life of every man may be rolled on to God and not weary Him, though it has wearied the man."

Pray! When you feel like it and especially when you do not. Expect God to answer because He will. He may not answer in the manner you wish Him to but He will send an answer that is best for you in your life, right now, at this time and He also has your future in mind. Trust Him to do what is right for you. You will not trust someone you do not know, so get to know God. Read His Word, it is His love letter to you. You will find He is the most trustworthy One you will ever meet.

"Be sure to remember that nothing in your daily life is so insignificant and so inconsequential that the Lord will not help you by answering your prayer." -O. Hallesby-

December 8

Trouble and praise go together.

"There are times when God asks nothing more of His
children except silence, patience, and tears."
-Charles Seymour Robinson

One of my favorite songs as a child and young woman was sung by Mahalia Jackson. The first line of the song was, "Trouble...it just won't go away." The older I get the more I realize how wise those words were. When we give our life to the Lord, we think everything will go great from here on out. Wrong! I found out life is much different when you become a believer and often it gets harder before it gets any easier. As long as I was living in disobedience the devil left me alone. The moment I became a believer, I discovered what spiritual warfare was. Anyone who even thinks of giving their life over to Jesus will face Satan's wrath. He is a deadly foe who doesn't play fair. The devil is a relentless foe and anything goes. If he can't take you down one way, he will try another and another...He came to steal, kill and destroy us. We don't fight against flesh and blood. No, our battle is a spiritual one. That is how God has equipped His children, not with swords or guns, but with spiritual body armor for a spiritual fight. God will provide exactly what we need, when we need it. He will never burden us with more than we can carry, although sometimes we do that to ourselves.

"I compare the troubles which we have to undergo in the course of the year to
a great bundle of faggots, far too large for us to lift. But God does not require us
to carry the whole at once. He mercifully unties the bundle, and gives us first one
stick, which we will carry today, and the another, which we will carry tomorrow, and
so on. This we might easily manage, if we would only take the burden appointed for
each day; but we choose to increase our troubles by carrying yesterday's stick over
again today, and adding tomorrow's burden to the load, before we are required to bear it."
-John Newton-

We burden ourselves by using human reasoning or emotions to solve our problems. God intended for us to come to Him for His wisdom for every situation we face. When He tarries, the hardest thing for us to do is wait on Him. It is against our nature to wait, yet we must.

"Oh, how great peace and quietness would he possess who
should cut off all vain anxiety and place ALL his confidence in God."
-Thomas a Kempis-

December 9

Launch out into the deep.
–Luke 5:4-

"Someday, friends, there comes a harvest. Someday there is
a payoff. Someday sinners become saints. And between now and then,
we get to keep spreading the message. We get to keep playing the
role we are meant to play. We get to keep planting seeds, trusting that
God will bring the increase. Because in due time – oh, the increase He brings!"
-Bill Hybels-

Have you ever gone fishing? I have, but I don't remember much about it except watching the poor little thing flop around on the deck of the boat and me crying and yelling, "Daddy, daddy, throw him back in the water, he's going to die!" Some of the greatest fishermen can fish all day and catch absolutely nothing. This was the experience of Jesus' disciples. They went fishing and caught nothing, at least until Jesus came along. Jesus had been preaching to a great multitude and he had used Peter's boat to do so. He asked Peter to push out from the shore and He began to teach. As he finished he turned to Peter and told him, now go back out fishing and you will catch many fish. Peter began to give all the reasons why he shouldn't go back out, they had already been out and caught nothing, we're tired, but instead he said, nevertheless, Lord, if You say so, we will give it one more try. The guys cast their nets out and as they began to bring in their nets they were so full of fish their nets began to break. They asked other fishermen to come help them and soon their nets were so full too, they almost sank. What was Peter's response to this miracle? He fell on his face before the Lord. Jesus then prophesized to Peter he would no longer be fishing for stinky old fish, but for stinky old people who were sinners. Thought for this day: Even though you attempted something and you failed, if Jesus tells you to go back out, don't give up, don't quit, go try again, then go try again! What miracle do you need from the Lord? Don't give up on it. Keep fishing! Wait on God, He will answer and then expect a big haul of fish. Often, we do not feel like obeying, that is the most important time to obey. A blessing is right around the corner and you don't want to miss it.

"There is only one thing worse than not
waiting on God and that is wishing you had."
-Charles Stanley-

December 10

There is no victory, until first there is a battle fought.

"It is never a power struggle between us and the enemy. It is a 'truth' encounter, Satan's *only* power is in the lie." -Neil Anderson-

Evil exists all around us. There was a point in time, evil was so rampant in the world, God elected to destroy the world, save a few souls, and start all over again. That is a frightening thought. Man, left on his own, became so evil, the only solution was destruction. Genesis 6:5 describes it this way: "The Lord saw how great man's wickedness on the earth had become, and that every inclination of the thought of his heart was only evil all the time." This is the reason for the flood. Man was utterly destroyed, all except for Noah and his family. The Bible talks about another time in the near future when the same thing will occur. It says in the end times, the world will be in a state such *as it was in the days of Noah*. Violence filled the earth. Today, untold violent acts are committed every day against the innocent. Recently, the terrorist group ISIS put to death anyone who refused to embrace Islam as their religion. They were given a choice, become a Muslim or die. Many chose death. This is just the beginning. God's people must be prayer warriors for their fellow brothers and sisters around the world.

"When we go to God by prayer, the devil knows we go to fetch strength against him, and therefore he opposeth us all he can." -Richard Sibbes-

Satan realized the power of a praying Christian more than the Christian does. If we really understood the power and the privilege given to the believer by Jesus we would become unstoppable at destroying the powers of darkness. We go to God for strength!

"No one is a firmer believer in the power of prayer than the devil; not that he practices it, *but he suffers from it.*" -Guy H. King-

This can best be illustrated by the prayers of a mother for her child. No devil in hell can come against that mother successfully, when she is on her knees interceding for her child. How many conversion stories begin with the statement, "I had a praying mom…or grandmother." God honors prayer and prayer honor God. When we go to Him in prayer we are saying, God I need Your help, I can't face this alone." Do you think God would ignore a request like that? Of course not. John Calvin is quoted as saying, "Against the persecution of a tyrant the godly have no remedy but prayer." This is a powerful reminder that when we have exhausted all of our warfare against the enemy, we will never exhaust the power of prayer." The New York Times writer, A.M. Rosenthal presented an awful truth, "One of the shocking untold stories of our time, is that more Christians have died this century simply for being Christians than in any century since Christ was born." More and more of us are suffering for our faith. An insidious campaign in America is well under way to rid America of God and our Christian heritage. We have sadly stood by while others removed God from our schools. They have redefined God's definition of 'family,' and have rewritten our history books to fit their pagan ideology. God no longer reigns, Wall Street does. Jesus asks, in the Book of Revelation, concerning the 'end times' that when He returns will He find faith on the earth?" Will He? That is a very sobering question and the way it is asked reveals the answer is no, He will not. You and I are either for Him or we are against Him. We can't be both. We must chose. The disciples chose and it cost them their life. What are you willing to sacrifice to be His child?

DECEMBER 11

Evil NEVER surrenders without a bitter fight.

"Do not be overcome by evil, but overcome evil with good."
Romans 12:21

Evil never surrenders without a bitter fight, but do we? What will it take to make me lay down my sword and walk away, or worse, run away from trouble? Sometimes, we get a little too smug for our own britches. We think of ourselves as Christians with a Super hero cape on, when we are really just one sin away from total devastation, but for the grace of God. One bad decision can affect your life forever. I think of Peter when He denied that he even knew Jesus. Under the same circumstances, fearing for my life, not understanding what was going on around me, seeing the Roman soldiers with swords drawn, would I have done the same thing? Would you? I would hope not, but I think God has shown us that the mighty saints can fall too, sometimes with just one push too many. If we depend upon our own strength we too can become a statistic in the hall of shame. We must realize that Satan will fight us to the bitter end. He is playing for keeps, but so is God and God's sword is bigger than Satan's. We can't forget, even for one moment, we are in a raging battle. It is so much easier to give up then to get back up after being knocked down by the enemy. God knows that and so He does not leave us to fight the battle alone. He provides us with everything we need for victory. Where Satan attempts to build a stronghold in our life, God will tear it down if we will call upon Him in our distress.

"We use God's mighty weapons, not mere worldly weapons, to knock down the devil's strongholds. With these weapons we break down every proud argument that keeps people from knowing God. With these weapons, we conquer their rebellious ideas, and we teach them to obey Christ."
II Corinthian 10:4-5

There isn't a worldly weapon made, despite today's sophisticated weaponry, that will take out the devil or his minions. You can't shoot them, you can't ignore them, you can't even see them, but they are there. Do not fear, they are no match for our God!

December 12

The problem of getting our prayers answered is trying to hold on for the last 30 minutes.
-unknown-

"I find the one thing in this world is not so much where we stand, as in what direction we are moving: To reach the port of heaven, we must sail sometimes with the wind and sometimes against it – but we must sail, and not drift, nor lie at anchor." -Oliver Wendell Holmes-

Perseverance...put your sails up and leave port for the unknown. This is much easier said than done. Keeping on when there is no light ahead, no hope and no help in sight. Life presents us with many situations. Some we cause by our own stupidity, some are caused by others, and some God uses to build our faith. I think this last category is the hardest to deal with. Everything wrong with this world has its root in sin. We want something, so we go after it even though God has said no. Others want something, and so they go after it, even if it means ruining someone else's life. Other times, well, other times life just deals us some blows we aren't capable of understanding this side of heaven and to make it worse the heavens appear silent to our pleas for understanding. The following story is an illustration of this:

"John Claypool, pastor of the Crescent Hill Baptist Church in Louisville, had a little daughter who was diagnosed with Leukemia. When she went into remission, everyone thought God had healed her. On an Easter Sunday morning she had a recurrence. In his book, Tracks of a Fellow Struggler, Claypool says his daughter asked, "Daddy, did you talk to God about my leukemia?" He said, "Yes, we've been praying for you." She asked, "Did you ask Him how long the Leukemia would last? What did God say?" What do you say to your daughter when you can't help her and the heavens are silent? A few hours later, the little girl died. The following Sunday John Claypool got up to preach, His test was Isaiah 40:31: "Those who hope in the Lord will renew their strength. They will soar on wings like eagles; they will run and not grow weary, they will walk and not faint." "There are three stages of life," Claypool said, "Sometimes we mount up with wings as an eagle and fly; we're on top of the world. Sometimes we run, we don't grow weary; we just go through the routine. Sometimes the best we can do is to walk and not faint. That's where I am right now. I need your prayers." At the moment Claypool was at his lowest, he preached probably his most influential sermon. Like Paul, he could say, "For when I am weak, then I am strong." (II Corinthians 12:10).
-R. L. Russell

If you have ever stood at the grave of a loved one you know what it is like to walk and try not to faint. I literally almost fainted, my knees buckled, as I walked to the gravesite to stand at my sister's grave, she left this world at the age of 31. I was only 27 and didn't have much faith at the time to understand much of what was happening. What I did have was a godly mother. Later in life I learned that would be my first experience to keep on walking, through the darkness, trying not to faint, until I was able to see the light of Jesus Christ again. I also learned that this life is not the end, but just the beginning of a new life in heaven with Jesus. He has promised eternal life that will never end as we close our eyes on this side of heaven and open them up to the face of our Savior on the other side. We should never be afraid of the 'other side.'

DECEMBER 13

Fire produces gold.

"The hotter the fire the purer the gold."
-Charles Stanley-

"When He has tested me, I shall come forth as gold."

How is a man tested? What would it take to cause you to fail the test? I think it is different for us all. For instance, I have no desire to rob a convenience store. No desire at all. However, if my family were starving, the thought might cross my mind. If the circumstances were right, we all might to do something we would not have even believed possible. Could I kill another human being? My gut reaction would be to tell you no, but if my children or grandchildren were threatened and I could save them, I believe the answer would be yes. Most mothers would say yes.

"Never think we have a due knowledge of ourselves till we have been
exposed to various kinds of temptations, and tried on every side. Integrity on
one side of our character is not voucher for integrity on another. We cannot tell
how we should act if brought under temptations different from those we have
hitherto experienced. This thought should keep us humble. We are sinners, but
we do not know how great. He alone knows who died for our sins."
-John Henry Newman-

That is a very powerful statement, "We are sinners but we do not know how great. Jesus alone knows." It was upon His shoulders at the cross that God the Father placed on Jesus the sins of the whole world. That boggles the mind. When I think of the horrors that have taken place in this world, I cringe inside and out that my sins too, were laid upon Him, the Holy Lamb of God. What pride is within man to think for one moment his good deeds will save him?

"See that you do not forget what you were before, lest
you take for granted the grace and mercy you received
from God and forget to express gratitude each day."
-Martin Luther-

Today would be a good day to give thanks to the Lord for all He has done for you. We end this day with the words of George Herbert: "Thou that has given so much to me, give one thing more – a grateful heart; Not thankful when it pleases me, as if thy blessings had spare days; But such a heart, whose pulse may be Thy praise."

DECEMBER 14

There is no way of learning faith except by trial.

"Oh, men and women, pray through! Do not just begin to pray and pray a little while and throw up your hands and quit, but pray and pray and pray until God bends the heavens and comes down!"
-R.A. Torrey-

Someone once said, "Faith and reason are not opposed, but where reason cannot take another step, faith can." Faith reaches for God's hand. Faith hopes when there is no hope. Faith believes even though it cannot see. Reason looks at circumstances, faith looks to God. Reason says, "I'm not sure God will..." Faith says, "He has already done it." Reason gives up. Faith gets on its knees and makes its requests known unto God. Faith never gives up and never gives in to despair.

"While reason holds to what is present, faith apprehends the things that are not seen. Contrary to reason, faith regards the invisible things as already materialized."
-Martin Luther-

Reason looks at the Red Sea, and then looks back at the enemy in pursuit, and trembles. Faith knows that God has said He will make a way where there seems to be no way and marches on. Reason looks at the hungry lions in the den and faints, faith watches as God shuts the mouths of those hungry lions and smiles at what an awesome God we serve. A good rule to follow in life is: Stop yourself mid-sentence if your words are negative or not words of faith. If you have to, pray, "Lord, shut my mouth!" When I hear those words, I have this picture in my mind of standing next to Jesus. He has one arm around my shoulder and with His other arm He extends His hand, and lovingly places it over my mouth. Words have tremendous power to hurt or power to heal. The Holy Spirit has often convicted me as the very words were coming out of my mouth, so I know it is possible to stop midsentence. It may be embarrassing, but oh so worth it not to offend God. Watch what you say, others are watching and so is God.

DECEMBER 15

Am I substituting feeling for faith?

"Faith is being sure of what we hope for and
are certain of what we do not see.
-Hebrews 11:1

It is foolish to think we could ever use our faith to manipulate God or our circumstances. Faith is a gift of God, not something you work for. It is our reliance on Him and Him alone. Not on self, not on others, but on Him. You cannot fool God, and to even try is a colossal waste of time. He knows not only what you do, but He knows the motive of your heart before you even do it. A good example of this is the story of the widow's mite. (Mark 12:42) She was a very poor, poverty stricken woman who came to the Temple in Jerusalem and put her only possession, one mite, into the offering plate. A mite was a ½ a cent in those days, the lowest denomination of money. Close by were wealthy religious men, Pharisees who gave much money, out of their wealth. Jesus said they gave out of their abundance whereas the widow gave everything she had. She even gave to the Lord all she had to live on. Many today who give their money to charities want the world to know of their generosity. They have wings in hospitals named after them, or plaques on a wall memorializing their gift. The widow on the other hand went unseen except by Jesus. I don't think anyone paid any attention to her that day except our Lord. She gave what she had. God knew the hearts of all and it was the widow who would receive eternal blessing. The others received their reward on this earth, from the accolades given them by others. This story teaches us that even in our deep poverty there is always something we can give, and who better to give it to than to God. God blesses our obedience to Him. Our faith is in His ability to accomplish something in our lives, not in my ability to try and make something happen. Most of us, myself included, have come up with a great plan, and asked God to bless it. That's not how it works. We are subject to God's plan for our life, that is what He promises to bless. Nowhere in the Bible will you find a verse that says, "Come up with a plan and I will bless it." My faith is in His Omniscience to do for me what is for my best and for His glory. He is all-knowing. He knows the end from the beginning, and all of the obstacles we will face in between.

"Faith is extending an empty hand
to God to receive His gift of grace."
-A.W. Pink-

December 16

When I cannot enjoy the faith of assurance, I live by the faith of adherence.
-Matthew Henry-

"What God asks is a will which will no longer be divided between Him and any creature, a will pliant in His hands, which neither desires anything nor refuses anything, which wants without reservation, everything which He wants, and which never, under any pretext, wants anything which He does not want."
-F. Fenelon-

Are you following God? Such a simple question, but the answer is a matter of life and death. Do you want God's will above all else in your life or just when it suits your purposes? If you call yourself a Christian, the world is closely watching. What do they see?
"More often people who claim to be Christian pursue the same selfish ambitions, worship the same worthless idols, enjoy the same sinful pleasures, watch the same ungodly entertainments, and grasp for the same possessions as everyone else. There is shockingly little difference between the way that Christians and non-Christians behave."
-Richard Phillips, Philip Ryken & Mark Dever-

Would some of your friends and acquaintances be astonished to learn you are a Christian? How sad would that be? I have heard it said, "If you were on trial for claiming to be a Christian, would there be enough evidence to convict you? Or would you go free? Many people will never pick up a Bible. They have no desire to read it and never will. The only living gospel they will ever see is watching your life and mine. I have heard some say they don't want to be a Christian because they are all hypocrites. Sadly, some are. Theirs is a life of compromise, so much so that it keeps people from seeing Jesus in their life. They can be seen sometimes hanging out in bars. Or going to movies that would make a harlot blush. They have potty mouths or use the Lord's name in vain. A good indicator of your life as a Christian is if you irritate your ungodly friends. They may not even realize it, but your godly life is convicting them. When it does they will mock you, make fun of you and sometimes call you names. They will comment you are holier than thou. They can say some very hurtful things. I know from experience. What they don't know is that we are not perfect, we are just forgiven. Where once we wanted to do a lot of things that brought shame to our Savior, our 'want to' is broken by the blood of the Lamb. We no longer 'want to' do most of the things we used to think were so much fun. He gave us a new 'want to.' I now want to go to church. I want to help others. I want to tithe. I don't want to lie. Let them laugh and mock all they want. Hopefully, one day they will look at your life and want what you have. Jesus. He will give them a new 'want to,' too.

DECEMBER 17

Make every attempt to see the face of Christ in those with whom you differ. -W.H Griffith Thomas-

"The truly humble soul is not surprised at its defects or failings; and the more miserable it beholds itself, the more it abandons itself to God, and presses for a more intimate alliance with Him, seeing the need it has of His aid."
-Francois Fenelon & Jeanne Guyon-

"Love covers, a multitude of sins. It forgives and disregards the offenses of others (1Peter 4:8)."

Love is one of the most powerful emotions man can experience on this earth. It alone can cover over over a multitude of sins, like anger, unforgiveness, jealousy, guilt and the list goes on and on. Love forgives. If it didn't, we would forever be lost in our sins. Love is a healer. If love did not heal, we would all be walking around with broken hearts. Love conquers all. Let love be the umpire of your life. Let it be the motivator for everything you do! Life hurts but love heals.

"If you accuse, accuse from love. If you correct, correct from love. If you spare, spare from love. Let love be rooted deep in you, and only good can grow from it." -Augustine-

Love put Jesus on the cross to die for your sins and mine. Love can turn a stranger into a friend. Love sees others as worthy. Most important, God is love. It is not just something He does, but it is who He is. His love has no limits, no boundaries. It is perfect and everlasting. His love never changes. He will never love me more than He already does. God's love, unlike man's love, is unconditional. He never says, "I will love you if…" He simply accepts us where we are, but loves us much too much to leave us there. His love is always pushing us up higher and higher. Satan tells us we are unworthy of anyone's love. God shouts from the rooftops, "I love you to the moon and back." That is a love even a child can understand.

"It helps to remember that as sinners we're all difficult people in our own ways. But God's love and grace have been extended to us all, and one of the requirements of following Him is that we extend grace to others." -Steve Stephens & Alice gray-

Where does your self-worth come from? If you answered anywhere but God, you answered wrong. He gives us our worth. Never forget that. It does not come from your friends. Love is <u>not</u> a feeling. "Today, I love you today, tomorrow I'm not so sure." Our love must be rooted in Christ's love for us.

"If we cannot show love for others, both for our neighbor and for our brothers and sisters in the Lord, it is a red flag that something is very wrong in our relationship with God."
-Dee Brestin & Kathy Trocolli-

How do you measure your love for others? Are you able to see others through the eyes of God? A child that lives with those who show their love for him or her, will learn to love others.

December 18

No earthly circumstance can hinder even one of God's promises.

"God's promises are like the stars; the
darker the night, the brighter they shine."
-David Nicholas-

William Barclay once said, "Jesus is the 'yes' to every promise of God." Our journey is just as important to God as our destination. There are two ways to go through life, with Him or without Him. I have done both. The first 27 years of my life I did my own thing. Crazy thing is I went to church regularly during that time, and yet I still did my own thing. God had my body sitting in a church pew, but He didn't have my heart. My heart belonged to the world and what it could offer. The wonderful thing about it all is I had a praying mom and grandmother. I wish I could say that one morning in church I heard a sermon, the light bulb went on in my head, I gave my heart to Jesus and lived happily ever after. That is not how it happened. I was going along in life, as I said doing my own thing, then God allowed a tragedy in my life of monumental proportions. The very foundations of my life were rocked. Nothing the world offered me could help me. I was alone with God, scared, confused, mourning the loss of my sister.

"We turn to God for help when the foundations of our life
are shaking only to find it is God shaking them."
-unknown-

There I was floundering, helpless, alone and afraid. It didn't matter what anyone said to me, no one could comfort me. Then one night, God came near. I truly had a 'come to Jesus moment.'
Nothing else mattered then, but Him. I cried, and He comforted me. I expressed my anger and confusion, He listened. Then I confessed all my sins, and He forgave me. He had brought me to the foot of His cross and required an answer. All those years in church I had heard about Jesus, that night I met Him. I met my Savior who was bloodied and bruised for my iniquities, hung on a cross and tortured for my sins. He died for ME. It became personal that night. Jesus died, not so I could become religious, but so I could have a personal relationship with Him.

"The acid test of our faith in the promises of God is never found
in the easy-going, comfortable ways of life, but in the great emergencies,
the times of storm and of stress, the days of adversity when all human aid fails."
-Ethel Bell-

I have walked with my Lord ever since that day. Well, honestly, some days He had to drag me, but He NEVER gave up on me. That was 41 years ago. Thought for the day: Don't make a tragedy the only way God can get your attention. If you have a godly mother, get down on your knees and thank God for her. More battles are won when a mom prays for her children than at any other time.

DECEMBER 19

*Closing your eyes in this world and opening them
to Jesus in the next, this is death for the Christian.*

"To die is gain (Philippians 1:21). That kind of talk is absolutely foreign to our modern, spiritual vocabularies. We have become such life worshippers, we have very little desire to depart to be with the Lord." -David Wilkerson-

After we die, then what? Some believe that is end of their existence, period! Others believe they will go to purgatory and continue to pay for their previous sins. Still others believe they will be reincarnated and return to earth in another form, as a dog, a frog, a cow...maybe a famous person. Others believe when they die, 70 virgins will be waiting for them. Christianity is unique in that it believes Jesus Christ died for the sins of the world and rose again. He then left this earth to prepare a place for us to live with Him for all of eternity. What rubs people the wrong way is that Christianity also teaches that to reject Jesus is to reject God the Father, who sent Him, and all that He offers to the repentant sinner. They don't necessarily like that part. That means there will be a day we are all held accountable for our actions. We will have to take responsibility for the life we *chose* to live. There will be no excuses that day. Why is Jesus the only way to heaven? because God says He is. Well, you may be asking, "I am a good person, so will God turn me away?" Read the following story by the daughter of evangelist Billy Graham, Anne Graham Lotz, as she writes about finding meaning in September 11, 2001:

"In my little book 'Heaven: My Father's House,' I tell about people who want to visit my father's home in western North Carolina. They drive up the long drive and come to the gate. they knock on the gate and say, "Billy Graham, let us in. We've read your books, we've watched you on TV, we've written to you, and we want to come to your house. And my father says, "Depart from me, I don't know you. You're not a member of my family, and you've not made any arrangements to come. But when I drive up that same driveway and knock on the gate, I say, "Daddy this is Anne, and I've come home." The gate is thrown right open, and I go inside, because I'm my father's child. Because heaven is God's house, he has the right to decide who comes in and who stays out. He says He will welcome anyone inside His home, but they have to be born again into His family through faith in Jesus Christ. That gives us a wonderful hope that when the time comes – whether death comes as a thief in the night, as it did for those in the World Trade Center towers, or as an angel of mercy after a long illness – we can be assured that at the end of the journey, we'll step right into our Father's arms. We will be welcomed because we are our Father's children."

Jesus always says what He means, and means what He says in John 3:3 –
"I assure you, most solemnly I tell you, that unless a person is born again (anew from above) he cannot ever see (know, be acquainted with, and experience) the kingdom of God."
What makes this statement even more sobering is that Jesus was talking to a very 'religious' man, Nicodemus. This shows us that religion doesn't save a man, Jesus does. "You must be born again!" That is His command, not a suggestion.

DECEMBER 20

Lay no conditions on God, He knows better what I need than I do.

"There is not a desire that arises in thy soul, but the Lord takes notice of it." -Thomas Brooks-

I wrote this in my journal years ago, I don't know who authored it, but it has opened my eyes to understanding exactly why I should let God run *His* world.

"If God would concede to me His Omnipotence for twenty four hours you would see how many changes I would make in this world. But, if He gave me His wisdom too, I would leave things just as they are."

God's will for my life is not to complain about how bad things are, but to live responsibly today and trust Him for tomorrow. It may seem things are out of control and the enemy is winning but that is not the case. In the end, God wins! In the end, when it is all over, every knee shall bow before Him, including every evil person that walked on this earth. We live in dire times. Right is wrong and wrong is right. No one tells the truth anymore. The changes I have seen in my sixty plus years are frightening, to say the least. We have removed God from just about everything that matters, government, schools, public places, and then wonder why our country is falling apart at the seams. Then I was reminded by a friend, "Our help comes from the LORD, not from Washington." We must stay in God's word during these perilous times. God reveals what the events will be that lead to the close of history as we know it. It gives new meaning to, "And they lived happily ever after," as Christians we can claim the promises of God, He wins, we win because He is our Father. So, don't get discouraged. Keep your focus on God, not on man.

"When the righteous cry for help, the Lord hears, and delivers them out of ALL their distress and troubles" Psalm 34:17

We cry out! God answers and delivers us from ALL our distresses and troubles. What good news that is, in days of distress, uncertainty and insecurity. God says, call on Him. It doesn't matter how big or small the trouble is, they are all small to an Omnipotent God. If He can hold the oceans in the palm of His hand, or sprinkle the heavens with stars, He can help you.

"The truth of Christ's supremacy over all powers in the universe is one which modern man sorely needs to learn…To be united to Christ by faith is to throw off the thraldom (bondage, slavery) of hostile powers, to enjoy perfect freedom, to gain the mastery over the dominion of evil – because Christ's victory is ours."
-F.F. Bruce-

Jesus came to set us free and that is exactly what He did.
"If the Son sets you free, you are free indeed." –John 8:36-

December 21

*Some things in life can't be reasoned out no matter how
hard we try, especially our failures.*

"I have lived a long time and the longer I live, the more
convincing proofs I see, that God governs in the affairs of men."
-Benjamin Franklin-

We all fail. We all come short of someone else's expectations or even our own. Failure doesn't have to be permanent. It is only fatal if you never get back up again to try once more. Christopher Columbus said God's Hand was in his explorations, "I recognized that our Lord has caused me to run aground at this place so that I might establish a settlement here. And so many things came to hand here that the disaster was a blessing." Wow! After the incident he had the understanding to say the disaster was a blessing. If only more of us could see that what we look at as a failure in our own life is really God running us aground, because there is no other way to get our attention.

"There is a deep peace that grows out of illness and loneliness and a sense
of failure. God cannot get close when everything is delightful. He seems to
need these darker hours, these empty-hearted hours, to mean the most to people."
-Frank C. Laubach-

God really gets our attention in the darkest hours. We are out of plans, out of excuses, out of ideas, out of friends, money, plans and out of faith. We are at the end of our rope, just where God wants us to be. We should be as the little child who misquoted Psalm 23, "The LORD is my Shepherd, that's all I want." If we will let Him, He will lead us. He may take us places we don't want to go, but His hand will be in ours and we can rest because He knows the way.
"The true recipe for a miserable existence
is to quarrel with Providence."
-James W. Alexander-

Quarrel or trust? To me that deserves a "duh!" It should be a no brainer for the child of God once we figure out that God doesn't lose any arguments. Never has. Never will.

December 22

"God reveals the future to us through prophecy – not for the purpose of satisfying our curiosity, but for us to change our behavior." -Unknown-

Every storm of life pushes me closer to home...Heaven.

God has revealed in His Word what will happen in the future. We don't have to wonder. He has laid out His plan for the end times in all of the Bible's prophetic books. The Books of Daniel, Isaiah, Ezekiel, Hezekiah and of course the Book of Revelation all tell of the events to come as the end of this age approaches. God always warns. The question is "Are we paying attention?" The warnings of God are to be taken *very seriously*. The people of Noah's day laughed and mocked as Noah slowly obeyed God and built an ark. He was jeered at and scorned until the day the rain began to fall. So it is with the events of our day. Every day there seems to be another crisis in the news. If you will listen carefully you can almost hear the hoof beats of the four horsemen of the apocalypse, approaching. This is described in the book of Revelation. America has been asleep at the wheel, but that will not change what is about to happen. The first white horse brings the Antichrist upon the stage of the world. He takes over the world without a struggle. Many bible scholars believe he is alive on the earth today. He is at war with God Himself. This will mark the final conflict. The second, a red horse follows, with war and the ability to banish peace from the earth. The Antichrist comes in by peace and immediately he begins his reign of terror to control the world and everyone in it. Killing breaks out everywhere. Another horse rides, the third, a black horse, brings starvation. A pair of balances is described, and mankind will be forced to pay a whole day's wages, for a single loaf of bread. This is a result of all of the wars and famines. Food will be scarce. Then follows a pale horse and its rider's name was 'death.' He was followed by another horse whose rider's name was 'hell.' They were given control of one quarter of the earth's population, to kill with famine and disease. Today there are 7.28 billion people on the planet. To kill one fourth of them is to slaughter 1.8 billion people! My friend, these are God's warnings, not mine. There is still good news for the Christian. God has promised to take all believers out of the world before these events happen. We will be safe in heaven, for God does not bring His wrath on His children. God disciplines His child, but His wrath is saved for the ungodly, saved for those who left Him out of their lives, those who mocked Him, ignored Him and blasphemed Him. Their consequences for such acts are right around the corner. They refuse to listen for the hoof beats. Jesus will take all believers to heaven before all hell breaks loose. It is called the 'rapture' of the church. It says we will be caught up to meet Him in the air one day.

"For the Lord, Himself will come down from heaven with a mighty shout and with the soul stirring cry of the archangel and the great trumpet call of God. And the believers who are dead will be the first to rise to meet the Lord. Then we who are still alive and remain on the earth will be caught up with them in the clouds to meet the Lord in the air and remain with Him forever. So comfort and encourage one another with this news."
II Thessalonians 4:16-18

All of these horrible events are God's wrath poured out on a godless world. Just as in the days of Noah, God warned the people, but they refused to listen. Today many still refuse to listen. The good news for the believer is we can comfort one another with these words written by Paul the Apostle in II Thessalonians. What an amazing thought. We know the devastation that is coming upon this world, yet God takes the time to comfort us. (If the reader would like more information on future prophetic world events please read Hal Lindsey's book, The Late Great Planet Earth.)

The Bible is the most up to date book on earth, because God is its author.

DECEMBER 23

God knows and understands when His child is too weary to pray.

"Carry one another's burdens." Galatians 6:2

Have you ever been there? Too weary and discouraged to get down on your knees to pray, and even if you could you wouldn't know what to say because things were really bad. God understands. The shortest prayer in the bible was prayed by the Apostle Peter as he was walking on the water and began to sink. "Jesus, help!" He didn't have time to pray much more before he found himself drowning in the storm and the waves. Peter's faith was soaring one moment, when he got out of the boat and found himself walking on the water to Jesus. Then as he took his focus off of Jesus and saw only the storm and the waves, his faith began to spiral down. Our life can be turned upside down and inside out in a moment's time, just like Peter's. Every trial that comes our way has been specifically designed for each of us individually. God will limit the weight, the burden the sorrow in our life while at the same time, developing our character and faith. We have a choice to fight God and complain and murmur or to submit to Him in this trial. We can resist Him out of fear for what might happen. We may resist because our pride gets in the way. Foolishly we think we have a better way out of the mess, a better plan. We may resist because the cost is too high. God may require us to let go of something very important to us, a relationship, a job, our pride. It hurts too much. One reason we resist God is out of a stubborn will. We simply don't want to do what He is asking us to do. Though we have the right to resist, it only causes God to turn up the heat in our life until we come into obedience with Him. He will get us on the right track or our life will spiral down and out of control. His way is always best. It may not be the least painful, but it is the best. God is not out to destroy us, but to build us up. To prepare us sometimes for an important task that may lie ahead of us. One of the hardest choices we have as Christians is to obey God regardless of the consequences. To obey Him when it hurts and I feel like my guts are falling out, when the sorrow is so great I wonder if I will make it through. It may seem as if every demon in hell has come against me. I may feel so all alone and it appears as if everyone has deserted me, even God. When God seems to be blessing everyone around me, just not me, and when I have nothing else left, I must trust Him. My faith will grow by leaps and bounds if I can feel all of these things and still say, "I trust you Lord. I don't understand, this really hurts, but I choose to trust you." God will honor your trust with blessings beyond anything He may have asked you to suffer.

"God is able to do abundantly, above and beyond anything I could ever dare to think, dream of or ask according to the power that is at work in us." Ephesians 3:20

With every trial that comes into my life I can profit from it or waste the opportunity. It is my choice alone. God may break your will, but He will never break your spirit. He sees the potential in each one of our lives so He will prune us to the point of pain, so we need to remember that those pruning shears are in the hands of my Heavenly Father. He knows when it is enough, and He will stop, but it is usually long after we want Him too. God's ultimate goal will be to conform us to the likeness of His Son. That means we have a long ways to go to reach that goal. In fact, we will not fully reach that goal until we go to heaven. Along the journey here on earth He will test our faith and devotion to Him. The good news is He will travel every step of the way with us. He will never leave us or forsake us.

December 24

God will not look you over for medals, degrees or diplomas, but for scars.

"In heaven we shall appear, not in armor, but in robes of glory. But here these are to be worn night and day; we must walk, work, and sleep in them, or else we cannot be true soldiers of Christ."
-William Gurnall-

The greatest acts of worship are to believe God and to obey Him. Believing and obeying God can come with a very high price tag. The world hates Jesus and the world hated Paul. The religious leaders did everything they knew how to do to get rid of them. Eventually they did, but not permanently. The Apostles paid with their lives for believing and following God. Paul was beaten and imprisoned on many occasions, yet he still went back out preaching the good news of Jesus Christ. I doubt there is a saint of God with more scars than the Apostle Paul. As he himself stated, "I have fought the good (worthy, honorable and noble) fight, I have finished the race, I have kept (firmly held) the faith. (II Timothy 4:7) Eventually, Paul was beheaded for his faith.

He has now exchanged his battle wounds for a robe of glory. Previously known as Saul of Tarsus, a Pharisee, he was on the road to Damascus, on his way to persecute and kill more Christians. Because he was a religious Pharisee, he believed it necessary to kill all Christians who were a threat to Judaism. God had a very different plan for Saul's life. Saul was blinded by a light, and knocked to the ground. He then heard a voice asking him, "Saul, Saul, why are you persecuting Me?" He replied, "Who are you Lord?" "I am Jesus, the one you are persecuting. Now get up and go into the city and there you will be told what to do. (Acts 9:5-6) Saul did as Jesus said, he met up with a man named Ananias, he received his sight back, and was filled with the Holy Spirit. His name was changed to Paul and the rest is history. Paul became the Apostle to the gentiles. It is because of him and his willingness to travel and suffer for Christ, that the gospel reached my ancestors and yours. Paul fought the good fight and so must we. We are in a spiritual battle every day of our lives, and we must never forget it. Yes, we will be scared. We will be rejected, laughed at, scorned and rejected, but so was Paul and so was Jesus. The good news of the gospel of Jesus will be received by those whose hearts are open. God alone knows who they are yet the good news is preached to *everyone* that they too might be saved. After that day on the Damascus road, Paul no longer lived for himself but for Jesus.

"For me to live is Christ, and dying is even better. Yet if I live, that means fruitful service for Christ. I really don't know which is better. I am torn between two desires; Sometimes I want to live, and sometimes I long to go and be with Christ. That would be far better for me, but it is better for you that I live." Philippians 1:21-24

During this Christmas season, take time to reflect on the virgin birth of Jesus. God Himself, in the person of the Son, left heaven's glory, entered into the womb of a virgin and was born sinless. He came to die. He was not a victim, He came for the sole purpose of dying for our sins. God's holiness demanded a perfect sacrifice, who was Jesus. God the Father sent Him to this earth to pay the debt of sin we owed. He is no longer a baby in a stable, but will soon return to this earth as King of Kings and Lord of Lords, where EVERY knee will bow before Him, either willingly or unwillingly, but bow we must. EVERY tongue shall proclaim that Jesus Christ is Lord, to the glory of God. Hallelujah!

December 25

He opened not His mouth.
– Mark 15:3-

"For unto us a child is born, to us a Son is given, and the
government will be on His shoulders. And He will be called
Wonderful Counselor, Mighty God, Everlasting Father, Prince of Peace."
Isaiah 9:6

Christmas celebrates the birth of Jesus. Immanuel, God with us. His purpose for coming to earth was to die. He was sent by God the Father to pay for the sins of the world. He came willingly. He came to a lost world, a world so corrupt that it did not want Him. A world that was threatened by His very words and actions, a world that chose to kill Him. He was falsely accused, yet never opened His mouth on His own behalf. He had come to die. God used the Romans and the Jews of that day to put Him to death just as the scriptures had prophesied years before. No one on this earth has lived a life like His. No one. His was indeed, a solitary life.

One Solitary life...
He was born in an obscure village
The child of a peasant woman
He grew up in another obscure village
Where he worked in a carpenter shop
Until he was thirty when public opinion turned against him
He never wrote a book
He never held an office
He never went to college
He never visited a big city
He never traveled more than two hundred miles
From the place where he was born
He did none of the things
Usually associated with greatness
He had no credentials but himself
He was only thirty three
His friends ran away
One of them denied him
He was turned over to his enemies
And went through the mockery of a trial
He was nailed to a cross between two thieves
While dying, his executioners gambled for his clothing
The only property he had on earth
When he was dead
He was laid in a borrowed grave

Through the pity of a friend
Nineteen centuries have come and gone
And today Jesus is the central figure of the human race
And the leader of mankind's progress
All the armies that have ever marched
All the navies that have ever sailed
All the parliaments that have ever sat
All the kings that ever reigned put together
Have not affected the life of mankind on earth
As powerfully as that one solitary life
-Dr. James Allan Francis © 1926.-

Christianity is about a relationship with a <u>risen</u> Savior, is He your Savior? He is alive and we will all come face to face with Him some day. Are you ready?

December 26

Seeking not the gift, but the giver which is God.

"Humility – Seeing myself as God sees me, first as a sinner, broken nothing without Him, undeserving. Then as His child with robes of righteousness, headed for glory."
-unknown-

Today's reflection is "How do you see yourself?" Do you believe the devils lies or do you see yourself as God does? I wasted many years of my life seeing myself through the eyes of the devil. I believed everything he said to me, not even realizing it was him saying them. I owned them as my own thoughts until I read the word of God. Satan tells us we are worthless, should be ashamed, a nobody, lonely, who would want you, you're ugly, you're fat, you're too skinny, you're stupid, you are going to hell. These were all lies. The trouble is I didn't understand they were lies until the day I met Jesus. That day I found out how much He loved me. That He would rather die than to live without me. That made me pretty special in His eyes. Was I perfect? Of course not, but Jesus takes us just as we are, He makes those changes I need. I love the song, "Just As I Am" In fact it was the song playing the night I accepted Jesus as my Savior. I had heard the song a thousand times before in church, that night was different. The words bypassed my brain and went straight to my heart as I laid there on the sofa, watching a Billy Graham Crusade, mourning the death of my sister. I no longer needed my brain to figure my life was in a mess, that night my heart was open to God as never before. I wasn't worthless. Jesus had died for me. I wasn't alone, He said He would be my constant companion and would never forsake me, as others had. No more excuses. I was what God said I was, a sinner who needed her sins forgiven. I needed Jesus. That night I accepted Him and I never looked back. That was over 40 years ago and though I have stumbled and fallen during my walk with God, He has been faithful. He has picked me up, dusted me off, and encouraged me not to quit. He wasn't done with me yet. Has the journey been easy? Absolutely not! There were many times I wanted to quit, many times I failed Him, not wanting to, but I did. Times I still insisted on doing things my way instead of His. Just a warning, that didn't work out so well, so I don't recommend you try it. It has not been easy to seek the Giver instead of His gifts, because He gives us so much. I am learning to be thankful for the little things, like a hot shower every morning. Most of the world doesn't have that luxury. Thankful, that even though my knees ache, I can still walk, on my own. I hope that one day 'stuff' won't matter to me anymore and the only thing I seek is Jesus. He will add the rest.

"For me to live is Christ, no longer for me to live is 'stuff.'"

December 27

Unbelief asks for a sign...faith stands at the red sea surrounded by the enemy knowing God will make a way where there seems to be no way.

Living for God can be a lonely battle sometimes. It can seem like an uphill fight. One that looks impossible to the weary saint. The good news is victory is always assured for the believer. No devil in hell can stand against a child of God who refuses to give up and who knows who they are in Christ and keeps pressing on, in His strength, not their own. We are more than conquerors and nothing can separate us from Him.

> "Can anything separate us from Christ's love? Does it mean He no longer loves us if we have trouble or calamity, or are persecuted, or are hungry or cold or in danger or threatened with death? For the scriptures say, "For your sake we are killed every day; we are being slaughtered like sheep." No, despite all these things overwhelming victory is ours through Christ who loved us."
> Romans 9:35-37

Despite all of these calamities that come into a Christian's life, we are victorious. So, we need not worry about God's love for us, even to the point of death. Paul goes on to give a long list of those things that CANNOT come between us and our Lord.

> "And I am convinced that nothing can ever separate us from His love. Death can't and life can't. The angels can't, and the demons can't. Our fears for today, our worries about tomorrow, and even the powers of hell can't keep God's love away. Whether we are high above the sky or in the deepest ocean, nothing in all creation will ever be able to separate us from the love of God that is revealed in Christ Jesus our Lord."
> Romans 9:38-39

What good news! Nothing can separate us. It doesn't matter where we go, or who tries to get in the way, God will not allow it. We are His forever. These words were written to churches in Paul's day that would face great persecution trying to get the good news of the gospel of Jesus Christ to the world. Many would give their lives in spreading the gospel. The disciples were all persecuted and killed for their faith, all except John, the writer of the Book of Revelation. The Church is still going despite the persecution. Jesus said the gates of hell would not prevail against His church. They have not and they will not. Rest in His love tonight, all warm and secure that no one has ever loved you like He has and does this very moment.

December 28

NOTHING *is too hard for GOD.*

"God's power does not diminish with any turn of events."
-unknown-

Someone has said, "God calms us in the storm, before He calms the storm." God can teach us things in the midst of the waves rolling over us, that we could never have imagined. We learn more in the storm than at any other time. Most of us don't respond very well to storms, but you have to admit they are a great teacher.

"If you are upset and disgusted with your disobedient
children, just imagine how God must feel about His."
-unknown-

We are all disobedient at one time or another, but God is very patient with every one of us. He sends us a test, it comes to us riding on a storm, we flunk the test, but it's okay because in God's classroom we get to take it all over again, until we do pass it. I don't think God is disgusted with us but I do think He is saddened by our behavior sometimes. There are always bad consequences to bad behavior or disobedience. He wants to spare us those consequences, but many times we force His hand and insist on them. Sometimes we want to do something so bad we are willing to suffer the consequences in order to do it. God's love does not change for us during those times. Hard to believe, but it is true. Love is not just something He does, it is who He is, God is LOVE! He will not love me anymore tomorrow or in 100 years, than He does today. We have all heard of 'tough love.' Well, God's love can get pretty tough some days. The Bible says, "He disciplines those He loves." Ouch! I know, and I am sure you do too, if you have been a Christian for a while. It's almost like those signs that say, "Wet paint," and we find ourselves reaching out to touch it just to make sure they know what they are talking about. God says don't touch it and we do. This year is coming to a close and a brand new year is beginning. We all will get a brand new start! No do overs from this year ending, no living life looking in the rear view mirror. What is done is done. Hopefully, we have learned from our mistakes and won't repeat them any time soon. God loves us, He wants only what is best for us, and that is why He requires our obedience. He is smarter than we are. We would be wise this coming year to do things His way.

DECEMBER 29

God doesn't give us great loads to carry without first telling us to 'cast our care on Him.'

"Give me a stout heart to bear my own burdens. Give me a willing heart to bear the burdens of others. Give me a believing heart to cast all burdens upon Thee, O Lord."
-John Baillie-

This is incredible that we may carry our burdens, help shoulder another's burden and in the end cast them all on Jesus. Our shoulders were never meant to carry the cares of the world. That is why there is so much pain and sickness in the world. Stress can do unimaginable things to the human body. We were not meant to carry stress. Hospitals are filled with patients who have been unsuccessfully dealing with stress. High blood pressure, ulcers, even some cancers are now thought to be caused by stress. Life is hard, and there is no arguing that issue. God knows our weaknesses. He knows that unless we have somewhere to place the cares of our life, we too will fall under its weight. He has given us a place. We are to bring them to Him. Not only bring them to Him, but leave them there. How many times do we go to the Lord, tell Him our problems, say thank you for listening, then pick them all back up and take them home with us. I am so guilty. God doesn't want us just to tell Him about our problems, he already knows. He wants to help. So, how do we find rest for our souls?

You have created us for Yourself, and our heart cannot be stilled until it finds its rest in You."
-Augustine of Hippo-

We find our rest in God. What exactly does it mean to rest: To have peace of mind or spirit, to repose, to take relief or respite; freedom from activity or labor.
Freedom from activity or labor means I stop fretting over my problems. I stop trying to reason them out or find a solution for them apart from God. He invites us to come to His throne of grace to find that peace and quiet we all crave. He strengthens us, He equips us, He directs us in the way that we should go, and I don't think He had in mind the hospital. He desires for us to be healthy and whole.

"Come to Me, all of you who are weary and carry heavy burdens, and I will give you rest. Take My yoke upon you. Let Me teach you, because I am humble and gentle, and you will find rest for your souls. For my yoke fits perfectly, and the burden I give you is light."
Matthew 11:28

You will never find a better deal than that. We all are weary at times, burdened down with the cares of this world. Jesus promises us rest. We give Him our problems, He gives us His rest. Jesus frees us from all of our burdens in this world. He starts with freeing us from the burden of sin. He then continues on to remove our guilt and shame, our unbelief, and anything that would keep us from Him. Where else are you or I going to find a deal like this? He will heal, He will give you peace and all the time He will wrap you up in His arms of love and if things get really bad, He will let you crawl up into His lap and hang out for a while. That is right where you will find me most days. The safest place on earth.

DECEMBER 30

Dare to dream again...

"Every challenge we face can be solved by a dream."
-David Schwartz-

What is on your bucket list for the New Year? Dare to do it! Take advice from Walt Disney: "If you can dream it, you can do it." He created the Magic Kingdom, the happiest place on earth, and it started with a dream and a piece of paper. Jiminy Cricket said, "When your heart is in your dream, no request is too extreme." Now when has Jiminy Cricket ever steered you wrong? So, go do whatever it is you have been putting off! Take a vacation, write a book, buy a motorcycle, take flying lessons, get a facelift, just make sure that people can still recognize you.

"Hold fast to dreams, for if they die, life is like
a broken winged bird that cannot fly."
-Robert Frost-

Make plans then do it. I am reminded of all the women on the Titanic that refused dessert that last night. I wish they had eaten it, that's why I make sure I never miss dessert, doesn't matter if I'm not on a cruise, there could be a tidal wave or an earthquake, you just never know. We all need to laugh more. Make a resolution to laugh more this coming year and stick to it better than you have to all of your other resolutions. I love Irma Bombeck's humor:

"Do you know what you call those who use towels and never wash them,
eat meals and never do the dishes, sit in rooms they never clean, and
are entertained till they drop? If you have just answered, 'A house guest,'
you're wrong because I have just described my kids."

Go hug your kids! They were a dream of yours once too. Just because that dream has changed to wanting them to move out, like yesterday, doesn't change the emptiness you will feel when they actually do. I know because the empty nest thing they talk about is real. Go get that bucket list of yours and go do something special or exciting. Call a friend you haven't talked to in a long time. Go visit a relative you haven't seen in a while. Tomorrow is promised to no one. It takes a September 11th to remind us of that sobering fact. Live with no regrets and start this New Year surrounded by people who make you laugh and enjoy life! It is the only life you will have! Try not to mess it up...but if you do, whisper His name...He will hear and He will answer. You can count on it.

December 31

"WATCH and pray. He is coming again! Maybe sooner than any of us think.

Jesus' message to the Church at Laodecia, the 'end time' church;
"I know all the things that you do, that you are neither hot
nor cold. I wish you were one or the other. But since you are like
lukewarm water, I will spit you out of My mouth."
Revelation 3:16

This is a dire warning to the end time church that is indifferent to the things of God. God says He will spit them out of His mouth. If this describes your church, get out now! Why bother to attend church if your attitude is one of indifference? Indifference says, you can take God or leave Him. Many have spent their whole life, leaving God out. The good news is, as long as you have breath, it is never too late to turn to Him. Sad part is, you will never find Him sitting in a church pew in Laodecia.

At the end of Revelation Jesus says, "Yes, I am coming soon." Come, Lord Jesus!

Are you looking for His return? If not, why not?

As this year comes to a close, keep in mind, God will defeat ALL evil in the end. Until then stay courageous!

Remember, courage doesn't always roar. Sometimes courage is the quiet voice at the end of the day saying, "I will try again tomorrow." Until then...WATCH & PRAY!

Lord, help me this New Year to live each
and every day as if I
am worth the price you paid to redeem me.

BIBLIOGRAPHY

I have been a Christian for 43 years and have collected many sayings, quotes and bible verses over the years, many of which did not include the author. Every attempt has been made to give credit to the authors of any copyrighted materials. Unfortunately, this was not always possible and I ask for forgiveness where this endeavor has failed.

- Life Application Bible; Tyndale House Publishers Copyright 1996.
- New Living Bible Paraphrased Copyright 1971 by Tyndale House Publishers, Wheaton, IL
- The Journey Is Too Great For Thee, Copyright 2005 by Authorhouse, Cindy Joanne Balch
- The New Encyclopedia of Christian Quotations: Copyright 2000, Baker Books

Copyright 2000 John Hunt Publishing Ltd Published by Baker Books
Bible Quotations The Holy Bible, New International VersionE Copyright 1973, 1978, 1984 By the International Bible Society, Tyndale Charitable trust
New American Standard Bible Copyright 1960, 1962, 1963, 1968,1971, 1972, 1973,1975,1977, 1995 by Lockman Foundation
The Message: New Testament Copyright 1993 by Eugene H. Peterson
King James Version Copyright Oxford University Press
New King James Version Copyright 1979, 1980, 1982 by Thomas Nelson, Inc., Publishers
Good News Bible New Testament Copyright American Bible Society, New York 1966, 1971 and 4th Edition 1979 Old Testament Copyright American Bible society, New York
Amplified Bible (E-version) Copyright 1965 by Zondervan Publishing House

- Songs of the Church - Copyright 1971-1975 by Howard Publishing Co.
- The Complete Guide to Christian Quotations: Copyright 2011 by Barbour Publishing.
- Living Quotations For Christians by Harper and Row Publishers; edited by Sherwood Eliot Wirt & Kersten Beckstrom
- An Encyclopedia of Compelling Quotations by R. Daniel Watkins.; Hendrickson Publishers.
- 14,000 Quips & Quotes by E.C. McKenzie; Hendrickson Publishers

CPSIA information can be obtained
at www.ICGtesting.com
Printed in the USA
FSHW021439121120
75762FS